Taipei

TAIWAN

N

LUZON

PHILIPPINES

Manila

MINDORO

PANAY

LEYTE

NEGROS

MINDANAO

Sulu

Sea

PACIFIC

OCEAN

Molucca Sea

HALMAHERA

SULAWESI

BURU

SERAM

Banda

AMBON

Sea

IRIAN
JAYA

PAPUA
NEW
GUINEA

Dili

Arafura

EAST TIMOR

Sea

Government and Politics in Southeast Asia

Government and Politics in Southeast Asia

Edited by
John Funston

ZED Books

First published in 2001 by
Institute of Southeast Asian Studies
30 Heng Mui Keng Terrace, Pasir Panjang, Singapore 119614
http://www.iseas.edu.sg/pub.html
ISBN 981-230-133-X (soft cover)
ISBN 981-230-134-8 (hard cover)

Published in 2001 in the United Kingdom, North America and Europe by Zed Books Ltd,
7 Cynthia Street, London N1 9JF, UK and Room 400, 175 Fifth Avenue, New York, NY
10010, USA.

Distributed in the USA exclusively by Palgrave, a division of St Martin's Press, LLC, 175
Fifth Avenue, New York, NY 10010, USA.

Zed ISBN 1 84277 104 3 (hb)
Zed ISBN 1 84277 105 1 (pb)

A catalogue record for this book is available from the British Library.

Library of Congress Cataloguing-in-Publication data has been applied for.

*The responsibility for facts and opinions in this publication rests exclusively with the editor
and contributors and their interpretations do not necessarily reflect the views or the policy
of the Institute or its supporters.*

Photo of Wat Benchamobophit (Marble Temple) reproduced with permission from
thaistudents.com.

Photo of the Philippine President Gloria Arroyo at Edsa reproduced with permission from
the *Philippine Daily Inquirer*.

Photo of former Indonesian Presidents, Abdurrahman Wahid and Suharto, reproduced with
permission from *Tempo*.

Printed in Singapore by Seng Lee Press Pte Ltd

Contents

List of Contributors

Roger Kershaw was a Lecturer in Southeast Asian Studies at the Universities of Hull and Kent, and subsequently worked in Brunei, in the Ministry of Education (1984–94).

Sorpong Peou is Associate Professor of Political Science and International Relations in the Faculty of Comparative Culture, Sophia University, Tokyo. He was a Fellow at the Institute of Southeast Asian Studies from 1995 to 1999.

Anthony L. Smith is a Fellow at the Institute of Southeast Asian Studies.

Nick J. Freeman is a Senior Fellow at the Institute of Southeast Asian Studies.

John Funston was a Senior Fellow at the Institute of Southeast Asian Studies for four years, until March 2001.

Tin Maung Maung Than is a Senior Fellow at the Institute of Southeast Asian Studies.

Joaquin L. Gonzalez III is Director of the Executive Master of Public Administration Program, Golden Gate University, San Francisco, California and Kiriyama Fellow at the Center for the Pacific Rim, University of San Francisco.

Jon S.T. Quah is Professor in the Department of Political Science at the National University of Singapore.

Thaveeporn Vasavakul is Regional Director, Southeast Asia and Resident Director, Program in Vietnam, Council on International Educational Exchange, Hanoi, Vietnam.

Preface

From conception to completion this book was with me for most of four years in Singapore at the Institute of Southeast Asian Studies. It was an exciting, if sometimes worrying time to work in and on Southeast Asia — a Dickensonian best of times and worst of times. I had scarcely acclimatized when Thailand floated the baht on a fateful 2 July 1997, with economic, political and social consequences for the region that are still being worked out. ISEAS provided an ideal vantagepoint to track these developments, and ensure they are reflected in this work.

The book is largely an ISEAS in-house product. Six of the ten country chapters are by ISEAS staff, and the rest by authors who have had a close association with the Institute over the years — part of a wide network of people sometimes considered the ISEAS alumni. I am grateful to all for their willingness to adhere to a common framework, and their patience in entertaining a wide range of demanding editorial requests. Many others in ISEAS also made important contributions. The book would not have been possible without support from the Director, Professor Chia Siow Yue. The Administration provided sterling assistance, particularly in responding to complicated word processing requests through numerous drafts. The Publications Unit provided expert copy editing, indexing and design and production. The Library assisted with its unique collection on Southeast Asia, and Ms Susan Low compiled the material for the Key Statistics in each country chapter.

I am greatly indebted for the hospitality and friendship of numerous Southeast Asians from all walks of life during more than three decades of working in and on the region. In particular I have benefited from the generosity of academics, politicians and officials. Debts such as these cannot be repaid, but I hope at least that this book reflects accurately the insights conveyed to me, and thereby contributes to a better understanding of Southeast Asia's complex and diverse political landscape.

John Funston

INTRODUCTION

Attempting to explain government and politics for ten Southeast Asian countries in a single volume is an ambitious undertaking. Much has been written on the region in recent years, but most accounts focus on a single country or a single issue (such as democracy, or elections). There is, however, an obvious need for a concise, up-to-date, overview volume that addresses core political science issues — institutions of government, and the nature of political practice — in all Southeast Asian countries. In the writer's experience, academics, policy-makers, journalists and others have frequently spoken of such a need.

Several attempts have sought to meet such an objective in the past. Early works appeared soon after the term Southeast Asia was adopted — to define a war theatre during World War II — but the first detailed account was *Government and Politics of Southeast Asia*, edited by George Kahin. This was published by Cornell University Press in 1959, then reappeared in an extensively revised form in 1964.[1] Each of the then eight countries (minus Brunei, and with Singapore as part of Malaysia) was examined in terms of four headings: historical background; socio-economic setting; the political process; and major problems. This was a seminal work, and nothing that followed has matched its quality.

Another influential book, Lucian Pye's *Southeast Asian Political Systems*, was published in 1969, and followed by a second edition in 1974.[2] This looked at the region on a comparative basis, rather than country by country. Although a compact work of less than 100 pages, it was a well-written synthesis of major political issues. Early chapters examined geography, history, economy, social organizations and value systems. They were followed by others on ideology, political dynamics (the role of parties, leaders, the military, civilian bureaucracies, interest groups and communist resistance movements), organs of government (a broad look at the constitutional division of power) and performance (the government's ability to hold the state together and provide basic services).

Two further comparative works on Southeast Asia appeared during the 1970s, by Michael Leifer and Richard Butwell. These were less comprehensive than Pye in discussion of political institutions, and focused more on the themes of post-colonial difficulties, and the retreat from democracy to authoritarianism.[3]

Another trend in the 1970s was a shift to separate country studies with a common regional focus. Cornell university initiated a series entitled

"Politics and International Relations in Southeast Asia", under which it published separate volumes on Burma, Malaysia/Singapore, Indonesia, Thailand and Vietnam.[4] The Southeast Asian Studies Program, established in 1976 by regional scholars with the Institute of Southeast Asian Studies in Singapore acting as co-ordinator, produced books on Thailand, Malaysia, Singapore and the Philippines.[5]

A volume on *Politics in the ASEAN States*, edited by Diane Mauzy, appeared in 1984.[6] Like the Kahin edited volume this is organized on a country basis. Chapters begin with historic and socio-economic overviews, followed by sections on major political cleavages, and the nature of government (who rules, by what means, on behalf of whom). In the 1990s Clark Neher added to the country-focused literature, producing three editions of *Southeast Asia in the New International Era*.[7] The country chapters have a general socio-political history introduction, followed by sections on institutions and social groups, democratization, economic development, the state, and foreign policy.

A number of comparative works have appeared since the 1980s. Neher's *Politics in Southeast Asia*, which first appeared in 1981 (second edition in 1987) was one of the most comprehensive.[8] This adopts a largely political history approach, with a comparative look at political culture, rural politics, and political dynamics (categorising and analysing countries in terms of whether they are military-authoritarian, civil-authoritarian, communist authoritarian, or democratic). Several more thematic works also appeared, focused on issues such as political economy,[9] democracy,[10] the military,[11] elections,[12] and the politics of traditionalism ("the ways Southeast Asian countries have preserved, recovered, and adapted traditional models of political power in the face of external pressures to change from the West").[13]

What This Volume is About

Where does this book stand in relation to those that precede it? The main focus is on addressing core political science concerns over the nature of political systems, and key political issues. Recognizing that political systems do not exist in a vacuum, country chapters begin with a broad description of history, society, geography and economy. This is supplemented by Key Statistics, covering area, population, gross national product (GNP), income distribution, human development and armed forces. Such statistics must be treated with caution — different criteria are sometimes used for different countries, and results sometimes change as new methodologies are adopted — but as far as possible the same sources have been used so they can serve as at least broad comparative indicators.

Political Systems

Analysis of political systems begin with a very broad description of governmental structure, based largely on national constitutions. Among the issues addressed are whether the focus country is unitary or federal, a monarchy or a republic, has a parliamentary or presidential form of government, and the nature of governmental structures at the sub-national level.

Having established the broad governmental framework, chapters then move to a more detailed study of the nature and importance of major political institutions — the word "institutions" used here to include both formal structures (such as parliament) and more diffuse political practices (including ideology and human rights). The main institutions included in this study are heads of state, the executive (cabinet, and both the military and civilian bureaucracies), the legislature, elections, the judiciary, political parties, ideology, civil society and human rights.

Political Issues

After setting the institutional framework, chapters move to focus on major political issues in each country. The approach adopted here combines traditional political science concerns with another of more recent origin. From at least the time of Aristotle, political theorists have asked questions about who rules, and who benefits. The issue of who rules has focused on the number of citizens involved in making important decisions, and which group/s are dominant — whether political parties, a particular class, or institutions such as the military or civilian bureaucracy. The closely related question of who benefits looks at which individuals or groups gain most from government policies. Benefits may accrue in economic or other forms. In Malaysia, for instance, constitutional benefits for Malays are not limited to concrete advantages in areas such as education, government employment and reserved land, but also include the prestige associated with having *Bahasa Melayu* as the national language, Islam as "the religion of the Federation", and a Malay as head of state.

Another issue of concern to theorists for many years is political legitimacy — meaning the extent to which citizens obey governments not out of fear or coercion, but because of a belief that it is morally right and proper to do so. In a classic articulation of this concept, sociologist Max Weber focused attention on three different bases of legitimacy, tradition, charisma and legality. More recently theorists have added a fourth basis, namely effectiveness — in particular the ability to deliver rapid economic growth. Assessing legitimacy involves difficult and sometimes conjectural judgements about the extent of popular support for political systems or governments. Some political systems may enjoy high legitimacy — such as constitutional monarchy in Thailand, or presidential democracy in the Philippines — while specific governments have low legitimacy. Elections may be an indicator of legitimacy, if reasonably free and fair. Other indicators may include demonstrations of popular support, or in some cases simply an absence of opposition.

Finally, in the last two decades a new concern has arisen over the concept of governance. The World Bank has defined governance as "the manner in which power is exercised in the management of a country's economic and social resources for development".[14] Good governance is generally described as the exercise of governmental power in a manner that is effective, honest, equitable, transparent and accountable. This requires judgements about governmental integrity, and ability to formulate policies and deliver services, in partnership with competent and honest bureaucracies; the existence of effective legal and regulatory frameworks (rule of law); provision for personal security (controlling social disturbances and crime); and meeting basic needs in such areas as education, housing, health, and transport. More recently, proponents of governance have also argued that elements such as effectiveness and accountability can only be ensured when there is public participation (democracy), including an important role for civil society.

Political Systems and Issues: The Linkage

When this book was conceived, the section on the political system was envisaged as essentially static — a simple description — while that on issues would be dynamic — explaining the interplay of institutions in practice. Once we began to write, it quickly became apparent that such a neat juxtaposition was not possible. The Thai Constitution, for example, cannot be explained without reference to the 15 constitutions that have gone before it, and the circumstances that gave rise to its birth. Yet in touching on such matters the writer inevitably intrudes into the area of issues. Similarly, executive dominance in many countries cannot simply be stated, it has to be explained — though again this intrudes into the area of issues. The balance between the two areas is handled differently in the following chapters, but in most cases both are viewed dynamically, with *issues* often emerging as a summing-up of conclusions reached in relation to *institutions*.

Regional economic crisis and the future

Since Thailand floated its currency on 2 July 1997, the regional economic crisis has been uppermost in the minds of Southeast Asia's political observers. Political fallout from the crisis has already been profound, and its effects are still being felt. This is not the major focus of the book, and there is no specific heading dealing with it, but it permeates much of the analysis.

A concluding chapter seeks to draw some of the major threads together. What are the similarities and differences in regard to institutions and issues in the region? How have these been affected by the economic crisis?

Having begun this Introduction citing the need for a book that is up-to-date, it should be acknowledged that such an objective can never be fully achieved. Since this volume was conceived, East Timor has gained its independence, and would warrant a chapter of its own were there any further editions. Between the time of completing the manuscript and its printing, new and important political events may well occur. However, every effort has been made to ensure it is up-to-date at the time of going to press. And since political change is more usually by evolution than revolution — even sharp changes such as those associated with Soeharto's overthrow in Indonesia occur alongside notable continuities in political institutions and practice — it is hoped this book will remain useful for some years to come.

Note

1   George McT Kahin, ed., *Government and Politics of Southeast Asia* (Ithaca: Cornell University Press, 1959 and 1964).
2   Lucian W. Pye, *Southeast Asia's Political Systems* (Englewood Cliffs, NJ: Prentice Hall, 1969 and 1974).
3   Michael Leifer, *Dilemmas of Statehood in Southeast Asia* (Singapore: Asia Pacific Press, 1972); Richard Butwell, *Southeast Asia. A Political Introduction* (New York: Praeger, 1975).
4   Those with a domestic political focus were: Josef Silverstein, *Burma: Military Rule and the Politics of Stagnation* (Ithaca: Cornell University Press, 1977); Stanley S. Bedlington, *Malaysia and Singapore: The Building of New States* (Ithaca: Cornell University Press, 1978); Harold Crouch, *The Army and*

Politics in Indonesia (Ithaca: Cornell University Press, 1978); John L. S. Girling, *Thailand, Society and Politics* (Ithaca: Cornell University Press, 1981); Gareth Porter, *Vietnam: The Politics of Bureaucratic Socialism* (Ithaca: Cornell University Press, 1993).

5 Jon S. T. Quah, Chan Heng Chee, Seah Chee Meow, eds., *Government and Politics of Singapore* (Singapore, Oxford University Press, 1985); Somsakdi Xuto, ed., *Government and Politics of Thailand* (Singapore: Oxford University Press, 1987); Zakaria Haji Ahmad, ed., *Government and Politics of Malaysia* (Singapore: Oxford University Press, 1987); Raul P. de Guzman, Mila A. Reforma, eds., *Government and Politics of the Philippines* (Singapore: Oxford University Press, 1988).

6 Diane K. Mauzy, ed., *Politics in the ASEAN States* (Kuala Lumpur: Maricans, 1984).

7 Clark D. Neher, *Southeast Asia in the New International Era* (Boulder: Westview Press, 1991, 1994, and 1999).

8 Clark D. Neher, *Politics in Southeast Asia* (Cambridge, Mass: Schenkman, 1981 and 1987).

9 Richard Higgott and Richard Robison, eds., *Southeast Asia: Essays in the Political Economy of Structural Change* (London, Boston, Melbourne and Henley: Routledge and Kegan Paul, 1985); Richard Robison, Kevin Hewison, and Richard Higgott, eds., *Southeast Asia in the 1980s: The Politics of Economic Crisis* (Sydney, London, Boston: Allen & Unwin, 1987); James Clad, *Behind the Myth: Business, Money and Power in Southeast Asia* (London: Unwin Hyman, 1989); and Kevin Hewison, Richard Robison, and Garry Rodan, eds., *Southeast Asia in the 1990s: Authoritarianism, Democracy and Capitalism* (St Leonards: Allen & Unwin, 1993).

10. Anek Laothamatas, ed., *Democratization in Southeast and East Asia* (Singapore: Institute of Southeast Asian Studies, 1997); and Clark D. Neher and Ross Marlay, *Democracy and Development in Southeast Asia: The Winds of Change* (Boulder: Westview Press, 1995).

11 M. Soedjati Djiwandono and Yong Mun Cheong, *Soldiers and Stability in Southeast Asia* (Singapore: Institute of Southeast Asian Studies, 1988). An earlier work on this theme was Stephen Hoadley, *Soldiers and Politics in Southeast Asia* (Cambridge, Mass: Schenkman, 1975).

12 R. H. Taylor, ed., *The Politics of Elections in Southeast Asia* (Cambridge, New York and Melbourne: Woodrow Wilson Press and Cambridge University Press, 1996); Wolfgang Sachsenroder and Ulrike E. Frings, eds., *Political Party Systems and Democratic Development in East and Southeast Asia* (Brookfield: Aldershot, 1998).

13 Michael R. J. Vatikiotis, *Political Change in Southeast Asia: Trimming the Banyan Tree* (London and New York: Routledge, 1996), p. 211.

14 World Bank, *Governance and Development* (Washington, D.C.: World Bank, 1992), p. 3.

BRUNEI
Malay, Monarchical, Micro-state

Roger Kershaw

INTRODUCTION

The micro-state Brunei Darussalam ("The Abode of Peace") regained its full independence on 1 January 1984. It is the rump of a once extensive empire covering Borneo and surrounding islands, whose "Golden Age" is linked to the name of Sultan Bolkiah (late 15th or early 16th century). Bruneian influence began to erode after Spanish settlement in the Philippines in the late 16th century, then at the hands of a dynamic former vassal, Sulu, in the mid-17th. In the 19th it lost most of its territories on Borneo to Sarawak under the "White Rajas" (Brookes) and North Borneo (Sabah) under Chartered Company rule. Today's Brunei is totally enclosed — as well as bisected — by Sarawak (Malaysia), except to seaward on the north side.

Brunei was saved from extinction by the establishment of a British "Residency" in 1906, a system of classic Indirect Rule which lasted until 1959 (apart from the Japanese interlude). In 1959, thanks mainly to the strong will and dynastic vision of Sultan Omar Ali Saifuddin III, but in part because Britain feared the Indonesian-style radical nationalism of the Parti Rakyat Brunei (PRB or Brunei People's Party), the Colonial Office yielded executive power over domestic administration to the monarchy. This was contrary to London's original intention of establishing elected government, corresponding to developments in the neighbouring Federation of Malaya, and Singapore.

Brunei's 1959 Constitution did, however, make provision for future elections. When these were held three years later the PRB's victory was overwhelming. This placed the party in a position — even in a Legislative Council only partly elected — to stall the merger of Brunei with Malaya and the remaining territories of "British Southeast Asia" as "Malaysia", on which the Sultan seemed to have set his heart. The Sultan delayed convening the Council, as if to forestall the passing of an anti-Malaysia resolution. (This was how PRB perceived it, and the British did have a motive for hoping the Sultan would prevaricate.) The PRB's military wing rose in revolt in December 1962, and thereby played into the hands of conservative interests. British forces from Singapore crushed the Rebellion. After this, a Gurkha battalion of the British Army was stationed in the Sultanate. Tentative steps towards democracy were resumed with elections in 1965, but again with no elective majority in the legislature or control over the executive. In 1970 elections were abolished, and government was conducted increasingly by decree, facilitated by rolling over the State of Emergency every two years. Just after independence even the fully appointed Legislative Council was suspended, and had not been restored at the time of writing.

The security role of Britain in the background has remained important for royal consolidation. Although handing over formal administrative responsibility in 1959, and internal security in 1971, Britain maintained its responsibility for foreign affairs and defence until "Full Independence" in 1984. A British Gurkha battalion has remained in the country to this day — at Brunei's expense. Up to 1984, and even beyond, the credibility and development of administration were guaranteed by the presence of British contract personnel in senior positions, including the Armed Forces. Brunei's external security remains linked to a bilateral treaty with Britain — though this has been supplemented by diplomatic efforts to strengthen relations with regional neighbours, particularly through the Association of Southeast Asian Nations (ASEAN). In fact, the only hint of a security dimension in the 1979 Treaty of Friendship Cooperation is its reference to a "common interest in the peace and stability of the region". The essence of the security relationship is buried in a confidential exchange of letters governing the deployment of the Gurkha battalion. External threat is assumed to be "covered" in some way, but not any internal unrest or insurgency. Brunei has remained outside the Five-Power Defence Arrangements but takes part in joint exercises with Commonwealth forces, and bilaterally with ASEAN partners.

Sultan Omar Ali Saifuddin abdicated in 1967. This move may have been part of his manoeuvres to ward off British (Labour Government) pressures for democratization at that time. Certainly the Seri Begawan Sultan (thus known from the time of his abdication — a title, meaning "Glorious Sage", as befitted the "Architect of Modern Brunei") did not withdraw from the political scene, but continued to play an active role

FIGURE 1.1

Brunei: Key Dates

1905/06   Supplementary Agreement to the 1888 Treaty of Protection establishes British Residency.

1941–45   Japanese administration.

1950   Succession of Sultan Omar Ali Saifuddin III.

1959   The Brunei Constitution transfers supreme executive authority to the Sultan, with a Chief Minister and provision for a partly elected legislature.

1961   Foundation of Royal Brunei Malay Regiment.

1962   First indirect elections to the Legislative Council. The Brunei Rebellion.

1963   Abortive negotiations to join Malaysia.

1965   Direct elections to the Legislative Council.

1967   Succession of Sultan Hassanal Bolkiah at the abdication of his father, Omar Ali Saifuddin (henceforth "Seri Begawan Sultan").

1970   Abolition of elections to the Legislative Council.

1971   Amended Agreement with Britain transfers control of internal security to the Brunei State.

1979   Treaty of Friendship and Co-operation with Britain sets Independence for 1984, whereby Brunei will take control of foreign relations and defence.

1984   Brunei recovers "Full Independence", joins UN, ASEAN, etc. Suspension of Legislative Council. Establishment of "cabinet system" with seven ministers. Prince Jefri becomes Director of Brunei Investment Agency (BIA).

1985   Foundation of Universiti Brunei Darussalam (UBD).

1986   Death of the Seri Begawan Sultan. Ministers increased to eleven; Prince Jefri Minister for Finance.

1997   Prince Jefri resigns as Minister for Finance.

1998   Prince Jefri dismissed as Director of BIA. Proclamation of the Sultan's eldest son as Crown Prince.

2000   Civil suit against Prince Jefri for recovery of BIA funds.

behind the throne, until his death in 1986. His son, Sultan Hassanal Bolkiah, was the pre-eminent beneficiary of pre-independence political developments.

Apart from — indeed, overshadowing — these changes, the emergence of Brunei's modern monarchical system owed much to the development of the oil industry. Oil had been discovered in one of Brunei's four surviving districts, Belait, in 1929. The industry expanded in the 1950s, and the previously poverty-stricken state became rich. The role of oil as a factor in British calculation in mid-1963, when it worked to secure Bruneian membership in Malaysia, is difficult to determine. Much easier to answer is the question about the role of oil in the Sultan's calculation as the moment of decision loomed. Kuala Lumpur's demand for control of the oil revenues within ten years proved to be a sticking-point, even as the discovery of oil offshore made it feasible for Brunei to contemplate an eventual independence outside Malaysia. The new discoveries held the promise of much greater reserves of wealth than hitherto, from which it would be possible to deliver "development" to a restless people and at the same time consolidate dynastic power during the years of residual British protection. Also crucial was the fact that Malaysia, antipathetic and even interventionist until 1977, became conciliatory thereafter and no longer posed an active security threat. This made it possible for Britain to shed its residual responsibilities under the Agreement of 1979, which set 1984 as the date for independence, with the Brunei Government's somewhat hesitant consent.

The Economy: A Shellfare State

What could not be foreseen in 1963, either by Malaysia or Brunei, was the rise of OPEC and the extraordinary, windfall oil-profits accruing to OPEC members and non-members alike in the decade of the oil-price revolution, up to the early 1980s. Brunei was transformed into a rentier state twice over: firstly through the flow of oil profits from the activities of an international company (Shell); secondly through the flow of interest from the astronomical financial reserves which the oil revenues were creating — managed by the government's Brunei Investment Agency (BIA) since 1983. Although in the past decade or so oil prices no longer left a surplus over annual expenditure for investment in the reserves, in principle income from the investments is constantly available for reinvestment. Meanwhile, current revenue is still the mainstay of one of the highest standards of living enjoyed anywhere in Southeast Asia. It is mainly through government employment that "oil rent" is distributed and filters down among the population, with an astonishing 75.6 per cent of all Bruneian citizens in the workforce government-employed on the eve of Independence.[1] (Even when the foreign work-force is included, government employment is a high 47 per cent.) Other mechanisms of distribution include the extensive welfare services, particularly education and health, which benefit the people in kind rather than cash.

Particularly favoured within this fortunate population are not only the royal family but an extensive bureaucratic class, drawn from and reflecting the traditional social structure, yet also allowing a degree of mobility for the more talented, in some cases far above inherited status. Bureaucratic salaries in the middle-to-higher reaches show a distinct unevenness *vis-à-vis* disbursements to the less privileged parts of the population. A Brunei Economic Planning Unit study of 1986 found a high degree of inequality, with the top 10 per cent accounting for over 40 per cent of all income (see Figure 1.2). The differentials have, however, been very slightly eroded by a series of cost-of-living allowances to middle and lower ranking bureaucrats since 1987.

The government has taken even more to heart a looming problem of youth unemployment, now that the bureaucracy has difficulty in expanding its recruitment in step with population increase, and in view of an ominous decline of discipline in schools and spread of the drug culture. That has meant constant stress on the need for economic diversification in successive National Development Plans. Unemployment was officially at 4.7 per cent of the would-be work-force in 1996, but such figures reflect registration at employment centres and miss those who are not actively seeking work.

More than 40 per cent of the work-force is made up of foreigners. "Westerners" play a significant part in the upper levels at Shell, engineering and architectural firms, executive positions in the great international banks, and in secondary education and the university. Chinese are numerous in branch offices of Singapore and Malaysian companies, as managers, sales representatives and technicians, and are also in education. Other important components of the foreign labour force include Indian engineers, the backbone of the Public Works Department for years, and many Indian teachers; Ibans from Sarawak, a vital component of the Shell work-force; Thais, the work-force for the construction industry; and Bangladeshi labourers, a familiar sight in road maintenance gangs. The Bruneian middle class also depends on Filipina, Indonesian and Pattani Malay girls for domestic service.

FIGURE 1.2

Brunei: Key Statistics

Land area: 5,765 sq. kilometres

Population:[a] 323,600 (1998)

GNP:[b] Current exchange rate — US$8.1bn (1997);
US$7.2 bn (1998)

GNP Per Capita: Current exchange rate — US$25,753 (1997);
US$22,278 (1998)

Income Distribution (1981):[c]

Gini Index	56.4
% share of income or consumption:	
Lowest 10%	0.83
Lowest 20%	3.08
2nd 20%	6.58
3rd 20%	9.94
4th 20%	16.60
Highest 20%	63.80
Highest 10%	48.31

Human Development Index (HDI) Ranking:[d]

World ranking	25 (1997); 32 (1998)
Value	0.878 (1997); 0.848 (1998)

Armed Forces:

Total no.[e]	5,000 (1999)
Expenditure[e]	US$378 m (1998)
% of GNP	—

Sources: [a] Official national sources.

[b] International Monetary Fund Staff Country Report No. 99/19, April 1999.

[c] Sritua Arief, *The Brunei Economy* (East Balmain, NSW: Rosecons, 1986), based on the 1981 census. Hj Ismail Bin Hj Duraman, using a 1986 Economic Planning Unit survey of personal income, found a Gini Index of 48.0, with the top 10 per cent earning over 40 per cent, and the lowest 56 per cent only 24.6 per cent. "Income Distribution in Brunei Darussalam", *Singapore Economic Review* XXXV, no. 1 (1990): 68–69.

[d] United Nations Development Programme (UNDP), *Human Development Report* (New York: Oxford University Press, 1999 & 2000).

[e] International Institute for Strategic Studies (IISS), *The Military Balance, 1999–2000* (London: Oxford University Press, 1999).

Per capita GDP in this "hydrocarbon economy" is sensitive to oil price fluctuation, and also to the population growth (a rise of 40 per cent since 1985) which prosperity has facilitated. Around 60 per cent of revenues are hydrocarbon-derived.[2] Government sources show per capita GDP stood at B$35,544 in 1985, B$25,685 in 1990, and B$24,980 in 1995, at current prices.[3] An International Monetary Fund estimate for 1998 puts this figure at US$15,009 (around B$26,200), while that for GNP is considerably higher (see Figure 1.2). An apparent decline from the 1980s may not reflect a declining "quality of life" as the government continued to invest heavily in social services, and the Brunei currency (linked to the Singapore dollar) appreciated sharply against many other currencies in this period, to the benefit of consumers' purchasing power. At any rate, clearly per capita GDP is one of the highest in the region.

At the time of writing, policies of diversification have clearly brought little change to the overall structure of state finances. Some state-run services have been privatized. (The best known example to date is perhaps Muara Port, but it is too early to judge the results.) But attempts to develop textile exports, built on joint-venture capital and imported labour, earned only a modest B$40m in 1994. Nonetheless, Brunei leaders do place importance on this strategy because of doubts about the longevity of oil reserves. Standard sources for 1996 gave figures of 1.4 billion barrels of oil and 0.40 trillion cubic metres of gas, which in terms of years to run at present rates of extraction meant 23.24 years for oil, 34 for gas. In practice, however, estimates of reserves always move ahead as new discoveries are made or new technologies make more difficult strata accessible. "The end of the road" for Brunei has always kept a generation ahead of any given present. Ministerial warnings of the finiteness of the mineral reserves may often be read as rhetoric in support of diversification, whose most important purpose, in turn, is to reduce unemployment and its undesirable social side-effects.

Because of persistently depressed oil prices the government jacked up production at the time of the Gulf War, when there was a temporary price boost, and has maintained it at historically high levels, touching 180,000 barrels per day. Even at a higher production level, however, prices have not been strong enough to fund government expenditure from current revenue alone. Since 1995 — reading between the lines of official data on the national accounts — it appears that the potential budget deficit has been made up by transfers back from the BIA. Drawing on the investments, if confirmed, is a radical departure from the earlier, almost sacred doctrine that they were being kept by the monarchy "in trust for future generations".

Initially this was only a matter of drawing on some investment income: the underlying capital continued to increase until mammoth drawings by the Sultan's brother, Prince Jefri, the reality of which is now in the public arena.

From 1998 much media speculation began to centre on capital losses sustained by the BIA, including more especially the rumoured diversion of funds by Prince Jefri, when Finance Minister and Director of the Agency. Prince Jefri resigned his Finance portfolio in February 1997, and was removed as Director of BIA in July 1998. Estimates and rumours of the level of losses have varied enormously. It is possibly relevant for the future stability of the country that even the highest suggested level of losses in 1998 commentary, US$16 billion, would still be only 14.5 per cent of the latest (highest) "guesstimate" at the value of foreign reserves, US$110 billion.[4] However, a "leading London banker" associated with BIA has suggested reserves were as little as US$47 billion before the losses.[5] And now we have a figure for losses as high as US$35 billion from the Lord Chief Justice at the opening of a civil action against the Prince (March 2000). The more critical, immediate impact of economics on society came, however, from the reduced levels of activity by ASEAN-based companies during the Asian financial crisis, and collapse of the market in rented property as foreign workers left the country (but some of these were certainly employed by Amedeo, Prince Jefri's company). This affects the Brunei middle class, which has invested heavily in rental accommodation for expatriates. The less well paid are affected by the introduction of sundry new fees and taxes on consumption — such as TV satellite decoders, previously supplied free by a company of Prince Jefri's son.

Land and People

The total area of modern Brunei Darussalam is a mere 5,765 square kilometres. Administratively it comprises four districts, namely (from west to east) Belait, Tutong, Brunei/Muara (location of the capital city, Bandar Seri Begawan), and Temburong (divided from the rest of the country by the territory of Limbang, Sarawak).

Only the coastal zone is at all densely settled. Rural villages are taking on more and more the appearance of suburbs, as workers commute to and fro, and the rice-fields revert to swampy wilderness. The undulating, wooded topography of the coastal zone has been revolutionized by the contouring of hills for housing sites, or their complete excavation for infill for house construction on low-lying ground. (The government claims "forests" cover 75 per cent of the land area, but not all is primary jungle.) Transportation within and between the districts is by motor-vehicle on an increasingly modernized road network, but travel to Temburong from "Bandar" still depends mainly on motor-launches plying the connecting waterways through Malaysian territory. Access to the uninhabited, jungled interior in the south of Temburong, Tutong and Belait districts is by river (using a motor-launch, or outboard-driven longboat), or by air (helicopter). But many Bruneians are more familiar with jet travel to Singapore (for shopping), or to Medina (for the pilgrimage), than trips to their own *ulu* (the up-country).

Brunei's population was officially estimated at 305,100 in 1996. This includes foreign workers without stating their numbers; the 20 per cent or so "temporary residents" are overwhelmingly foreign workers. For the resident population, the Nationality Enactment of 1961 recognized seven ethnic groups as properly indigenous and entitled to citizenship by operation of law: the Bruneis, Kedayans, Tutongs, Dusuns, Bisayas, Belaits and Muruts. Geographically speaking, the Bruneis originate from the old capital ("Kampong Ayer") and Brunei-Muara. The agricultural Kedayans are native to that district but are also found in Temburong and Tutong. The Muruts are the most ancient community of Temburong. The Tutongs take their name from Tutong town and district. Tutong district is also home to most of the Dusuns, but they are found in small numbers in Brunei-Muara, as well as Belait. The few Bisayas are in Brunei-Muara, bordering the Bisaya heart-land, Limbang. The diminishing or disappearing Belaits are called after the name of their district. But Belait is more celebrated today as the location of the oilfield, the "oil-town" of Seria, and the "gas-port" of Lumut, than for its native people. Its population and lifestyle have become distinctively cosmopolitan. In this, it presents a considerable contrast with the more sedate, Muslim-dominated villages of Brunei-Muara, even of the modern capital, Bandar Seri Begawan — though Brunei Shell leans over backwards to inculcate its Western expatriate personnel with "cultural propriety".

Sociologically speaking, the separate identities of the seven constitutionally-indigenous groups are becoming blurred; linguistically there is a contributory convergence too, from separate languages and dialects into the modern lingua franca of "Standard Brunei Malay". These are the effects of education, new employment patterns and urbanization, together with extensive intermarriage, but also of conversion to Islam, which is promoted by the State with a "nation-building" motive and is also compulsory under State law for a non-Muslim marrying a Muslim.

Current official statistics make no distinction between the constitutionally indigenous races (originally defined in the Constitution, before the Nationality Enactment of 1961). All 204,000 estimated for 1996 are classified as "Malay", regardless of religion or language. In 1981 the non-Muslim Dusuns, Bisayas and Muruts were recorded in unpublished statistics as 6.62 per cent of the constitutionally indigenous, though this was probably subject to under-reporting.[6] "Other indigenous", of whom many would be Iban (and thus include a significant group from Sarawak with Malaysian passports, working in the oil industry), were estimated at 18,100 in 1996.

The Chinese (of whom a sizeable number will be Malaysian passport-holders) numbered 46,300 in 1996. Just over half are residents (55.9 per cent in 1981). In 1981 14,016 of these resident Chinese had "Permanent Resident" status, while only 8,043 had citizenship. Since then, a steady stream of professionally qualified "P.R.s" has emigrated, but access to citizenship for those remaining (via Registration for the increasing number of locally born) has recently improved. However, whereas banks and Shell were previously required to discriminate against Permanent Residents, preferential policies for *"bumiputera"* (native race) employees now have the same effect for ethnic Chinese who are citizens. The Chinese remain predominantly the shop-keeping class of Brunei. Even the more substantial capitalists are not on a par with Malaysian or Singaporean counterparts. A handful of locally born Chinese have made moderate progress in the government service, but only one (Pehin Dato Paduka Lim Jock Seng, at Foreign Affairs) as high as Permanent Secretary.

Brunei has a young, rapidly growing population. Over 40 per cent (126,500) is under the age of 20, by 1996 official estimates. This has strengthened government anxieties about unemployment. Yet the very welfare which has boosted population growth has also inhibited the development of a cultural orientation towards private sector employment.

English is becoming more widely understood among younger-generation Bruneians as the State pursues "bilingualism" in Malay and English (i.e., the sciences in English, "soft" subjects in Malay). Before 1985 there were selective English-medium schools, but "bilingualism" has been compulsory in all schools since then. This policy was imposed on the private Chinese schools after 1991, and the government Arabic schools are not excluded, though still teaching partly in the Arabic medium in the interests of students bright enough to contemplate an eventual career in the religious bureaucracy via higher education in the Middle East. The form of Malay used in education, official communication and the media is Malaysian, with a Brunei accent and a few dialect words. The linguistic factor binding young Bruneians of all races, however, is vernacular "Brunei Standard Malay", as stated above. As the privately-funded schools of the Chinese have been brought under the national curriculum and approved language media since 1991, education in Mandarin is now effectively at an end (but the academic standards and discipline of Chinese schools are highly regarded, and attract numbers of Malay pupils). Colloquially, Hokkien dominates in Chinese society at the capital, Cantonese and Kheh at the western end of the country.

Brunei society is extremely hierarchical, with the Sultan and immediate members of the royal family at the apex. Social standing is determined largely by proximity to the royal family by birth — indicated by the title *Pengiran Anak* for the most proximate — or achieved status in the bureaucracy (or in rare cases, commerce). Both inherited and bestowed titles are matters of the highest importance, with top non-royal achievers conferred the title of *Pehin*, and those just below, *Dato*.

Islam provides a strong bond for its Brunei followers (*ummat*). Much time is taken up with activities centred on the mosque, or State-sponsored Koran-reading competitions and celebrations of religious feast-days. The extended family is also important, reflected particularly in elaborate wedding festivities that preoccupy Bruneians most weekends. Any spare time left will often be devoted to sport — particularly badminton and soccer — organized largely on an inter-departmental basis among government servants. In some respects Bruneian society might, however, be considered "anomic". Repeated campaigns — promoting neighbourhood cleanliness, courteous and safe driving, politeness in behaviour generally, or respect for "public property" — expose the depth of the problem. The low level of civic consciousness is due in part to the depoliticization of the last thirty years, and is also a guarantee that there will be little demand for repoliticization in the foreseeable future.

THE POLITICAL SYSTEM

Brunei is an absolute monarchy in which the Head of State is also the Head of Government. At the present time, there is no institution of a legislature, nor are elections held, except to offices at village level. Political parties are occasionally granted registration.

The Brunei Constitution, promulgated in 1959 as the first, fundamental step in the transfer of powers from the British Residency, was a comprehensive but conservative document, comprising twelve Parts.[7] Although elections were provided for, the elected members of the

Legislative Council were not in the majority. (There were to be 16 indirectly elected and 17 appointed or *ex officio.*) There was a change to direct elections in 1965, but with no significance for control of the executive. The Chief Minister (and through him, his assisting officers such as the State Financial Officer) were responsible to the Sultan, in whom the "supreme executive authority of the State" was vested. The Sultan made laws "with the advice and consent of the Legislative Council", but no matter concerning finance or security could even be discussed without the Sultan's consent. The Constitution does not include any guarantees of individual rights. Emergency orders and constitutional amendments were, however, originally subject to the Legislative Council's approval.

The marginally democratic features were subject to a process of dilution in due course, starting with the abolition of elections in 1970 and moving on to the "suspension" of the Legislative Council in early 1984. At the point of "Full Independence" the post of *Menteri Besar* (Chief Minister) was converted into Prime Minister, and assumed by the Sultan. The authority of the Constitution continues to be invoked biannually, in the Government Gazette, as the legal basis of the "State of Emergency", and indirectly for the many Legislative Orders issued in this framework. In official speeches the Constitution is seen as embodying the values of the State ideology — particularly the executive power of the Sultan and the official status of the Muslim religion. The Constitution has also been described as "the highest law of the land", while being said to have been "adapted" in the light of changing needs. But when the Constitution was amended at the end of 1983 to empower the Sultan to appoint Ministers, and in early 1984 to suspend the Legislative Council, these amendments were effected by Emergency Order, not through the Legislative Council. Since then it seems to have become a practice to extend the Sultan's powers through further Emergency Orders (Subsidiary Legislation) which invoke the authority of the Constitution yet do not amend its text in the relevant Sections. Whereas in the Constitution as originally drafted, amendments had to be laid before the Legislative Council, now amendment itself is done by Emergency Order. Indeed, under a 1984 amendment, any Order under a Proclamation of a State of Emergency by the Sultan is deemed to have validity even though the previous Proclamation had expired or not been properly laid before the Legislative Council. By a further amendment that year, the Sultan transferred authority over the State finances from himself acting as "Sultan in Council" to the Minister for Finance acting "with the approval of His Majesty". This enabled him to assume full financial control, then delegate it without bureaucratic scrutiny.[8]

Reflecting its declining importance, the Constitution has not been published for general sale since the early 1970s. Constitution Day (29 September), after being effectively moribund for some years, was replaced, from 1991, by Teachers' Day (23 September) as an annual mark of honour to the late Seri Begawan Sultan. However, 29 September was restored as "Civil Service Day" in 1994.

For a more authentic expression of élite aspiration for the development of the polity, it is better to turn from the British-drafted Constitution of 1959 to the Bruneian-drafted Independence Declaration of 1984. Here we learn that Brunei Darussalam "shall be forever a sovereign, democratic and independent Malay Muslim Monarchy [founded upon] the teachings of Islam according to Ahlis Sunnah Waljamaah and based upon the principle of liberty, trust and justice..."[9] Bruneian commentators have had little to say on the meaning to be attributed to "democratic" in this context, but have made suggestions that it should mean the people's will is expressed through the supremacy of Islam, or that their welfare and national aspirations are completely understood and cared for by the monarch. Certainly, theorists of the national Malay Muslim Monarchy ideology (*Melayu Islam Beraja*, or MIB) emphasize the unsuitability of Western democracy to Brunei's "cultural circumstances".

Nevertheless, a Constitutional Review Committee has been in existence since the first half of 1994, chaired by the first of the Sultan brothers, Prince Mohamed, the Foreign Minister (holding the title of *Perdana Wazir* — i.e., "the Premier Wazir"). A source close to the chairman intimated to the writer that liberalization was definitely on the agenda in 1994: even steps towards making the government and royal family justiciable in the courts were mooted. The committee's initial findings were forwarded in that year, but no details were made public, and nor did any constitutional change eventuate. The *Perdana Wazir* again mentioned the committee in mid-1998, at a press interview coinciding with a British state visit, possibly with a British audience in mind. He did, however, refer to forthcoming "change" in a speech in January 1999, delivered to a Bruneian audience while deputizing for the Sultan, and following this, in an interview with *Asiaweek*.[10] Nonetheless, the dramatic suit against Prince Jefri launched in February 2000 was not announced as a prosecution, only a civil suit for recovery of BIA funds, and by May it had been settled out of court.

Head of State

Brunei remains an absolute monarchy, unconstrained by parliamentary institutions, or the judiciary. There is no test of "the legality of laws"; nor can any government action be challenged, in the absence of any provision for the government, let alone the Sultan, to be sued. (As stated above, the suit against Prince Jefri appeared to be for recovery of funds by the government: it was not a suit against the government by a citizen, or even a prosecution of Prince Jefri by his government.) The Sultan is the embodiment of the nation, heads the executive, legislative and judicial arms of government, is Head of Islam, and Supreme Commander of the Royal Brunei Armed Forces. These are not legal fictions as in many countries: he rules as well as reigns. He is assisted by a Privy Council on matters related to the royal household, and by a cabinet and bureaucracy on most other matters.

The Privy Council includes the more senior ministers, but also a predominant leavening of royalty and holders of traditional titles. In 1998 there were 31 members: 9 cabinet ministers; 9 senior officials or retired officials, including holders of senior Pehin titles; 9 aristocracy, including retired officials with Cheteria titles; and 4 members of the Royal Family, i.e., brothers-in-law of the Sultan. The most "political" of the reported activity of the Privy Council is to advise the Sultan regarding the prerogative of mercy. More often, it will tender "advice" on matters such as seating arrangements and the wearing of insignia at State ceremonies; the appropriate precedence for Muslim and Christian Era dates in official documents and correspondence; and the appointment of a Deputy Sultan during the Sultan's absence abroad.

This is not to play down the importance of the Privy Council, for the Sultan's ceremonial or ritual role is at least as important as that of the Heads of State of Thailand and Malaysia. The crucial difference between Brunei and these two political systems is that the ceremony and ritual do not provide supplementary legitimacy for an executive power based on elections, but cast a transcendental aura over the power exercized by the monarch himself. In fact, absolute power and supreme ritual status confirm and reinforce each other. At the heart of this synthesis is the power to detain any subject deemed to be subversive, literally "at His Majesty's pleasure", and to require a religious oath of loyalty to the Sultan as a condition of ultimate release after "rehabilitation". These features are not found in the Internal Security Act (permitting detention without trial) — but nor does the Act itself accord any role to the courts.

The Sultan is Head of Islam, as are the Sultans of the States of Malaysia. He is Chairman of the Religious Council and the notion of the ruler as "Caliph" has been built upon in official discourse. Royal wealth has been increasingly channelled into religious endowments. The Office of the

Mufti, which issues theological rulings, is under the Sultan within the Prime Minister's Department. However, in keeping with his absolute power and the endeavours of functionaries to cultivate charisma, the present incumbent in Brunei is much more venerated as a "Caliph" than the Peninsular Sultans are in their domains. Importantly, there are some signs that the Sultan of Brunei himself takes his divine calling seriously, not only as to the duties entailed but also with regard to self-perception. The Sultan first performed the Haj pilgrimage to Mecca in 1987, and delivered his first sermon in April 1992.

On the administrative side, educated Bruneians generally recognize a distinction between Orders which originate in the bureaucracy but are issued with the Sultan's formal or presumed consent (*titah berkenan*), and commands or utterances which the Sultan makes personally (*titah*). However, the colonial-period formula of "the royal assent" to legislation is becoming redundant as Subsidiary Legislation, simply signed by the Sultan in the framework of Emergency Orders, increasingly takes the place of Enactments or Acts. These are initiated within the Prime Minister's Department and drafted by the Ministry of Law (see further in the "Legislature and Elections" section, below).

The masses are not generally encouraged to perceive any distinction between the Sultan's munificence and that of the government — it is all attributed to the Sultan — yet a quite important distinction is sometimes claimed, between State funds and the Sultan's "private wealth". The "private wealth" enables the Sultan, as an independent actor in the system, to bestow direct patronage without going through the budgetary process, and to be praised for his "personal charity". There has been some discussion among "observers" as to the validity of the epithet "the Richest Man in the World". Although the Brunei Government denies that all the wealth of the State is the Sultan's personal fortune, the fact that he has absolute power, as monarch, over the disposal of all State funds, and delegated a significant part of that power to his younger brother, may seem to show that the distinction between "public" and "private" wealth is a little academic. Certainly the original source of the "private" element was not private, as may be intuited from the appearance of a new, non-legislated head of "Charged Expenditure" in the revenue statistics just prior to national independence, designated "royalty" and approximate in value to current hydrocarbon income — a category distinct from the "Civil List". (The British-style Civil List — i.e., allowances, under Charged Expenditure, to individual members of royalty — continues, but the new type of Charged Expenditure vastly overshadows the old type.)

Under the Law of Succession 1959,[11] succession to the throne is by primogeniture in the line of Sultan Hashim (reigned 1885–1906). By custom, ceremonial confirmation of the heir apparent has become institutionalized, and politically requisite. This development seems to imply that the Council of Succession or leading court figures could play a part, if a ruler were to die intestate. Indeed, in 1985, as part of the last conflict of will between the Sultan and his ailing father, the Sultan changed the composition of the Succession Council, apparently fearing that the Seri Begawan might in some way divert the succession. At the time of writing there is no "succession question" in Brunei, since the Sultan's eldest son by his first (the royal) wife, was installed as Crown Prince (*Paduka Seri Pengiran Muda Mahkota*) in August 1998.

The Succession Council is slightly smaller than the Privy Council, with a good deal of overlap but no group of cabinet ministers. There can be little doubt that its Chairman, Prince Mohamed, is very much the power "next to" the throne. This is widely recognized in Bruneian society, and his chairmanship of both the Succession Council and the Constitution Review Committee attest to it.

Inheriting an institution with a reputedly unbroken history extending back over five centuries, the current Sultan — *Kebawah Duli Yang Maha Mulia Paduka Seri Baginda Sultan Haji Hassanal Bolkiah Mu'izzaddin Waddaulah, Sultan dan Yang Di-Pertuan Negara Brunei Darussalam*, to give his correct title — attracts loyal support from a majority of Bruneians. His birthday is the social event of the year, with months of bureaucratic planning culminating in construction of elaborate, brightly-lit arches over all main roadways, and a tightly packed programme of entertainment. He presides over most important national and religious events, and makes regular tours of the countryside. He greets tens of thousands of Bruneians annually at such functions, reaching out to touch hands in a manner sometimes akin to that of a populist Western politician. (See also section on Extent of Legitimacy).

The Executive

The Executive Council of the 1959 Constitution is now named Council of Ministers. In practice, its procedures vary from most foreign models. Ministers and Deputy Ministers are appointed by the Sultan. It appears to be normal for ministers to request, or to be called for, individual audience with the Sultan, rather than to gather round a table under his chairmanship. In audience they relate to him as their Sovereign, not as a Prime Minister, *"primus inter pares"*. It is in "His Majesty the Sultan and Yang Di-Pertuan", not a Prime Minister, that the supreme executive authority is vested. The fact that the Sultan himself is Prime Minister provides an illustration of his power, but is somewhat incidental to the relationship and interaction with an individual minister.

Apart from the premiership — the capacity in which he attends Heads of Government summits abroad — the Sultan assumed the Finance and Home Affairs portfolios in the first, seven-man, Cabinet of 1984–86. He took over Defence from October 1986, after the death of his father, with his brother Prince Jefri and close adviser Pehin Isa taking over Finance and Home Affairs respectively in a twelve-member Cabinet. He again took on Finance, without giving up Defence, in 1997, when Prince Jefri resigned. His many powers exercised under pre-Independence law as "the Sultan in Council", include: the granting or refusal of consent to various types of land transaction; the grant or withdrawal of certain categories of citizenship; the approval or rejection of overseas scholarship applications by Bruneian students; and appointments of expatriate employees proposed by the Public Service Commission. The royal prerogative of pardon also has roots in the era of colonial Indirect Rule. But it is not a power that can be exercised with any detachment, as in other political systems, for the original decision to imprison may have been made by the Sultan himself.

An awesome workload is implied by this list of responsibilities — which goes with a busy schedule of public appearances and speech-making at home, and many trips abroad. Indeed, there were symptoms of paralysis in

---

FIGURE 1.3

Brunei: Government Ministries

Prime Minister's Department
Ministry of Defence
Ministry of Foreign Affairs
Ministry of Finance
Ministry of Home Affairs
Ministry of Education
Ministry of Law
Ministry of Religious Affairs
Ministry of Industry & Primary Resources
Ministry of Development
Ministry of Health
Ministry of Culture, Youth & Sports
Ministry of Communications

the government machinery in the first few years of independence. A solution has been sought in the development of an élite unit of administration to manage the royal prerogatives and functions from within the Palace, as well as supervise the good functioning of the bureaucracy as a whole: the Prime Minister's Department. By the end of 1994, 15 departments were located within "JPM" (*Jabatan Perdana Menteri*) itself, several of them "annexed" from other ministries at various times. The Public Service Commission, Establishment, Audit are under JPM; also, importantly, the Police.

This development has done much to strengthen and vindicate the monarchical system of government. The JPM is the hub of government in every sense. The Sultan's speeches drafted by the department communicate the main lines of policy to both bureaucracy and public with the absolute authority of royal *titah*. This is tantamount to saying that the most powerful man in Brunei next to the Sultan himself is the self-effacing Special Adviser to the Sultan-cum-Minister for Home Affairs, Pehin Orang Kaya Laila Setia Bakti Diraja Isa bin Ibrahim, son of the first *Menteri Besar* of Brunei (1959–61).

The task of other ministers is to implement policy conceived at a higher level. However, their leadership within their own segment of the bureaucracy may contribute to the relative success or failure of policies. The four most powerful ministers after, or alongside, Pehin Isa have been Prince Jefri, (Minister for Culture, 1984–86; Finance Minister, 1986–97; Director of BIA, 1984–98); Prince Mohamed, (Minister for Foreign Affairs, 1984 to the present); Pehin Aziz (Minister for Education and Health in the first Cabinet, 1984–86; Minister for Education, 1989 to the present; Acting Minister for Health and Director of BIA, since 1998); and Pengiran Bahrin (Minister for Law, 1984–98).

Although there was some switching of responsibilities between the twelve ministries (listed at Figure 1.3), there was a striking continuity of personnel holding Cabinet office between 1986–98, comprising only twelve men (including the Sultan). Of these, three were royal (the Sultan, Prince Mohamed and Prince Jefri), two minor aristocracy (Pengiran Bahrin and Pengiran Dr Ismail), and seven commoners (including Pehin Isa and Pehin Aziz). This pattern may be contrasted with the small Cabinet of 1984–86 in which four members of the royal family, including the Seri Begawan Sultan, outweighed one minor aristocrat and two Pehins in the share of ten ministries, reflecting the desire of the Seri Begawan for a "royal independence".

Occasional differences between Cabinet members have been discernible over a range of issues, perhaps most notably in relation to Islamic affairs.

Objecting to religious authorities changing arrangements for the annual Maulud (birth of the Prophet) procession in 1985 (by segregating male and female) the Sultan stayed away from the ceremony; so did all the cabinet, except Education and Health Minister, Pehin Aziz. (Pehin Ustaz Badaruddin, Director of Information and the creator of MIB, was blamed for the decision, but the revision of the marching plan was not, it is understood, on "religious" grounds, but rather for the convenience of the ladies.) About a year later, the Sultan acted against Aziz by demoting him in a Cabinet reshuffle after the death of the Seri Begawan, and prior to that, Badaruddin was sent into ambassadorial exile in Jakarta. In 1988 religious elements began to reassert influence. At Radio and Television Brunei both female and male news readers put on head-coverings. In November 1988 Pehin Aziz regained the front-line Education Ministry, and the following month Pehin Badaruddin returned as Permanent Secretary in the Prime Minister's Department with responsibility for government information and media. In subsequent years relations between the "Islamic" elements and others sometimes proceeded uneasily as Brunei opened up to international "sky" TV and rock concerts by the likes of Michael Jackson, but a broad accommodation was reached. Brunei has certainly never appeared in danger of travelling down the path of Islamic "extremism". Perhaps the greatest barrier to it is the growing preference of the younger generation for secular, cosmopolitan styles.

Although correctly described as a "monarchy" first and foremost, Brunei Darussalam is also a "bureaucratic state". All ministers except royalty have been promoted from the bureaucracy. All appointments to government jobs are handled by the Public Service Commission, while transfers and promotions are in the hands of the powerful Establishment Department. The most powerful civil servant, with the highest rank of Pehin, is the head of the Public Service Commission. In general, the pervasiveness of careers in government service permeates society with a culture that is very much oriented towards a "governing" perspective, i.e., amenability to the idea of the legitimacy of administration and State authority.

At the sub-national level the four districts are administered from their respective District Offices, under a District Officer answerable to the Minister for Home Affairs. The District Officer liaises with the Police on a district security committee. The district administration communicates policy to the people, and hears their grievances, through village and commune (*mukim*) headmen and a network of village and commune councils. The headmen are appointed after soundings are taken in their communities, sometimes culminating in an election, but the candidates all have to pass tests of acceptability with the district administration first. The headmen receive an attractive government stipend (over B$1,000 per month), and are increasingly recruited from among retired minor officials, army NCOs or policemen.

Military and Police

There are four weapon-bearing organizations in the country: the Royal Brunei Armed Forces (RBAF or ABDB), the Brunei-employed Gurkha Reserve Unit, British Army Gurkhas at Seria, and the paramilitary Royal Brunei Police. The first two of these organizations come under the Ministry of Defence funded by a budget of B$490.7 million for fiscal 1989, as an example. That was 14.9 per cent of the total appropriation to the Consolidated Fund. The Royal Brunei Police Force comes under the Prime Minister; it received a budget of B$63.8 million in the same year. The initial appropriation to Defence in 1993 was B$625.4 million, to the Police B$77.5 million. His Majesty is Supreme Commander of the Armed Forces, and Inspector General of Police. His first and second wives (Raja Isteri Pengiran Anak Saleha and Pengiran Isteri Mariam) are patronesses to the charitable organizations of the Armed Forces and Police wives respectively. Pengiran Isteri is also honorary Colonel of the Women's Wing of RBAF.

The RBAF have been divided into their three separate forces — a land army, navy and airforce — since 1991. Hardware consists typically of armoured cars, coastal patrol vessels, and helicopters, respectively. A fixed wing Hawk squadron has been promised since 1989, and a trickle of pilots trained abroad for this purpose, but insufficiency of pilots and other vital personnel have constantly delayed implementation.

The armed forces and the police forces have both stayed outside politics. A testing moment occurred in 1985, when conflict between the Sultan and Seri Begawan resulted in the latter appearing to "lay claim" — at least by insinuation that was read in this sense by the Sultan — to the Sultan's own office and the position of Supreme Commander that goes with it. But any prospect of military revolt against the existing Sultan was soon removed when the police, followed by RBAF, publicly pledged support to the incumbent. The Sultan's 1991 speech announcing the separation of army, navy and airforce caused a minor stir when he warned of the dangers of "weapons consuming their masters", and was taken to have said — mistakenly as it transpired — that to forestall such a possibility he was assuming direct command.

Physically, the Armed Forces are more than strong enough to take over the State (there are now three infantry battalions), but the rapid circulation of senior army officers between field commands and staff posts, and their even more rapid retirement after reaching the top, seem to limit the possibilities for any individual officer to develop political pretensions. In the absence of any active external threat, but knowing that internal upheaval might trigger an external intervention which Brunei's relatively minute forces would be unable to repel, there is little prospect of a war that could raise the military's profile and create heroes. Moreover, the Gurkha Reserve Unit guards key government installations, while the British Gurkha Battalion in Seria is an "uncertain quantity" at best, even though not formally part of internal security dynamics as far as the British Foreign Office is concerned. British Special Forces are believed to "drop in" for jungle training from time to time, and the Singapore Armed Forces has a permanent training base in Temburong.

Senior military personnel generally give the impression of being well contented by a large budget which provides them with regular opportunities to update their equipment in line with other ASEAN forces, as well as comfortable salaries. The main difficulties they must contend with are poor recruitment and retention of Other Ranks (reflecting the widespread prosperity), and an even more serious paucity of technological sophistication (reflecting Brunei's small population and educational deficit).

Legislature and Elections

The Legislative Council provided for in the 1959 Constitution was to consist of sixteen members elected indirectly from four elected District Councils, and seventeen appointed and *ex officio* members. Such a body took shape out of the August 1962 elections, with the PRB gaining almost immediate control of the whole elective element. This Council was never convened, but after the Rebellion elections were held in March 1965, resulting in a Council comprising ten directly elected members and eleven appointed and *ex officio*. The electorate returned a number of presumed PRB candidates, masked as "Independents". This result, combined with increasing British pressure for a Cabinet responsible to the Legislature, seems to have hardened the Sultan's opposition to democratization — a position he promoted from a less exposed position after he abdicated in 1967. The abolition of elections followed (1970), then the "suspension" of the Legislative Council (1984). The government still maintains that laws are issued by a "legislature" — or at least it can be inferred from references in some Orders that there is a "process of legislation". In most cases laws are issued as Emergency Orders, with a Subsidiary Legislation (S) number — rarely as Enactments (E) as used to be the case in the days of a Legislature.

As noted earlier, some elections remain for village (*kampong*) heads. A national-level "Assembly of Kampong Councils" was convened for the first time in May 1996. This had no legislative function, but was apparently intended to create the appearance of "representation". But in any democratic sense this is still awaited. The Assembly's function looks more like that of passing resolutions of support to the government — which is also the employer of all the village officials in the Assembly.

Ever since 1962 the government has been able to discourage democratic aspirations by playing on the trauma of the Rebellion, which set brother against brother and caused much suffering. And in 1998 the political turbulence in Indonesia and Malaysia provided a more up-to-date "admonition" about the "perils of democracy". Most Bruneians remain willing to "count their blessings" and not flirt with ideas of change.

Political Parties

In an interview on the eve of independence, the Sultan ruled out any immediate role for institutions such as political parties. In spite of this, and the suspension of the Legislature Council, two parties were permitted in 1985 — the Brunei National Democratic Party and a break-away known as the Brunei National Solidarity Party (*Parti Perpaduan Kebangsaan Brunei*). This seemingly liberal approach to parties ended in January 1988 with the banning of the BNDP and arrest of its two main leaders under the Internal Security Act. Ostensibly the party had failed to lodge annual reports in accordance with the Societies Act, and had established an illegal affiliation with an international organization (the Pacific Democratic Union). Perhaps more important were calls by the party leadership for the Sultan to assume a figurehead role and hand power to the people. The BNSP assumed a low profile thereafter, but resurfaced in 1995 and held its first National Congress. Every would-be political party faces the fundamental liability that the government forbids membership of political organizations to government servants — a major block of potential educated support and intellectual participation. Many less educated Bruneians will listen to "guidance" from their educated kinsmen in the government service. The natural constituency for parties, and social background of their office-holders, is the small business class — a group who invariably feel disgruntled because the government is giving "too few contracts to locals" or is not paying their invoices promptly after contracts are awarded. But they must be cautious so long as the government is the source of their livelihood. In terms of policy, there is little to distinguish the two parties which have arisen since independence, albeit alongside their pledges of loyalty to the Sultan and adherence to the State ideology BNDP was radical enough to say that it would "peacefully try to achieve a system of parliamentary democracy under a constitutional monarchy".

Two generations of Bruneians have now come to maturity who have never experienced a general election, let alone the heady democratic hopes of the PRB era. The return from exile of PRB leader Zaini Ahmad by early 1994, and his "rehabilitation" into a non-political, private exist-ence in July 1996, after a period of penance in prison, signalled and symbolized the triumph of the monarchical system over its main ideological alternative.

Judiciary

The judiciary is the most independent institution within the State, notwithstanding that the Sultan is the head of it. The current Chief Justice is a Briton on contract, formerly Chief Justice of Hong Kong. A succession of "Commissioners" of the High Court have served "on circuit" from Hong Kong. The hierarchy of courts in Brunei consists of Magistrates Courts; the High Court; the Appeal Court; and appeals to the Privy Council in London, but only, since 1995, for civil cases. The Kathi Courts deal essentially with family matters within the Muslim community. A *Syariah* Court to deal with a range of offences under Islamic law was announced in 1996, but has been slow to come into action. The full "Brunei-ization" of the judiciary is within sight, as local magistrates gain experience in the lower courts, followed by promotion in the Ministry of Law and emergence on the Bench.

In terms of the independence of the courts in dealing with cases brought, and in terms of the meticulous gazetting of laws with no retroactive effect, it is certainly possible to say (as the former Minister for Law often did) that Brunei is subject to a "rule of law". Further, the government and even members of the royal family are willing to be cited as defendants in foreign courts, and to accept foreign arbitration in commercial disputes. This gives important assurance to foreign investors.

However, although the State may on occasion conduct a prosecution against an errant official, no member of the public may sue the government through the Brunei courts — at most, a government employee may be sued for personal negligence. Seriously errant royalty have been customarily dealt with by detention "at the Sultan's pleasure" rather than by the courts. The first breach in this principle occurred about four years ago, when the son of the Sultan's eldest sister was prosecuted for kicking a policeman's helmet. And although the choice of the "civil" route against Prince Jefri upheld the taboo on prosecution of high royalty, it had important symbolic significance — despite the early settlement. A limiting factor for reform so far has been that the private advocates in Brunei are mainly of foreign nationality, acutely aware that they depend on the government's goodwill to renew their licences to practise, and thus nervous about proposing change.

Ideology

The official ideology, as noted, is styled *Melayu Islam Beraja* (MIB) — a "Malay Muslim Monarchy". Although claimed to have existed as the defining principle of society and polity since time immemorial, it began to be systematized around the time of independence by the then Director of Information, Ustaz (later Pehin Udana Khatib) Badaruddin bin Othman. It is now taught in secondary schools up to Form III, and is a subject of both instruction and research at the national university, Universiti Brunei Darussalam (UBD, founded 1985).

Foreign analysts tend to perceive tensions between the principle of absolute monarchy and certain tendencies within modern Islam, let alone Malay nationalism as experienced in Brunei during the PRB era. However, the purpose of the ideology, precisely, is to unify these "opposites" by co-optation and conservative interpretation of both Islam and nationalism under monarchical authority. One way of doing this is by depicting a shared, ethnic identity of kings and people in the remote past, infused with patriotism, to forestall and disqualify the "aberration" of selfish nationalist politics under non-royal leadership in the mid-20th century. Particularly crucial is the claim that the kings of yore had long anticipated the modern Brunei doctrine of the "caring Caliph", even if expressing it in less elaborate or well-funded ways than a welfare state.

Little attempt has been made to describe the relationship of the indigenous non-Muslim masses to the Sultan, in those reputedly formative times of yore when they were the majority, or even for the present day when they are still a significant minority. As for the Chinese, they find no niche within this ideological formulation.

In the early days of the ideology — that is, in the early days of its formal, intellectual articulation — senior bureaucrats privately bemoaned the lack of any authoritative source-book on the subject, and would leave it to their staff to work out what the ideology required in terms of action. Many officials, high and low, intuited that the "I" (religion) was going to be the dominant element among the three. In this light, MIB was seen by many as a radical innovation, hostile to Brunei tradition with its easy-going Malay-style Islam. There was some satisfaction at the fall from grace of the Islamically-minded Minister for Education, Pehin Aziz, and his transferral to the Ministry of Communications in late 1986. The Sultan seemed to be swinging away from too strong an Islamic orientation. However, as noted, after two years the Sultan was in some way constrained to change his mind, and brought both Pehin Aziz and close ally Pehin Badaruddin back into prominence.

By this time (late 1988) the Head of the History Centre — de facto official historian, Pehin Orang Kaya Amar Diraja Mohamed Jamil al-Sufri bin Umar (half-brother to Pehin Aziz) — had already published, in private edition, a series of lectures given to teacher trainees during 1984–85.[12] It could not receive government funding because the future status of MIB was in the balance from late 1986. But it represented an enterprising, perhaps even courageous, attempt to put some content into both the "M" (giving an account of Brunei Malay custom and cultural characteristics); the "B" (mainly royal custom and the traditional polity); and the "I" (dominant in the text, and presented with a striking panache, given that the author is not a "religious-trained" intellectual). Missing, however, was a systematic attempt to integrate the three components.

The first group in society to experience a more systematic exposure to MIB were the early cohorts of UBD students, in the form, especially, of the lectures by an Indonesian economist, soon published internally.[13] The discourse was boldly anti-Western and Islamic-modernist, with little that made it uniquely Bruneian. Students were very much a captive audience, given that the course, introduced in the 1989/90 session, was compulsory for all. A pass in it was not a condition of graduation at first, but became required in the following year. Since the early 1990s the many students studying overseas on government scholarships have also been put through MIB courses during their vacations back home.

Within a few years the university had also sponsored collections of academic work which gave pride of place to "scientific" and "sociological" rationalizations of MIB.[14] The Academy of Brunei Studies (the unit within UBD which undertook the editing of these works) was intended, from its inception in 1990, to serve as the research directorate to a "Supreme Council on Malay Islamic Monarchy". Characteristically, research into

MIB focuses on demonstrating that current structures and behaviour have existed since time immemorial. It should be stressed that systematization is not an approach which contradicts the claim of "long-standing reality", but indeed takes its very legitimacy from this.

Notwithstanding a stream of speeches, newspaper essays and TV lectures on MIB across the years, it was not until 1998 that there was a book-length attempt to integrate the strands of the ideology, as among themselves, and with their purported historical origins.[15] Its predominant content is theological, as befits the author who is Minister for Religious Affairs, and its overall coherence derives more from theology, and Middle Eastern history, than from insights into Brunei's own past. The chronic difficulties facing the enterprise of systematization, and even the inadequacies of the school text-books produced to date, were admitted in 1994 by no less a personage than the Director of the UBD Academy of Brunei Studies. He urged teachers to look outside the textbooks and simply imagine MIB as "the Brunei way of life", with emphasis on Brunei-Malay culture as the primary matrix, with the religion of Islam and rule by a Sultan as significant components.[16]

More than fifteen years on from Brunei's independence, and ten years after the last piece of pioneering work by Ustaz Badaruddin,[17] the momentum appears to be in decline. The reasons for this can only be speculated upon. One possibility is that the Sultan has been persuaded that the search for compatibility or intellectual integration between the parts has been made superfluous by allowing his own role to be entirely defined by Islam, which has its own corpus of ready-made answers to what makes a "good" ruler. Nonetheless the ideology — as formal programmme — is now deeply entrenched. It is integrated into the Bruneian educational system, and in its basic form draws on a perception that most ethnic Bruneis and Kedayans can identify with — namely that they share a unique common identity, shaped over centuries by Malay ethnicity, Islam and the institution of the Sultanate. The ethnic minorities whose history is divergent from this "discourse" are subject to sundry doctrinal pressures to incorporate it into consciousness as their own.

Civil Society and Human Rights

From all that has been said about the structure and mechanisms of absolute monarchy, it will not be surprising if independent institutions associated with "civil society" are difficult to identify. Their development is inhibited, for one thing, by the fact that many in the middle class — and nearly all outside the bureaucracy — are drawn from the Chinese community, not the Malays. They are small in number, and the scale of their businesses is also small. Although many Chinese are citizens, the advantages of their citizenship are clearly limited in a political structure where status and power are still determined substantially by ethnicity and inherited rank. Besides, every businessman is vulnerable to withdrawal of contracts, and even his trading licence, if he shows any inclination towards social leadership outside the Chinese community itself. In a similar way, expatriate teachers in the secondary schools are discouraged from acting as social leaders, while students are urged to be wary of the moral influence of these non-Muslims.

All clubs and social organizations in the country are subject to strict regulation, and mainly serve as extensions or channels of State power — the Federation of Youth Movements is a conspicuous example. Initial registration is subject to the rigorous scrutiny of the police Special Branch and the Ministry of Home Affairs, and will be withdrawn for any breach of conditions, especially any activity that begins to smack of politics. The Internal Security Act (ISA) provides a ready legal framework for taking potentially subversive leaders out of circulation. Printing presses are subject to strict regulation. In 1998 special Emergency regulations were promulgated for the control of places of entertainment too. Yet an atmosphere of greater openness was noticed by readers of the Brunei commercial press during 1998, and as the extent of the scandal of the missing billions began to enter the consciousness of some strata, government ministers, especially Pehin Aziz, acknowledged a need for greater transparency. A programme enshrining such objectives was set out by Pehin Aziz in March 2000.

"Human rights", like other issues, have been little discussed in Brunei, unless on terms set by the government in TV "Forums" or its weekly print organ, *Pelita Brunei* — basically affirming that the people's interests are well understood and protected by the benevolent monarchy, upholding the principles of MIB and warding off unwholesome influences from "the West". There are no human rights groups in Brunei. But nor are there egregious "human rights abuses" to attract international condemnation, in the absence of a restive population needing to be tightly controlled. (Symptomatically, Amnesty International reports may list executions in the United States but never mention Brunei at all). All or nearly all the dissidents of the older generation have now been "rehabilitated".

POLITICAL PRACTICE

Who Has Power?

Power is intensely concentrated in the Sultan's hands, and is secured there by the traditional (but self-consciously cultivated) aura surrounding the monarchy. The real power is not as ancient as the aura, however, but goes back effectively to the settlement with the British in 1959. Given the way that royal hegemony dominates foreign imagination, it must be stressed again that nine Ministries apart from Defence, Foreign Affairs and Finance have been almost continuously held by non-royals, who have risen by higher education and merit within the bureaucracy.[18] These Ministers, along with Permanent Secretaries, must be regarded as significant participants in the exercise of power — even counterbalancing royal power in subtle ways, though always on condition of overt loyalty to the Sultan who appointed them.

Strikingly, the Ministry with the greatest potential to become a rival for power has not seemed to be Defence, but rather Religious Affairs, on which the Sultan depends for vital legitimation of State authority in the absence of democracy. Inter-ministerial differences have, as noted above, focused largely on Islamic issues (though this does not mean that "debates" take place — in a Cabinet which rarely convenes as such). Not entirely coincidentally, during his voluntary exile in 1998, Prince Jefri claimed to have lost his power in a struggle with "religious conservatives".[19]

Who Benefits?

Brunei society is obsessed with the belief that "connection" counts for everything, including immunity from government regulations. As has just been shown, the perception is misled if one means that "the royal family occupy all top positions". However, the sons and daughters of "good family" (not only families of the minor aristocracy — the *Pengiran* class — but those in which the rank of *Pehin* has been bestowed in successive generations) do begin life with a head start.

Ethnically, the Brunei Government is committed to promoting the economic interests of the *bumiputera* (indigenous) races, e.g., with credit facilities for small businesses, scholarships for higher education, cheap housing. This policy mirrors the practice of the Malaysian Government, as well as being the most concrete expression of the monarchy's claim to embody "Malay nationalism" in Brunei. As in Malaysia, where the term *bumiputera* was coined in order to extend economic preferences to the non-Muslim indigenes of Sarawak and Sabah, Brunei officially gives priority to all its "constitutional indigenous". Yet with the rise of MIB, the subjective superiority of the coastal Bruneis over "backward" groups in the interior has received a boost. Many Dusuns, for example, believe, rightly or wrongly, that advancement in government service depends on conversion and assimilation to Malay culture.

Compared with Malaysia, the Sultan of Brunei is endowed with a more potent religious charisma than any of its Rulers, and Islamic legitimacy has been promoted as an alternative to democratic and nationalist legitimacy and symbols. The Malay language is still enshrined as the official language, but proper command of it is increasingly confined to the graduates of the "Arabic" (i.e., religious) schools, as the language declines in the rest of the education system under the name of bilingualism. Again in contrast to Malaysia, there are no "Malay Reservations", though the government purports to manage the huge reserves of State land in a spirit of "custody" for the native people, and has indeed allocated large areas for housing estates for landless indigenes.

Meanwhile, even the private sector, including foreign banks, are required to give priority to the recruitment of *bumiputera*. Thus ethnic Chinese citizens of Brunei, let alone those with only Permanent Resident status, have found the doors closing on one of their traditional arenas of employment. Promotion to higher levels has also become more difficult. The effects of this have been most dramatic in Shell, which has by now lost a significant cadre of technical staff to emigration. Young Chinese who seek higher education overseas often do so in order to increase their international mobility.

But for indigenous citizens, the affluence dispensed by the "rentier state" filters down to the lowest economic levels. Even citizens who have never been government employees in their lives receive a modest non-contributory pension. Those in government service enjoy car and house loans at low interest, or in any event low-cost accommodation of a high standard. Petrol is subsidized and there is no income tax. The poorly housed are being rehoused in government housing estates, where the houses may be owned freehold in the long run after repayment of government credits. All these facilities indirectly benefit strings of dependants. The Haj is organized for the faithful, conveyed in jumbo jets to Medina at subsidized fares. The general effect is that society is enveloped by a sense of benefiting from the political structure through the prosperity associated with it. The "middle-class" in the form of a large bureaucratic class, and military officer corps, owe their very affluence and prestige to the State. Nor do the masses feel "left out" when they contemplate the extraordinary change in their economic fortunes in the course of a generation, and the promise of social mobility for their children.

One group who benefit little are the children of low-income earners with large families, where both parents have to work to make ends meet. The children are left to fend for themselves, deprived of the traditional family-based working environment in which to be socially nurtured, and denied an adequate modern education in schools which are floundering in a sea of problems. Much to the concern of authorities, these problems lead to indiscipline, rootlessness, juvenile delinquency and drug-taking.

Extent of Legitimacy

Legitimacy is difficult to determine in the absence of political openness, elections or opinion surveys. The only public statements on the matter come from government sources, and are designed to promote legitimacy itself, or the belief that it exists.

However, even allowing for the role of some historical "invention", the ancient aura of the monarchy and the traditional notion of *daulat* (a sacred quality of "sovereignty" vested in the ruler) gives the Brunei State a considerable advantage over democratically-based systems in other "transitional" societies. To date, we also see signs of success in combining the courtly tradition (royal ceremonies, award of traditional ranks) with Islamic revival, at least in the old Sunni mould which upholds monarchy. In this framework, the Sultan's legitimacy is enhanced by his role as the leader of Islam, not weakened by modernist theological debate. His profile as a leader and exemplar of piety has been emphasized by his now almost annual pilgrimages.

There is certainly a connection between these two strands of legitimacy and the widespread conviction that "the Sultan can do no wrong". At the same time, the statecraft of the late ruler, the Seri Begawan Sultan, showed the way in highlighting the errors or rumoured venality of some high officials, as grounds for dismissing them. Ironically, the dismissal of "bad officials" gives such enormous popular satisfaction that it enhances the Sultan's prestige. Even when a popular grievance remains unanswered for months or years, the people seem willing to blame the officials, for "not letting the Sultan know". If this appears inconsistent with the principle that the Sultan has access to all information as Head of Government, or with the fact that he allows envelopes containing complaints to be slipped into his hand when he mixes with the people, we may have to conclude that the people of Brunei in their great majority have a deep craving to believe that, whatever else might be questionable about the system, the virtue of the ruler can be trusted. This obviates the problem which some high officials anticipated when the Sultan made himself Head of Government, that the authority of the State would be compromised if the fount of its sovereignty were to be blamed for political error. In the event, although the Sultan has been Prime Minister for fifteen years, he is still able to make other Ministers bear the vital burden of "ministerial responsibility", whereby he preserves his own sovereign sanctity intact. Visitors to Brunei in the months following Prince Jefri's dismissal from government do not record any lessening of the Sultan's prestige on account of the Prince's apparent misdeeds.

The Sultan's personal popularity is constantly augmented by mixing with the people in their homes. He not only receives private petitions, thrust into his hands, but has shown his detachment from officialdom and protocol by remarking sardonically on the fine furnishings, even air-conditioners, which are installed by the District Offices for the duration of a royal visit to a selected home. The surging crowds at the Sultan's return from his first Haj in 1987 bespeak a potent mixture of charisma inherent in the monarchical office, multiplied by the state of grace of a pilgrim, and an incipient popularity attaching to the present Sultan as an individual.

Government legitimacy is also definitely generated by government expenditure on religious pursuits, even in office hours. A distinct religious revival has taken root among middle-level officials "of a certain age", and there is no radical tendency waiting to capture it for the time being. Multiple, subsidized pilgrimages have become possible for every Muslim.

Finally, the recent economic and political turmoil in Indonesia and Malaysia — particularly the social unrest in the former — has served to confirm the value of the present political arrangements of Brunei, in the eyes of most citizens. Recent losses from the national reserves, even if the precise amount were known, would be beyond the capacity of most citizens to assess and pass a judgement on. For most Bruneians the economic and social costs of the Asian Crisis have been minor.

The Bruneian state does, of course, have a formidable array of means — both legal instruments such as the ISA, and police and military forces — to enforce acquiescence. Fear of these powers ensures that *surat layang* ("flying letters", from opposition sources) are read furtively and passed on quickly or destroyed. But for the most part these powers are not invoked, and the public obey the government out of respect rather than fear.

Governance

Most of the material requirements of modern government are handled with a degree of competency by regional standards. There are no social disturbances, and the Police have kept the wave of burglaries more or less in check. On the largely materially-weighted Human Development Index of the U.N. Development Programme, Brunei ranks at the top of the Southeast Asia scale, just behind Singapore. (See Figure 1.2) There has, however, been a potentially debilitating perception among the public that government efforts to stamp out corruption have been targeted at the "small fry", not the "big fish". The handling of the Prince Jefri case may have dissipated this perception to some degree, though the sudden withdrawal of the suit in May 2000 leaves a slight doubt.

Only if "governance" is defined purely in quantitative terms — leaving out accountability, which in the last analysis would depend on democratic institutions — could Brunei's governance be hailed as "good". External pressure might notionally be brought to bear on the accountability front if Brunei were receiving international aid, but it is not: indeed as Brunei pays for the Gurkha Battalion in Seria, the former colonial power itself receives a significant Bruneian contribution to its armed forces. Whether the recent signs of government interest in greater accountability and transparency — e.g. in the correspondence columns of the commercial press[20] — represent a new commitment, or should be read only as "lip-service", may still be too early to tell.

STATIC BUT STIRRING: ON THE THRESHOLD OF TRANSITION?

Brunei did not emerge completely unscathed from the regional financial crisis that swept Asia after Thailand floated its currency in July 1997. A fall in world oil prices, and the collapse of Amedeo, Prince Jefri's conglomerate — both events related at least indirectly to the Asian Crisis — unsettled Brunei's proverbial calm. In face of public anxiety, the government hinted that it was interested in more open and transparent administration. The need to introduce new types of tax added some credibility to the promise of openness. However, there are institutional obstacles to its rapid fulfilment.

Thus the scene may be "stirring" for Brunei-watchers, but what remains less clear is whether fundamental changes are in prospect. The country's economic future seems secure for some time yet. With constantly improving technologies, oil production could be increased without the fear of drastic depletion of the reserves. There is no lack of calls to the people to "count their blessings" compared with other peoples of ASEAN, and to give thanks for these blessings in the mosque. And the message may well be taken to heart through long habituation — though not without mild stirrings of anxiety and conscience for some, either stimulated by religion or provoked by a material factor such as the collapse of the market for rented property. Occasionally, before the crisis, concerns surfaced in public but unreported expression. Still, if thousands of isolated individuals continue to opt for "realism" in face of a system which still fundamentally works, Brunei will continue to confound the theorists who see a statistical or historically necessary correlation between economic achievement and the rise of democracy.

Theorists from both East and West are fascinated with nexuses of politics and growth — whether the postulated flow of cause-and-effect puts "economics" first, as in Western liberal thought, or "politics" in the lead, as in "Asian Values" discourse. In the case of Brunei, the focus should perhaps be on control of economic resources, whatever their derivation. It might then gradually become apparent that a State in firm control of national economic assets, with a goodly quotient of political acumen, will be in a strong position to perpetuate the political structure handed down from the recent past, whatever form that structure may take. Contrary to liberal theorists, the economic development which is supposed to foster democracy by way of a nascent "middle class" may strengthen the hand of the State in dictating authoritarian scenarios. This may also pose a difficulty for radical theorists, who similarly deplore the absence of a bourgeoisie, a class considered historically "necessary", not just for the rise of liberal democracy but for the second transformation that is believed to lie beyond. If its economy remains intact, the mould of Brunei's recent past may well define its future.

Notes

1   See Christopher Colclough and Martin Godfrey, "Brunei Manpower Master Plan" (A study conducted for the Government of Brunei by the British Council, London, 1982), pp. 49–50.

2   Mark Cleary and Wong Shuang Yann, *Oil, Economic Development and Diversification in Brunei Darussalam* (London: St Martin's Press, 1994), p. 73.

3   Ministry of Finance, *Brunei Darussalam Statistical Yearbook 1996/1997* (Bandar Seri Begawan: Department of Economic Planning and Development, 1997), p. 177.

4   Dana Rubin, "Prince playboy", *Institutional Investor*, December 1998, pp. 89–91.

5   "Oil is Brunei's best bet: financial experts stress need to boost reserves", *Borneo Bulletin*, 23/24 (January 1999).

6   For discussion, see Roger Kershaw, "Marginality then and now: shifting patterns of minority status in Brunei Darussalam", *Internationales Asienforum* 29, nos. 1–2 (1998): 86.

7   *The Constitution of the State of Brunei, 1959* (Subsidiary Legislation, S. 97). The Parts are: I. Preliminary; II. Religion; III. Executive Authority; IV. Privy Council; V. The Executive Council; VI. The Legislative Council; VII. Legislation and Procedure in the Legislative Council; VIII. Finance; IX. The Public Services; X. The State Seal; XI. Miscellaneous; XII. Amendment and Interpretation of the Constitution.

8   See *The Constitution of Brunei Darussalam (Order under Section 83 (3)): The Emergency Orders, 1984* (Subsidiary Legislation, S. 34); *The Constitution of Brunei Darussalam: The Constitution (Transfer of Functions and Consequential Provisions) (No. 4) Order, 1984* (Subsidiary Legislation, S. 36) (Brunei: The Government Printer.) (Government Gazette, Part II, No. 16).

9   Department of Information, Negara Brunei Darussalam, *Proclamation of Independence of Brunei Darussalam* (Wall poster, 1984).

10 *Pelita Brunei*, 10 February 1999, and *Asiaweek*, 13 August 1999.

11 State of Brunei, *The Brunei Agreement, 1959; The Constitution of the State of Brunei, 1959; The Succession and Regency Proclamation, 1959* (Brunei: Government Printer, n.d.).

12 Mohd. Jamil al-Sufri bin Umar, *Melayu Islam Beraja* (Bandar Seri Begawan: published by the author, n.d.).

13 Moehammad Nazir, "Masalah dan Cabaran atas Identiti Kebruneian", mimeographed (Bandar Seri Begawan: Universiti Brunei Darussalam, 1989). Reproduced in *Pelita Brunei*, 13 June–4 July 1990 [4 weekly issues].

14 The collections were: Abu Bakar bin Apong, ed., *Sumbangsih UBD. Essays on Brunei Darussalam* (Bandar Seri Begawan: Akademi Pengajian Brunei/ UBD, 1992) to honour the Silver Jubilee of the Sultan; Abdul Latif bin Ibrahim, ed., *Purih. Universiti Brunei Darussalam dalam Satu Dekad.* (Bandar Seri Begawan: Akademi Pengajian Brunei/UBD, 1996) marking UBD's Tenth Anniversary.

15 Mohd. Zain bin Serudin, *Melayu Islam Beraja: Suatu Pendekatan* (Bandar Seri Begawan: Dewan Bahasa dan Pustaka, 1998).

16 Abdul Latif bin Ibrahim, "Melayu Islam Beraja: suatu pendekatan huraian takrif". Mimeographed paper presented at a seminar on MIB for Senior Government Servants sponsored by the Public Service Institute with the co-operation of Academy of Brunei Studies, 1994, p. 21.

17 Badaruddin bin Othman, "Keberkesanan ke arah penerapan konsep M.I.B. dalam struktur Kerajaan dan Negara", *Pelita Brunei,* 26 April, 3 May, 10 May 1989.
18 The situation is quite different from that imagined by Neher and Marlay, who state: "every bureaucrat, and military officer, is related to the Sultan". Clark D. Neher and Ross Marlay, *Democracy and Development in Southeast Asia: The Winds of Change* (Boulder: Westview, 1995), p. 145.
19 See Jefri Bolkiah, Prince, "Une lettre du prince Jeffri Bolkiah, frère du sultan de Brunei", *Le Monde*, 23 September 1998.
20 Mark Cleary and Simon Francis, "Brunei Darussalam: The Outside World Intrudes", in *Southeast Asian Affairs 1999* (Singapore: Institute of Southeast Asian Studies, 1999), pp. 67–76.

Further Reading

Cleary, Mark and Wong Shuang Yann. *Oil, Economic Development and Diversification in Brunei Darussalam.* London: St Martin's Press, 1994.
C. Gunn, Geoffrey. *Language, Power and Ideology in Brunei Darussalam.* Athens, Ohio.: Ohio University Center for International Studies, 1997.
Horton, A.V.M. ed., *Report on Brunei in 1904 by M. S. H. McArthur.* Athens, Ohio: Ohio University Center for International Studies, 1987.
Hussainmiya, B.A. *Sultan Omar Ali Saifuddin III and Britain. The Making of Brunei Darussalam.* Kuala Lumpur: Oxford University Press, 1995.
Leake, David Jr. *Brunei. The Modern Southeast Asian Sultanate.* Kuala Lumpur: Forum, 1990.
Singh, Ranjit D.S. *Brunei 1839–1983. The Problems of Political Survival.* Kuala Lumpur: Oxford University Press, 1984.

2

CAMBODIA
After the Killing Fields

Sorpong Peou

INTRODUCTION

Cambodia is one of the oldest states in Southeast Asia, but longevity has not provided a shield against political turmoil. The Khmer Rouge government gained international notoriety in the 1970s, turning the whole country into killing fields, and subsequent governments have found it hard to escape this legacy.

From the ninth to the thirteenth centuries Cambodia's Angkor dynasty ruled over much of the Southeast Asia mainland. It left historical remains that are among the wonders of the world, and evidence of a highly developed civilization. From the fourteenth century Cambodia began to contract, squeezed by Thailand on one side and Vietnam on the other. France made it a protectorate in 1863, and the state assumed its present form after Battambang and Siem Riep were wrested from Thailand in 1904 and 1907. Apart from a brief Japanese interlude during World War II, it remained a French colony until independence in 1953.

Cambodia shares long and often contested borders with Laos (in the north), Thailand (in the west), and Vietnam (in the east). It remains a predominantly agrarian society, with 75 to 80 per cent of the population earning their living from agriculture. Forests are among the country's most important natural resources, but have been depleted rapidly (often illegally) since the mid-1990s. Despite being resource-rich, Cambodia remains poor. This is largely the legacy of the civil war in the first half of the 1970s and the Khmer Rouge reign of terror. In the early 1980s, a socialist government started to rebuild the economy from scratch. Faced with economic stagnation, the government moved to adopt a policy of liberalization late in the decade. A market-oriented economic system has

FIGURE 2.1

Cambodia: Key Dates

800–1300	Golden age of Angkor.
1863	Cambodia becomes French protectorate.
1953	Cambodia gains indepedence from France.
1970	Prince Norodom Sihanouk is ousted in a bloodless coup staged by his own defence minister, Gen. Lon Nol. The US-backed Khmer Republic comes into existence, but ends up fighting a war with a Khmer Rouge guerrilla force led by Pol Pot and supported by communist troops from North Vietnam.
1975	The Khmer Rouge revolutionary movement wins the war, takes control of the country, and starts to build a totalitarian regime, known as Democratic Kampuchea (DK).
1978	In late December, Vietnam invades Cambodia and drives the Pol Pot leadership out of power. Vietnam's army occupies Cambodia (until 1989) and installs the People's Republic of Kampuchea (PRK). The PRK is initially led by Heng Samrin, but he is soon succeeded by Hun Sen.
1982	The Coalition Government of Democratic Kampuchea (CGDK) is established as a government-in-exile, to co-ordinate resistance to the PRK. Its members include the ousted Khmer Rouge, the National United Front for an Independent, Neutral, Peaceful, and Co-operative Cambodia (FUNCINPEC) and the Khmer People's National Liberation Front (KPNLF).
1989	The PRK is renamed State of Cambodia (SOC). With the withdrawal of Vietnamese troops, Cambodia begins to open up by adopting a policy of economic liberalization.
1991	SOC and the CGDK sign the Paris Peace Agreement, permitting UN intervention to facilitate a free and fair election.
1993	The UN-organized election is won by FUNCINPEC. SOC, re-named the Cambodian People's Party (CPP), comes second, the KPNLF third, and the little-known Moulinaka fourth. The Khmer Rouge boycotts elections and continues armed struggle against the new government. The four parties form a coalition, with Prince Norodom Ranariddh (son of Prince Sihanouk) as First Prime Minister and Hun Sen as Second Prime Minister. The government adopts a new constitution. Sihanouk is reinstated as King.
1997	Hun Sen stages a coup against Prince Ranariddh. The Khmer Rouge movement begins to disintegrate.
1998	Hun Sen wins national election, and emerges as the sole Prime Minister. The Khmer Rouge rebellion ends, after Pol Pot's death and the capture of his top military commander, General Ta Mok.
1999	Cambodia becomes a member of the Association of Southeast Asian Nations (ASEAN).

since been publicly recognized, even in the current Cambodian Constitution.

In the current population of around 12 million, the Khmer remain the dominant group. There are at least 20 identifiable minority groups, representing about 3.83 per cent of the population. According to official statistics in 1995, most noticeable minority groups include the Cham (203,881), Vietnamese (95,597), Chinese (47,180), and Laotian (19,819). These generally live peacefully alongside the Khmer, except for the Vietnamese who are viewed with suspicion and distrust because of deep historical animosities. This homogeneity has not, however, prevented large-scale civil conflict and war.

Buddhism is the official religion of the country, and followed by an overwhelmingly number of inhabitants (90 per cent). It remains an important unifying factor, nothwithstanding Khmer Rouge attempts to extinguish all religions. It is estimated that by the mid-1990s, there were more than 3,000 Buddhist temples (wats) in Cambodia and some 30,000 monks, compared with 3,369 temples and 65,000 monks before 1975. At the same time Buddhism has also been linked with a fatalistic acceptance of misfortunes, and deference to authority — an omnipresent reality in Cambodia's hierachical society. Other religions do, however, enjoy considerable freedom. The Muslim community numbers more than 200,000, and in the 1990s the number of Christians grew from just 200 to around 60,000.

Since it gained political independence, the country has been racked by a series of tragedies. Prince Norodom Sihanouk, King from 1941 to 1955, then Head of Government, was deposed by a coup on 18 March 1970. Civil war followed, and a revolutionary movement known as the "Khmer Rouge", led by Pol Pot, finally brought down Lon Nol's new Khmer Republic on 17 April 1975. The new regime conducted a reign of terror that led to internal rebellions and foreign intervention. In late 1978, Vietnam sent at least 100,000 troops to oust the Khmer Rouge, and returned the country to war again. The Vietnam-backed People's Republic of Kampuchea/Cambodia (PRK/SOC) fought with three major Cambodian resistance groups, the royalist FUNCINPEC, founded by Prince Sihanouk but later headed by his son Norodom Ranariddh, the Khmer People's National Liberation Front (KPNLF), led by former Prime Minister Son Sann, and the surviving Khmer Rouge army and leadership.

It was not until 23 October 1991 that the warring Cambodian factions signed a major peace accord, generally known as the Paris Agreements, which invited the United Nations to intervene. The United Nations Transitional Authority in Cambodia (UNTAC) received a mandate to

FIGURE 2.2

Cambodia: Key Statistics

Land area: 181,035 sq. kilometres

Population:[a]   11,700,000 (1999)

GNP:[b]   Current exchange rate   — US$3.2 bn (1997);
                                              US$2.9 bn (1998)
                  Purchasing Power Parity — US$12 bn (1997);
                                              US$14 bn (1998)

GNP Per Capita:[b] Current exchange rate   — US$300 (1997);
                                              US$260 (1998)
                  Purchasing Power Parity — US$1,290 (1997);
                                              US$1,246 (1998)

Income Distribution (1997):[b]
                  Gini Index   40.4
                  % share of income or consumption:
                  Lowest 10%   2.9
                  Lowest 20%   6.9
                  2nd 20%   10.7
                  3rd 20%   14.7
                  4th 20%   20.1
                  Highest 20%   47.6
                  Highest 10%   33.8

Human Development Index (HDI) Ranking:[c]
                  World ranking   137 (1997); 136 (1998)
                  Value   0.514 (1997); 0.512 (1998)

Armed Forces:
                  Total no.[d]   149,000 (1999)
                  Expenditure[d]   US$100 m (2000)
                  of GNP[b]   3.1% (1995)

Sources: [a] Official national sources.
          [b] World Bank, *World Development Indicators* (Washington, D.C.:
             1999 & 2000).
          [c] United Nations Development Programme (UNDP), *Human
             Development Report* (New York: Oxford University Press, 1999 &
             2000).
          [d] International Institute for Strategic Studies (IISS), *The Military
             Balance, 1999–2000* (London: Oxford University Press, 1999).

create a neutral political environment for free and fair elections. Election took place in May 1993, with FUNCINPEC winning 58 seats, the SOC, reconstituted as the Cambodian People's Party (CPP) 51 seats, the KPNLF 10 seats, and the independent Moulinaka, one seat. The new 120-member Constituent Assembly adopted a constitution, which was promulgated by the reinstated King Sihanouk. On 26 July 1998, Cambodia held another national election, this time without any massive international intervention. The number of the Members of Parliament increased to 122. The CPP won with 64 seats, FUNCINPEC gained 43, and 15 went to the new Sam Rainsy Party.[1] In late 1998, a new coalition government between the CPP and FUNCINPEC was formed (with Hun Sen as Prime Minister), leaving the Sam Rainsy Party as the only opposition in parliament.

According to some critics, the regime under Prime Minister Hun Sen remains "communist" or "fascist". Most observers tend to view Hun Sen as Cambodia's "strongman", thus implying that the country is under a kind of draconian rule by one dominant leader. This chapter argues that Cambodia is neither a communist nor dictatorial regime in any strict sense, partly because the Constitution is based on the principles of liberal democracy. The country has adopted a parliamentary system of government. But the system remains fragile, largely because of the immature character of factional politics, and remains susceptible to anti-democratic practices. Evidence suggests that the current government has consolidated its power by seeking to institutionalize its political control. Cambodia may therefore emerge and remain an illiberal democracy in the foreseeable future, with elections held on a regular basis but only to help legitimize the CPP.

THE POLITICAL SYSTEM

The legal framework for Cambodian politics is mainly determined by the 1993 Constitution.[2] A 26-member multi-party committee within the newly elected Constituent Assembly was formed on 30 June 1993 and then began working on a draft constitution. After a short period of parliamentary debate, the Assembly adopted the Constitution. It was further amended in March 1999, as a result of opposition parties arguing the case for more checks and balances. The major change was establishment of a Senate.

The Constitution is recognized as the "Supreme law of the Kingdom of Cambodia" (Article 150). That is, "[laws] and decisions by the State institutions shall have to be in strict conformity with the Constitution". Cambodia adopted a "two-tier" legal system, with the Constitution being the "highest law of the land", standing above all statute laws passed by the

National Assembly. The current written or codified Constitution, which is closely linked to liberal values and democratic aspirations, rejects any form of political authoritarianism.

The Preamble of the Constitution declares the principle of popular sovereignty. The Khmer people "have awakened, stood up, are determined to stand united, strengthen national unity and defend Cambodia's territory and its sovereignty". The Preamble further states they are determined to defend the Angkor civilization as well as to "build Cambodia as a 'Land of Peace' based on a multi-party liberal democratic regime guaranteeing human rights and the respect of law". Article 51 makes clear that "Cambodia adopts a policy of liberal democracy and pluralism" and that "the Cambodian people are the master of their own country". Moreover, "All powers belong to the people who exercise them through the National Assembly, the Senate, the government, and the judiciary".

Cambodia's parliamentary system is based on the principle of a "fusion of powers". All powers are fundamentally concentrated in the parliament rather than separated, as is generally the case in a presidential system. Besides this it is fundamentally a unitary state, built upon the principles of political hierarchy. According to Article 145 of the Constitution, the administrative structure is divided into provinces and municipalities. There are 20 provinces and four municipalities (Phnom Penh, Sihanoukville, Kep and Pailin). The provinces are divided into districts (*srok*), which are in turn divided into communes (*Khum*). Each province is divided into 183 districts, which are in turn divided into 1,609 communes, then into 13,406 villages (not part of formal administrative structures). Each municipality is also divided into sections (*khan*), and each section into quarters (*sangkat*).

Seen in this context, the idea of participatory democracy in Cambodia is non-existent. While much has been talked about participatory democracy and decentralization to encourage public feedback or input, the government continued to make efforts aimed at centralizing state control. The draft Law on Commune Administrative Management, as part of the so-called reform attempts at promoting local governance is yet another example of the state seeking to centralize its political authority. The Ministry of Interior still contemplated the idea of providing direct funds to every elected Commune Council from the national treasury. The draft law also conferred the Ministry with the power to give instructions to the commune chief on the duties and responsibilities between the deputies on the Commune Council. The central government's intrusion into local government also includes the draft law's requirement to have one administrative clerk within each Commune Council, who would work for the Ministry which would also have the power to remove the clerk from office. As of May 2000, the government was still in the process of drafting two laws related to the initiative of decentralization, deconcentration and local governance.

This does not mean that the hierarchical nature of power distribution in the country is clear-cut. The Constitution makes no mention of the sub-national governments' powers and responsibilities. Neither has the Legislature passed any law regarding the division of powers and sharing of responsibilities between the different levels of government. The Council of Ministers and the Ministry of Interior control lower-level administrations by such administrative orders as sub-decrees (*anu-kret*), announcements (*prahkas*), and circulars.

Any initiative to review or amend the Constitution is the prerogative of the King, the Prime Minister and the President of the National Assembly, at the suggestion of one-fourth of all the assembly members. Any amendment has to be approved by the Assembly, with a two-thirds majority. The Constitution forbids any revision or amendment that affects "the system of liberal and pluralistic democracy and the regime of Constitutional Monarchy" (Article 153).

Head of State

The motto of the Kingdom of Cambodia in the Constitution is "*Cheat, Sasna,* and *Mohaksath*" "Nation, Religion, and King". As one of the oldest institutions in the country, the monarchy remains politically relevant. The governance structure locates the King as Head of State (see Figure 2.3).

Though derived from the people and not from any divine power, the King's political authority has been a cause for concern to some observers. A number of articles in the Constitution make it appear as if the King presides over a very powerful institution and may thus work against liberal democracy. According to the Constitution, he is "Head of State for life" and "remains inviolable" (Article 7). He is Supreme Commander of the Armed Forces (Article 23), and as Chairman of the Supreme Council of National Defence has the power to declare war (Article 24). He also has the right to grant partial and complete amnesty (Article 27). All major policy and political decisions must be made by Royal Decree.

Nonetheless, the King as Head of State does not enjoy absolute power. The Constitution makes it clear that the King "shall reign but shall not govern" (Article 7). Worth stressing is the fact that this clause "absolutely shall not be amended" (Article 17). The King "shall be a symbol of unity and eternity of the nation" (Article 8), and as such is not to engage in partisan politics. Second, he is not self-appointed. The Royal Council of the Throne — made up of the President and Vice-Presidents of the National Assembly, the Prime Minister, Buddhist Chiefs of the two major Orders (Mohanikay and Thammayut) — will choose the new King when the incumbent dies. Third, the King can act only after receiving approval from the Prime Minister and the National Assembly. Article 22 stipulates that "When the nation faces danger, the King shall make a proclamation to the people putting the country in a state of emergency after agreement with the Prime Minister and the President of the National Assembly and the President of the Senate". Article 24 further stipulates that "the King declares war after having gained approval from the National Assembly". He shall also sign the law (*Kram*) promulgating the Constitution, laws adopted by the National Assembly and reviewed by the Senate, and decrees (*Kret*) presented by the Cabinet.

Overall, the constitutional monarchy has lost much of its influence on Cambodian politics. King Sihanouk still enjoys a high degree of traditional legitimacy, but that alone is insufficient to make him a leading political force within contemporary Cambodia.

The Executive

As Head of State, the King cannot in reality be serving as the chief executive; this role lies with the Prime Minister. Approval of a new Prime Minister rests with the upper and lower chambers of the National Assembly. After elections the winning side must seek a vote of confidence by a two-thirds majority. Since the proportional voting system makes it unlikely that any party will emerge with a two-thirds majority, at least two parties will have to agree on coalition. The Assembly President advises the King on the appointment, drawn from assemblymen of the largest party (usually the leader). The King then formally appoints the new leader. The issue was initially complicated further, however, by transitional provisions in the 1993 Constitution which allowed for the appointment of First and Second Prime Ministers with equal powers and prerogatives based on the principle of "co-decision". This transitional provision no longer exists. There is only one Prime Minister (assisted by Deputy Prime Ministers) who leads the Council of Ministers.

The Prime Minister appoints and leads the Council of Ministers (generally known as Cabinet) which is the Royal Government of Cambodia whose

FIGURE 2.3

The System of Government in Cambodia, 1999

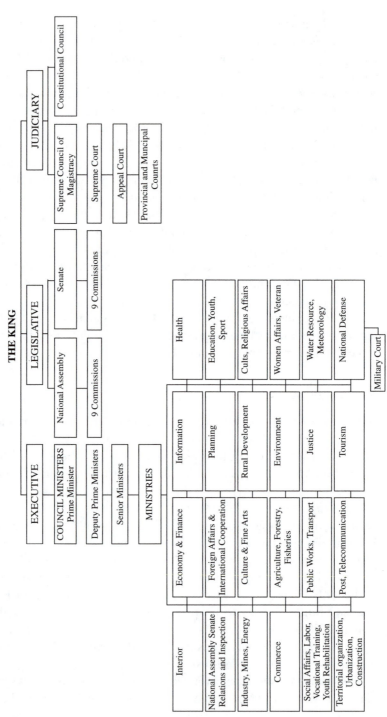

members also include Senior Ministers, Ministers and State Secretaries. After receiving a vote of confidence by the National Assembly, the King issues a Royal decree appointing the entire Council of Ministers (Article 119). Non-Assembly members may be appointed, though they must be members of political parties represented in the Assembly. Having made the appointment, however, the Prime Minister can only dismiss Council members with the support of two-thirds of the Assembly.

Council members are individually responsible to the Prime Minister and Assembly for their actions, and collectively responsible to the Assembly for all policy decisions. A vote of parliamentary confidence in the Prime Minister or any members of Council can be proposed at any time, but requires a two-thirds majority for approval.

The Council of Ministers is the focal point of administration. It meets every week in plenary session and in a working session. The Prime Minister chairs the plenary sessions and may assign a Deputy Prime Minister to preside over the working sessions. As its head, the Prime Minister manages and commands all aspects of government activities. The Office of the Council of Ministers, headed by a senior minister, is the highest administrative unit, managing and setting the agenda of the government aimed at achieving policy co-ordination and ensuring administrative functions. All draft laws, decrees and sub-decrees prepared by line ministries must be submitted to the Office for review. The Office has a secretariat of its own, with a staff of over 900, and also two attached independent secretariats related to Public Function, and Civil Aviation.

As of 1999, the Council of Ministers comprised 24 ministries (Figure 2.3), and the aforementioned independent secretariats. Each ministry usually has one minister, supported by two Secretaries of State and five Under-Secretaries of State. Next to the position of Prime Minister, the Interior and Defence portfolios are the most important. Both have co-ministers from the CPP and FUNCINPEC, because the two parties still cannot trust each other. Interior has control over local administration. Provinces and municipalities are run by a governor, assisted by first, second and third deputies. Governors are appointed by the Prime Minister, and are currently drawn from three political parties: one municipal and 11 provincial governors from the CPP, nine provincial and two municipal governors from FUNCINPEC, and one municipality (Pailin) is under Khmer Rouge defectors (Democratic National Movement). Provincial governments have authority over the lower-level administrations, and appoint chiefs of those levels, but have very limited power over revenue-expenditure and other areas of decision-making.

The central government controls the bureaucracy, whose administrative personnel as well as those of the military and security apparatuses are supposed to implement public policies. The civilian bureaucracy has 163,000 regular staff (excluding 21,000 others with special status, such as commune personnel and village chiefs). The bureaucracy is highly politicized and dependent on the political leadership, particularly the CPP. Very few bureaucrats have strong technocratic credentials, which in other countries make them indispensable to political leaders.

Political Role of Military and Police

The roles of the military and security forces have never been clearly spelt out. Cambodia has yet to publish a White Paper on National Defence, though one is in preparation. According to government sources, the current number of personnel within the Royal Cambodian Armed Forces (RCAF) is 140,693, with 15,551 "ghost soldiers" having just been removed from the military payroll. The police total about 66,000, officially under the control of the Ministry of Interior. In addition, special status staff (military and commune militia) total about 40,000.

Although the military and security forces have not played a dominant role in Cambodia, they have served as the political leaders' best instrument in advancing their political interests. During the coup in July 1997, the Chief of the General Staff General Keo Kim Yan (CPP) initially refused to get involved in the factional fighting, perhaps because of his rumoured close ties with General Nhek Bun Chhay, FUNCINPEC's top military leader. This inaction reportedly upset Prime Minister Hun Sen, who had to depend on his armed body guards and police elements led by the National Chief of Police Hok Lundy. This is not to say that the RCAF has no political role. In fact, it even has its own radio station.

The military and police forces continue to pose a credible challenge to good governance. Rumours persist of "ghost soldiers" who are either dead or have left the Armed Forces. Under intense pressure from donors, Hun Sen is committed to military reform, including substantial demobilization. But reform efforts have been complicated by a lack of funds. Members of the security and military forces do not enjoy public confidence because of their corruption and criminal activities, such as drug trafficking, illegal logging, armed robberies and kidnappings. Such criminals have almost never been prosecuted.

Bicameral Legislature

Cambodia has a bilateral legislature, which includes a National Assembly and a Senate. The 122-member directly elected National Assembly is the dominant chamber. It provides the Prime Minister, and has the primary role for legislation and other functions. Members serve for 5-year terms, unless elections are held ahead of schedule.

According to the Constitution, the notion of parliamentary supremacy is crystal-clear: the executive does not exercise its authority apart from the legislature. The head of the executive, namely the Prime Minister, must come from the Assembly, and both he and his government require a two-thirds vote of approval before they can take office. After that the Assembly may at any time bring down the executive with a vote of no-confidence, if it can muster a two-thirds majority. The executive, however, cannot dissolve Parliament on a whim — this can only happen after it has been defeated on two parliamentary votes within twelve months.

This does not mean that parliamentary sovereignty enjoys absolute power or can exercise its rights without any limitations ("elective dictatorship"). Laws adopted by the Assembly will be considered null if they violate the principles of national independence, national sovereignty, territorial integrity, and affect the political unity or administration of the nation. According to the Constitution, Cambodia remains a neutral, non-aligned state (Article 53). While Parliament represents the sovereign rights of the people, the legislature is not entrusted with the power to turn against liberal democracy. The legislature does not stand above the people.

The Assembly's power is clearest in relation to legislation. All members have the right to initiate, though in practice executive members such as the Prime Minister are likely to take the initiative. The Assembly also holds the basic "power of the purse". Under the Constitution the Assembly's financial functions include approving the national budget, state planning, loans, lendings, and the creation of changes and annulment of tax.

While the executive is the principal body in charge of making decisions and implementing them, the Assembly also has some executive powers. It must approve all appointments, transfers and dismissals of high-ranking civil servants and military personnel. It also has an important role in foreign affairs. It must approve or annul treaties or international conventions negotiated by the executive. It must also approve a declaration of war. These aspects can be decided by a simple majority of all members.

The Assembly also has "investigative" and "quasi-judicial" functions. Article 126 of the Constitution stipulates that, "each member of the Royal Government shall be punished for any crimes or misdemeanors that he/she has committed in the course of his/her duty". The Assembly can file charges against any member of the government that it finds has committed serious offences. The Prime Minister, and/or his Ministers, can also be collectively called to explain matters within their competencies. The Minister must reply within seven days.

The Senate was only established following the elections in 1998 and amendment of the Constitution in March 1999. It currently comprises 61 members, and may not exceed half the number of Assembly members. The Senate's main role is to review draft laws approved by the National Assembly, though it also has the right to initiate legislation. The Senate may return a law to the Assembly for reconsideration in its entirety, or parts of it, or reject outright. Laws can be promulgated only if the Senate approves or offers no opinion. The Senate's review can take no longer than one month, and only five days on urgent matters. Draft laws are then submitted to the King for his signature and promulgation, and go into effect within 20 days. In case of urgency, a law can take immediate effect throughout the country after promulgation.

According to the Constitution two Senators are appointed by the King, two others by the National Assembly and the rest are to be elected by a "non-universal election" (meaning appointment by political parties). Senators serve a fixed six-year term, and may be re-appointed. Current Senators include 31 from the CPP, 21 from FUNCINPEC, seven from the Sam Rainsy Party, and two appointed by the King.

Elections

Cambodia has an Election Law, which seeks to ensure that the electoral system is based on the principles of parliamentary democracy. Article 2 affirms that Assembly elections "shall be conducted in accordance with the principles of multi-party, liberal democracy". Furthermore, the Law is based on the democratic principle of proportional representation (Article 5). The electoral system was adopted after Cambodian leaders had realized that a first-past-the-post plurality system (based on the idea that a candidate who receives the largest number of votes, regardless of how small the margin, shall be declared the winner) would not work. Proportional representation was adopted not just because it was seen as more democratic, but more importantly because it offered a means of overcoming the country's deep political divisions. This ultimately forced the major parties to agree on the need to create a system that would help build trust by not allowing anyone to banish another from the political arena.

The National Election Committee (NEC) was established by the National Assembly prior to the 1998 elections, primarily to prevent electoral fraud and ensure free and fair elections. Composed of Chairman (a Khmer dignitary), Vice-Chairman (another dignitary) and other members (one from each political party currently having seats in the Assembly, two high ranking officials from the Ministry of the Interior, and one from local non-governmental organizations), it is intended to be an independent and neutral body in the carrying out of its duties. Under its direct control are Provincial/Municipal Electoral Commissions, Commune Electoral Commissions, and Polling Station Commissions.

To date elections have only been held for the National Assembly. Plans have also been announced for the election of commune council members, now scheduled to take place in 2001. Currently, the heads of the 1,609 communes are political appointees, most of whom remain loyal to the CPP. Future elected councils will work to promote socioe-conomic development, to facilitate the delivery of certain services for citizens in their localities, to protect natural resources and to draft and implement small-scale development projects within their own communes.

Judiciary

The Cambodian judicial system has been transformed in the last two decades. Completely destroyed by the Khmer Rouge regime, it had to be built virtually from scratch. In the 1980s, Cambodia had conciliatory bodies and authorities (at all local levels), one tribunal for each of the 21 provinces, a military tribunal (located in Phnom Penh), and a Supreme Court (in Phnom Penh). The Court was established in 1985, but did not function until after 1989. Its role included acting as a reviewing body of the tribunals' judgements, and receiving complaints filed by citizens against the public administration. By the early 1990s, however, the Court had not yet pronounced any judgement.[3] The judiciary lacked independence from the ruling party, partly because there were few legal experts — most Cambodian lawyers were killed under the Khmer Rouge regime, or left the country to resettle in other countries — but more importantly because the country was still at war. The Revolutionary People's Party of Kampuchea (RPPK), then the only party in the country, and other communist-controlled mass organizations, exercised a high degree of influence and control without any checks and balances or separation of powers.

The concept of an independent judiciary was introduced during the transitional period under UNTAC, when the Cambodian signatories of the

Paris Agreements agreed to set up at least one trial court (composed of one judge and one prosecutor) in each province. The judiciary was to be independent of the executive and legislative branches of government. Judges were to be appointed, promoted, and dismissed by the existing administrative structures, of course under the supervision of UNTAC. The factions also agreed to set up at least one appellate court (composed of three judges and one prosecutor) in each zone or province under their control, and to improve the SOC Supreme Court. While the appellate courts would judge both law and fact, the Supreme Court would perform such functions as reviewing judicial review of the law, appellate judgements and sending cases back to an appellate court if found conforming to the Supreme Court's judgement.

A two-tier court system was subsequently re-established. The system consisted of Municipal and Provincial courts, Courts of Appeal, and a Supreme Court. Municipal and provincial courts were the lower or first level courts located in every municipality and province. There are four municipal Courts in Phnom Penh, Sihanoukville, Kep and Pailin (with 14 judges and 6 prosecutors) and 20 provincial courts (with 75 judges and 41 prosecutors). They adjudicated legal cases and administrative litigation. Based in Phnom Penh, the Court of Appeal (with nine judges and four prosecutors) had complete jurisdiction over the entire country and dealt with criminal and civil cases in case of appeal against the lower court's decisions. The Supreme Court (with nine judges and four prosecutors) will only look at issues related to the application of law. There are also military courts under the jurisdiction of the Ministry of National Defence. The government plans to create specialized courts, in such areas as commerce and administrative.

The judiciary depends on the Gendarmerie, a special police force, to carry out its decisions. Established in 1994, the force has a number of tasks, one of which falls in the area of judicial police. It is separate from the National Police, under the Ministry of Interior. Its tasks include recording crimes and infractions, recording violations of law, collecting evidence for prosecution, investigating offenders and bringing them to the court of law under warrants for arrest issued by the court, and performing duties delegated from court authorities.

The post-1993 governments have committed themselves in principle to building an independent judiciary in line with the concept of liberal democracy. Article 128 of the Constitution stipulates that the judicial body "shall be an independent power" and "shall guarantee and uphold impartiality and protect the rights and freedoms of the citizens". In order to ensure judicial independence, the Constitution includes clauses such as Article 130 which states that "Judicial power shall not be granted to either the legislative or the executive branch".

To further protect the Constitution from being violated, Cambodia also created other public institutions associated with the judiciary: a Constitutional Council (CC) in March 1998, the Supreme Council of Magistracy (SCM) and prosecutors. The CC has a duty to safeguard the Constitution, and also the right to examine the constitutionality of any laws promulgated by the King, and to examine and decide on contested cases related to the election of assembly members. The CC consists of nine members with a nine-year mandate, of whom one-third shall be replaced every three years. Of the nine members, three shall be the King' appointees, three the National Assembly's appointees, and the SCM appoints the rest. All members must be selected from among dignitaries with a higher-education degree in law, administration, diplomacy, or economics, and with considerable work experience.

The nine-member SCM has a critical role to play in the judicial system. Chaired by the King (who is the guarantor of the independence of the judiciary, according to Article 132), the Council "shall make proposals to the King on the appointment of judges and prosecutors to all courts" (Article 134). The SCM also has the power to take disciplinary action against any delinquent judges — the only organization with the power to do this. Decisions are by secret ballot, without participation of the Chair, except when there is a deadlock.

The independent nature of the SCM remains, however, questionable, as the Minister for Justice (a politician rather than a neutral figure) is an important member. Although SCM meetings may be convened by the Chairman for the Council or at least three members, it is normally the Minister for Justice who "shall convene a meeting, following a consultation with the Chief of the Supreme Court and the Appeal Court" (Article 7).

Political Parties

Cambodia has a multi-party system. In 1993, 19 parties were registered to compete in the elections, and by 1998 this had increased to 39. However, as noted, in both elections only three or four parties gained enough support to win seats in Parliament. In both cases the CPP and FUNCINPEC were by far the largest parties, alternating for leadership of the Assembly. The Sam Rainsy Party is currently the only other party with significant parliamentary representation, and is the only opposition in Parliament.

Parties are governed by the Law on Political Parties, which like the Constitution is based on the principles of political pluralism and democracy. A political party is defined as, "a group of persons of like ideas who voluntarily form a permanent and autonomous association in order to participate in national political life". This means that no one can be forced to join a political party against his or her own will and that political parties are independent from the state and have the right to take part in politics.

The law further indicates that "[all] political parties shall have the same rights and privileges and shall receive equal treatment from the Royal Government and authorities at all levels". The terms "same rights and privileges" underscore the liberal foundation of democracy, which is essentially based on the idea of free and fair competition and political tolerance based on individual rights and freedoms. To avoid past anti-democratic practices in the country political parties must *not* "create an autonomous zone to the detriment of national unity and territorial integrity", "subvert the multi-party, liberal democratic regime by employing violence in order to seize power", or "establish any kind of armed forces". All this implies that competition for political power must be carried out by legitimate means and through the ballot box.

Political parties are generally based on strong leaders. They function without the support of strategists and policy analysts capable of helping them formulate party policies and implement party decisions. None of the major parties has developed a coherent ideology.

State Ideology

Cambodia has no official state ideology. Frequent changes of political regimes in recent decades have made it difficult to develop one. Nonetheless, one theme that has emerged in Cambodia's contemporary history is that the state rests its political foundation on a set of ideas related to the motto of the Constitution: "Nation, Religion, and King". The national flag and national anthem reinforce this view. The flag with the picture of Angkor Wat in the middle symbolizes Cambodia's glorious civilization. This aspect of the state ideology is mentioned in the Preamble of the Constitution, which also states the Cambodian people's commitments to the restoration of Cambodia into an "island of peace" based on multi-party liberal democracy and respect for human rights, the rule of law and responsibility for the nation's future. Seen in this context, state ideology is liberal.

However, the liberal foundation of state ideology is counterbalanced by other traditionalist ideas. The national anthem features the King, the ancient temples and Buddhism as part of the national soul. The people wish the King glorious victories and ask to live under the shadow of his might. The anthem also depicts Angkor Wat as something that helps the Cambodians remember that their ancient kingdom was great and the Khmer race is rock-like, which stays intact and strong. Buddhism is also seen as part of the national soul, reflecting a popular slogan that "to be Khmer is to be Buddhist". If the people follow Buddhism, says the anthem, angels will intervene and provide benefits to keep their kingdom great.

Civil Society and Human Rights

Defined in terms of a set of institutions such as religious institutions, the media, non-governmental organizations (NGOs), economic and financial businesses and so on, civil society in Cambodia has emerged, but still lacks real influence. Religious organizations have also flourished.

Another bright spot is the Bar Association, established on 16 October 1995. It started with 38 lawyers, who were sworn in before the Court of Appeals. It now has a membership of 216 lawyers. Its role includes training, supervising and professionalizing a new generation of lawyers, as well as promoting and protecting human rights and strengthening the rule of law. However, it has had difficulty regulating its own affairs let alone influencing legal processes, and still suffers from a severe lack of material resources needed to provide legal training to its members and the public.

Several hundred NGOs have also been in operation since the early 1990s, but they are small, have failed to achieve effective collective action, and are thus far from influential. A number of policy-relevant institutes have developed their research agendas and sought to influence government decision-making. Among them are the Cambodia Development Resource Institute (CDRI), the Cambodian Institute for Co-operation (CICP), the Khmer Institute of Democracy (KID), Cambodian Institute of Human Rights (CIHR), and the Center for Social Development (SCD). These institutes are, however, under-institutionalized and weak measured in terms of their impact on public policy. CDRI is the most institutionalized of all and has benefited from a pool of national and foreign experts and financial support from foreign donors. It has a number of publications to its credit, focussing on economic development. Most institutes do not receive any funding support from the government or the private sector.

The business sector began to emerge in 1989 when the SOC adopted an economic liberalization programme giving economic rights and freedoms such as the right to private ownership. The Constitution further strengthens these rights. But the business community and the middle class have not grown strong enough to influence government policy. Limited economic development has prevented the business sector from maturing.

Other civil society organizations continue to face an uphill battle. Their positive impact on government policies and actions has proved rather limited. There are about 200 newspapers and magazines now available to the public. However, Cambodia can be described as a country allowing freedom of expression, but not freedom after expression. Although political violence has declined markedly, journalists have been silenced and face imprisonment for speaking out against senior government leaders' corruption.

MAJOR POLITICAL ISSUES

The Constitution and ideology are only statements of intent on the part of the parties who draft and adopt it. The legislature and the judiciary are key state institutions aimed at encouraging the public to see the system of government as "rightful". Even if they are based on democratic principles of political governance, they do not ensure that a government always acts lawfully. By themselves, they are not credible guarantees against tyranny. Even totalitarian states have such institutions as national assemblies, though without any independent legislative power. This section examines who in Cambodia has the power, who benefits from the system, how legitimate the government is, how strong civil society has become, and to what extent the government has been able to perform its functions. As shall be discussed, the democratic principles of parliamentary supremacy, judicial independence, civil and political rights have often been violated.

Authoritarianism Still at Work

In theory, the Cambodian people exercise power through Parliament. To a large extent, Parliament remains stable. Since the election of 1993, no Parliament has been dissolved — unlike frequent change in the 1950s, 1960s and 1970s. The 1993 Assembly completed its five-year term and was replaced by representatives elected in 1998. This was an improvement on previous legislatures. However, Parliament has not had full control over legislation, nor has it always been able to prevent the government from exercising power arbitrarily.

Despite Parliament's apparent legislative dominance, it has played a minor role in initiating or drafting legislation. Usually, the government drafts laws and submits them to the Assembly for review and approval.

Even during the review process, government officials are often involved in meetings held by Assembly commissions. Governmental input, partly due to Assembly members' lack of expertise and skills and partly due to political interference by the Council of Ministers, gives it undue influence on the legislative process. The legislative body usually plays a passive or reactive law-making role.

Government leaders have consciously sought to minimize the Assembly's role as much as possible. They often leave little time for the Assembly to review or scrutinize technical matters related to complex policy proposals or draft laws. When the government wants the Members of Parliament to adopt the annual budget law, for instance, the documentation usually arrives at the Assembly in mid-December, just two weeks before the new fiscal year starts, leaving little time for parliamentary review and debate.

The government has also sought to demonstrate its dominance over Parliament in a more direct way, by muzzling or expelling from the Cabinet and the National Assembly those who dared challenge their political authority. Finance Minister Sam Rainsy (FUNCINPEC) was first relieved of his duty in the Cabinet in 1994, then expelled from his own party, and finally removed from Parliament in 1995. Sam Rainsy had spoken out against graft at the highest levels, putting him at odds with First Prime Minister Ranariddh and Second Prime Minister Hun Sen. While Prime Ministers have responsibilities to reprimand and discipline their cabinet members, only the Assembly has the power to dismiss a cabinet minister, by a vote of two-third majority. The two Prime Ministers reportedly twisted their party members' arms to the extent that they went along with their wishes without waiting for the National Assembly to decide on Sam Rainsy's political fate. What all this meant was that, although party discipline is normal in parliamentary democracies, if unrestrained it could undermine the ability of assembly members to represent their constituents, thus undermining the idea of representative democracy.

Government leaders' harsh treatment of dissidents within their parties often violated the democratic principle of transparency and accountability. Sam Rainsy was dismissed from power mainly because he had spoken against high-level corruption within the coalition government, not because he acted unconstitutionally. While corruption is not confined only to anti-democratic regimes, it runs counter to the spirit of accountability. Elected Members of Parliament were powerless to address this issue.

Another example of parliamentary subordination was when Hun Sen forced the National Assembly to strip Prince Norodom Sirivudh of his parliamentary immunity, after learning that the Prince had verbally threatened to kill him. (Prince Sirivudh was King Sihanouk's half-brother, and thus Prince Ranariddh's uncle; he had served as FUNCINPEC's Secretary-General, and as post-1993 Minister for Foreign Affairs.) On 17 November 1995 the Prince was placed under house arrest. His alleged "crime" was seen as against the state. Then, 105 Members of Parliament voted to lift his parliamentary immunity without any open debate, contrary to what the Minister for Justice had promised earlier.

The coalition government began to fall apart when First Prime Minister Ranariddh started to become more assertive *vis-à-vis* the CPP in general and Hun Sen in particular, and disintegrated when the Second Prime Minister staged a violent coup in early July 1997 against his co-premier. The ousted Prince was later charged with crimes against the state — colluding with Khmer Rouge hard-liners and illegal importation of weapons. In March 1998, he was sentenced to 20 years in prison and fined more than $50 million. Ranariddh did all this in his capacity as First Prime Minister; Hun Sen had done virtually the same in his negotiations with other Khmer Rouge leaders. Parliament was helpless in the face of such violence. Even the word "coup" was prohibited in Cambodia. After the coup, Parliament was forced into taking action against the ousted Prince. FUNCINPEC Members of Parliament were under considerable pressure to conform to Hun Sen's wishes and had to choose Ung Huot, FUNCINPEC Foreign Minister, to replace Prince Ranariddh. Ung Huot then became First Prime Minister, and showed much deference to Hun Sen's authority.

The government, or more particularly the CPP, has also strengthened its dominance by influence over the judiciary. The legal principle of due process has regularly been violated. Criminal trials proceed after the accused have been charged by prosecutors and subsequently investigated by judges. Judges have enormous power, ranging from investigating cases, to reviewing evidence to examining witnesses and to compiling case files. They have the power to decide whether there is enough evidence to bring the accused to trial. Because they compile case files and have full access to them, they usually decide what to do prior to the trial process. When they prosecute cases, prosecutors usually depend on judges' case files. Rarely are police officers or witnesses allowed to testify at trial because they might interfere in prosecutors' cases or judges' decisions.

At present, there are no effective mechanisms to ensure transparency in the process of collecting and weighing evidence to be used during trial. The court system is not, in any shape or form, independent from the executive body, partly because the courts' entire budget comes from the

Ministry of Justice and partly because most of the judges were appointed by the CPP in May 1993, the day prior to the UNTAC-organized elections. Their appointments were not merit-based. Most of them are former teachers, who had received training in the pre-Khmer Rouge period with no formal education in the law. Moreover, eight of the 117 judges work within the Ministry. There is no doubt that the CPP has a firm grip on the judiciary. Unsurprisingly, Cambodian judges hardly hide their pro-CPP stance. When Sam Rainsy was expelled from FUNCINPEC in November 1995, he filed a complaint with the Phnom Penh court, protesting the illegality of his expulsion. The court refused to hear the case. But when four FUNCINPEC members, who had positive relations with Hun Sen, rebelled against Ranariddh in April 1997, the court ruled in their favour by issuing an injunction against the expulsions, offering no grounds for the decision.

In another instance, a royalist colonel in the Gendarmerie was arrested, sent to Phnom Penh for trial, and sentenced to 15 years in prison, after a prominent businessman openly associated with the CPP was implicated in drug trafficking involving approximately 700 kilos of marijuana. The Director General of the National Police, Hok Lundy, a CPP political appointee, "publicly exonerated the businessman and accused FUNCINPEC of planting the evidence".[4] What is interesting about this legal case is that it grossly contravened Article 51 of the Law on Civil Servants, which stipulates that no civil servants may be arrested or prosecuted for any crime unless the government or the concerned minister consents in advance. Although Article 51 includes military and police personnel, it did not apply when action was taken against the royalist party officer.

Hun Sen has not shown any serious willingness to punish human rights abusers. No one involved in the execution of royalist party members during the 1997 coup has been put on trial. The Gendarmerie has even become an agent of human rights abuses, "enjoying the same impunity as the other security forces".[5] Members of this security force, for instance, were involved in human rights abuses during the coup in 1997, but have never been taken to justice. Military courts have also interfered in non-military cases. Although the jurisdiction of military courts is over "military offences", they have handled cases not involving military personnel, and non-military individuals have been detained in military prisons.

Although the post-1998 election Minister for Justice was chosen from FUNCINPEC, it remains unclear whether CPP-appointed judges can stand above politics. They still operate within a political environment dominated by CPP loyalists, especially those within the security apparatus. Recent evidence indicates that the judiciary remains at the mercy of governmental officials. In 1998, the Minister for Justice sacked three judges in the Appeal Court after they had overturned a verdict and set free a defendant involved in a politicized drug case. Late in 1999, the Minister for Justice suspended the Chief Judge and Chief Prosecutor of the Phnom Penh Municipal Court on the grounds of judicial misconduct — an action that violated the Law of the Supreme Council of the Magistracy, which forbids the Minister for Justice from attending SCM meetings involving disciplinary actions against judges or prosecutors. Another example of government officials undermining judicial independence occurred when Hun Sen issued a directive late in 1999 for the re-arrest of individuals who had been released by courts for lack of evidence or on bail or parole. As of 10 December 1999, at least 54 people had been re-arrested, without any new evidence or warrants.[6]

Even more alarming, the government has also sought additional means to tighten its control over the judicial system. Within the Ministry of Justice, the Secretaries of State have been given the responsibility to prepare laws related to the judiciary as well as inspection of courts' work, to manage "staff" which may include ministry personnel, court clerks and judges. They are to examine and control the prosecutors' work and also have the authority to make recommendations to the files of criminal, civil, labour, administrative and commercial cases.

The strengthening of authoritarian rule is also a consequence of a civil society that — for reasons already discussed — remains woefully weak. After assuming power as Prime Minister after the 1998 elections, Hun Sen declared that civil society must serve as a "partner" with the state rather than as challenger to its authority. Similarly, in Parliament the idea of a "loyal opposition" means that opposition parties are to play an advisory role in assisting the state by way of making contributions and giving valuable direction to help the leadership do its job effectively. These weaknesses, and the lack of judicial independence, means that the executive, particularly from the CPP, can do largely as it pleases.

Winners and Losers in the Political System

Hun Sen and CPP party members have benefited from the system. The benefits can be measured in terms of his ability to put down any challenges to his authority. Although his party did not win the 1993 elections, he managed to force the royalists to share power and then worked his way to weaken and exploit his coalition partners' internal weaknesses. After the successful coup in July 1997, Hun Sen was able to control effectively the security environment, which eventually worked to his ultimate political advantage: the CPP victory in the 1998 elections.[7] He subsequently emerged as the sole Prime Minister of Cambodia.

Politically, the King and other royal members are among the losers in the new system of government. The monarch's traditional authority has been on the steady decline. Due to his poor health, old age, and past tragic involvement in politics that led the country into disaster in the 1960s and 1970s, King Sihanouk has faced an uphill battle in his attempts to play a role as Head of State. As noted earlier, his half-brother (Prince Sirivudh) was pushed out of power, leaving those loyal to the King more and more powerless. Although his son Prince Ranariddh (when still in power) had never shown any deep sense of loyalty and deference to his father, the coup that ousted him in July 1997 further weakened royalty, to the point where the monarchy no longer plays a significant role in Cambodian politics. Constrained by the Constitution, the absence of a popular prince, who would inherit the throne after King Sihanouk's eventual death, and the CPP's political dominance, it is very unlikely that the monarch will bounce back as a powerful traditional ruler.

It would be misleading, however, to suggest that Hun Sen alone has benefited from the fragile system of government. While he has often been characterized as Cambodia's "strongman", the Prime Minister's political survival continues to depend on the goodwill of other CPP officials and military leaders who have also reaped the benefits from the CPP's political hegemony. Those who have benefited from Hun Sen's grip on power are those who have helped to keep him in power. Hun Sen was not alone in staging the July 1997 coup, which paved the way for his victory in the 1998 election, through a peaceful but unfair electoral process. One prominent person involved in the execution of royalists during and after the coup was none other than chief of the national police, General Hok Lundy.

The CPP-dominated military and security apparatus also benefited in other ways. While government could barely pay its employees, defence budgets remained huge. In 1998, despite a 5 per cent reduction from a year earlier, military and security expenditures still represented a full 45 per cent of total spending, roughly US$397 million.

Other senior government officials have also benefited from the political status quo. One method has involved illegal logging. Despite the fact that log production and forest products trade have increased, tax revenues to the government have not experienced a corresponding increase. In 1997, for instance, only $12.4 million (representing 10 per cent of log production) was paid to the government. Yet several government ministries and other organizations were involved directly and indirectly in the forestry sector.[8] The Geopolitical Drug Observer of France noted that "everyone, from

Members of Parliament to princes to former Khmer Rouge officials, is now involved in drug trafficking".[9] Although Hun Sen has been favouring a tough policy against drug trafficking, "too many people around him are involved or ensnared in drug trafficking".[10] Corruption remains rampant and not limited only to senior public officials.

The economy expanded in the mid-1990s — at least till the 1997 crisis — but not everyone has benefited equally. Among financial beneficiaries of Hun Sen's hegemonic power were prominent businessmen who have enriched themselves through dubious and sometimes illegal means. Teng Bunma, Cambodia's best-known and wealthiest businessman with total assets estimated at around $400 million, has long been closely associated with the CPP. He even spoke openly about giving Hun Sen $1 million to bankroll the 1997 coup, and about rewarding several royalist party rebels, each with $50,000.

Those who have gained least included low-ranking state employees, students, vulnerable workers (i.e., cyclo drivers, porters, small traders and scavengers) and peasants. Early in 1999, for instance, university students launched picket lines and set tires on fire in their demands for better employment prospects. In February, students from 13 faculties of the Royal Phnom Penh University threatened to take to the streets if the government did not raise their lecturers' salaries from $15–20 to $300 per month. Hun Sen was not assuring when saying, "we have no money". All he could do at the time was simply wish he could pay the lecturers $3,000 per month, but the harsh reality was that "it cannot be done".[11]

Although 80 per cent of the population earn their living from agricultural production, they are the most disadvantaged group within society. The incidence of poverty is the lowest in Phnom Penh (11.1 per cent), followed by urban areas outside Phnom Penh (29.9 per cent) and rural areas (40.1 per cent).[12] Only 3 per cent of rural inhabitants have access to electricity, compared with 67 per cent in Phnom Penh. One sign indicative of peasants' predicaments is Cambodian labour migration to Thailand, numbering around 82,000. According to a preliminary study there are many reasons people seek work in Thailand. Most were poor and, some had no land to cultivate rice. Although they would have preferred to work in Cambodia, those who owned cultivated land to keep them at work for a few months each year apparently had low earnings and faced the problem of few job opportunities for the rest of the year. Other incentives for migration labour include higher wages earned in Thailand (twice as much for comparable work in Cambodia) and financial gains that benefited their villages and helped some repay their heavy debts.[13]

Peasants have benefited from the current system of government only to the extent that the political leadership keeps encouraging foreign donors to allocate more of their aid for rural development. Government policies have placed emphasis on the need to build basic infrastructure for transportation, farm-to-market roads, irrigation systems, basic education, and health services. One of the Ministry of Rural Development's position papers issued in 1996 viewed rural development as the "vision for the 21st century" and stated "Returning to the Village" as "the theme" for rural development activities. By and large, the government has left the responsibility for alleviating poverty with the donor community. Between 1992 and 1997, for instance, the disbursements of foreign aid have amounted to US$2 billion, though rural development accounted for only 13.8 per cent.[14] Benefits vary from region to region: per capita health spending was much larger in Phnom Penh than in remote areas.

For various reasons, demographic growth being one, the peasantry now faces a new crisis: "For the first time in its history, Cambodia experiences a lack of cultivable land."[15] This has been highlighted in recent anti-government protests. On 1 March 2000, for instance, hundreds of poor farmers, led by opposition leader Sam Rainsy, marched through Phnom Penh in an angry protest over the growing problem of land-grabbing. While such protests were small-scale, they revealed new potential crises. Most of the people who have filed land dispute complaints in provincial courts are poor farmers, but about 75 per cent of the accused in such disputes involved either government officials or members of the military.[16]

The uneven distribution of benefits from the status quo can also be measured in terms of socio-economic differences across the country. Cambodia's current Human Development Index ranking of 136 (see Figure 2.2) is a stark measure of the country's backwardness. The percentage of people living below the poverty line has declined only modestly from 39 per cent in 1994 to 36.1 per cent in 1997, but recently rose to 38 per cent, with indications that the anti-poverty momentum was "being lost" after the 1997 coup. Basic facilities in areas such as health, education and housing are grossly inadequate. Public spending on education, for instance, is only 9 per cent of the national budget, while military and security budgets consume about 45 per cent.[17]

Hun Sen's Conditional Legitimacy

The uneven distribution of benefits by the various sectors or groups has enormous implications for the current regime's legitimacy. Still, assessing the degree to which the Hun Sen government is legitimate is a difficult task. While the degree of legitimacy may be measured in terms of how citizens obey the state on the basis of the government's perceived right to rule — in traditional terms, or based on leaders' personal charisma, or government performance — it is important to bear in mind that these domestic sources of legitimacy are inadequate in contemporary politics. Another key source of legitimacy is recognition and support by the world community. The key sources that maintain Hun Sen's legitimacy are the last controversial election, international diplomatic recognition, and foreign aid.

Both international institutions and other states presented their vote of confidence in the 1998 electoral process. The Joint International Observation Group (JIOG), the UN Electoral Assistance co-ordinating body for delegations from almost 40 countries, which had approximately 500 observers and was responsible for drafting statements on the conduct of the 1998 election, concluded the process "was free and fair to an extent that enables it to reflect, in a credible way, the will of the Cambodian people". The European Union (EU), which had provided $12 million for the July 1998 election preparations and dispatched some 200 observers, also showed a positive attitude towards election results and declared officially on 29 July that it was satisfied with JIOG reports. The EU Chief observer Sven Linder also found no "flaws and frauds of a magnitude that could have distorted the will of the Cambodian voters".[18] More importantly, the UN Secretary-General took a similar position by accepting the JIOG's judgment and urged the Cambodian parties to accept the election results. On 7 December 1998, the UN General Assembly approved the seating of the Cambodian Government.

ASEAN, which had postponed Cambodia's entry into its membership right after the Hun Sen-led coup, also quickly accepted the JIOG assessment. Singapore Foreign Minister S. Jayakumar (then Chairman of ASEAN) issued a public statement saying that the group was looking forward to admitting Cambodia as a member "in the near future". Cambodia finally became a member in April 1999, and quickly stepped up bilateral interaction with other ASEAN countries.

Cambodian relations with states outside the region have since improved noticeably. Between late 1999 and May 2000, multilateral and bilateral donors pledged greater financial assistance to Cambodia. At a donors meeting in Paris, May 2000, aid pledges reached $548 million, more than the $500 requested. The large infusion of aid has propped the economy up, and helped sustain Hun Sen's political legitimacy. However, should aid fatigue hit donors, this form of conditional legitimacy may weaken considerably or simply disappear.

The great powers also improved relations with Cambodia. Japanese Prime Minister Keizo Obuchi visited Cambodia, the first visit by a Japanese head of state in over forty years. A number of high-ranking Chinese officials also made contact at around the same time. Among them was Vice-President of the Chinese National People's Congress, paving the way for a visit of Chinese President Jiang Zemin, in November 2000.

The Hun Sen government has also enjoyed warmer relations with the United States. U.S. lawmakers had initially claimed that the election was neither free nor fair, and in October 1999, the House of Representatives passed a resolution urging the administration to collect evidence against Hun Sen's crimes for a future UN International Criminal Court. Soon after, however, Washington officially recognized the new coalition government. In January 1999 the two states reached the first-ever trade agreement, on textiles.

While the Hun Sen government has enjoyed a high degree of international legitimacy, it still does not enjoy a high degree of political legitimacy at home. Although the election appears to be more acceptable than expected, it was not uncontroversial. The voter turnout was large (more than 5.3 million, or 97 per cent of the potential voters.) The National Election Committee was professional in performing its tasks, and the elections were held in a relative peaceful environment. But if the post-coup political intimidation directed against opposition party leaders such as Prince Ranariddh is taken into account, the electoral process cannot be accepted as fully free and fair. The fact that the CPP collected 41.4 per cent of the votes in a not truly free and fair electoral process indicates that the ruling party's level of legitimacy at home was low. Opposition parties strongly disputed the election results.

Allegations about irregularities and fraud made by opposition parties may have been over-exaggerated, but the crux of the matter is that the majority of the Cambodian people did not seem to believe that Hun Sen was the man they wanted to represent their interests. Other parties turned down the CPP call for a coalition. Hun Sen had to threaten them by warning that the current National Assembly dominated by the CPP could amend the Constitution to allow a party to form a government with only a simple majority. Stalemate ensued as the opposition parties' call for Hun Sen's resignation fell on deaf ears. Sam Rainsy refused to join what he called a "Mafia-led" government. But the CPP finally voted to confirm Hun Sen's nomination as prime minister-elect. On 24 August the two main opposition parties — FUNCINPEC and the Sam Rainsy Party — began to organize public protests to demand a resolution of their complaints about election irregularities. Encamped at the park in front of the National Assembly, a place dubbed as "Democracy Square" with all the pretense of imitating China's Tiananmen Square in 1989 or the Philippines' 1986 "people power" revolution, protestors increased in size to more than 10,000. The government had to use security forces to end these protests.

Prime Minister Hun Sen does not enjoy a high degree of traditional legitimacy. He was born into a rural, not royal, family. Divisions between city and the countryside have often polarized Cambodian society. Moreover, traditional legitimacy is based on the idea that only the king had the right to rule. King Sihanouk remains popular (if not powerful in political or military terms) because of who he is. There is still a myth, though waning among young Cambodians, that "without a king, the kingdom is shattered".

The Hun Sen government can take advantage of King Sihanouk's traditional legitimacy by showing the latter respect, but it is important not to exaggerate the Prime Minister's "borrowed" traditional legitimacy. This form of dependency is temporary, as it depends on how Hun Sen manipulates the King, at least in public. Although he was conferred the honourable title "Samdech", traditionally given to very high officials, the title does not make him part of the royal family.

The extent to which Hun Sen has charismatic legitimacy is difficult to assess. King Sihanouk has been considered a charismatic personality. Besides his traditional right to rule, he also emerged as a leader who had fought for independence from France, and came to be known as the "Father of Independence" (*Beydaa aek-reach-cheat*). Compared with Sihanouk in terms of charisma, Hun Sen lags far behind. Although Hun Sen can claim legitimacy on the basis of what he did to liberate Cambodia from the Khmer Rouge reign of terror, his rule at the time depended heavily on Cambodia's arch-enemy, Vietnam. Some Cambodians, especially urban dwellers and opposition parties, still label him "Vietnam's puppet".

Prime Minister Hun Sen has made numerous efforts to enhance his personal charisma by repairing his old communist or Khmer Rouge past, by working hard to build some sort of a "cult of personality", and by projecting his image as "a man of the people". He has, for example, built around 1,500 schools, most of which carry his name. However, this kind of personal effort seems to have borne little fruit, one reason being that these schools lacked teaching staff and facilities, and the educational system remained in a shambles. Moreover, the CPP remains unpopular because of its communist past.

Hun Sen's political image was also severely damaged after the bloody coup in 1997. His unpopularity immediately soared, especially after the economy worsened. If free and fair elections had been held immediately after the coup, according to one Canadian report, "the CPP might lose, provided a credible and effective alternative could be presented".[19] Even within the CPP Hun Sen encountered opposition, with Deputy Prime Minister Sar Kheng often viewed as a potential rival.

In bureaucratic terms, the government cannot claim legality built on the concept of legal rationality. Attempts at administrative reform have made little headway, despite many promises of restructuring and disciplining these engaged in illegality. To be fair, recent efforts, such as the creation of the Council of Administrative Reform (CAR) in June 1999, a sub-decree establishing an "anti-corruption" council associated with the Secretariat General of the CAR, and the plan to downsize the civil service, are commendable. But such efforts require political will and the extent to which they will succeed remains to be seen.

Nor can the Hun Sen government claim economic achievement as a strong basis of legitimacy. While growth did occur in the early 1990s — increasing from around 3 per cent in 1992 to 7 per cent in 1996 — the economy subsequently went into a sharp decline. Cambodia was beset by such problems as high inflation, declining foreign reserves, and low levels of foreign investment. The regional crisis was undoubtedly a reason for this, though the decline started after a grenade attack on opposition demonstrators in March, and was also linked to the 1997 coup. The growth rate of real GDP was 1 per cent in 1997 and in 1998. According to government claims the growth rate for 1999 rose to 4.3 per cent. However, even these modest achievements were largely the result of foreign aid.

While the Hun Sen government's political legitimacy remains precarious, it is not about to collapse. Not a single political group is in the position to provide an alternative. The Khmer Rouge movement has ceased to exist. The system as a whole enjoys some legitimacy, with all factions having accepted, in principle, liberal democracy as the best form of political governance. But liberal governance faces many obstacles.

Governance

It should be apparent from the foregoing that Cambodia's attainments in terms of good governance have been modest. It does not have a comprehensive legislative framework, nor adequate trained, independent court officials or non-corrupt security forces, to ensure the rule of law. The government's record on combating corruption and improving socio-economic conditions also has remained woefully inadequate — indeed the small progress that has been made is primarily due to the international donor community.

The government has, however, made some efforts to promote good governance. It plans to reduce the strength of the RCAF to around 100,000 by late 2002. The 5-year programme for administrative reform (1999–2003) is a good start. The Council of Administrative Reform (CAR), which was mandated by the Council of Ministers to co-ordinate and monitor government activities in relation to administrative reform and governance, is another bright spot. In March 2000, the Office of the Council of Ministers, with the support of the Asia Development Bank (ADB) and Konrad Adenaur Foundation, sponsored a symposium on "Democracy, Good Governance and Transparency in the Asian Context". The Ministry of National Assembly, Senate Relations and Inspection was in the process of drafting anti-corruption legislation. Late in 1999, a National Anti-Corruption Action Plan was drafted. The government also signed a sub-decree creating an anti-corruption unit within the CAR and has been open to governance analysis on legal reform, anti-corruption and public sector, commissioned or supported by the World Bank and other international agencies. At a donors' meeting in Paris on 25–26 May 2000, the Hun Sen government affirmed its commitment to good governance as "a necessary condition to sustainable socio-economic development and social justice",[20] and presented two key documents: "Position Paper — Good Governance in the Cambodian Context" and "Cambodia — Governance Action Plan" (to have been finalized by September 2000).[21] The language of governance — the importance of transparency, accountability, predictability and participation — is now on the government agenda in Cambodia.

Current government plans seek to enhance good governance on the basis of six priority actions. First, the government is to establish "priority groups", made up of officials subject to stringent performance and practices. Establishment of these groups is an immediate priority of administrative reform and would be under the supervision of the concerned ministries and "stakeholders" (particularly foreign donors). The aim is to break the logjam of productivity, to dampen the brain drain as well as to enhance service delivery, while long-term initiatives are being implemented. Second, the government is committed to democratize the country further by decentralizing and de-concentrating government functions and activities. Third, the government seeks to accelerate and better co-ordinate reform of the state in several areas, such as demobilization, reform of the military, administrative reform, judiciary reform, budget and financial reform. Fourth, the government is committed to accelerating legal and judicial reform programmes to ensure that the judiciary becomes an effective branch of the state. Fifth, the government seeks to facilitate the development of a comprehensive Governance Action Plan of prioritized initiatives with the active involvement of all stakeholders (the state, civil society and the donor community). Sixth, the government has pledged to establish partnership arrangements, consulting all stakeholders and providing means to lay out mutual responsibilities and accountabilities.

At the heart of the problem standing in the way of socio-economic and political development, however, lies the persistent structural fragility of the state. Formidable obstacles to enhancing good governance come from the fact that the state structure remains dominated by one party (CPP), and is fragmented along the line of sub-factional and interest groups unwilling and/ or unable to transcend their parochial interests. Political leaders generally have lacked the political will to undertake reform. Cambodia's embryonic civil society is not yet in a position to pressure them to do so. Similarly, the bureaucracy lacks the requisite human resources, and appropriate organization. While the government's good intentions to demobilize and reintegrate some members of the military have indicated a degree of willingness to promote good governance, it is unclear how fast this process would go. By May 2000, only a pilot plan aimed at demobilizing and reintegrating 1,500 soldiers had been initiated. The government does not have the necessary funds to implement this plan because the departure allowance per demobilized solider is $240. It will need more foreign donor assistance to carry the scheme forward. In short, while good intentions to promote good governance by the government and the donor community have been sufficiently expressed, it remains to be seen as to how much real action will be taken. State- and civil-society building is indeed a formidable task.

THE CASE FOR PARLIAMENTARY DEMOCRACY

Because of the state's structural fragility rooted in factional politics and poverty, genuine change towards good governance in Cambodia will take many decades. Any violent revolution aimed at solidifying the state structure would only bring the country to its knees again, as the Khmer Rouge once did. Peaceful reform remains the best path towards peace and stability, but the transition towards liberal democracy has been and will be painfully slow. The challenge for Cambodia is to establish a system of government that can avoid the twin evils of anarchy and civil war that have afflicted it over recent decades. This requires a political system capable of enforcing the rule of law, ensuring security and promoting respect for human rights and equity. Can the current system achieve these goals?

For those who take the issue of governability or governance seriously, a concern has been that Cambodia is difficult to govern. They tend to call for establishment of a strong system of government, capable of solving complex problems and of securing compliance with its policies. The current system is not seen as capable of doing this.

Many who take this view believe that the SOC/CPP should have been left to rule the country. They argue that the United Nations-introduced Western-style government cannot work in a country where the people remained largely uneducated. Moreover, a multi-party election might further fragment the state and society. The SOC was considered capable of rebuilding the country, sustaining itself, and meeting the people's basic needs.

This view, however, ignores the problem of political legitimacy the SOC faced before the 1993 election. The Hun Sen regime came to power after Vietnam invaded Cambodia and overthrew the Khmer Rouge regime. The new communist, pro-Vietnam regime was structurally weak and could not afford to wage war indefinitely, without some sort of political accommodation or legitimization through the ballot box. The fact that the SOC continues to exist as a political party today owes much to the UN intervention, which recognized the CPP as a legitimate player in Cambodian politics. Prior to that, the United Nations only recognized the Coalition Government of Democratic Kampuchea (CGDK) made up of three resistance factions (FUNCINPEC, the KPNLF, and the Khmer Rouge).

For staunch royalists, however, the monarchical rule seems to be the only way out for the war-torn traditional society. To them, King Sihanouk is the only leader who enjoys the legitimacy to bring peace and stability to his people. He benefits from a perceived traditional right to rule, possesses a high level of personal charm and charisma, and is definitely more socially acceptable to all power contenders than anyone else.

While this argument appears attractive, even to many foreign observers, it has little merit. King Sihanouk's poor health, old age and past failures as a politician would not make him the ideal national leader. He failed in almost all his major efforts to end the war during the 1980s and early 1990s, and to tame the CPP, even after the Hun Sen coup in 1997. A second problem is that the dominant CPP is unprepared to revive the old monarchy. Although it no longer claims to uphold communist ideals, the CPP leadership is by and large anti-monarchical. Thirdly, the King still does not have a promising candidate who would inherit the throne and restore its lost credibility.

Nor is a presidential system the answer for Cambodia. It could be argued that a politically unstable country like Cambodia needs a political system in which the winning candidate could take executive control and form a strong government. While this argument has some merit, presidential systems are not necessarily better at promoting political governability within structurally weak states such as Cambodia. Disagreement and stalemate between the legislature and executive bodies are quite common in presidential systems. In weak states, such political crises and the zero-sum character of presidential elections may encourage a strong president not to tolerate any challenges to his political authority. A rigid presidential system, which gives little priority to political accommodation through consensus building, may invite political dissidents to stage coups d'état or to take violent subversive, revolutionary action.[22]

On empirical grounds, the arguments in favour of a "strong" political system for Cambodia are indefensible. Between 1954 and 1991, the country adopted different anti-democratic political systems: paternalistic under Prince Sihanouk, republican under Lon Nol, revolutionary totalitarianism under Pol Pot, and socialist dictatorship under Hun Sen.[23] For various reasons, these regimes remained, in different degrees, repressive and politically unstable. None could give what the country needed most, namely peace, stability and security.

The arguments against a strong, anti-democratic political system do not suggest that a parliamentary system is perfect. Parliamentary politics failed in the 1950s. The post-1993 parliamentary system has also had many shortcomings and failures. Between 1993 and 1997, for instance, there were at least five coup attempts, the last successful. In some democracies government is constantly subject to parliamentary votes of confidence, making the system inherently unstable. Moreover, a parliamentary system may even lead to what is seen as anti-democratic, namely an "elective dictatorship". It is not impossible that parliamentary democracies also end up in a "winner-take-all" situation.

Whatever the case, parliamentary democracy in Cambodia should be seen as the byproduct of power relations among the political factions, rather than as the outcome of conventional wisdom of any political theory. Factionalized Cambodia needs a democratic system that is flexible enough to allow political accommodation to work, and that encourages power sharing. The Paris Agreements, the Constitution and the proportional representation electoral system bear witness to this political reality.

This is why the chances for Cambodia to return to any of the past political systems (paternalistic or republican authoritarianism, revolutionary totalitarianism, and socialist dictatorship) are slim, unless the incumbent leadership is willing to risk bringing the country back into violence and war. The potential risk is enough to demonstrate the virtues of parliamentary politics in Cambodia.

Despite its problems, including coup attempts, Cambodia's new system has demonstrated a degree of relative stability in recent years. If allowed to mature, it may prove better than any other system adopted in the past. A strong argument for this is that the electoral system of proportional representation does seem to work, because it allows room for political compromise. Elections in 1993 and 1998 illustrate this, despite the fact that some scholars spoke against the "undemocratic" nature of post-UNTAC coalition politics. Some analysts contend that in 1993 it was irresponsible for Prince Ranariddh and the international community to share power with the Hun Sen-led CPP.[24] Against this it is worth remembering that without the CPP inside the political arena, the royalist leadership would probably not have lasted as long as it did. Had the secessionist movement succeeded (led by prominent dissatisfied members of the CPP right after the 1993 elections), it would have resulted in a renewed civil war. The habit of compromise would not have been given any chance to help temper unscrupulous behaviour. Was it also irresponsible for the CPP to strike a political compromise with FUNCINPEC by agreeing to share power with the latter after the 1998 elections? The answer is no.

Much, however, is still at stake. Cambodia's power structure remains deeply hegemonic and hence still has a large capacity to undermine the parliamentary system. The destruction of political democracy under Sihanouk (from the mid-1950s until 1970) had much to do with his initial hegemonic ascendancy through the use of repressive violence. Hun Sen's hegemonic re-ascendancy after the 1998 elections, if not effectively restrained, could thus mark the beginning of an end to the country's nascent democracy. The drive for hegemony causes the politics of envy and perpetuates an atmosphere of mutual suspicion and fear. All this could create a dynamic known as the security dilemma, meaning attempts to increase power actually brings greater insecurity, as everyone else seeks to do the same.

The basic rules of the parliamentary game provide all factions with opportunities to promote transparency and build trust, based on a set of liberal principles, norms, rules and procedures that can reduce future uncertainties and political risks. But the parliamentary system will mature only if the present government and other factional leaders realize the imperative of democratic compromise and foresee the danger of heavy-handed policies. It is important to understand the tragedy of Cambodian history and all the forces behind all past destruction. In a highly fragmented state like Cambodia, a presidential or monarchical system does not appear to offer the best solution. There is no sure guarantee that the current parliamentary system will last, either. Unless all power-contenders learn to play the democratic game by its rules, the system is bound to collapse, largely because the level of the power-holders' political legitimacy remains low and the state/social structures unconsolidated.

Notes

1 For background analysis of the UN intervention, see Sorpong Peou, *Conflict Neutralization in the Cambodia War: From Battlefield to Ballot-box* (New York, Singapore & Kuala Lumpur: Oxford University Press, 1997). See also contributions by scholars who examined contemporary Cambodian politics in Sorpong Peou, ed., *Cambodia: Change and Continuity in Contemporary Politics* (Hampshire, UK: Ashgate, forthcoming). For a comprehensive analysis of the post-colonial Cambodian regimes, see Sorpong Peou, *Intervention and Change in Cambodia: Towards Democracy?* (New York, Bangkok & Singapore: St. Martin Press, Silkworm & Institute of Southeast Asian Studies, 2000).

2 This study is based on the Constitution (Khmer version) adopted in 1993 and amended in March 1999. This (before amended) and other public documents such as the Paris Agreements, the Law on Parties, and the Election Law, can be found in the appendix of Sorpong Peou, *Intervention and Change in Cambodia: Towards Democracy?*

3 For more details, see UN, "Report of the United Nations Fact-Finding Mission on Present Structures and Practices of Administration in Cambodia" (United Nations: June1990), pp. 118–33.

4 "Report of the Secretary-General on the Situation of Human Rights in Cambodia", UN Document A/52, 26 September 1997, p. 22.

5 Ibid., p. 19.

6 Human Rights Watch, *Cambodia: HRW World Report 1999* (New York: 10 December 1999).

7 Sorpong Peou, "The Cambodian Elections of 1998: Democracy in the Making?" *Contemporary Southeast Asia* 20, no. 3 (December 1998): 279–97.

8 For more details, see Department of Forestry and Wildlife, "Forest Policy Transition Paper on Cambodia" (Phnom Penh: May 1998).

9 Cited in *Bangkok Post*, 23 July 2000, p. 4.

10 Ibid., p. 4.

11 *AFP*, 3 February 1999.

12 Cambodian Ministry of Planning, *Cambodia Human Development Report 1999*, p. ii.

13 Chan Sophal and So Sovannarith, "Cambodian Labour Migration to Thailand: A Preliminary Assessment" (Phnom Penh: Cambodia Development Resource Institute, Working Paper 11, June 1999), p. 11.

14 Council for the Development of Cambodia, *Development Cooperation Report, 1997/1998* (Phnom Penh: June 1998), p. 16.

15 Serge Thion, "What is the Meaning of Community?" *Cambodian Development Review* 3, no. 3 (September 1999): 13.

16 Shaun Williams, "Land Disputes in Cambodia". Paper presented at the National Workshop on Institutional Cooperation about Resolving Land Disputes in Cambodia, organized by Oxfam GB-ADHOC, 15–16 July 1999, p. 10.

17 So Chunn and Sopote Prasertsri, "Literacy Rates Much Lower than Estimated", *Cambodia Development Review* 4, issue 2 (June 2000).

18 Sven G. Linder's (Confidential) final report on "Support for the Democratic Electoral Process in Cambodia". Project ALA 97/0513.

19 John Bosely, Stephen Owen and Greg Armstrong, "Program Assessment Mission to Cambodia" (Ottawa: Final report, 19 September 1997), p. 9.

20 Royal Government of Cambodia, "Position Paper of the Royal Government on Good Governance in the Cambodian Context". Document presented at the CG meeting, 25–26 May 2000, Paris, p. 1.

21 The two documents can be found in Royal Government of Cambodia, Council for Administrative Reform, "Good Governance". Document presented at the CG meeting, 25–26 May 2000, Paris.

22 For more on problems with presidential systems, see Juan J. Linz, "The Perils of Presidentialism", in *The Global Resurgence of Democracy*, edited by Larry Diamond and Marc F. Plattner (Baltimore and London: Johns Hopkins University Press, 1993).

23 On the different types of political systems in Cambodia, see Sorpong Peou, *Foreign Intervention and Regime Change in Cambodia: Towards Democracy?*

24 Julio Jeldres sees the pitfalls of power sharing between FUNCINPEC and the CPP after the 1993 election (Julio Jeldres, "Cambodia's Fading Hopes", pp. 149–51). See also Abdugaffar Peang-Meth, "Understanding Cambodia's Political Developments", *Contemporary Southeast Asia* 19, no. 3 (December 1997): 286–308.

Further Reading

Chandler, David. *A History of Cambodia*, 2nd ed. Chiang Mai, Thailand: Silkworm Books, 1993.

————. *Brother Number One: A Political Biography of Pol Pot*. NSW, Australia: Allen & Unwin, 1993.

Curtis, Grant. *Cambodia Reborn? The Transition to Democracy and Development* Washington, D.C. & Geneva: Brookings Institution Press and United Nations Research Institute for Social Development, 1998.

Heder, Steven and Judy Ledgerwood, eds. *Propaganda, Politics, and Violence in Cambodia: Democratic Transition under United Nations Peace-keeping.* Armonk, NY: M.E. Sharpe, 1996.

Human Rights Watch. *Cambodia: HRW World Report 1999.* New York: 10 December 1999.

Jackson, Karl D. *Cambodia: 1975–1978, Rendezvous with Death.* New York, NJ: Princeton University Press, 1988.

Kiernan, Ben. *The Pol Pot Regime.* New Haven, CT: Yale University Press, 1996.

_____ , ed. *Genocide and Democracy in Cambodia: the Khmer Rouge, the United Nations, and the International Community.* New Haven, CT: Yale University Southeast Asia Studies, 1991.

Mabbett, Ian and David Chandler. *The Khmers.* Oxford, UK & Cambridge, MA: Blackwell, 1995.

Osborne, Milton. *Sihanouk: Prince of Light, Prince of Darkness.* NSW, Australia: Allen & Unwin, 1994.

Peou, Sorpong, ed. *Cambodia: Change and Continuity in Contemporary Politics.* Hampshire, UK: Ashgate, 2000.

_____ . *Intervention and Change in Cambodia: Towards Democracy?* New York, Bangkok & Singapore: St. Martin Press, Silkworm & Institute of Southeast Asian Studies, 2000.

_____ . *Conflict Neutralization in the Cambodia War: From Battlefield to Ballot-Box.* Singapore, New York & Kuala Lumpur: Oxford University Press, 1997.

Vickery, Michael. *Kampuchea: Politics, Economics and Society.* Boulder, CO: Lynne Rienner, 1986.

_____ . *Cambodia: 1975–1982.* Boston, MA: South End Press, 1984.

3

INDONESIA
Transforming the Leviathan

Anthony L. Smith

INTRODUCTION

Indonesia is in transition, from authoritarian rule under former President Soeharto to an uncertain future. It is attempting to build a more democratic and economically sustainable state in one of the most heterogeneous and archipelagic countries in the world. With more than 216 million citizens, it bestrides Southeast Asia as a colossus. The region is hostage to its future.

Modern Indonesians view themselves as heirs to some great and refined civilizations. Two of these kingdoms assume pride of place. The first is the Hindu-Buddhist Srivijaya empire, established in Sumatra on the trading route between India and China, which came to exercise a loose suzerainty over parts of Malaya, Borneo and west Java from the 8th century until the 14th century. The second is the later Majapahit empire (1293–1520), based in Java, which extended to Sumatra, the Malay peninsula, Bali and parts of Borneo, though how far it covered eastern Indonesia is the subject of conjecture.

For post-independence Indonesian governments these two empires provide an indigenous rationale for modern state boundaries. This "Hindu-Buddhist past" remains important to many Indonesians, particularly in Java and Bali (the latter remains Hindu), notwithstanding the coming of Islam in the thirteenth century. Both the wording of the Indonesian state motto, and the official ideology of Pancasila, are Sanskrit, not Bahasa Indonesia (or the Indonesian language). Sanskrit names are common in Java (Sukarno and Soeharto to give just two examples), and the language occupies a similar status position as Latin for English or European language speaking peoples.

Europeans first reached Southeast Asia in the sixteenth century, seeking spices and spreading Catholicism. First to arrive were the Portuguese, who established footholds throughout the Indonesian archipelago after conquering Malacca in 1511. In later years Portugal surrendered these to the Netherlands, except East Timor.

Arriving in 1596, Dutch authority over Indonesia expanded slowly over 350 years. Largely eschewing the christianizing mission of the Portuguese, the Dutch were primarily interested in the spice trade, controlled by the Dutch East India Company (VOC or Vereenigde Oostandische Compagnie). The Dutch gradually found it necessary to control more of the interior for security, and greater land area to grow transplanted spices. The Dutch East Indies was reduced to an agricultural fief to service European markets.

Resistance to Dutch expansion was strong in places but lacked coordination. Full scale wars were fought in West Sumatra (1821–37), Java (1825–30), and Aceh (1873–1903). The Java War took some 200,000 lives at a time when the population of Java was around three million. Aceh's resistance was the most sustained, continuing on a smaller scale after 1903 and virtually bankrupting the Netherlands.

Dutch strength was never great, with a modest bureaucracy under the governor general, a Royal Netherlands Indies Army of 35,000, and a small navy.[1] They were supported, however, by the indigenous aristocratic class (*priyayi*), and auxiliary forces recruited locally (particularly in Ambon). This "divide-and-rule" had a profound impact, particularly on the generation that won independence, and helps explain occasional outbursts against perceived external interference.

From the early 1900s the Netherlands, under pressure from the liberal forces at home, and building on important social changes undertaken by Stamford Raffles during a British interregnum in Java (1811–16), decided to implement the so-called "Ethical Policy". This was largely undertaken to expand health and education services. An embryonic parliament was formed, called the *Volksraad*, and although it was dominated by the Dutch, it did facilitate greater interaction between leaders of the different islands. The Ethical Policy was a major factor in helping forge a collective Indonesian consciousness, training the first generation of nationalists.

As Dutch authority was finalized in the early 1900s, nationalist movements began. Some nationalist leaders favoured working within the system to achieve an evolutionary path to independence. Others rejected any cooperation with the Dutch. A turning point in the creation of an Indonesian identity was the 28 October 1928 *Sumpah Pemuda* (Youth Pledge), at a congress in which the delegates were introduced to the Indonesian national anthem, *Indonesia Raya* (Great Indonesia), followed by a pledge to unite around "*satu nusa, satu bangsa, dan satu bahasa*" (one land, one nation and one language). Nationalists adopted Malay, already a common *lingua franca*, as the language to unite an ethnically and liguistically divided people.

Dutch obfuscation and prevarication over independence strengthened the hand of non-cooperators, led by the charismatic Sukarno and technocratic Mohammed Hatta. When Japan invaded and defeated the Dutch in January 1942 these leaders headed a Japanese-sponsored government. However, they cooperated with the Japanese only as a means to independence, while other nationalists made contact with the allies and resistance forces. When Japan surrendered on 17 August 1945, Sukarno proclaimed independence. This date is still celebrated as independence day. The first Constitution was promulgated a day later.

The Dutch sought to reestablish control, launching a euphemistically named "police action" in July 1947. This marked the beginning of a massive Indonesian struggle (*perjuangan*) for nationhood. After the Dutch captured Sukarno, Hatta and other civilian leaders in December 1948, the military, based on the 65,000-strong Japanese trained forces, continued to resist — establishing a role for itself as defender of the nation even in the absence of political leadership. The Dutch finally quit in December 1949, with their legacy in tatters. They had failed to prepare their colony for full independence, destroyed much of the country through warfare, and unwittingly given a role to the Indonesian military that they have yet to fully relinquish. The struggle for independence was, however, a defining event for Indonesia, forging solidarity among the country's diverse ethnic groups.

The new state of Indonesia had a troubled birth. During the independence struggle, and the decade that followed, there were three main uprisings. Communists staged the Madiun Rebellion in August 1948, while the Darul Islam movement fought for an Islamic state in the provinces of Aceh, West Java and South Sulawesi, from around 1950 until 1962. Local army commanders in Sumatra and Sulawesi proclaimed rival governments in 1958, for an array of personal, regional and political motives.[2]

Instability continued after Indonesia held its first elections in 1955. Sixteen parties emerged with at least one seat, and a stable governing coalition could not be established. In December 1956 independence hero Hatta, a Sumatran, resigned as Vice-President after differences with Sukarno, heightening concern among non-Javanese. By 1958 state institutions were beginning to run down due to political infighting.

In reaction to political instability Sukarno banned elections in 1959 and announced that he would preside over a "guided democracy", promoted as being more in keeping with the Indonesian cultural values of consultation (*musyawarah*), consensus (*mufakat*), and mutual assistance (*gotong royong*). He suspended the 1950 Constitution, reverting to the original 1945 Constitution (still in force today) which gives greater power to the president. He also established a National Advisory Council "to save the country from ruin",[3] and permitted only ten political parties.

Sukarno then became increasingly radical. He drew close to the People's Republic of China and the domestic communist party (PKI or Partai Kommunist Indonesia), withdrew Indonesia from the global "neo-colonialist" economy, forced the issue over the possession of Irian Jaya (now Papua) through the introduction of troops and then a rigged plebiscite in 1969, and in 1963 started *Konfrontasi* over the formation of Malaysia, alleging it was a British colonial creation. He played a balancing act between sworn enemies, the three million-strong PKI, and the military, but increasingly leaned to the PKI.

On 30 September 1965, under circumstances that remain contentious, six leading generals were arrested and executed. The coup attempt was blamed on the PKI, and in the next few months between 500,000 and 1 million people were murdered, not only destroying the communist party but also allowing villagers to settle economic, religious and racial scores.[4] According to the Central Intelligence Agency, this was "one of the worst mass murders of the 20th century, along with the Soviet purges of the 1930s, the Nazi mass murders during the Second World War, and the Maoist bloodbath of the early 1950's".[5]

General Soeharto, head of the Strategic Reserve (Kostrad), and the most senior officer left in command, crushed the coup attempt, then gradually eased Sukarno aside. He assumed full governmental powers on 11 March 1966, moved to reorganize the economy, and dropped Sukarno's more adventurous foreign policies, including war with Malaysia.

Dubbing himself "the father of development" Soeharto called his regime the New Order (*Orde Baru*), to distance himself from the failed economic and supernationalist policies of Sukarno's "old order". He based his legitimacy on economic growth, and brought dramatic improvements in the living standards of most Indonesians. He also moved to depoliticize Indonesia, allowing only three political parties: Golkar (Golongan Karya, or functional groups) his own vehicle, based on a party founded in secret by leading army officers in the early 1960s; an Islamic party called the United Development Party or Partai Persatuan Pembangunan (PPP); and a nationalist-secular party, the Partai Demokrasi Indonesia (PDI). Both PPP and PDI became compliant to the ruling Golkar, always agreeing to

FIGURE 3.1

Indonesia: Key Dates

800s	Emergence of Kingdoms in Central Java and the construction of the Borobudur and Prambanan temple complexes. The Sumatran-based Sri Vijaya trading empire flourishes through to the 14th century.
1293	Majapahit empire established. Extended through much of what is current day Indonesia until the early 16th century.
1596	Dutch begin a 350 year expansion that eventually includes all of what is now Indonesia. Ruled until 1799 through Dutch East India Company, established in 1602 in order to dominate the spice trade.
1811	Stamford Raffles begins a five-year control of Java during what is known as the British Interregnum.
1927	Sukarno and other nationalist leaders form the Indonesian Nationalist Union which was soon renamed the Indonesian Nationalist Party (PNI).
1942	Japanese occupation of the Dutch East Indies in March.
1945	Two days after the Japanese surrender, Sukarno proclaims Indonesia independent on 17 August. The new constitution is promulgated the next day.
1945	War of independence against the returning Dutch authorities begins.
1949	Dutch give authority to the Republic of the United States of Indonesia (RUSI) on 27 December. Abandoned in favour of a unitary state in 1950.
1955	Indonesia's first general election on 29 September — and the freest until 1999.
1959	Sukarno announces Guided Democracy and restores the 1945 Constitution giving full executive power to the president.
1963	Sukarno takes control of Irian Jaya and begins a three-year war (*Konfrontasi*) with Malaysia.
1965	An alleged communist coup on 30 September, during which six leading generals were killed, saw General Soeharto launch a counter-coup. Over the next year more than 500,000 suspected communists were killed.
1966	Formal executive power transferred to Soeharto on 11 March.
1973	Soeharto's regime further depoliticizes the political system by recognizing only three parties: Golkar (the ruling party); the United Development Party (PPP); and the Indonesian Democratic Party (PDI).
1975	Invasion of East Timor on 7 December, resulting in an estimated 200,000 deaths.
1998	Soeharto resigns after widespread rioting in Jakarta and across Indonesia, and is succeeded by Vice-President, B.J. Habibie, on 21 May. Habibie presides over *reformasi* in the Indonesian political structure.
1999	Landmark general election on 7 June, from which Megawati Sukarnoputri's party, PDI-P, emerges as the front-runner. Former ruling party, Golkar, comes a distant second.
1999	A referendum in East Timor reveals 78.5 per cent want independence. Anti-independence groups and the military destroy much of the territory before international forces restore order.
1999	Nahdlatul Ulama leader, Abdurrahman Wahid, is appointed the fourth president of Indonesia by the MPR on 20 October. The general public are placated with the appointment of Megawati as Vice-President.
2000	Wahid apologizes to the nation at the August session of MPR, to try to counter rising public anger at financial scandals, continuing regional violence, and ineffective economic reform.
2001	In February the DPR overwhelmingly votes to set in motion the process of impeachment. This culminates in the selection of Megawati as president on 23 July.

support Soeharto's nomination for president, until the mid-1990s when elements of the PDI began to exhibit genuine opposition to the New Order regime. Playing off various factions or constellations within Jakarta's political elite with an adroit touch, Soeharto faced no real opposition until 1996.

A second major human rights violation occurred under Soeharto following the 1975 invasion of East Timor, and its annexation as the "27th province". This move was not recognized by the United Nations, which continued to accept Portugal as the legal representative. The deaths of around 200,000 East Timorese made it one of the worst human rights violations *per capita* since the end of World War II. East Timor gained independence from Indonesia after Soeharto left office, in 1999, following a UN-run referendum in which the independence option gained 78.5 per cent support.

Beginning in 1971 elections were held at five yearly intervals, but Golkar's resounding victory was never in any doubt. In 1988 Soeharto talked of *keterbukaan* (openness), but it soon became clear that this was empty rhetoric when three newspapers were shut down in June 1994, and the government became increasingly intolerant of opposition voices. In 1996 Megawati Sukarnoputri, the daughter of Sukarno, was overthrown as leader of the PDI in a rigged selection process. This sparked domestic unrest and was the beginning of sustained public opposition, which escalated dramatically after the Indonesian economy crashed in December 1997. Many blamed corruption, collusion and nepotism (known by its Indonesian acronym — KKN, or *korupsi, kolusi, nepotisme*), largely centred on the Soeharto family, for the economic collapse. By May 1998 demonstrations had broken out all over Indonesia. Student-led demonstrations demanded greater democracy, while the urban poor rioted against the removal of subsidies on basic commodities (mandated by the International Monetary Fund) and soaring prices. Elements of the military organized chaos and violence against the Chinese community, seemingly in a bid to provoke martial law and thus save Soeharto's teetering regime.[6] However the Jakarta elite turned against Soeharto, including 13 senior ministers, the speaker of parliament, Harmoko, and leaders of Golkar. Sensing the chance to gain the presidency, Habibie also helped convince Soeharto to step down. Finally, military head, General Wiranto, reportedly refused to act against demonstrations, removing Soeharto's last hope of retaining power.

Coming to power amidst a period of high public demand for *reformasi* (political and economic reform), Habibie was forced to make wholesale changes. The most important was a dramatic re-politicization of Indonesia through greater freedoms of speech and assembly. This included legislation to allow for the creation of new political parties, early general elections, and alterations to the composition of parliament. Hundreds of political prisoners were released. Free elections were held in June 1999, the first since 1955. Parliament reassumed its role as a check on executive power, as specified in the 1945 Constitution.

Nonetheless, the changes represented an evolution of the New Order, not a complete revolution as many *reformasi* activists demanded. Half of Habibie's cabinet were inherited from the preceding Soeharto cabinet, and Habibie was never was able to shake a reputation as a continuation of the New Order regime. A turning point was the 11 November 1998 Ciganjur Agreement signed at Abdurrahman Wahid's residence between four leading opposition figures, Wahid (or Gus Dur), Megawati Sukarnoputri, Amien Rais and the Sultan of Yogyakarta, Hamengkubuwono X. Their agreement was to work within the existing political structure towards *reformasi*.

In the June 1999 general elections Golkar came a distant second to Megawati's Indonesian Democracy Party–Struggle or Partai Demokrasi Indonesia–Perjuangan (PDI-P), a break-away from the original PDI. Habibie's hopes of retaining the presidency were dashed when parliament rejected his accountability speech on 20 October 1999 — a signal that he did not have the votes. Through a series of negotiations, promises and double crosses, Wahid came from behind to gather the support of the *Poros Tengah* (the Central Axis of Muslim parties) and Golkar, to capture the presidency. He presided over further democratization and economic reform, but a high degree of political instability and socio-political violence continued. On 23 July 2001 Wahid was removed by parliament and replaced by his vice president, Megawati.

Geography

Indonesia's current borders were founded by the Dutch, notwithstanding Indonesia claims for continuity with pre-colonial Srivijaya and Majapahit civilizations. The name "Indonesia" itself is derived from the Greek words *Indos Nesos* (the Indian islands), and gained popular usage amongst nationalists for its non-colonial (or non-Dutch) etymology.

By sheer size, both area and population (see Figure 3.2), Indonesia is the *primus inter pares* for Southeast Asia, and the Association of Southeast Asian Nations (ASEAN). Since the formation of ASEAN in 1967 Indonesia has had generally peaceful and constructive bilateral relations with its neighbours, though border problems and political differences have occasionally caused tensions.

FIGURE 3.2

Indonesia: Key Statistics

Land area:	1,904,569 sq kilometres
Population:[a]	216,108,345 (1999)

GNP:[b] Current exchange rate   — US$221.5 bn (1997);
                                              US$130.6 bn (1998)
                  Purchasing Power Parity — US$679 bn (1997);
                                              US$490 bn (1998)

GNP Per Capita:[b] Current exchange rate   — US$1,110 (1997);
                                              US$640 (1998)
                  Purchasing Power Parity — US$3,390 (1997);
                                              US$2,407 (1998)

Income Distribution (1996):[b]

Gini Index	36.5
% share of income or consumption:	
Lowest 10%	3.6
Lowest 20%	8.0
2nd 20%	11.3
3rd 20%	15.1
4th 20%	20.8
Highest 20%	44.9
Highest 10%	30.3

Human Development Index (HDI) Ranking:[c]

World ranking	105 (1997); 109 (1998)
Value	0.681 (1997); 0.670 (1998)

Armed Forces:

Total no.[d]	298,000 (1999)
Expenditure[d]	US$1.498 bn (1999)
% of GNP[b]	1.8% (1995)

Sources: [a] Official national sources.
      [b] World Bank, *World Development Indicators* (Washington, D.C.: 1999 & 2000).
      [c] United Nations Development Programme (UNDP), *Human Development Report* (New York: Oxford University Press, 1999 & 2000).
      [d] International Institute for Strategic Studies (IISS), *The Military Balance, 1999–2000* (London: Oxford University Press, 1999).

Indonesia is in turn dominated by Java. Although only 7 per cent of the total area, it has 60 per cent of the population, and is the centre of government, business, and higher education. In a bid to ease overcrowding in Java, Indonesia has tried, with some success, to limit its population growth, primarily through the support for birth control.

Indonesia has vast natural resources to draw on. Much of the soil is volcanic, which has made islands such as Sumatra, Java and Sulawesi extremely fertile for tropical agriculture. Oil and gas, mainly from East Kalimantan and the eastern coast of Sumatra, have provided capital necessary to fund development. Petroleum has been an important component of exports since the 1970s. Other mineral wealth includes tin, nickel, bauxite, copper and iron. Timber is also a major resource, with the largest forest reserves in Asia. Forest fires in Kalimantan and Sumatra, most started by companies wishing to clear land, have had a devastating impact on these reserves in recent years. Under Soeharto, investment by MNCs led to an increase in manufacturing exports, although this was pegged back somewhat during the Asian financial crisis.

Society

Among Indonesia's more than 200 different ethnic groups, the main components are Javanese (45 per cent), Sundanese (14 per cent), Madurese (7.5 per cent), and coastal Malays (7.5 per cent). Efforts to forge a single nation/state from an extremely heterogeneous society have been based on stressing the anti-colonial struggle against the Dutch, and promoting a sense of being "Indonesian" through the adoption of Malay as the national language (Bahasa Indonesia), the promotion of state symbols, and schooling in the national ideology of Pancasila. Transmigration and intermarriage have also played a role. While ethnic identities are still very real, large numbers – especially from urban sectors — have mixed parentage (like Sukarno and Habibie), and many have come to identify solely as Indonesians and thus defy ethnic classification. Nonetheless, regionalism remains strong in parts of Indonesia, with Aceh and Irian Jaya exhibiting strong secessionist movements. Recent inter-communal violence, notably in Maluku, demonstrates the continuing potential for civil disorder.

Indonesian Chinese are between 3–5 per cent of the population, but dominate commerce. As non-*pribumi* (non-indigenous) they have often faced open discrimination from both government and society. The victims of violent pogroms in, *inter alia*, 1965 and May 1998, the community was until recently also forbidden to possess Chinese written characters, medicines or to engage in some cultural displays and their identity papers were specially marked. Most restrictions are no longer enforced, and may be repealed in the coming years, but the Chinese community still technically faces legal as well as societal discrimination.

Religion in Indonesia is more complex than official statistics indicate: Muslims are 88 per cent, Protestants 5 per cent, Catholic 3 per cent, Hindu 2 per cent, and Buddhist 1 per cent. During Soeharto's time, the state ideology *Pancasila* (literally "the five pillars") was rigidly enforced, which meant that Indonesians had to follow the first "pillar" stipulating a belief in one God. Those who did not belong to a recognized religion were considered atheists, which was invariably associated with Communism.[7] Second, the Islamic community (almost exclusively Sunni) is divided between what anthropoligist Glifford Geertz called *abangan* and *santri* strains.[8] Although these divisions are not always rigid, *abangan* Muslims of Java have tended to synthesize Islamic belief with the Hindu-Buddhist past into what is known as Javanese mysticism (*kebatinan*). *Santri* Muslims, found in urban Java and outer islands, are now probably in the majority, and follow a purer version of the faith. Within the *santri* stream are "traditionalists" and "modernists". The former represented by Gus Dur's Nahdlatul Ulama organization, while the latter are represented by Amien Rais' Muhammadiyah. The differences reflect a division between interior and coastal peoples, as sea-borne traders from Islamic countries established Islam during different time periods and with differing intensity, though in recent years a growing Islamic revival and expanded religious education have given greater numbers access to a more orthodox understanding of Islam.

The Hindu faith is found mostly in Bali, which held out against conversion to Islam, while the Chinese community are mostly Buddhist or Christian. Other Christians tend to be concentrated in clusters, notably Sumatra (Toba Batak), south and central Sulawesi (Toraja), North Sulawesi (Minahasa), Ambon, Flores, Kalimantan, Irian Jaya and in urban Java. For the most part, Christian and Muslim communities live in relative harmony, the major exception being Ambon where sectarian violence claimed the lives of around 5,000 people in recent years. Christians generally have better access to education than other Indonesians, and this has given them greater influence on government and society than their numbers would tend to suggest.

In line with urban drift in many other countries, 35 per cent of Indonesians now live in urban areas. While data remains uncertain in the aftermath of the financial crisis, the middle classes represent around 5–10 per cent of the population, while perhaps 15–20 per cent of the population is now below the poverty line. Those living in Jakarta have average incomes two or three times higher than the rest of the country.

Indonesia is a stratified society in two senses: hereditary status and wealth. The Javanese in particular have historically been divided between *priyayi* (aristocrats) and non-*priyayi*. An important symbol of power for Soeharto, himself of rural non-*priyayi* origins, was his marriage to a member of Solo's royal Mankunegara household. The presence of a stratified society has not led to significant class conflict as the fault lines, where they exist, are ethno-religious.

In the Constitution women are listed as having the same rights as men, but in practice this has not always been the case. Women have had a limited political role. Both Nahdlatul Ulama and Muhammadiyah, Indonesia's largest Islamic groups, have publicly stated that a woman could be president,[9] over the objections of more hard-line Islamic groups. Megawati Sukarnoputri, as leader of Indonesia's largest political party, PDI-P, and President, stands out as the obvious candidate — though her power has come from association with a popular male relative. Since Soeharto's time there have usually been one or two women in cabinet, but women still remain underrepresented at all levels of government in Indonesia. Male society, and most religious leaders, expect women to be wives and mothers first, and subordinate to their husbands.

Economy

Indonesia's per capita GNP is around US$1,110. The World Bank has classified the economic structure in 1999 as consisting of agriculture at 17.3 per cent, industry 43.1 per cent, and services 39.6 per cent. Agriculture has recently enjoyed a slight increase as primary exports have become highly competitive with the low rupiah, and at the same time manufacturing has declined since the onset of the financial crisis.

After a debilitating war of independence, Indonesian governments from 1950–59 attempted to foster indigenous industry, though foreign investment faced little opposition because of a shortage of capital. However during Guided Democracy, Sukarno, like many third world leaders at the time, sought to limit the influence of "neo-colonialism". Indonesia increasingly embarked on a course of economic nationalism which involved insulation from the global economy through public ownership and high tariff barriers. By the time Soeharto seized power Sukarno had run Indonesia's economy into the ground, with inflation running at over 1,000 per cent. Sukarno used much of the state budget on military spending, to engage in military adventurism against Malaysia. He also set about establishing exorbitant Eastern bloc style statues, including the massive torch-shaped Monumen Nasional (Monas) made entirely from Italian marble, with a large amount of solid gold in the flame at the top.

Until the eve of the recent Asian crisis, Indonesia's economic growth under Soeharto was among the most remarkable the world has seen, bringing poverty levels down from 60 per cent to around 14 per cent pre-crisis. Soeharto practically gave *carte blanche* to U.S.-trained liberal economists to open the economy more to trade and investment, while pursuing a tight monetary and fiscal policy. After 1966 growth rates averaged between 5 and 7 per cent. This was considerably assisted in 1973 by the first oil shock. As an oil rich nation, Indonesia did well out of high prices, although the state oil company, Pertamina, was often mired in debt due to over-expansion. From the 1980s foreign direct investment in light manufacturing played an increasingly important role.

There were, however, flaws in economic policy. The late 1980s saw the emergence of the technologs — or mercantilists — led by then Minister for Research and Technology, B.J. Habibie. Habibie wished to use state industrial policy to close the technological gap with the developed west, most infamously through the establishment of the hugely expensive and economically unviable Industri Pesawat Terbang Nusantara (IPTN) aircraft company. President Soeharto's children, and other select businessmen, were also allowed to control hundreds of companies, acquiring a business empire worth tens of billions of dollars. Indonesia's richest man, Liem Sioe Liong, was estimated to control 5 per cent of the Indonesian GNP by 1990,[10] in part through the sole rights to the steel production industry.

In December 1997 Indonesia plunged into a deep economic crisis that in turn caused a political upheaval culminating in Soeharto's ouster. When the regional crisis began in July, Indonesia had strong economic indicators including, *inter alia*, balanced books for government expenditure, strong exports, and a healthy balance of payments. However, structural micro-economic flaws — including corruption and an apparent unwillingness to adhere to terms negotiated with the International Monetary Fund (IMF), the presence of monopolies and oligarchies, and an under functioning legal system — saw investors lose confidence in the Indonesian economy. The IMF concluded one of the largest bail-outs in its history of US$43 billion, but even this brought no immediate respite. The currency crashed from a high of Rp. 2,432 to the US$ on 1 July 1997 to its lowest point on 24 January 1998 of 14,800. For 1998 as a whole the economy contracted by

14 per cent. The financial crisis exposed and exacerbated problems in the banking system, whereby most banks were (and still are) technically insolvent. IMF reforms to end "toll-gate enterprises" were welcomed, but the removal of energy and food subsidies in May 1998 sparked widespread chaos in Indonesia. Attempts to impose austerity, especially through a balanced budget, also exacerbated this crisis, and were soon dropped in favour of a Keynesian-style 5 per cent of GDP budget deficit as a pump priming measure. Some of the social and economic gains of the Soeharto regime were undermined, and the crisis continues to grip Indonesia despite a return to modest growth after 1998.

THE POLITICAL SYSTEM

Indonesia is a republic with a presidential system of government. The main features of government are prescribed by the 1945 Constitution. This had been replaced in 1950 by a constitution that established a parliamentary system of government, but Sukarno reinstated the 1945 Constitution in 1959 to restore presidential power. However, several amendments have been made since then, particularly since the fall of Soeharto, most in order to strengthen democracy through more effective checks and balances. Amendments require a three-quarters majority in the senior parliamentary body, the People's Consultative Assembly (Majelis Permusyawaratan Rakyat or MPR). The Constitution notes a requirement of approval by referendum, but this has not been applied.

The Constitution defines the roles of the organs of state and separates power between institutions. Six organs of state are identified: the Presidency; Parliament — the MPR and the House of Representatives (Dewan Perwakilan Rakyat or DPR); the Supreme Advisory Council (Dewan Pertimbangan Agung); The State Audit Board (Badan Pemeriksa Keuangan); and the Supreme Court (Mahkamah Agung). How these institutions relate to one another has often proven open to interpretation.

Although Indonesia has a presidential form of government it is, as former presidential adviser Dewi Fortuna Anwar has written, "more like a quasi parliamentary system".[11] The politicians elect the president through the MPR, and there is an expectation that the president will choose a cabinet that at least partially reflects the partisan composition of parliament (although Wahid ignored this for his second cabinet line-up).

Indonesia's basic policies of government are prescribed by the Guidelines of State Policy, drafted and approved by the MPR every five years to coincide with the presidential term. The Guidelines are a rather broad statement of intent, often concentrated on issues such as development and a greater distribution of wealth.

Indonesia adopted a unitary rather than a federal system of government because federalism had come to be associated with colonial attempts to weaken the state. The Dutch ceded authority to the Republic of the United States of Indonesia (RUSI) after the 1949 settlement, but this was dissolved in the face of growing regional tensions on 17 August 1950. Even discussion of the term "federalism" has been treated with disdain since then.

Indonesia is currently officially divided into 32 provinces,[12] below which are districts and subdistricts. Elected councils exist at all levels except the subdistrict. There are three types of provinces: 29 *provinsi*; the two special provinces (*daerah istemewa*) of Yogyakarta and Aceh; and the capital city, Jakarta (*daerah khusus ibukota*). Yogyakarta was given special status to allow the hereditary sultan to remain head of the province, while Aceh gained the same recognition in order to try to placate the independence movement. *Daerah istemewa* does not entail any real devolution of authority although in 1999 Aceh was entitled to implement some aspects of *syaria* (or Islamic law).

Local assemblies have not had much power in the past, but devolution has recently gained popularity as a means to address the widespread regional unrest towards the end of Soeharto's rule and after his ouster. Laws 22/1999 (local autonomy) and 25/1999 (revenue sharing with provinces and districts), signed in May 1999, allow district autonomy from May 2001. Devolution has not been granted at the provincial level, most probably because of fear that this will give sustenance to either federalism or even full-blown independence movements. The central government will retain defence, foreign affairs, justice, overall monetary and fiscal policy, religious affairs and the development of strategic natural and human resources, while the districts will control the residual functions. Several questions remain over the proposal. First of all, will Indonesia have the human resources at the district level to cope with managing a budget and providing core services such as transport, health and education? Second, the issue of the division of finances has been the subject of much debate and speculation. The Ministry of Finance has announced that 61.5 per cent of Indonesia's revenue will go to the provinces and districts. Currently Jakarta allocates around 25 per cent of its expenditure to the provinces, while nearly 90 per cent of revenue goes to Jakarta making the relationship heavily weighted in favour of the centre. How this will work in practice is still unclear as some resource rich provinces provide enormous revenue for the state (such as East Kalimantan and Riau) while others are net beneficiaries (such as East Nusa Tenggara). Third, the legislation on regional autonomy is opaque and contradictory, with a strict reading of the laws suggesting that the same powers are simultaneously transferred to more than one level.

Discussion surrounding the role of religion in public life has been part of Indonesian political culture since independence. As noted, the Pancasila stipulates belief in God as a necessary requirement but does so in a generic way. Belief in a deity is not defined in Muslim terms by any of the founding documents. This decision was over the opposition of those promoting the so-called Jakarta Charter. While there is a vocal minority who wish to promote either a state where Islam is recognized as the primary faith, or even the introduction of Islamic law, most Muslims, as represented by Muslim and secular parties, accept a pluralistic society.

Head of State

The Indonesian head of state is the president, a position that is both ceremonial and executive. The balance between these two functions has changed over the years. The 1945 Constitution initially gave the president extensive executive powers. The shift to parliamentary democracy under the 1950 Constitution made the office more ceremonial in form. Sukarno's reinstatement of the first Constitution in 1959 again strengthened presidential powers, but the position has become answerable to parliament since the fall of Soeharto.

The President must be a native born Indonesian citizen. Candidates do not have to be a member of the DPR or the MPR to be considered for the role. First and foremost, the Head of State is officially the "Mandatary" of the MPR in that he/she receives his/her mandate from this body said to represent the will of the people. The office is held for five years and is renewable only once. This limit was imposed by a constitutional amendment in 1998, in order to limit the amount of power accruing to one individual. Unitl May 1998, only two men had occupied this post — Sukarno (1945–66) and Soeharto (1966–98).

As ceremonial Head of State the president's main duties include granting mercy, amnesty or pardon, bestowing all state titles and decorations, appointing ambassadors, and receiving foreign emissaries. Following constitutional amendments in 1998 the president is required to consult on all these matters with the DPR, apart from the receiving of emissaries.

The Vice-President is elected separately in the same manner as the President. His/her only constitutionally defined role is to assist the president.

In practice, the influence of this office holder has varied over time. Mohammad Hatta (1945–56), had a distinguished nationalist record, and for a time was almost an equal of Sukarno, but with his resignation the position was held open until Soeharto's appointment of the then Sultan of Yogyakarta, Hamengkubuwono IX, in 1971. Soeharto never allowed a vice-president to consolidate influence by having more than one term.

The vice-president succeeds if the president is incapacitated, removed or decides to resign. Soeharto's departure in May 1998 saw Vice-President Habibie automatically take over. After the vice-president succession falls to a triumvirate of the Minister for the Interior, the Minister for Foreign Affairs and the Minister for Defence (deemed to cover the three sectors of government).

Executive

The president holds the main executive power in Indonesia. He/she has the sole right to appoint government ministers. The president is the nation's top diplomat, able to declare war and negotiate international treaties. He/she is commander-in-chief of the armed forces, and can declare a state of emergency in time of crisis, and assume all the state's functions.

The president has ultimate power over legislation and even has an important legislative role, initiating most laws that go before parliament. The Constitution requires that both the president and the DPR be in agreement before a bill can become law. A constitutional amendment requires that legislation passed through the DPR must become law after thirty days even if the president does not sign, but in practice the situation still favours the executive. The executive is consulted in all four stages of the passage of a bill through the DPR, but during the third reading in select committee an indication is given from cabinet as to whether a given bill is acceptable. If so, only then will it proceed to the fourth stage to be voted on. The only potential scenario for the DPR overriding the president's refusal to sign would be if the executive gave approval to parliament at the third reading of a given piece of legislation, but the president subsequently changed his or her mind about its acceptability.

The president may also issue an executive decree (*Keppres* or *Keputusan Presiden*) but such decrees are considered supplementary and subordinate to DPR approved legislation. (There are also similar ministerial decrees known as *Kepmen* or *Keputusan Menteri*.)

FIGURE 3.3

Government Organization in Indonesia

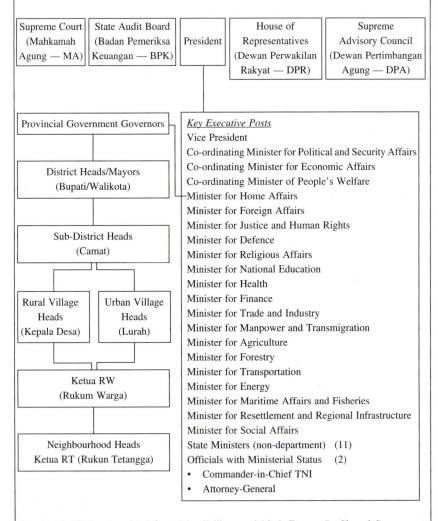

People's Consultative Assembly
(Majelis Permusyawaratan Rakyat — MPR)

| Supreme Court (Mahkamah Agung — MA) | State Audit Board (Badan Pemeriksa Keuangan — BPK) | President | House of Representatives (Dewan Perwakilan Rakyat — DPR) | Supreme Advisory Council (Dewan Pertimbangan Agung — DPA) |

Provincial Government Governors

District Heads/Mayors
(Bupati/Walikota)

Sub-District Heads
(Camat)

| Rural Village Heads (Kepala Desa) | Urban Village Heads (Lurah) |

Ketua RW
(Rukum Warga)

Neighbourhood Heads
Ketua RT (Rukun Tetangga)

Key Executive Posts
Vice President
Co-ordinating Minister for Political and Security Affairs
Co-ordinating Minister for Economic Affairs
Co-ordinating Minister of People's Welfare
Minister for Home Affairs
Minister for Foreign Affairs
Minister for Justice and Human Rights
Minister for Defence
Minister for Religious Affairs
Minister for National Education
Minister for Health
Minister for Finance
Minister for Trade and Industry
Minister for Manpower and Transmigration
Minister for Agriculture
Minister for Forestry
Minister for Transportation
Minister for Energy
Minister for Maritime Affairs and Fisheries
Minister for Resettlement and Regional Infrastructure
Minister for Social Affairs
State Ministers (non-department)   (11)
Officials with Ministerial Status   (2)
• Commander-in-Chief TNI
• Attorney-General

Source: Modified and updated from John Halligan and Mark Turner, *Profiles of Government Administration in Asia* (Canberra: Australian Government Publishing Service, 1995), p. 34.

Both Sukarno and Soeharto exercised executive power almost unchecked by other branches of government. Now, however, greater politicization has significantly changed the role to one that is genuinely answerable to parliament.

The president is accountable to the people of Indonesia through its (mostly) representative body, the MPR. As noted, this meets every five years to appoint the president and vice-president, and approve the Guidelines of State Policy. Under Soeharto more than half of the MPR members were his appointees, enabling him to determine the outcome of this process. Since his fall the overwhelming majority are elected representatives, and it has come to possess a real ability to influence the presidency.

The changing nature of checks and balances on the presidency can be seen in Habibie's tenure. While Habibie was constitutionally able to continue as president until 2003, pressure from his own cabinet and the MPR forced him to hold general elections in 1999, which were followed by the election of Wahid.

The president is assisted by a cabinet. Ministers are drawn from inside and outside parliament, but are directly responsible to the president alone. It meets weekly on Wednesdays. Indonesian cabinets have always tended to be large, as positions are used to establish patronage or to reward political allies. Soeharto's first "development cabinet" contained 30 ministers, which had grown to an unwieldy 41 in the fifth and sixth cabinets.[13] Wahid tried to trim this number but found that in order to pay back favours he had to settle at 33 for his inaugural "cabinet of national unity". After the MPR session in August 2000 Wahid reduced the number of ministers to 26. A practice inherited from Soeharto was the appointment of coordinating ministers (*menteri koordinator* or *menko*). Wahid initially retained four, but later reduced them to two, while Megawati has opted for three. They are supposed to marshal the other ministers who are placed under their supervision.[14]

The process of choosing a cabinet has become increasingly complex. While Soeharto had to satisfy factions within his ruling elite, notably powerful members of the Golkar party, the bureaucracy and the military, Wahid found it necessary to include, initially, ministers from all the major parties of parliament. His sacking of two cabinet ministers from rival parties in April 2000, for no apparent reason, caused suspicions that Wahid hoped to replace cabinet ministers with his own party members and allies. Wahid's second cabinet was controversial because it mainly consisted of those linked to the president or his PKB party, a minority party in parliament with around 10 per cent of the seats. Magawati's first cabinet is a mixture of political appointees — rewarding her supporters and those parties backing her — and technocratic professionals.

From August 2000, Wahid opted to devolve the "technical aspects" of Indonesia's cabinet to the Vice-President, Megawati. While Megawati and supporters wanted a binding legal document to confer authority on the Vice President, this was deemed unconstitutional. Wahid therefore delegated authority to the Vice-President, a move endorsed by the MPR, but that authority remained at the President's wish.

The state bureaucracy is coordinated by the Civil Service Administration Agency (Badan Administrasi Kepegawaian Negara — BAKN). BAKN deals with issues of recruitment, secondments, and regional placements, and forms policy on issues that effect the civil service as a whole. Until 1998, all civil servants had to belong to Golkar, the ruling party. Now bureaucrats at all levels must take leave to become politically active, and they must serve ministers irrespective of ministerial political allegiances. Severing the link between Golkar and the bureaucratic elite has been an important step in terms of democratization.

Unlike former British and American colonies, Indonesia did not have a well trained bureaucracy at the time of independence. A lack of expertise was exacerbated by corruption, which became systemic under Sukarno and Soeharto. Most bureaucrats (and members of the armed forces) took *pungli* payments ("informal taxes") to supplement meagre salaries. The government expected this, reducing the need for more formal taxation. Transparency International has listed Indonesia as one of the most corrupt countries in the world as a result of this practice. World Bank president, James Wolfensohn, has stated that corruption had caused 10–40 per cent of World Bank disbursements to be squandered.[15] To combat this pressing problem the Wahid administration has increased civil servant salaries by two 10 per cent increases during 2000, with greater increases for top level officials. The Attorney General has also promised an anti-graft agency, which has received support from a number of the DPR members.[16] All of these steps are necessary to provide a professional and independent bureaucracy.

Political Role of Military and Police

Until recently, the 300,000-strong Indonesian military or TNI (Tentara Nasional Indonesia — Indonesian National Military), previously known as ABRI (Angkatan Bersenjata Republik Indonesia — Armed Forces of the Republic Indonesia), was the most powerful political institution in

Indonesia. The TNI has seen itself as a participant in the political process since the nascent military continued to fight the Dutch during the war for independence after civilian leaders surrendered. Holding to the notion of *dwi fungsi* (dual function), the military argued that it had two roles: security and socio-political. *Dwi fungsi* effectively gave the TNI the rationale for a role in domestic affairs.

The military was a key player under Sukarno, but became dominant under Soeharto. The doctrine of *dwi fungsi* was incorporated into law in 1982. With a focus particularly on its socio-political role, the military has divided the territory of Indonesia into territorial commands (*kodam*) — there are currently eleven – for military units to build a "supply chain" to make each defensive area autonomous and self funding. They, in effect, establish a parallel administration to the civilian administration throughout the country. Also, around one third of troops are involved in the construction of infrastructure, education, health, and related activities. This has allowed the military to interfere with civil affairs and become involved in commerce at the same time.

The military has evolved a series of business linkages in order to achieve a certain amount of "self funding". A vast network of "institutional" companies (known as *yayasan*), ranging from forestry, insurance, hotels and resorts, an airline, and even a university.[17] Some senior officers established personal fiefdoms. This is evidenced by the vast holdings, or "non-institutional" businesses, of retired officers and their families, including generals Benny Moerdani (notable for his involvement in the sale of East Timor's coffee) and the late Ibnu Sutowo (who bankrupted Pertamina). None of these business operations have been disrupted by the political changes that have swept Indonesia (except in the territory of East Timor).

In addition, large numbers of military officers were seconded to cabinet posts and prestigious bureaucratic positions (including ambassadorial postings, and provincial and district positions) through a process known as *kekaryaan*. For ambitious Indonesians, joining the officer corps became the best way to gain advancement and the resulting material and status benefits.

The military has had a curious role in the post-Soeharto government. Though serving officers can no longer hold ministerial posts, Both Wahid's and Megawati's cabinets have included four retired generals, one a coordinating minister. Soldiers may not vote in elections, but TNI retains 38 seats in the DPR. Ten per cent of representative seats in provincial and district assemblies are appointed from the ranks of active or retired military personnel, while a number of retired senior officers remain in the ranks of Golkar, and a handful in PDI-P.

The TNI has demonstrated that it cannot always be controlled by its political masters, and sometimes it cannot control dissenting factions within its own ranks. In recent times several events have highlighted this: widespread chaos in Jakarta and other major cities in May 1998, including systematic attacks on the Chinese community, most likely organized by elements of the TNI; the killing of hundreds of Islamic scholars attached to Nahdlatul Ulama in East and Central Java through paramilitary "ninja killings" in 1998, again most likely backed by elements of the TNI; wholesale destruction of property and mass killings in East Timor by the TNI sponsored militia after the referendum of August 1999; and units of the TNI and the police failing to enforce peace in Ambon and in the Malukus, and taking sides in these conflicts. A number of observers report a split along "red/white" (nationalist) and "green" (Islamic) lines. Although there was some truth to this in the past, it is one of a number of cleavages (religious, ideological, geographical, commercial and not least of all, personal) within a pattern of shifting allegiances.

However, the military has undergone some major changes since the fall of Soeharto. First of all, the public reputation of the military is at an all time low because of its perceived role in buttressing the Soeharto administration and then failing to bring order during the May 1998 riots. This makes a military coup difficult given the widespread opposition that it would provoke. Second, the Indonesian police force was taken from the military aegis in 1999, and now has independence — although it will take years to end military-police linkages built up over decades in remote areas. Third, Wahid asserted some civilian dominance by dismissing several top generals (including the then Army CIC General Wiranto) and appointing civilians as Minister of Defence, for the first time since pre-Soeharto days. Megawati has also appointed a civilian (Matori Abdul Jalil) as Minister of Defence.

TNI influence has been reduced, but potentially it remains a formidable player in the Indonesian political scene. A warning of a possible "Pakistan-style coup" by the then Indonesian Minister for Defence, Juwono Sudarsono, in November 1999, was taken seriously by many observers. Although *dwi fungsi* is now downplayed, the influence of the TNI remains strong. The military is not as confident as it once was, but it will continue to play a role in domestic affairs due to its network of business interests, direct participation in national and provincial politics and the bureaucracy, and the ability to hold the president to ransom through the enforcement or non-enforcement of potential disorder.

The Indonesian police force (Polisi Republik Indonesia or Polri) was created in 1945 and remained independent until 1965. After Polri sided with Sukarno during Soeharto's counter-coup it was merged with the military. Formally separated from the military in 1999 the 180,000 strong force remained under the Ministry for Defence until 1 July 2000, when it was transferred to become directly answerable the President. It is thus accountable to central government, not to local authorities. The police also have a special unit called the Mobile Brigade (Brimob), which receives military training and is used in situations of civil disorder.

A third element of Indonesia's security apparatus are the two intelligence agencies — Bakin (Badan Koordinasi Intelijen Negara or State Intelligence Co-ordinating Agency) and Bais (Badan Intelijen Strategis or Strategic Intelligence Agency). Bakin is answerable to the President, while Bais reports to TNI central command. Bais was dominant during the early 1980s when Benny Moerdani, who came from Bais ranks, was head of the armed forces. There is ongoing discussion about reform of the intelligence services, with Bakin set to take over the sole role of intelligence coordination and gathering, while Bais will focus strictly on military intelligence.

Legislature

Indonesia's legislature, as noted, is comprised of two components. The 500 member DPR (reduced to 495 members after East Timor's departure) is popularly elected, except for 38 military appointees. The MPR includes the DPR, plus 200 others chosen by provincial assemblies and the National Election Commission. The legislature, or parliament, has been reinvigorated in recent times, having served as little more than a rubber stamp in the Soeharto era.

All bills must obtain the consent of the DPR to become law. The DPR can also initiate legislation with 30 signatures of DPR members to any given bill, although most legislation begins with the executive. If the president refuses any bill, it can only be resubmitted during the subsequent session of the DPR. In New Order days legislation was often passed by "consensus", and in the event that it was not, referred to a Steering Committee to be put to a vote at a later date. In the new environment unanimity is near impossible to find. Voting on legislation is now the established practice, for which a quorum of two-thirds must be present.

Each bill goes through four readings: the first announces the bill to parliament, the second is followed by a general debate; the third involves a referral to the appropriate committee (of which there are eleven), and the fourth includes a final debate and vote. Executive approval of legislation is indicated prior to the vote and the president must sign a bill before it becomes law (see earlier section on the Executive). Should the president issue "regulations" during an emergency, these must be approved, *post facto*, when the DPR is able to hold its next session.

The DPR also controls the purse strings, through the annual state budget. In the event that it is delayed or rejected, the last approved budget, which would generally be the preceding year's, is adopted by default. Financial powers are strengthened by the requirement that the State Audit Board — which audits expenditure by the executive — report directly to the DPR.

Another DPR function is to nominate candidates from government and society for the 45 member Supreme Advisory Council. The final selection rests with the president, and the Supreme Advisory Council is charged with responding to queries from the president on matters of state and policy. The Council has four permanent committees: (1) political; (2) economic, financial, and industrial; (3) social welfare; and (4) defence and security. Although this body is specifically mentioned in the Constitution it does not exercise great influence over the decision making process.

DPR affairs are managed by a chairman (sometimes called the "speaker" by the foreign press), elected by secret ballot. The chairman is an influential political figure, as he/she has the power to set the agenda of discussion.

During Habibie's tenure, and even more so under Wahid, the DPR became a highly politicized debating chamber. Parliament now has a dynamic multi-party environment, where coalitions have to be constructed to get legislation passed. No party whips enforce discipline, leading to coalitions that are intra- and inter-party combinations.

Currently there are four major groupings within the DPR. The largest political party, PDI-P, has 153 seats. Golkar is second, with 120 seats. A third group, the *Poros Tengah*, or the central alliance, can muster nearly 170 votes from various Muslim parties (or sometimes around 200 with sympathetic elements of Golkar). The 38 TNI officers representing the military (reduced from 75 in Soeharto's time), is also an influential faction. However, the four groups are fluid, with a degree of overlap and a series of shifting alliances.

The growing influence of the DPR was illustrated just prior to the 1999 general election when Habibie found it politic to visit the chamber and symbolically meet with party heads. And on 20 July 2000 Wahid answered a "summons" to explain the sacking of two ministers in April. The then president was under no obligations to obey such a request, but chose to do so, citing "transparency and democracy" as the reason to front up. Although he actually failed to explain the sackings, and was jeered by representatives, the changed dynamics between the executive and legislature were clear to all.

The DPR has the power to initiate proceedings that may result in the censure or even dismissal of the president. It may call a Special MPR session although the Constitution does not set out a detailed process. An MPR decision has provided a series stages for the removal of the president. The DPR may pass a memorandum of censure, giving the president three months to provide a satisfactory response to allegations of wrong-doing. If there is no response, or a response deemed unacceptable, a second memorandum is issued giving the president a further 30 days to comply. After that a Special MPR session will be called to consider the president's future. This process was in fact begun on 1 February 2001, when the DPR issued the first memorandum against President Wahid over his failure to explain his alleged involvement in two financial scandals. None of Wahid's responses were deemed acceptable and on 23 July the MPR appointed Megawati as president just hours after Wahid had attempted to suspend parliament and declare a state of emergency.

The MPR, in constitutional terms, is the highest legal body in Indonesia. The President of the Republic is in theory subordinate to the MPR. Although international media sources tend to use the terms "Upper House" and "Lower House" to refer to the DPR and the MPR respectively, this is not an entirely accurate reflection as the DPR is actually a subset of the MPR. The DPR members now occupy a dominant position in the MPR. The Constitution does not stipulate the proportion of DPR members and others. During the New Order additional officials numbered 500, allowing a system whereby Soeharto appointed the majority of the MPR and they in turn re-elected him. Of the current 200 additions, 135 are chosen by the elected provincial assemblies (5 representatives each). The Komisi Pemilihan Umum (KPU) or National Election Commission also selects 65 "functional representatives" consisting of religious leaders (20), sectoral groups (9), the artistic and intellectual community (9), war veterans (5), women (5), youth (5), ethnic minorities (5), and the disabled (2).

The MPR, as already noted, has several important tasks. It chooses the president, drafts and approves the Guidelines of State Policy, and evaluates executive preference against the Guidelines. It may also change the Constitution, or impeach the president if he or she is deemed to have broken the law or not followed the State Guidelines, with a two-thirds majority. The MPR must meet at least every five years to elect the president, but a convention has now developed (post-Soeharto) of holding a *Sidang Tahunan* (Annual Session) to evaluate the president's performance. These meetings, lasting a week to 10 days, have so far been landmark events. The 1998 session determined that there would be an early election and limited the president to a maximum of two five-year terms. The 1999 session (the regular post-election meeting) rejected Habibie's accountability speech, dashing his hopes for a second term, then surprised all by electing Wahid as president ahead of the more popular Megawati. The August 2000 session saw an abject apology to the nation during Wahid's accountability speech in order to avoid a politically damaging rebuke, while the 2001 special session saw Wahid's removal. Apart from the annual meetings, a Special MPR session can also be called by the DPR if needed.

Elections

Indonesia's first general elections were held in 1955, and these remained the most democratic ever until 1999. Under the New Order the government exercised a tight rein over political parties' campaign issues. Elections were based on a proportional representation system, under which successful candidates were chosen from party lists on a provincial basis. Golkar always won comfortably in five-yearly contests, with majorities ranging from 62.8 per cent in 1971 to 74.5 per cent in 1997. Elections were accompanied by vigorous campaigning, and violence — 1997 was the worst of all, with around 300 fatalities.

The 7 June 1999 election was a watershed for Indonesia. The MPR in November 1998 had determined that a free and fair election would be held between May–June 1999. Habibie commissioned a "Team of Seven" to rewrite the election laws. Based on the Team's recommendations the election was under the authority of the National Electoral Commission (KPU), consisting of 48 party members (a cross-section of major parties) and 5 government representatives. The PPI (Panitia Pemilihan Indonesia) or the Indonesian Election Commission assisted with administrative preparations.

After the Habibie administration passed the Party Law 150 parties emerged, but only 48 were allowed to contest the election. A "Team of Eleven" was established under the leadership of noted Islamic scholar, Nurcholish Madjid, to decide which parties would confest the election. Parties were selected on their ability to establish branches in 50 per cent of the districts in at least nine provinces. This precluded parties based solely on one island or ethnicity. At the time of the election, Sumatra, the island with the largest number of provinces, had eight (this has now been increased to nine). Furthermore, the law also states that the parties must acknowledge the Pancasila, even if their membership is not Pancasila based (ie not multiethnic and/or multireligious). With 48 parties standing there was a lot of potential for confusion, with 6 parties claiming to be successors to Sukarno's old PNI.

Each of the 48 parties that stood were allocated public funds of Rp. 150 million (c. US$17,000), which favoured those parties with access to supplementary funding. Golkar had a distinct advantage here with press speculation that the party had up to US$40 million at its disposal. PDI-P appears to have benefited from the patronage of sections of the business community who wished to cover all options. Currently all major political parties are scrambling to secure funds in order to fight the next election in 2004.

The electoral system adopted was a compromise between supporters of a district system (such as Golkar) and those favouring proportional representation. Former U.S. President, Jimmy Carter, an election observer in 1999, described the process as "the largest and most complex democratic procedure in which we had ever participated".[18]

In the elections percentages gained by parties, and therefore seats gained in the House, were determined at the provincial not the national level. Thus, for electoral purposes Indonesia was split into its then 27 component provinces. While the allocation of seats is based on population numbers, the electoral law also stipulated that there must be a minimum of one seat at the district (*kabupaten* and *kotamadya*) level. At the time of the 1999 election, Indonesia's 27 provinces had 327 *kabupaten* and *kotamadya*. The rest of the 135 elected seats were allocated by the KPU on the basis of population to give provinces of higher population density a fairer representation. However the reallocation of seats did not completely alter inequalities in the number of people represented by a single seat. This explains why the percentage of votes gained by parties does not neatly tally with seats gained in the DPR.

In order to determine who is actually elected, a complicated process is followed. The number of seats a party receives will be determined by the number of votes it obtains in each province. Once the number of Members for a given party is determined, based on its proportion of the vote for a given province, the central committee of that party then decides who should be chosen to sit in the DPR. Theoretically (and according to the electoral law) this should be done with consideration to reward those who polled highest *and* to give representation to every district. However, this could not be achieved in practice. It is possible for a candidate to "win" a district seat but fail to be selected for the DPR. Additionally, not every district ended up with a representative.

Parties that failed to gain more than two per cent of the vote are ineligible to contest the next election, although exactly how this will work remains unclear since those disqualified could presumably register as "new" parties. Elections for provincial and district authorities are held simultaneously with the national election.

The 1999 election did encounter problems. In the troubled province of Aceh large numbers boycotted the election, while in Maluku 109 per cent voted! Overwhelming support for Golkar in East Timor, where international observers were not stationed because of contested sovereignty claims, suggests that widespread cajoling occurred there. Irian Jaya also seems to have posted returns for Golkar far higher than might realistically be expected. Money politics and old patronage links continued to play a role, particularly in the outer provinces. The results of the election took nearly six weeks to be decided, as a consequence of the sheer difficulty of counting the huge number of votes and attempts by some members of the KPU to hold up the process in order to try to favour their own parties. To avoid a wider crisis Habibie issued a presidential decree on 4 August to declare the elections valid.

Still, the elections were largely peaceful, and judged by international observers to be "vastly improved", in democratic terms, from previous

	% Election Vote	% DPR Seats	Number DPR Seats
PDI-P	33.8	30.6	153
Golkar	22.5	24	120
PKB	12.6	10.2	51
PPP	10.7	11.6	58
PAN	7.1	6.8	34
PBB	1.9	2.6	13
TNI	—	7.6	38
Others	11.38	6.6	33

contests.[19] Turn out rates averaged 95 per cent across Indonesia — far higher than in established democracies — amounting to more than 112 million voters.

The election was a strong endorsement for the PDI-P, which gained nearly 34 per cent of the vote. Golkar was its nearest rival with almost 22.5 per cent of the vote. Most of the remaining seats were won by Islamic parties — Partai Kebangkitan Bangsa (PKB), PPP, Partai Amanat Nasional (PAN) and Partai Bulan Bintang (PBB) with around 13 per cent, 11 per cent, 7 per cent and 2 per cent respectively. These results were broadly reflected in DPR representation, with PDI-P and PKB slightly under-represented and Golkar and PPP slightly over-represented.

Presidential Election

The first post-Soeharto election of the president by the MPR took place on 20 October 1999. Most commentators and diplomatic corps expected a contest between Habibie and Megawati, and yet Abdurrahman Wahid, whose party gained just below 13 per cent of the vote in the June election, won office. The final result was 373 to Wahid and 313 to Megawati, showing that in a multi-party environment coalition-building skills may count for more than gaining the highest vote. Wahid's victory resulted from his ability to pull together various parties, including the Poros Tengah and a substantial number of Golkar representatives. It is likely that compromise figures, or even popular non-partisan leaders, will emerge in the future.

It might be premature, however, to see the presidential election process only in terms of coalition building. Strong public expectation had built up that Megawati should be elected, followed by anger when this did not occur. The masses were only placated when Megawai was elected Vice-President. At the very least a strong performance in general elections would need to be carefully noted by the MPR in future presidential contests. With Wahid's ouster on 23 July 2001, Megawati assumed the presidency with PPP's Hamzah Haz taking the vice president's role — thus indicating the importance of the Muslim parties. Megawati won the MPR vote by an overwhelming 591–0 (with Wahid's supporters boycotting the session).

Judiciary

Indonesia's constitution recognizes the judiciary as a separate branch of government. Law No. 14/1970 provides courts with autonomy from political interference, though in practice under the Soeharto administration no court decisions against it were tolerated. Overall judicial power rests with the Supreme Court, the final court of appeal. Under this are high courts located in a number of regional capitals throughout Indonesia. Beneath that are more than 250 district courts. There are also four distinct juridical spheres: the general court deals with criminal and civil issues; the religious court (*pangadilan agama*) applies to all Muslims (and only Muslims) in the family matters of marriage, divorce and inheritance; the court martial for military discipline; and the administrative court for disputes with the bureaucracy. A separate commercial court has also been established recently to hasten the process of bankruptcy.

The administration of courts, including the overall budget as well as appointments, placements, and promotions, used to be under the Ministry of Justice — which gave the executive undue influence on the process. While the Ministry of Justice still oversees the justice system, the Supreme Court is more of a stand alone institution in terms of general management and has complete responsibility for the affairs of the courts below it. The president makes the appointment of Chief Justice, but from nominees proposed by the DPR.

Indonesian law is based on the antiquated Dutch legal code of colonial times. However, at another level many decisions, as it is applied to Indonesians, are decided on the basis of the uncodified *hukum adat* or local customary law which can vary markedly throughout the archipelago.

Although ostensibly to interpret laws and provide a check on executive power, the judiciary was badly run down during the New Order. The Supreme Court (consisting of 51 judges) is widely regarded as graft ridden and chronically inefficient. In early 2000 the Attorney General found it necessary to announce a plan for non-career judges outside the Supreme Court to be appointed on an ad hoc basis to overcome a backlog of cases.[20] The courts have often proved unable to bring justice to bear.

In recent landmark cases, the courts have shown more regard for the due legal process. In May 2000 24 soldiers and a civilian were sentenced to up to ten years in jail for the murder of 57 Acehnese (although senior officers were spared and the sentence considered relatively light). In June a district court dismissed a case brought by Soeharto's lawyers against *Time* magazine for claiming the Soeharto family fortune stood at US$15 billion. In August legal proceedings were brought against Soeharto himself, but the case dismissed on the grounds of Soeharto's ill-health. His son, Tommy Soeharto, has been sentenced to 18 months in jail for fraud, though at the time of writing his disappearance prevents enforcement.

Political Parties

In the past half century Indonesian political parties have come nearly full circle. During the 1950s there were around 50 parties, with the main four or five linked to leading *aliran* (cultural streams). *Abangan* and non-muslim Indonesians were largely represented by the PNI and PKI, and *santri* by Masjumi and NU. Although *aliran* forms have changed over this period, in today's multi-party system *abangan* and non-muslims are represented by PDI-P and Golkar, and the *santri* by the *Poros Tengah* led by PAN and PPP (although PKB initially aligned with this alliance to secure the Wahid presidency, the impeachment precedings created an open split). The correlation between parties and *aliran* is not, however, complete. For example, perhaps half of the PDI-P's support has come from the Muslim community, including the modernist stream.

Parties remain loosely organized, often around a strong leader, and lack both adequate structures for pursuing party interests and systematic ideologies. They all generally share agreement about issues such as macroeconomic reform, regional autonomy provisions, the retention of a secular society, and greater democratization. All of this is summarized by the slogan *"reformasi"*, which has swept the political environment like a tidal wave — with even former members of the New Order showing the zeal of new converts.

There are few restrictions on establishing parties, but the communist party (PKI), banned in 1966, remains prohibited. Parties advocating regional secession are also not allowed. The number of parties is not restricted, except by requirements on membership and gaining 2% in elections, leaving 48 parties to contest the 1999 general elections. A similar number contested the 1955 elections, though subsequently party numbers were limited to 10 under guided democracy and three under the New Order.

The Partai Demokrasi Indonesia–Perjuangan (PDI-P) is Indonesia's largest party. When Megawati Sukarnoputri was ousted from the party leadership of PDI in a government rigged vote in 1996, the bulk of the party left with her to form the PDI-P. Megawati's charisma amongst the masses could best be described as "inherited" as it derives from the immense popularity the late Sukarno still enjoys. She clearly believes she is destined to lead Indonesia, not through the force of her ideas but because she has the right to rule based on lineage. This seems to invoke the Javanese concept of *wahyu*, or the spiritual blessing to rule, which many associated with Sukarno and Soeharto at their zenith. She seldom speaks on policy issues, or participates in day-to-day party affairs, but seems untouchable in her position as PDI-P leader.

Megawati has critics inside PDI-P, most vocally from a deputy chairman Mochtar Buchori, who express the concern that the party is becoming wracked by internal feuding and that Megawati is failing to modernize the party. Professional members have tried to transform it into a "modern political party", based on democratic procedures and policy discussion, but with little success. An attempt by two officials in 2000 to challenge Megawati's chairmanship was subject to physical harassment and intimidation from other members who failed to understand the ideal of democratic procedure. PDI-P also has its own paramilitary wing, and Eurico Gutteres, leader of the Timorese Aitarak militia is a prominent member of the party.

PDI-P is one of the few truly national political parties, with a strong presence in all 32 provinces. The party's popularity is not based solely on the person of Megawati. It is viewed as the successor to PNI and is the only decidedly secular party. Its main support comes from Central Java, Jakarta, Bali, parts of Sumatra and East Kalimantan.

Golkar was Soeharto's vehicle for managing political activity. During the New Order, Golkar included military officers, all civil servants and the heads of functional groups, such as unions and sectorial associations — thus the line between government and party was well and truly blurred. By the late 1960s Golkar had a network of 270 associations to represent all manner of functional groups. As power attracts, a number of professionals and Islamic leaders also became associated with what was then the natural party of government.

The fall of Soeharto thrust the party into a more democratized era and forced it to dissociate itself from excesses of the past. An open split in the party emerged in 1998 when Habibie loyalist Akbar Tanjung squared off against retired general Edi Sudradjat (often linked to Soehartoist conservatives but also a friend of Megawati) in the first ever open political contest for Golkar chairman amongst the party leadership. Tanjung won by 16 to 11. Golkar now consists of various factions, highlighted in the party's nomination of no less than five candidates for the presidency in 1999, with reports that a few secretly favoured a sixth — Megawati. It currently seems divided at least three ways. Party chairman, Akbar Tanjung represents the modernist Muslim wing; Deputy party chairman and former Attorney General Marzuki Darusman, represents a reformist faction (White Golkar); while DPR member Baramuli champions a "conservative" (or pro-New Order) grouping.

Golkar suffered a dramatic decline of fortunes in the June 1999 elections, and may decline further as patronage opportunities are reduced. Still, it has a strong base in the outer islands and is in a solid position to form part of future governments. It retains a large number of experienced professionals who have tried to reconstruct themselves in post-Soeharto Indonesia. Support for Golkar remains extremely strong in Sulawesi (a combination of a strong regional economy and support for Habibie, who is from this island), while it also did well in Eastern Indonesia.

The three major Islamic parties enjoy similar levels of support. The National Awakening Party (Partai Kebangkitan Bangsa or PKB) is largely the creation of Abdurrahman Wahid, although he has never held an official position in the party and it remains under the chairmanship of Matori Abdul Djalil. The PKB is based on the membership of the 34 million strong conservative Islamic organization, Nahdlatul Ulama (NU or Association of Islamic Scholars), founded by Wahid's grandfather. Both NU and PKB have little appeal outside Java — in the election, as expected, support came from East and Central Java.

Wahid is noted for his defence of a secular society, the Chinese minority, Christians and other faiths, and controversially his support for legalizing the PKI and establishing links with Israel. Something of a political maverick, he is far more liberal than the political forces he represents. The PKB is in some respects an authoritarian party, and NU has been linked to the violence of 1965–66. There remains, within the party, a paramilitary militia known as the *Banser*. Wahid's actions and views are tolerated, as many PKB members see him as invested with the *wahyu*, a clear reflection of Indonesia's tradition — and personality-driven politics.

The one New Order party able to retain its share of the popular vote was the United Development Party (Partai Persatuan Pembangunan or PPP). Under the leadership of Hamzah Haz, PPP has thrived under the new rules and earned a reputation as a force for political reform, most notably by urging a reduction in the number of DPR and MPR seats gifted to the TNI. PPP has been more outspoken than other major Islamic parties in promoting Muslim concerns (particularly broader application of Islamic laws for Muslims), and has supported Malaysian-style affirmative action share for *pribumi* (indigenous) Indonesians. The principal support bases for the party are in Jakarta and Kalimantan.

The National Mandate Party (Partai Amanat Nasional or PAN) of Amien Rais is based on the 28 million member modernist Islamic organization, Muhammadiyah, which Amien formerly chaired. Muhammadiyah is strong on parts of coastal Java and Sumatra. Sometimes regarded as a political chameleon, Amien tried to shed his image as a highly conservative and firebrand Islamic scholar and became a supporter of the student-led demonstration for reform in 1998. A noted orator, he tried to turn his high profile during student demonstrations to political advantage.

Amien's attempt to make the transition from an *aliran* leader to a national leader may have led to the party "falling between two stones". PAN recruited non-Muslims as candidates (unlike other Islamic parties) and loudly espoused *Pancasila*. This apparently alienated Muhammadiyah supporters, some of whom voted for other parties in the general election. In July 2000 Muhammadiyah decided to remove references to the Pancasila from the organization's brief. Chairman Ahmad Syafii Maarif stated that "[the] Pancasila is no longer recognized as our founding statute".[21]

Amien is the only party leader that will publicly mention the word "federalism" — discredited by its perceived association with Dutch attempts to weaken the Republic in 1949. He is also something of a "king maker" within the political system. By cobbling together the Poros Tengah, Amien was able to secure the position of chairman of the MPR, and in turn helped deliver crucial votes to Wahid to win the presidency. Amien remains a central figure within the Indonesian political structure despite his party's disappointing showing in the elections. PAN is factionalized along two lines: a moderate group, led by Faisal Basri, an experienced politician and respected economist until his recent resignation from PAN and a more radical Islamic group led by Islamic teacher and activist A M Fatwa. In the election PAN appealed to middle class Muslims in Jakarta, as well as large numbers of people in western and northern Sumatra (including Aceh).

The Crescent Star Party (Partai Bulan Bintang or PBB) claims its lineage from the old Masyumi party banned by Sukarno. PBB is perhaps more radical than the three more mainstream Islamic parties, and has generated a lot of publicity. Its platform advocates the promotion of a society based on Islamic values, primarily through changing the Constitution to make Muslims subject to Islamic law. It is led by Yusril Ihza Mahendra, a presidential candidate in 1999 who had close links to the Habibie administration and was Minister for Law and Human Rights until February 2001 (and now re-enters the Megawati Cabinet as Minister of Justice).

State Ideology

The state motto of Indonesia, *Bhinneka Tunggal Ika* or "unity in diversity" indicates tolerance of religious and cultural difference. All administrations have endorsed this concept, spread its message through the education system, and to a greater or lesser degree practiced it.

Indonesia's official state ideology is known as the Pancasila, or the "five pillars": belief in the One and Only God; just and civilized humanity; the unity of Indonesia; democracy guided by the inner wisdom in the unanimity arising out of deliberations amongst representatives; and social justice. Under Sukarno the document was taken seriously, but under Soeharto it was greatly emphasized as a way of shoring up legitimacy. Every school child in Indonesia is required to memorize the "five pillars" and their applications to politics and society.

The reference to God in the first pillar is generic in form, and not linked to Islam. *Pancasila* is often used by the Indonesian media as short-hand to refer to political leaders and parties that favour recognition of a multireligious or secular society, as opposed to Islamic society. Religious freedom of a kind is guaranteed, however atheists fall outside this provision. Under the New Order communism and atheism were identified as one and the same — which often meant death during the killings of 1965–66 and imprisonment as a Marxist thereafter.

The remaining Pancasila components also require brief elaboration. The provision for a "civilized humanity" is a reference to the promotion of human rights as a universal principle. Talk of secession also defies the state canon under the third principle. Thus political parties or movements that openly advocated independence were ruthlessly suppressed in Soeharto's time (Aceh, East Timor and Irian Jaya), while recent talk of independence in Aceh and Irian Jaya (Papua) has provoked a stinging reaction from the DPR. The fourth principle, that of democracy, is also firmly embedded, though under Sukarno and Soeharto it meant preserving some outward forms (those "appropriate to Indonesian culture") while running authoritarian states. The final principle is understood to mean that Indonesia's wealth must be used for the welfare of all its people.

Civil Society and Human Rights

The burgeoning number of civil society groups, or non-governmental organizations (NGOs), has been a notable feature of recent change in Indonesia. Independent unions have become more active in the workplace (to the chagrin of some investors and economists). A myriad of human rights groups have been established, exposing atrocities and human rights abuses from the past and in more recent times. Indonesian NGOs were well represented during the East Timor referendum in 1999 and served as monitors in the 1999 general election. Campuses have also been the centre of political activity in recent years. It was the actions of students that highlighted disenchantment with the New Order regime from early 1998. The tremendous upsurge in political consciousness has continued, with demonstrations and protests a regular occurrence in Jakarta and other university cities.

The most prominent NGOs in Indonesia are the Islamic organizations, some with a long history. The 34 million strong NU, representing traditionalist Muslims in central and eastern Java, is known for its *pesantren* (Islamic schools) and other social services. Wahid, for many years the chair of NU, took the organization out of politics and transformed it into a non-partisan grouping, then subsequently brought it back to the political field. Muhammadiyah, 28 million strong, plays a similar role for modernist Muslims of coastal Java and parts of Sumatra. During the New Order an organization of Muslim Scholars, Ikatan Cendekiawan Muslim se Indonesia (ICMI), became influential, and was run by Habibie for a time.

There are also several research centres in Indonesia which have had varying influences, at different times, with policy makers. The Centre for Strategic Studies (CSIS) was well known for its role in policy construction (particularly foreign policy) during the earlier years of the New Order regime. Other think tanks have also played advisely roles from time to time, notably, Lembaga Ilmu Pengetahun Indonesia (LIPI or Indonesian National Institute of Sciences) and the Center for Information and Development Studies (CIDES). Habibie has now established the Habibie Center to promote good governance and democratization.

The Soeharto government did tolerate a degree of political pluralism. In 1988, the regime talked of *keterbukaan* (political openness) in line with political changes sweeping the globe. However the June 1994 closure of three newspapers — *Editor, Detik,* and *Tempo* — most probably because of their criticism of Habibie as Minister for Research and Technology, was a major setback. While there was a degree of freedom in academic and press comment — and this grew louder as the regime began to unravel — criticism of the person of the president was treated as *lèse majesté*.

During the New Order the media was controlled by the Department of Information, while literature was screened by the Department of Education and Culture (2,000 books were banned including those by Indonesia's most famous writer, Pramoedya Ananta Toer). The Department of Information had the power to revoke print media licences, which was used extensively in the 1960s but less so after that. The major news dailys, only some of which had formal or informal links to the Soeharto family and/or

Golkar, largely survived by depoliticizing their content. The leading newspaper was, and remains, *Kompas*, followed by *Suara Pembaruan*, *Jawa Pos*, and *Media Indonesia*. *Suara Karya* and *Republika*, both popular papers, are linked to Golkar and Ikatan Cendekiawan Muslem se Indonesia (ICMI) respectively. There were and are a host of regional papers, many controlled by the Kompas-Gramedia group and several English language newspapers of which the *Jakarta Post* is the most well-known and was an outspoken critic of the Soeharto regime. (Being published in English allowed it near complete freedom.) In 1999 the right to revoke permits ended and 500 new permits were issued for new publications. Newspapers are now able openly to print stories embarrassing to the current and former governments (and they frequently do). Press freedom seems almost complete, although there were restrictions on East Timor news stories during 1999. Radio has been dominated by state-run Radio Republik Indonesia (RRI) and television (especially news broadcasts) by Televisi Republik Indonesia (TVRI). Both broadcasters still operate but there are also now independent actors, particularly in radio.

In April 1999 Habibie amended the 1963 Anti-Subversion Law, press freedom was legislated for, human rights laws were strengthened and a National Human Rights Commission (KOMNAS-HAM) established. Some provisions of the Anti-Subversion Law have been retained including the ban on the progagation of marxism and separatism, but the act has been applied sparingly. During sixteen months in office Habibie released 213 political prisoners,[22] including East Timorese leader Xanana Gusmão, labour leader Dita Indah Sari, and economist and Muslim activist Sri Bintang Pamungkas.

Wahid took such measures further. He released prisoners associated with the struggles in East Timor and Aceh, strengthened religious freedom, looked at lifting bans on Chinese written characters, medicines and cultural displays, and even proposed legalizing the PKI.

There is still a long way to go to improve basic human rights. During 1999 the whole world focused on the violence in East Timor which claimed the lives of thousands, all with the acquiescence of elements in the Indonesian military. The TNI and the police also continue to abuse public rights in Indonesia, including through extra-juridical killings, torture and arbitrary detention. Labour is exploited, including child labour, in light manufacturing sweat shops. Nonetheless Indonesian democracy has strengthened civil society, and as the U.S. State Department's human rights report for 1999 states, "there has been a general improvement in the institutionalization of human rights protections."[23]

MAJOR POLITICAL ISSUES

Who Has Power?

According to the Constitution the people of Indonesia are deemed to be sovereign. What this means in practice has changed over time. Although the Soeharto regime argued that its method of government was a culturally appropriate form of democratic government, this model is currently discredited. The idea that the "people are sovereign" has taken on new meaning. Legitimacy is now seen as deriving from a free and fair vote in an environment of open debate and discussion of political issues, and sensitivity to the public will between elections. The "people" of Indonesia, particularly those who favour *reformasi*, have become a strong factor in the power equation. Unpopular decisions now result in public demonstrations by a range of civil society organizations. As noted, Wahid's 1999 election to the presidency threatened to re-ignite street protests, and crowds were only placated when Megawati was elected as Vice-President.

Besides civil society, the public also exercises influence through parliament. The public will is not perfectly represented here as both the DPR and MPR still contain non-elected or indirectly elected representatives. Where close contests occur such members may exercise the balance of power, as many believe occurred in Wahid's 1999 election by the MPR. Also, the 1999 general election was not completely free of fraudulent behaviour, with Golkar using existing patronage links to mobilize support in some of the outlying areas. Nonetheless parliament does reflect the public will far more accurately than predecessors under Soeharto's New Order.

The Constitution specifies that executive power resides with the presidency, supported by cabinet and the bureaucracy. Under Soeharto the executive exercised this power with few checks and balances. Now, parliament and civil society exert rigorous checks on the executive powers. The President retains overall executive power in modern times, but must negotiate legislation with the DPR. While the balance of power has moved to the civilian leaders, the military remain powerful in political and commercial life in Indonesia. A number of changes are still needed before the military can be said to have returned to the barracks.

Who Benefits?

Under President Soeharto state power was exercised quite blatantly to give a particular benefit to the family and friends of the president himself.

Estimates of the Soeharto family's worth at its zenith range from US$15–30 billion. Thousands of companies controlled by the Soeharto family or leading businessmen like Bob Hassan and Liem Sioe Liong were given monopoly rights over key economic sectors. This market favouritism stands out as one of the most excessive examples of crony capitalism in recent history.

Many Indonesian Chinese thrived economically under the New Order, and the Soeharto regime sought to harness this domestic source of capital. There were no economic barriers to ethnic Chinese business people. However, there was discrimination of another kind. The banning of aspects of Chinese culture, in particular the written script, made it difficult for the community to pass on Chinese language. Aside from official discrimination, many *pribumi* became resentful of the Chinese community's business success — this was to manifest itself during the riots of May 1998.

Since 1998, the Soeharto family have come under investigation for so-called ill-gotten riches, and their business linkages have seemingly withered away. However, many of the large companies, and notably Indonesia's largest conglomerate, the Salim group of Liem Sioe Liong, have survived intact. Many Chinese businesspeople who fled Indonesia in 1998 have now returned, and official discrimination has largely come to an end.

Attempts are currently underway to reduce conglomerate control of the economy. Anti-monopoly laws have been passed by the DPR in line with IMF mandates. There is much discussion in policy making circles about the need to assist SMEs in a number of ways, including direct and indirect incentives, limiting corruption (which always favours larger companies), and improving bureaucratic procedures. In the DPR many parliamentarians, across various parties, are calling for the development of an *Ekonomi Rakyat* (People's Economy), which means a greater level of participation in commerce at lower levels. Some Muslim parties have promoted Malaysia's affirmative action New Economic Policy (NEP) as a possible role model. Others in the DPR have pointed out that this ignores the reality that not all the rich are Chinese, while not all the poor are *pribumi*.

Under Soeharto's rule many in the outer islands came to believe that Indonesia was the domain of the Javanese, a belief not entirely without foundation as Javanese held powerful positions in government and the military out of proportion to their numbers. However, while the New Order undertook policies to stress or force "unity", lip service was paid to "diversity", symbolically in Jakarta's *Taman Mini* (the miniature garden) where all of Indonesia's more than 200 cultures were subordinated to 27 provincial displays of house structure, costume and dance. Soeharto's departure has brought much of this discontent out into the open.

In the past, development has come mostly to urban Java and some of the mineral rich provinces such as Riau. Incomes vary markedly, with the highest average on Batam at Rp. 350,000 per month, and the lowest on Jambi at Rp. 173,000 per month. Generally the regions to the east of Bali are poorest. Some provinces have been "held back" by the Jakarta-based government. Riau, which produces 50 per cent of Indonesia's oil, received only Rp. 821 billion (US$108 million) of the wealth generated in the 1999 financial year, or 1.4 per cent of the total returns from the oil resource.[24] The fact that 98.6 per cent of returns go to Jakarta has increased demands for greater autonomy over resource use. Aceh has been unable to take advantage of its strategic location on the Malacca Straits to build port facilitates as these would have competed with those further south. Provinces outside Java are also poorly served by tertiary educational institutions and thus many *seberang* (outer islanders) move to Java for educational and professional reasons. Current plans for regional autonomy seek to address these issues, but are not sufficiently coherent or well-advanced to inspire confidence. While another disaster similar to East Timor is not an immediate prospect, these are serious challenges to central control in Aceh and Irian Jaya.

However, the Soeharto regime did preside over a dramatic expansion of the Indonesian economy which saw much of the population gain as a result. From 1969 to 1994, Indonesia embarked upon its first development phase. Per capita income rose from US$70 to more than US$700. Education levels and life span also dramatically increased as a result. (See further in the Governance section, below.)

Numbers below the poverty line have undoubtedly increased since the regional economic crisis, but the actual percentage is disputed. Some economists argue it is between 13 and 15 per cent, the World Bank maintains 20 per cent, while the International Labour Organization (ILO) has stated that it is close to 50 per cent. The real figure would probably be at the lower end of this range, with the greater impact in Java, East Nusa Tenggara and parts of Sumatra and Kalimantan. Other parts of Indonesia were not so badly affected, including Sulawesi which enjoyed a trading boom due to the plunging rupiah. The government must be concerned about alleviation for the poor as in the aftermath of the crisis large numbers of people entered the poorly paying informal sector. In post-Soeharto Indonesia trade unions are more active, and from 1 April 2000 the minimum wage[25] was lifted to ameliorate the fall in real wages.

The most common method of poverty alleviation in the past was to provide subsidies on fuel and foodstuffs. That continues to some extent, and has been broadened to health care products, including the provision of free contraceptives to maintain Indonesia's population policy. There is strong pressure to remove or reduce subsidies, because of the distortions these create, but no one in government has forgotten that the catalyst for the May 1998 riots culminating in Soeharto's resignation was the removal of kerosene and food subsidies.

Amidst the trauma of Indonesia's recent regime transition, Muslim groups and parties have filled a leadership void as their political fortunes have been boosted. As the New Order regime crumbled, religious subnational groups and their leaders were viewed increasingly as providing both an alternative organizational structure and an order that was morally detached from the corruption of Soeharto's government. Although the two leading parties in Indonesia at the time of writing are secular, the Muslim parties together have a significant impact, and will continue to do so in the foreseeable future.

Legitimacy

Events in Indonesia since 1997 demonstrate a marked change in the nature of legitimacy. Sukarno founded his legitimacy on his charisma and status as the "father of independence". Soeharto sought to ground legitimacy in economic and social development, as the "father of development". These days legitimacy is linked to *reformasi*, a touchstone word to mean greater political and economic reform, including democratization.

To what extent the Indonesian people have come to believe in democracy for its own sake, or simply as a way to remove an unpopular leader in the short term, remains an open question. A number of scholars have noted a tendency in Indonesia for people to follow charismatic leaders.[26] In an Indonesian sense charisma does not necessarily revolve around policy ideas or eloquence — although these may be factors from time to time — but often through a sense of lineage and the mantle of power. Both Sukarno and Soeharto claimed lineage back to ancient kingdoms and/or famous leaders, as Megawati and Gus Dur do in contemporary times. With Indonesia's re-emerging *aliran* as political identity markers, anointed leaders will be said to have the *wahyu*. Dewi Fortuna Anwar notes:

> Although intellectuals have argued that as Indonesia moves towards democracy the focus should be on developing democratic systems and institutions rather than on personalities, it cannot be denied that at this early stage of its democratic transition Indonesians remain transfixed by personalities.[27]

Wahid's accession to the presidency with only minority popular support for his political vehicle, the PKB, caused some disillusionment with the system. Further, Wahid was unable to tackle Indonesia's problems with as much energy and professionalism as many had hoped. Although he enjoys overwhelming support from the regions in Java where Nahdlatul Ulama is dominant, this does not extend to the rest of Indonesia. However, currently there is not one political leader (or party) who could be said to enjoy the overwhelming popular support of the majority in the way that Sukarno did after Independence. However the democratic process enjoys widespread legitimacy at the moment, largely in reaction to Soeharto's autocratic rule. Still, belief in democratic governance remains vulnerable in a population with a short history of democratic practice. If the democratic system proves capable of delivering results in terms of leadership, then its legitimacy will grow.

The popular legitimacy of Indonesia as a nation/state has also been questioned by some international commentators. While regional tensions clearly exist, the idea of "Indonesia" and being "Indonesian" enjoys widespread support throughout the archipelago, with the exceptions of Aceh and Irian Jaya where this is very much open to question. The common struggle against the Dutch and the use of a common language serve as two important factors in holding the Republic together. Indonesian nationalism is still strong outside of Aceh and Irian Jaya, and currently this would seem to preclude suggestions of a break up of Indonesia along the lines of the former Soviet Union.

Governance

Under the New Order (1965–98), the Soeharto regime instigated development programmes in education, industry and agriculture designed to improve living standards. It has generally been accorded high marks for its ability to plan and implement these policies. From 1969 to 1994, Indonesia embarked upon its first development phase achieving near universal schooling, dramatic improvements in literacy, increasing life expectancy (increasing by around 10 years to an average of 65), and effective birth control programmes. In that time absolute poverty officially went from 60 per cent of the population to 14 per cent. In 1994 the Indonesian government claimed that poverty levels had been reduced to 27 million people. At the onset of the Asian Financial Crisis the official levels of poverty were 11 per cent. Jeffery Winters has pointed out that the official poverty line was measured at an income of US$9.30 (then

Rp. 20,000) per month for rural workers and US$13 (Rp. 28,000) per month for urban workers, which was about enough to buy food alone,[28] but it remains true that considerable progress towards alleviating poverty was made. With economic contraction in 1998, poverty climbed back to 14 per cent (official statistics) while disposable incomes were reduced. Official unemployment increased to 6.4 per cent by February 1998 (up from 5.1 per cent in February 1997), and large numbers were forced into the informal sector, where underemployment and reduced incomes are still a major problem.

Indonesia's economic performance has improved with growth of an expected 4–5 per cent in 2000, but the Soeharto administration has left many unfortunate legacies. Soeharto's industrial policy fostered a series of conglomerates, or "crony capitalists", often family and friends, who were protected from international and domestic competition. Many of these industries were rent-seeking exercises, such as collection of taxes, tolls, or the establishment of a single desk seller (for example, clove growers had to sell at a fixed price to the Humpuss company owned by Tommy Soeharto, from which the cloves were on-sold to *kretek* manufacturers for twice the price). Lax rules and enforcement allowed many large corporations and banks to fall into serious liquidity problems. The recapitalization of the banking sector will amount to around US$800 billion, or a massive 80 per cent of GNP. The allowance of an extremely low capital asset ratio (CAR) has bankrupted the banking system, threatening to bring down linked businesses. Corruption remains at the heart of many of these problems. In newly democratized Indonesia this is now subject to media scrutiny. However the problem remains endemic with regard to virtually any government service — a situation that favours those with higher disposable incomes.

The financial crisis in Indonesia has probably made personal security more of an issue for the general population than it was before. The police force seem unable to control the rise in petty crime, with the emergence of vigilante violence now one of the most common responses to criminal suspects.[29] The military and the police are unable to deal effectively with communal tensions also, which remain serious in particular regions. Indonesia faces the prospect of growing inter-communal violence.

Compounding such problems is the fact that the armed forces of Indonesia are seemingly powerless (or, sometimes, unwilling) to prevent conflict. The TNI is not entirely responsive to the command of the Indonesian president, or the TNI chief-of-staff. Despite *reformasi*, the military have still functioned as a law unto themselves in outlying areas, committing an array of unpunished breeches of justice against citizens, particularly in

Aceh, East Timor, Irian Jaya and Ambon. At times the enforcement agencies even seem divided in themselves.

The notion of governance in Indonesia is largely captured in the term *reformasi* — leaders and opinion-makers are searching for ways to adhere to issues such as democracy, the rule of law, transparency, accountability, effectiveness and opposing corruption. Considerable progress has been made in terms of improving democracy in Indonesia, though much still remains to be done. Gains in other areas have been slower, and must surmount the legacy of missteps by the New Order government.

CONCLUSION

In spite of attempts to give substance to *reformasi*, Indonesia faces a host of serious challenges. Amongst others it must nurture fragile new democratic political institutions, contain violence caused by outbreaks of ethnic conflict, address pressing economic and social needs of tens of millions of poor, contain a range of potential ecological disasters, repair a financial and corporate sector flattened by the economic crisis, and begin drafting laws to put in place an adequate rational/legal framework. Even its territorial integrity is under threat — though adherence to a common nationalism makes "fraying at the edges" more likely than a total break up — as challenges in Aceh and Irian Jaya remain serious. Addressing such issues would test any government, let alone one trying to proceed by democratic means.

How should current politics in Indonesia be categorized? Commentators who see the political structure as a successor to Soeharto's authoritarian structure are partly right. Key aspects of government remain from that time, notably the 1945 Constitution (with modification) and a military that has not been completely removed from its position of influence. But such critics ignore wholesale changes that have occurred. While the democratic process is not yet consolidated, the emergence of political pluralism and a genuine division of powers mean that the system is more than just the façade of democratic rule evident in the New Order. Reform is best characterized as being evolutionary within the existing Constitutional framework.

Since May 1998 Indonesia has been repoliticized. Soeharto's departure has seen the emergence of a multi-party environment, with PDI-P by far the largest party. The former ruling party, Golkar, has suffered greatly as many associate it with abuses of the past. In common with many regime changes around the world, ecclesiastical authority often emerges to challenge authoritarian states because of their independent authority structures and moral commitment. Political Islam has a prominent role in recent events, and will continue to influence the immediate future, though the generally tolerant character of Indonesian Islam is an important assurance that this will not take on a extreme form.

Indonesia's new politicized environment is not irreversible, but provides a strong check on the return of authoritarian rule. The idea of dictatorship — whether it is based on the military or a powerful family — is currently in recession.

Notes

The author would like to thank Riyana Miranti, of the Institute of Southeast Asian Studies, Singapore, for assistance with aspects of this chapter.

1 David Joel Steinberg, ed., *In Search of Southeast Asia: A Modern History* (Revised edition) (Honolulu: University of Hawaii Press, 1987), p. 193.

2 Secession was not proposed by these army commanders, who still continued to use the symbols of the Indonesian state. See Kenneth Conboy and James Morrison, *Feet to the Fire: CIA Covert Operations in Indonesia, 1957–58*, (Maryland: Naval Institute Press, 1999).

3 Cited in D.R. Sar Desai, *Southeast Asia: Past and Present*, 4th ed. (Colorado: Westview Press, 1997), p. 267.

4 See Robert Cribb, ed., *The Indonesian Killings 1965–66: Studies from Java and Bali* Monash Papers on Southeast Asia No. 21. (Clayton, Victoria: Centre of Southeast Asian Studies, 1990).

5 Central Intelligence Agency, Directorate of Intelligence, *Intelligence Report: Indonesia — 1965, the coup that backfired* (Washington, D.C.: Central Intelligence Agency, 1968), p. 71n. Cited in Robert Cribb, ed., *The Indonesian Killings 1965–66: Studies from Java and Bali*, p. 5, n. 8.

6 See Stefan Eklöf, *Indonesian Politics in Crisis: The Long Fall of Suharto, 1996–98* (Copenhagen: NIAS, 1999).

7 By way of illustration, in East Timor membership of the Catholic Church was 30 per cent in 1975. Soon after the invasion membership had climbed to 90 per cent as the East Timorese, many of whom have strong animist traditions, found Catholicism the best alternative.

8 Clifford Geertz, *The Religion of Java* (London: The Free Press of Glencoe, 1964). The term Santri is used by Geertz to describe pious or orthodox Muslims. In Indonesia the Santri are only those who have graduated from Pesantren schools. In this chapter Geertz's definition is employed.

9 See Bernhard Platzdasch, "Islamic Reaction to a Female President", in *Indonesia in Transition: Social Aspects of Reformasi and Crisis*, edited by Chris Manning and Peter van Dierman (Singapore: Institute of Southeast Asian Studies, 2000).

10   Michael Vatikiotis, *Indonesian Politics Under Suharto: The Rise and Fall of the New Order*, 3rd ed. (New York: Routledge, 1998), p. 177.

11   Dewi Fortuna Anwar, "Indonesia: the presidential election and its aftermath", *Asian Affairs*, no. 9, (Autumn 1999), p. 84.

12   At the time of the 1999 general election there were 27 provinces, as there had been since 1976. East Timor ceased to be a province in 1999, and since then 6 new provinces have been added — North Maluku, Banten (Java), Irian Jaya has been split into three from the original province, Bangka and Belitung (South Sumatra), and Gorontalo (North Sulawesi).

13   Ramlan Surbakti, "Formal Political Institutions", in *Indonesia: The Challenge of Change,* edited by Richard W. Baker, M. Hadi Soesastro, J. Kristiadi, Douglas E. Ramage (Leiden and Singapore: KITLV Press and the Institute of Southeast Asian Studies, 1999), p. 65.

14   For a full listing, see <www.thejakartapost.com/resources/cabinets/cabinet.asp>.

15   "Graft in Indonesia rife, says World Bank", *Straits Times*, 21 February 2000. Wolfensohn also added that he had been prohibited for three and a half years from using the word "corruption".

16   "Anti-Graft Agency Soon for Jakarta", *Straits Times*, 18 February 2000.

17   For a full list of the TNI's institutional and non-institutional companies, see Indria Samego et al., *Bila ABRI Berbisnis* (Bandung: Mizan, 1998).

18   Jimmy Carter, "Visit to Indonesia, June 1–11, 1999", *Trip Report* (Carter Center), <www.cartercenter.org>.

19   See National Democratic Institute, "Statement of the National Democratic Institute (NDI) and the Carter Center International Election Observation Delegation to Indonesia's June 7, 1999, Legislative Elections" (Jakarta, 9 June 1999), <www.ndi.org>.

20   Marianne Kearney, "Indonesia acts to clean up its courts", *Straits Times*, 6 April 2000, p. 24.

21   Lindsay Murdoch, "Jitters at switch to Islam", *Sydney Morning Herald*, 13 July 2000.

22   U.S. State Department, "Indonesia", *1999 Country Reports on Human Rights Practices*, 25 February 2000.

23   Ibid.

24   Margot Cohen, "Chorus of Discontent", *Far Eastern Economic Review*, 17 February 2000, p. 24.

25   Indonesia has 37 administrative regions for the purposes of judging wage levels, and the increases varied from 15–50 per cent.

26   See Clifford Geetz, *The Religion of Java* (London: The Free Press of Glencoe, 1964) and Benedict R. O'G. Anderson, *Language and Power: Exploring Political Cultures in Indonesia* (Ithaca and London: Cornell University Press, 1990).

27   Dewi Fortuna Anwar, "Indonesia: the presidential election and its aftermath", *Asian Affairs*, no. 9, (Autumn 1999), p. 83.

28 Jeffery A. Winters, "Suharto's Indonesia: Properity and Freedom for the Few", *Current History* 94, no. 596: 422.
29 See Dini Djalal, "The New Face of Indonesian Justice", *Far Eastern Economic Review*, 13 July 2000.

Further Reading

Anderson, Benedict R. O'G. *Language and Power: Exploring Political Cultures in Indonesia*. Ithaca and London: Cornell University Press, 1990.

Booth, Anne. *The Indonesian Economy in the Nineteenth and Twentieth Century: A History of Missed Opportunities*. New York: St Martin's Press, 1998.

Budiman, Arief, Barbara Hatley and Damien Kingsbury, eds. *Reformasi: Crisis and Change in Indonesia*. Clayton: Monash Asia Institute, 1999.

Crouch, Harold. *The Army and Politics in Indonesia*. Cornell University Press: Ithaca, 1978.

Cribb, Robert, ed. *The Indonesian Killings 1965–66: Studies from Java and Bali*. Monash Papers on Southeast Asia no 21. Clayton, Victoria: Centre of Southeast Asian Studies, 1990.

Eklöf, Stefan. *Indonesian Politics in Crisis: The Long Fall of Suharto, 1996–98*. Copenhagen: NIAS, 1999.

Emmerson, Donald K., ed. *Indonesia Beyond Suharto: Polity, Economy, Society, Transition*. New York: the Asia Society and M E Sharpe, 1999.

Feith, Herbert. *The Decline of Constitutional Democracy in Indonesia*. Ithaca, New York: Cornell University Press, 1962.

Geertz, Cliftord. *The Religion of Java*. London: The Free Press of Glencoe, 1964.

Hill, Hal. *The Indonesian Economy*, 2nd ed. Cambridge: Cambridge University Press, 2000.

Liddle, R. William. *Leadership and Culture in Indonesian Politics*. Sydney: Asian Studies Association of Australia and Allen & Unwin, 1996.

Lloyd, Grayson and Shannon Smith. *Indonesia Today: Challenges of History*. Singapore: Institute of Southeast Asian Studies, 2001.

Manning, Chris and Peter van Dierman, eds. *Indonesia in Transition: Social Aspects of Reformasi and Crisis*. Singapore: Institute of Southeast Asian Studies, 2000.

Schwarz, Adam. *A Nation in Waiting: Indonesia's Search for Stability*, 2nd ed. Sydney: Allen & Unwin, 1999.

Suryadinata, Leo. *Interpreting Indonesian Politics*. Singapore: Times Academic Press, 1998.

Thomson-Zainu'ddin, Ailsa G. *A Short History of Indonesia*, 2nd ed. Stanmore, NSW: Cassell Australia Ltd, 1980.

Vatikiotis, Michael. *Indonesian Politics Under Suharto: The Rise and Fall of the New Order*, 3rd ed. New York: Routledge, 1998.

4

LAOS
Timid Transition

Nick J. Freeman

INTRODUCTION

Though often caught in the middle of regional strategic rivalry, Laos remains relatively isolated, and is perhaps Southeast Asia's least understood state. Now, it is moving tentatively onto the world stage, opening its economy and joining the regional mainstream with membership of the Association of Southeast Asian Nations (ASEAN) in 1997.

The origins of a unified Lao state arguably date back to the Buddhist kingdom of Lan Xang Hom Khao (Kingdom of a Million Elephants and the White Parasol), founded in the mid-fourteenth century under Fa Ngum, and initially centred on the town of Luang Prabang. During the early eighteenth century, as a result of a conflict over royal succession, Laos divided into three smaller and independent kingdoms, centred on Vientiane (the capital of Lan Xang after 1560), Luang Prabang, and Champassak. By the nineteenth century, all three kingdoms had become vassals of Siam, and their combined territorial extent comprised large areas of what is now northern Thailand (i.e., the Khorat Plateau and land west of the Mekong River), as had unified Lan Xang before them. By the time the French arrived in the latter part of the nineteenth century, just the kingdoms of Luang Prabang and Champassak were still functioning, after Siam's overthrow and destruction of Vientiane in 1828.

The current territorial extent of landlocked Laos is largely a product of French colonial acquisition and administration. Laos' present borders were defined in 1893 — and slightly extended westward in 1904 and 1907 — by forcible French acquisition, and subsequently recognized by a series of treaties between France and Siam. Initially seeking to use the Mekong River as a "back door" into China, France gradually annexed all Lao territory east of the river, and merged the three Lao kingdoms under its remit into a single protectorate. In doing so, all ethnic Lao (about half the total) that resided west of the Mekong River found themselves territorially divorced from those living east of the river. Vientiane was chosen by the French as the administrative capital — a status it has kept to this day. The King residing in Luang Prabang was permitted by the French to continue as monarch, and the town remained the royal seat until the abolition of the monarchy in 1975. Under the French, Upper Laos became a "protected kingdom", and Lower Laos (which was of greater pertinence to French commercial activities in Vietnam) was deemed a "directly administered territory".

When the river route to China proved elusive, France came to regard Laos as a hinterland for the more concerted colonial exercise conducted in Vietnam, a buffer against competing British colonial expansion to the west, and a bridgehead for a possible extension of French influence into Siam at a later date. Throughout the pre-World War II colonial period, the French regarded Lao as "a means to ends that lay elsewhere".[1] Both colonial governance and economic exploitation were rather rudimentary and lacklustre, since the country was regarded as being only marginally useful to more profitable activities in neighbouring Vietnam. Producing and exporting relatively little (small quantities of tin, rubber, coffee and opium), Laos only accounted for a tiny fraction of French Indochina's cumulative export earnings and revenues. In terms of expenditure, colonial Laos was a loss-leader for France, even though great efforts were made to ensure that administrative costs were kept to a bare minimum. Just 600 French nationals were resident in the country by 1940, aided by a far greater number of imported (and cheaper) Vietnamese administrators. Prohibitively heavy fiscal obligations (including corvée labour duty) were placed on the local populace. The country's colonial rulers did little to develop any sense of state- or nation-hood within their new territorial construct. The only local political entity formed during this period was the Indigenous Consultative Assembly for Laos, established in 1923, which was a toothless, advisory, and non-elected body. At the onset of World War II, "... Laos still remained a charming backwater of inconsequential economic importance, still requiring to be subsidized from the revenues of Vietnam".[2]

Under pressure from Japan, King Sisavangvong declared Laos' independence in April 1945, immediately following imprisonment of the Vichy administration. However, seeking the return of French rule to protect his monarchy, the King retracted this statement four months later, after

---

FIGURE 4.1

Laos: Key Dates

1353	Kingdom of Lan Xang founded by Fa Ngum, centred on Luang Prabang.
1560	Capital of Lan Xang relocated to Vientiane.
1893	France gained suzerainty over the territory now known as Laos.
1936	Lao section of the Indochina Communist Party formed.
1941–45	Japanese occupation of Laos.
1953	Independence granted to Laos. Soon embroiled in First Indochina War.
1954	Geneva conference on Indochina. Laos designated a neutral country.
1955	Pathet Lao (Lao People's Party) established.
1957	First coalition government to include the Pathet Lao.
1961	Geneva conference on Laos starts.
1962	Geneva Accords signed, according Laos neutral status and recognizing Pathet Lao position in government alongside right-wing and neutralist groups.
1964	Coalition government breaks down. Commencement of U.S. "secret war" in Laos, as part of the Second Indochina War.
1972	LPP renamed the Lao People's Revolutionary Party (LPRP) at Second Congress.
1973	Ceasefire agreed to end civil war and third coalition government formed.
1975	Lao People's Democratic Republic (LPDR) established under Kaysone Phomvihane, and monarchy abolished.
1977	25-year treaty of friendship and co-operation signed with Vietnam.
1978	Co-operativization of agriculture programme commenced.
1979	Seventh Resolution ended forced co-operativization and relaxed various social restrictions.
1986	Fourth Party Congress, economic reform process unveiled. Supreme People's Assembly replaced by a National Assembly.
1991	New constitution promulgated.
1992	Death of Kaysone Phomvihane.
1997	Laos gained full membership status in ASEAN.

Japan's surrender in August that same year. Prince Phetsarath, as leader of the fledgling Lao Issara (Free Laos) nationalist movement, then re-asserted Lao independence a month later. Despite the Lao Issara's bid to gain national independence, France forcibly regained possession over the country in 1946. The Lao Issara leaders fled to Thailand — where the movement was to fracture in 1949 — and much of the country's Vietnamese population (some 40,000) returned to their home country. Belatedly, France now began to view Laos as distinct from Vietnam, and as its hold on Indochina began steadily to erode made Laos an "independent associate state" in 1949. Four years later, in October 1953, Laos secured full sovereign status as a constitutional monarchy, the Royal Lao Government (RLG).

The following 22 years saw domestic Lao politics overwhelmed by Cold War rivalry. Leaderships in Hanoi, Beijing and Moscow assisted the domestic communist forces, the Lao People's Revolutionary Party (LPRP) and its Pathet Lao (Land of the Lao) army, in an integrated political and military campaign to seize power. Washington and Bangkok led an opposing coalition that wished to see the RLG remain a non-communist state. Despite the Geneva accords of 1962, which formally recognized Laos' neutrality in the international arena, and three attempts by Vientiane to form coalition governments with the communists (in 1957, 1962–63 and 1973–75), the history of the RLG period was primarily one of military conflict.

Headquartered in the highland areas under its control, the communist LPRP displayed a noteworthy unity of purpose, and remained wholly focused on its ultimate objective. Between its founding in the early 1950s and its assumption of power in 1975, the leadership profile of the secretive LPRP barely altered, and was led throughout by Kaysone Phomvihane. In the crucial period between 1963 and 1973, the LPRP's main headquarters was located in a series of caves in north-eastern Sam Neua province (closer to Hanoi than Vientiane), which provided some degree of safety from heavy United States bombing. The hardship of living in these grim surroundings was in stark contrast to the decadent lifestyle of the LPRP's adversaries in the Lao capital during that same period. The military and civilian leadership in Vientiane was riddled with clannishness and in-fighting, and often distracted by the lucrative temptations of relatively massive corruption.

During the Cold War years, power struggles, coups and counter-coup attempts within the RLG regime were a common occurrence. Rivalry was inadventenlly exacerbated by U.S. assistance, as part of Washington's overall policy to thwart the bid for communist rule across Indochina. The

U.S. bankrolled most of the national budget, bloating the economy of the RLG almost beyond recognition and making its exploitation by a corrupt élite a relatively easy task. Although regular U.S. forces were never employed in Laos, the U.S. Air Force bombed LPRP-controlled parts of Laos intensively from Thai bases, and the CIA undertook what became known as a "secret war", roughly between 1964 and 1973, using hill tribe (Hmong) irregulars and Thai "volunteers".[3]

The character and progress of civil war in Laos were largely a by-product of the more intensive conflict waged in neighbouring Vietnam. Hanoi's primary logistical supply channel for its troops in the south — the "Ho Chi Minh trail" — traversed large parts of eastern Laos. U.S. attempts to sever this important conduit resulted in Laos receiving one of the most sustained and punishing bombing campaigns ever witnessed. On a per capita basis, no country has endured greater bombing than Laos. And this grisly legacy is still apparent today, with about 11,000 Lao civilians having been reported either killed or wounded by unexploded ordnance since bombing ceased in 1973, and large areas of land still too dangerous for cultivation.

In February 1973, a ceasefire agreement between the RLG and Pathet Lao brought an end to two decades of armed conflict. In the next two years the LPRP worked systematically towards taking sole power. Like communist victories in South Vietnam and Cambodia, success came earlier than the LPRP had anticipated, and left them unprepared for the considerable tasks that lay ahead. But unlike the communist victories in South Vietnam and Cambodia, the final seizure of power in Laos was attained largely through political manoeuvres, and not brute military force. Initially at least, the LPRP's capture of power was not wholly unwelcomed by the two-thirds of the population that had not previously lived under its authority — as they had seen at first hand, and grown increasingly disenchanted with, the utter venality of much of the RLG leadership.

The current regime in Laos, the Lao People's Democratic Republic (LPDR), was formally established in December 1975. This political transition, after a civil war that had divided the country in two for more than a decade, came very shortly after parallel transfers of power in neighbouring Cambodia and Vietnam. It drew a line under the complete supremacy of communist forces across the Indochina sub-region. The new regime abolished the monarchy and constitution of the RLG regime. Buddhism was given a much smaller, if not wholly insignificant, role. The King was initially given the titular status of advisor to the President, but in 1977 he and his family were sent for "re-education" in remote

Hua Phan, from whence they never returned. Prince Souphanouvong — the "Red Prince" — who had been the primary public face of the LPRP for much of the previous twenty years, became President, a largely ceremonial post.[4]

Flush with the euphoria of victory, the LPRP, under Prime Minister Kaysone Phomvihane, embarked on an ambitious programme to transform under-developed Laos into a socialist state. Marxist-Leninist orthodoxy was imported wholesale, with Laos striving for socialism by ambitiously leap-frogging the capitalist phase of its development. The newly unified Socialist Republic of Vietnam provided a model that Lao leaders sought to emulate. They announced that Laos would be transformed from what was in effect a "semi-feudal agricultural economy" into a proletarian dictatorship, despite the very evident paucity of a working class. In order to do so, the LPDR would undergo three parallel revolutions, pertaining to the means of production, science and technology, and ideology and culture. Paralleling a similar initiative in Vietnam, several thousand senior members of the former RLG regime and its armed forces were sent to re-education camps (*samana*).

One fairly immediate consequence of these policies was a mass exodus of urban, middle class and educated citizens, fearful that the new Laos envisaged by the LPRP held scant prospects for them. The loss of such people was to prove a costly burden for Laos. Fortunately, the avidity with which the more radical elements within the LPRP leadership attempted to transform Laos after 1975 was relatively short-lived, as popular opposition mounted. A 1978 attempt to transform agricultural production — which a majority of the populace depended on for their livelihood — into state-run co-operatives was abandoned after little more than a year.[5] In late 1979, Kaysone Phomvihane, as both general secretary of the LPRP and Prime Minister made a speech to the Supreme People's Assembly — later known as the "Seventh Resolution" — which signalled a markedly less puritanical stance towards the enactment of socialist policies and central planning techniques. This change in policy direction included a more relaxed approach towards Buddhist (and other religious) worship, a recognized (albeit still small) role for the non-state sector in the economy, greater freedom of movement, a slowing down in the pace to attain socialism, an end to most co-operatives, and even permission to wear traditional dress. The leadership began to pursue a more gradual — and arguably a more Lao-oriented — version of socialist endeavour. Implementation of socialist methods was diluted even further at the Fourth Party Congress in late 1986, when the LPRP signalled the commencement of an economic liberalization programme, similar in format to that unveiled by Hanoi earlier in the year.

Geographic and Strategic Determinants

With a land area of almost 237,000 square kilometres Laos is a similar size to Britain, but just 15,000 square kilometres is currently under some form of agriculture. Two main geographical features dominate the physical profile of the country: the mighty Mekong River, which delineates much of the country's southern border with Thailand; and the Annamite mountain chain that broadly marks Laos' extended border with Vietnam to the east. The country's relatively flat lowland plains that bracket the Mekong River are in sharp contrast to the steep, often heavily wooded, mountains and high plateaux that dominate roughly two-thirds of the country. Almost 70 per cent of Laos was forested in 1940, but that has now dropped to below 50 per cent, due to both swidden (slash-and-burn) practices by some minority hill tribes, and extensive logging activity by state-owned firms. The difficult topography of Laos makes domestic travel and communications something of a challenge, with heavy reliance placed on river traffic. Up to a quarter of Laos' five and a half million inhabitants reside in remote locations not accessible by roads. Roughly 20 per cent currently live within urban areas (up from 10 per cent in 1970). The numerous rivers feeding into the Mekong River also provide the country with immense hydropower generating potential, of which only a very small fraction has been harnessed to date, primarily for export to Thailand.

The Lao state is currently divided into 16 provinces, with Vientiane governed as a prefecture with provincial status. The most populace city is the capital Vientiane, with less than 150,000 residents, though about half a million citizens reside within the greater Vientiane area. Other major towns include Luang Prabang (the former seat of the King) to the north, and Savannakhet and Pakse in the southern "panhandle". Almost all the major towns of Laos are to be found on the eastern banks of the Mekong River.

Laos is a landlocked country, sharing extended borders with China, Vietnam, Cambodia, Thailand and Myanmar. As such, its domestic fortunes have consistently been influenced by relations with neighbours and regional rivalries — most notably during the Second Indochina War. The post-1975 alliance with Vietnam resulted in a fairly tense relationship between Laos and China to the north, particularly after Hanoi and Beijing came to blows over the vexed issue of Cambodia. However, as a rapprochement

FIGURE 4.2

Laos: Key Statistics

Land area: 236,800 sq. kilometres

Population:[a]   5,407,453 (2000)

GNP:[b]   Current exchange rate   — US$1.9 bn (1997);
                                     US$1.6 bn (1998)
          Purchasing Power Parity — US$6 bn (1997);
                                     US$8 bn (1998)

GNP Per Capita:[b] Current exchange rate   — US$480 (1997);
                                       US$320 (1998)
          Purchasing Power Parity — US$1,300 (1997);
                                     US$2,247 (1998)

Income Distribution (1992):[b]
                  Gini Index   30.4
                  % share of income or consumption:
                  Lowest 10%   4.2
                  Lowest 20%   9.6
                  2nd 20%   12.9
                  3rd 20%   16.3
                  4th 20%   21.0
                  Highest 20%   40.2
                  Highest 10%   26.4

Human Development Index (HDI) Ranking:[c]
                  World ranking   140 (1997); 140 (1998)
                  Value   0.491 (1997); 0.484 (1998)

Armed Forces:
                  Total no.[d]   29,100 (1999)
                  Expenditure[d]   US$70 m (1998)
                  % of GNP[b]   4.2% (1995)

Sources: [a] Official national sources.
         [b] World Bank, *World Development Indicators* (Washington, D.C.
            1999 & 2000).
         [c] United Nations Development Programme (UNDP), *Human Development Report* (New York: Oxford University Press, 1999 & 2000).
         [d] International Institute for Strategic Studies (IISS), *The Military Balance, 1999–2000* (London: Oxford University Press, 1999).

between Hanoi and Beijing developed in the late 1980s, this allowed a parallel thaw to occur between Laos and China, and relations between the two countries are currently deemed to be good.

Lao relations with Thailand, a country with which it shares close cultural, linguistic and economic ties, have often been problematic, particularly after the fall of the RLG government in 1975. Vientiane's move towards economic liberalization in the 1980s improved ties, as Thai companies led the flow of foreign firms seeking to enact business in newly-opened Laos. Bilateral relations have been generally civil over the last decade, and given tangible expression in the Friendship Bridge, opened in 1994, that spans the Mekong River between Nong Khai and Vientiane. However, a number of issues continue to prevent a fully relaxed understanding burgeoning. These include continued border demarcation disputes (a joint commission has been established, following armed conflict in the 1980s), sporadic spats between commercial river traffic and border patrol boats on the Mekong River, the occasional imprisonment of nationals from the other country (by both sides), and the presence of a few remaining Lao refugees in Thai camps. Vientiane is only willing to take back refugees prepared to return of their own volition.

The sense of close fraternity that exists between the ruling communist parties in Hanoi and Vientiane, first forged in the intense heat of anti-colonial struggle, continues to this day. Following communist victory in both Laos and Vietnam, the close affinity of the two new regimes was formalized in a 25-year treaty of friendship and co-operation, signed in mid-1977. Indeed, considerable numbers of Vietnamese troops were stationed in Laos for a decade after 1975, prompting some observers to regard the LPDR as a quasi-vassal state of Vietnam, and recreating a hierarchical relationship similar to that which had existed between the two countries under colonial rule.

Although the historical symmetry of "Hanoi hegemony" might be appealing, it is probably over-stating the case, particularly since the mid-1980s. Hanoi's influence on the leadership in Vientiane was — and continues to be — quite significant, but the enactment of economic reform measures since the mid-1980s illustrate the extent to which the Lao leadership has diverged from aspects of the Vietnamese model. Examples include widely differing attitudes and actions on state sector divestment and the handling of foreign currency exchange rates. A gradual reduction in the frequency of various delegation visits between the two countries could also be discerned in the early 1990s. However, recent years appear to have seen a halt in this trend, possibly spurred by Hanoi and Vientiane's shared concerns over the adverse effects of the Asian Crisis on their respective economic liberalization and development programmes. After being confirmed as Vietnam's new party secretary in December 1997, the first overseas trip made by Le Kha Phieu was a week-long visit to Laos in March 1998. Looking forward, it will be interesting to see if Vientiane and Hanoi renew their treaty of friendship and co-operation when the existing treaty expires in 2002.

Population and Ethnic Profile

The current population of Laos is estimated to total almost five and a half million. It is one of the most sparsely inhabited countries in Asia, with an average population density of just 19.5 people per square kilometre. (This compares with more than three times as many people per square kilometre in Myanmar, six times in Thailand, and over ten times in Vietnam.) The country has a youthful demographic profile, with approximately 55 per cent of citizens under the age of twenty. Population growth rate is about 2.5 per cent per annum.

Despite its small population, the ethnic profile of Laos is remarkably diverse. The government officially recognizes 68 different ethnic identities in the country, although this varied spectrum can be broken down into three main groupings. Roughly 60 per cent are defined as Lao Loum, or lowland Lao, and are akin to the much larger number of ethnic Lao residing in north-eastern Thailand. They are largely Buddhist, and inhabit the towns and lowland areas along the northern banks of the Mekong River. As a consequence of their location in the rice-growing and urban parts of the country, they tend to be the most affluent citizens. Secondly, the Lao Theung constitute about a third of the population, and typically reside in the mid-altitude (300 m to 900 m) slopes of the mountain areas in northern and southern Laos. Most are animist, although some follow the Buddhist faith. They tend to comprise some of the poorest people in Laos. Thirdly, the Lao Sung, which make up about 10 per cent of the Lao population, reside in the highest altitude areas of the country (typically above 1,000 m). They too are animist. The largest grouping is the Hmong, about 10,000 of whom played a major role in the civil war prior to 1975, as U.S.-funded irregular troops combating the communist Pathet Lao forces, under the leadership of General Vang Pao.[6] Both the Lao Theung and Lao Sung have a semi-subsistence lifestyle, with barter trade the primary form of economic interaction. Laos also has a small number of ethnic Chinese and Vietnamese, typically engaged in various commercial activities in the major towns. About 60 per cent of the Lao population are deemed to follow Theravada Buddhism, which is recognized as the national religion.

The Economy

The Lao economy is the smallest in Southeast Asia. The country's GDP is put at just US$1.2 billion, in current exchange rate terms. On average, the Lao economy grew by an exemplary 6.5 per cent per annum during the 1990s, largely as the direct result of the economic liberalization programme commenced in 1986. Despite this, by 1996 the average real per capita income of Laos was only around US$350 per annum and the country is firmly positioned in the bottom quartile of the UN's human development index. (See Figure 4.2) Due in part to better infrastructure and communications, the central provinces of Laos tend to be more economically active than the northern highland and southern "panhandle" areas. More than 80 per cent of the Lao population resides in rural areas, the majority of whom conduct a semi-subsistence lifestyle. In 1995, average life expectancy at birth in Laos was put at 52 years, infant mortality was 102 per 1,000 live births. The World Bank estimates that over a fifth of the population live below the food poverty line, and the UNDP notes that 46 per cent live below the national poverty line. The country's adult literacy rate was estimated to be only 43 per cent in 1995, with less than a third of children completing formal school education. Only around 4 per cent have some form of higher education. Needless to say, human resource development is one of Laos' primary areas of concern.

Agriculture accounts for about 55 per cent of the country's GDP, and employs about 75 per cent of the labour force. The main crop is rice, primarily grown in the lowland plains of the Mekong River. The mountain hill tribes traditionally employ swidden (slash-and-burn) agricultural practices, although the government has been trying to phase this practice out, with mixed success, in a bid to reduce the heavy toll being exerted on the country's forests. The service sector accounts for about a quarter of Laos' GDP, and is largely focused on trading activities. The country's tourism industry has great potential, although the government has tended to adopt a rather conservative approach, preferring to limit the inflow of foreign visitors to manageable levels. Nonetheless, tourism is now the country's fourth largest source of foreign exchange earnings. Industry accounts for just a fifth of the Lao GDP and tends to be focused on light industry (such as textiles, garments and motorcycle assembly) or handicrafts, power generation, some forms of agricultural and forestry product processing, as well as construction and some mining. Despite the country's apparent mineral wealth, the mining sector has been slow to develop in Laos, and does not yet play a very significant role in the domestic economy. The main export earners include wood products, garments, electricity, and coffee.

As the country must import most of its consumer needs and investment goods, and has not yet attained foreign currency earnings to match, Laos has registered a consistently substantial current account deficit — equivalent to 20 per cent of GDP in 1996. However, this is more than adequately cross-funded into the capital account by overseas development assistance and concessional lending by various bilateral donors and multilateral agencies, in addition to some foreign direct investment inflows. These sources of funding have come to almost wholly replace the considerable assistance provided to the LPDR by Vietnam, the Soviet Union and CMEA states prior to 1990, which in turn replaced equally substantial United States assistance to the RLG regime before 1975. Indeed, since colonial times Laos has never had a self-sustaining economy, and has always been partly dependent upon externally-sourced funding.

At the Fourth Congress of 1986, the LPRP unveiled an economic reform programme, sometimes referred to as "New Thinking", as it became increasingly apparent that socialist economic planning methods were wholly failing to improve the general development of the country and the living standards of its populace. It saw the Lao leadership concede that the goal of a socialist state could not be achieved by leap-frogging the capitalist phase, as first intended in 1975, and that a more gradualist approach would be necessary. The economic reform measures resembled closely the *doi moi* reform programme in Vietnam — primarily one of dismantling various central planning methods, ending fixed pricing, divesting non-strategic state firms, permitting greater private sector participation, ending the state sector monopoly on external trade, and generally liberalizing various areas of the commercial and financial environment. Added impetus followed the collapse of the Soviet Union and socialist bloc at the end of the 1980s. Much-needed venture capital, necessary to finance and equip the development of greater business activity in Laos, came from foreign investment inflows, which were approved in 1989. A surprisingly liberal foreign investment law was passed in 1994, and the Sixth Party Congress of 1996 confirmed the high priority given to foreign investment and the promotion of overseas capital inflows for various key sectors of the economy. Thailand alone accounts for just under half of total foreign investment approvals, with the United States a distant second. (By late

1997, it was estimated that roughly US$465 million of foreign investment had actually been disbursed in Laos, although the country has officially licensed a far larger quantity.) The main sectors to have received overseas venture capital interest include energy, telecommunications, tourism, industry and handicrafts.

Finally, it should be recognized that a relatively substantial parallel economy operates within the country, as in most transitional and less developed economies. Although it is desirable for this parallel economy to be ultimately integrated into the official economy (if only so that the government can derive greater tax revenues and thereby lessen its fiscal deficit), at present it plays a useful role in meeting those demands that the formal economy is unable to serve adequately. However, the existence of a parallel economy does make both the monitoring and macro-management of the Lao economy a much more difficult exercise for the government and its advisors.

THE POLITICAL SYSTEM

The Lao People's Democratic Republic (LPDR) remains an avowedly socialist-oriented state, within which the Lao People's Revolutionary Party (LPRP) enjoys a full monopoly on political power. As with China and Vietnam, recent economic liberalization efforts have not been enacted in tandem with moves towards political pluralism, and no parties other than the LPRP are legally permitted to function in Laos.

Officially at least, the primary responsibilities and powers of the organs of the state are defined by a written constitution dating from 1991. The head of state is the President, who appoints the Prime Minister (with the approval of the National Assembly). Executive power resides largely with the Prime Minister, who appoints the Cabinet of Ministers. An elected National Assembly acts as legislature. However, in practice it is the senior leadership of the LPRP — the Politburo — that is at the core of the Lao leadership, and represents the highest level of political power in Laos. The Politburo decides all major policies, which the executive then implements. Although not recognized in the constitution, a very high degree of overlap between the senior personnel of the LPRP leadership and that of the executive has been apparent since the LPDR's founding in 1975, blurring the distinction between the two bodies. Indeed, the extent to which political power is contained within a relatively small group of people has prompted some observers to draw parallels with earlier Lao regimes, and regard the current polity as resembling that of a patrimonial bureaucracy.

FIGURE 4.3

Laos: Key Figures in the LPDR / LPRP Leadership

Khamtay Siphandon

Born in 1924, from peasant stock in Champassak. He was appointed to the Central Committee of the LPRP in 1957 and the Politburo in 1972. Head of the Pathet Lao Armed Forces from 1962 to 1975, he then became Minister for Defence and a Deputy Prime Minister of the LPDR. Appointed Prime Minister in 1991, and LPRP general secretary in 1996. In 1998 he resigned as Prime Minister and was appointed State President (whilst retaining his position as LPRP party secretary). The primary political figure in Laos today.

Sisavat Keobounphan

Born in 1928, a military officer in the Pathet Lao, he was appointed to the Central Committee of the LPRP in 1972. In 1975 he became Interior Minister and Chief of the General Staff. Appointed to the Politburo in 1986, although removed from the leadership in 1991, following accusations of corruption. Re-joined the Politburo, and appointed Vice-President, in 1996. Appointed Prime Minister in 1998 (previously Vice-President) and regarded to be a close ally of Khamtay Siphandon.

Nouhak Phomsavan

Born in Savannakhet in 1916, he was a founding member of LPRP, and trusted deputy of Kaysone Phomvihane. In 1975, appointed Minister for Economy and Finance, and made a Deputy Prime Minister in 1982. Appointed President in 1989, and also LPRP general secretary after the death of Kaysone. He retired from this latter position in 1996, and retired as State President in 1998.

Kaysone Phomvihane (deceased)

Born in 1920 of Vietnam and Lao parents, in Savannakhet. Attended law university in Hanoi. Kaysone was the dominant figure of the communist movement in Laos, from its origins until his death in 1992. Appointed general secretary of the LPP in 1955, and remained head of the LPRP until 1991. Not seen in Vientiane prior to 1975, he was appointed Prime Minister of the LPDR in that year. In 1982 he also assumed the post of Prime Minister. He held the post of State President from 1991 until his death a year later.

Prince Souphanouvong (deceased)

Born 1909 in Luang Prabang, a younger half brother of leading RLG politician, Souvanna Phouma. Founding member of the LPP, and primary public face of the LPRP until victory in 1975. Appointed State President and head of the Supreme People's Assembly in 1975, and ranked third in the Politburo. Retired as President in 1991.

Following the LPRP's ascendancy to power, it took sixteen years for the new regime to promulgate a new written constitution, and so replace the one it abolished in 1975. This was unanimously passed by the then Supreme People's Assembly (subsequently renamed the National Assembly). It spans eighty articles, across ten chapters pertaining to: the political regime, the socio-economic system, rights and duties of citizens, the National Assembly, the state president, the executive, provincial and local administration, the judicial system, national symbols, and procedures for the amendment of the Constitution. Interestingly, no official reference is made in the document to the ultimate goal of attaining socialism — or a proletarian dictatorship — in Laos, and there is just one reference to the LPRP, as the "leading nucleus" of the Lao political system.[7] However, the role of the private sector and foreign investment are recognized, as are property rights. Economic management of the country is according to "the mechanism of [the] market economy with adjustment by the state" (Article 16). The LPRP is responsible for setting national policy, while policy implementation and day-to-day management of the country is placed in the hands of the government. Article 22 of the Constitution states that all Lao citizens are equal before the law, regardless of sex, social status, education, religious faith and ethnicity. Article 31 officially recognizes the "right and freedom of speech, press, and assembly", although this is not

---

FIGURE 4.4

Laos: Current Politburo Line-Up

(In order of ranking)

Name	Government Position
Khamtay Siphandon (general secretary)	State President
Saman Vignaket	President of the National Assembly
Choumali Sayasone	Deputy Prime Minister and Minister for Defence
Oudom Katthigna	Vice-President and President of the LFNC
Thongsing Thammavong	N.A.
Osakan Thammatheva	Minister for Culture & Information Deputy Prime Minister (and interior affairs supervision)
Sisavat Keobounphan	Prime Minister
Asang Laoli	Minister for Interior

apparent in practice. The Constitution may be amended by the National Assembly, with a minimum two-thirds majority.

The LPDR's national seal comprises a picture that depicts representations of paddy fields, an industrial wheel, a two-lane road, a hydropower dam, Pha That Luang (the country's most well-known Buddhist stupa), and a forest. This compilation of images is framed by two arched stalks of rice. Prior to 1991, Pha That Luang's place on the national seal was taken by a hammer and sickle, and the communist five-pointed star. The removal of the latter echoes the extent to which the 1991 Constitution recognized a dilution of communist ideological adherence by the LPRP leadership after the mid-1980s, and its replacement with Pha That Luang indicates the degree to which the state has permitted the return of the Buddhist faith as the national religion. The national slogan of the LPDR is "Peace, Independence, Democracy, Unity and Prosperity". The word "prosperity" was inserted in 1991 to replace "socialism", and has perhaps proved to be the most elusive goal for the people of Laos.

Prior to 1992, Laos' 16 provinces enjoyed a relatively high degree of autonomy from national government in the LPDR, with authority to collect taxes and enact expenditure broadly as they deemed appropriate. The decision to centralize the government's fiscal and budgetary process has been quite slow in taking hold, and the level of provincial autonomy remains fairly generous, aided by communication difficulties between the capital and some of the more distant provinces. The realities of Laos' challenging terrain makes this somewhat inevitable, and also mirrors the degree to which regional power centres (both political and military) were very apparent prior to 1975, thereby constraining the political remit of the national government under the earlier RLG regime. Today, however, the organizational tentacles of the ruling LPRP, and its various support organizations, extend well down into the provinces (*khwaeng*), and beyond to the district (*meuang*) and village (*baan*) levels. There is relatively little scope for provincial authorities to adopt differing policy stances to those of the national leadership, or for the national government to be unaware of most developments in even outlying provinces. A recent trend towards growing regionalization, driven by economic realities, is discussed below.

Head of State

The State President is the head of state in Laos, appointed by the National Assembly (see below) — albeit from a list provided by the LPRP, making this decision something of a rubber-stamping process. The term of office is five years.

The powers and responsibilities of the head of state are detailed in Articles 52 to 55 of the Constitution. The President formally promulgated the 1991 constitution, as well as all laws passed subsequently by the National Assembly. He must do so within 30 days, or request that the law be reconsidered. In the latter case, should the Assembly adhere to its initial decision, the law must be promulgated within 15 days. With the approval of the National Assembly, the President appoints the Prime Minister, and other Ministers in the Cabinet. Proposals, submitted by the Prime Minister, for appointing and changing provincial governors must be approved by the President. The President is commander of the Laos Armed Forces, and must approve top-ranking military appointments. He also has the authority to confer medals and honorific titles, grant pardons, appoint and recall diplomats, and set aside agreements previously signed with other countries. In theory, then, the powers of a President are extensive, but in practice he has generally followed advice.

Since 1996, there has also been the post of Vice-President, who is expected to act as an assistant, and act on the President's behalf when he is absent. Like the President, the Vice-President is elected by the National Assembly.

The Executive

Since the founding of the LPDR regime in 1975, the Prime Minister has enjoyed greater political power than the President. But while the Prime Minister may be the most powerful person within the *state* leadership, the post still does not rival that of the General Secretary of the LPRP (see below).

The Prime Minister has a five-year term of office. His powers and responsibilities are detailed in Articles 58 to 60 of the Constitution, and include: supervision of government work; guidance over ministries, municipalities and provinces; the appointment of deputy ministers and other officials down to the district level.

The country's highest executive body is the Ministerial Cabinet, which is officially selected by the National Assembly on the recommendation of the President. In practice, however, the composition of the Cabinet is decided on after widespread consultation within both the party and state leadership. Like most decision-making, the appointment of a Cabinet is conducted behind closed doors. It requires a broad consensus, and is the product of much jockeying for position among the contenders.

Greatest executive power is wielded by the Prime Minister, across whose desk most major (and sometimes even relatively minor) executive decisions must first be submitted and approved. This can cause a bottleneck effect on implementation of government policy, exacerbating the often ponderous decision-making process within the Lao leadership. In 1996 (following the ejection from the LPRP Politburo and Central Committee of its head, Deputy Prime Minister Khamphoui), the State Committee for Planning & Co-operation — responsible for all foreign investment and external assistance — was renamed the Committee for Investment and Foreign Economic Co-operation, and lost an earlier independence to come directly under the Prime Minister's office. Conversely, in the same year, responsibility for management of the civil service was passed from the Prime Minister's office to that of the LPRP central committee.

Under a programme of administrative reforms enacted in 1992–93, the number of ministries within the government was reduced from 25 to 13, with some being merged, others assuming wider responsibilities, and others dissolved. The current Cabinet is composed of all 13 ministers, plus heads of three "equivalent committees": the State Planning Committee,

---

FIGURE 4.5

Laos: Ministries and Equivalent Committees Represented in the LPDR Cabinet

Prime Minister's Office

State Planning Committee

Ministry of National Defence

Ministry of Interior

Ministry of Foreign Affairs

Ministry of Justice

Ministry of Finance

Ministry of Agriculture and Forestry

Ministry of Communication, Transport, Post and Construction

Ministry of Industry and Handicrafts

Ministry of Commerce (including Tourism)

Ministry of Information and Culture

Ministry of Social Welfare

Ministry of Education

Ministry of Public Health

Bank of the Lao PDR

the Prime Minister's Office, and the Bank of the Lao PDR (the central bank). (See Figure 4.5). In tandem with a similar development in Vietnam, the Lao government leadership now has multiple Deputy Prime Ministers (currently four), with specific policy remits, sometimes above and beyond those of their own (or others') ministerial portfolios. For example, the current Minister for Defence also has Deputy Prime Minister status, as does the Foreign Minister. Another Deputy Prime Minister is responsible for the supervision of interior affairs (Bounyang Vorachith), above the interior ministry portfolio held by another Member of the Cabinet. Deputy Prime Minister Khamphoui Keoboualapha also holds the finance ministry portfolio and is responsible for matters relating to foreign investment. Of the four Deputy Prime Ministers, two are also LPRP Politburo members, and a further two Ministers and the Prime Minister are also in the Politburo. Or put another way, more than half of the nine-person LPRP Politburo is represented in the current Cabinet line-up.

After a programme of retrenchment in the first half of the 1990s, the current number of civil servants in Laos is put at around 65,000, equivalent to 1.3 per cent of the total population. Along with senior military officers, they comprise the bulk of the LPRP's membership, and at higher levels represent a new social and political élite in the LPDR. As noted above, responsibility for the civil service was transferred in 1996, from the Prime Minister's Office to the LPRP central committee. This strange move provides further evidence of the extent to which the LPRP governs much of the Lao polity, including the state bureaucracy. Despite a large number of civil servants, the various institutions of the state structure remain relatively weak, and their professional capacities are in need of further development. This is concurrent with a general necessity in Laos to strengthen both the state institutions and human resources of the country, and rectify a shortage of adequately trained technocrats and other professional personnel. Some work in this regard has already been done over recent years, but much more will be necessary to overcome the vacuum left by the mass exodus of the Lao middle class after 1975. Besides being inadequately trained and resourced, Lao civil servants are remunerated at levels that make corruption a strong temptation. Junior ranks receive less than US$10 per month.

Political Role of Military and Police

Laos' military is currently thought to amount to about 30,000 men and 100,000 local militia, cumulatively representing about 2.8 per cent of the total population. Defence expenditure is about 4 per cent of GDP, roughly four times the expenditure budget for health. As in Vietnam, the political and economic roles of the Lao military are considerable. Extremely close links between the army and the LPRP — to the point where drawing a clear line of distinction becomes rather difficult — were forged in the intense heat of the protracted liberation struggle. Even in the aftermath of armed conflict the political importance of the military shows no sign of diminishing. In 1996, the military's representation on the nine-man Politburo increased from three to seven.

The Lao military has developed fairly substantial business interests since economic liberalization began. Most well known is the army-controlled BPKP, a company established in 1984, active in logging, tourism, construction, trade, and various other activities in the central part of Laos. The military undoubtedly enjoys privileges that give it an advantage in the Lao business environment, and might be regarded by some observers as an undesirable element in any attempt to develop a genuine market economy. However, the revenues generated from such commercial activity may ease pressure on the government's military expenditure budget, and may also provide some form of incentive for the military in supporting the economic reform effort, albeit within certain limits. Thorough liberalization of the business environment in Laos is unlikely to be supported by the military, as such a scenario would probably result in the end of many of its business privileges. In 1996, the BPKP was reported to have 32 separate business units, and has "won" various lucrative contracts, including the logging of a large area intended for flooding as part of the Nam Theun II hydropower project.[8]

The National Police Department is a branch of the Lao military. Like the Lao (riverine) navy and air force, the police force does not play a significant role in the political process in Laos.

The Legislature

The National Assembly is the legislative wing of the Lao political framework, with origins that pre-date the LPDR. Under Articles 39 to 51 of the 1991 Constitution, the powers of the unicameral National Assembly (née Supreme People's Assembly) were extended, and this legislative body has since been responsible for passing a series of laws that provide an important legal platform on which much of Laos' economic reform programme has depended. Under the Constitution, the powers of the 99-member National Assembly include the following: endorse, amend, or abrogate laws; elect or remove the State President and Vice-President, as well as the President of the Supreme People's Court and the Public Prosecutor-General; decide on the establishment or dissolution of ministries, province and municipalities; decide on matters of war and peace; and amend the Constitution. The Assembly may pass a vote of no confidence in the government, or members of the government, if proposed by the Standing Committee of the National Assembly (see below) or one quarter of all delegates. Under Article 61 of the Constitution, if a vote of no confidence is carried, the government must resign. The Assembly is typically in session twice a year, and is elected for a period of five years.

The National Assembly elects its own Standing Committee, which performs various support functions of the National Assembly when it is not in session, as detailed in Article 48 of the Constitution. The Standing Committee is headed by the President and Vice-President of the National Assembly. The State President, the National Assembly Standing Committee, the government, the Supreme People's Court, the Public Prosecutor-General, and mass organizations may propose draft laws to the National Assembly for consideration.

Elections

Elections to the National Assembly are by secret ballot, and are conducted on a first-past-the-post basis. Although all Lao citizens over the age of 18 are permitted to vote, and turnout is typically very high (reportedly 99 per cent in the 1997 polls), all candidates must first be approved by the LPRP's own Lao Front for National Construction (*Neo Lao Sang Sat*). This process allows the LFNC — and thereby the LPRP — effectively to determine the composition of the National Assembly. The vast majority of National Assembly delegates tend to be LPRP members, with only a token number of independents represented.

In the December 1997 National Assembly elections, of 159 candidates permitted to stand, only four were non-LPRP members. All were reportedly from the business community, and just one was elected — even less than the previous National Assembly, which had four independents. Six other non-LPRP members who sought to stand for election were rejected by the LFNC. A profile of the 159 approved candidates in the National Assembly elections of 1997 showed that: the average age was 50 (the eldest being 74 and the youngest 36 years old), just 27 (or 17 per cent) were women (of which 21 were later elected), and 46 (or 29 per cent) were from ethnic minorities. Lao women were first granted the right to vote, and stand for election, in 1958. Of 41 members of the previous National Assembly seeking re-election, 33 were successful.[9] Under the Constitution, candidates must be at least 21 years of age. It is conceivable that should the Lao leadership move to allow a greater diversity of non-LPRP representation within the government structure in the future, then it could take the form of more independent candidates standing for — and being represented in — the National Assembly. However, at the time of writing, there is no immediate prospect of this.

The Judiciary

The concept of the rule of law in the LPDR is relatively new, and continues to evolve. Prior to the 1991 Constitution the LPDR was largely governed by LPRP fiat, as an earlier body of law used by the RLG regime was abolished in 1975, along with the Constitution and the 600-year-old monarchy. As of 1996, the country's body of law was based on just 34 pieces of legislation, albeit supported by a far larger array of decrees and implementing regulations. All 34 laws have been promulgated since 1988, when the Lao leadership recognized that any inflow of foreign venture capital would necessitate some form of legal platform to recognize and protect property rights.

Legislation in Laos is depicted as a hybrid of French civil law, some remaining tenets of socialist planning concepts, and elements of Lao tradition lore. Under Article 67 of the Constitution, judges are appointed (and can be dismissed) by the National Assembly Standing Committee. At present, Laos could not be said to have a judiciary that is wholly independent of the Ministry of Justice, and therefore independent of the government or the LPRP. The re-establishment of the Lao Bar Association in 1996 may represent a small step in this direction.

Political Parties

As noted above, the LPRP (*Phak Pasason Patavit Lao*) is the only legal political party in Laos, and is recognized in the first chapter of the 1991 constitution as the "leading nucleus" of the country's political system. At the Fifth Congress of the LPRP in 1991, at which the current Constitution was unveiled, the notion or prospect of political pluralism in Laos was roundly rejected.

The LPRP's origins are to be found in the Indochina Communist Party (ICP), formed in 1930. Six years later, a Committee on Laos was established within the ICP, but it was not until 1955 that the Lao People's Party (LPP) was formed, with about 300 members. In 1972, at its Second Party Congress, the LPP was renamed the LPRP.

Regardless of any initial appearance to the contrary, all real political power and decision-making authority in Laos resides firmly within the senior LPRP leadership. Both the executive and legislative branches of the state structure are largely obedient to the wishes of the LPRP, and neither would consider acting in a manner that was independent of, or contrary to, the directions of the ruling party. Indeed, the high degree of overlap between the senior leadership of the party and the state leadership make any refutation of this view difficult to substantiate. As Martin Stuart-Fox observes: "In practice, ... the Party makes policy decisions which the government then executes. In practice, also, the overlap in membership between the Party and government ensures that power continues to reside in the hands of the Party."[10]

Almost all leadership decision-making is consensus driven, arrived at behind closed doors and away from the public domain. The possible exception to this is the National Assembly gatherings, although as noted above, this legislative body appears to enjoy relatively little autonomous power in actual practice. The emphasis on consensus can help guard against erratic and blatantly erroneous policy initiatives, but it does tend to reduce Vientiane's ability to react to events in a timely manner. It also runs the risk of more long-term government indecision on issues where a consensus simply cannot be found. A general reluctance to delegate responsibility, or to undertake personal initiatives (for fear of being reprimanded later if proved wrong), can further exacerbate the rather ponderous decision-making process within the Lao leadership. Such an ambience also tends to stifle creative thinking within the leadership, and benefits those willing to obediently "toe the line".

During the LPRP's Sixth Congress in 1996, membership of the party was reported to be around 75,000 (up from 60,000 at the party congress in 1991, and 35,000 at the Third Party Congress in 1982), or about 1.5 per cent of the country's total population. The majority of members are derived from the more senior ranks of the government bureaucracy and army.

In terms of organizational structure, the LPRP closely resembles the Vietnamese Communist Party, on which it is largely modelled. The Politburo is the "locus of political decision-making"[11] within the party, and therefore within the LPDR. The highest ranking official in this body is the General Secretary. The Politburo is elected by the Central Committee at the party congress. It currently has nine members, two less than the

Politburo appointed in1991. It includes five members from the previous Politburo, with three of the four newcomers originating from ethnic minority groups.

Positioned under the Politburo is the 49-person Central Committee. Attached to it are various permanent commissions pertaining to areas such as party personnel, inspection, and ideological adherence, and a secretariat responsible for the day-to-day running of the LPRP's affairs. The following profile was released after the election of the current central committee at the Sixth Congress in 1996: average age of 53 (youngest 40 and eldest 72), three-quarters were members of the LPRP prior to the founding of the LPDR in 1975, 90 per cent participated in some way during the previous years of struggle, only four were women, and just five had some form of higher education.

The Central Committee gathers several times a year for party plenums, and is made up of senior LPRP representatives from across the country. Discussions conducted at these plenums feed into the policy-making process of the Politburo, and provide feedback on policy initiatives proposed by the senior leadership.

The LPRP also operates a number of support organizations, including the Lao Front for National Construction (LFNC), which is similar in form and mandate to the Fatherland Front in Vietnam. The LFNC replaced the Lao Patriotic Front (Neo Lao Hak Sat) organization in 1979. Its formal mandate is to foster national solidarity and promote socialist economic development. Technically speaking, the LFNC is the umbrella organization that spans all the LPRP-related bodies, including the LPRP itself, although in reality the LPRP directs the LFNC. Other LPRP support bodies include the Association of Women, the Federation of Lao Peasants, the Youth Union, and Federation of Lao Trade Unions. Far from diluting the power of the LPRP, these support organizations are intended as supplementary arms of the party, providing valuable channels of communication between the LPRP leadership and various elements of society. They act as important conduits to pass down national policy instructions, and pass up community feedback; additional eyes and ears of the LPRP.

Official Ideology

Despite the economic reforms of the last decade, on the political front the leadership of the LPDR still professes filial loyalty to Marxist-Leninist ideology. Laos remains an avowedly socialist state, albeit not a fundamentalist one. Indeed, the actions of the leadership over the last ten years tend to suggest a gradual dilution in — if not wholesale jettisoning of — this ideological stance, particularly since the abandonment of the avid central planning and co-operativization programmes of the late 1970s. If constructing a socialist state remains the final destination of the current regime, then its leadership appears to be taking the scenic route to get there.

A pragmatic need to govern the country in a manner that does not incur popular opposition and provides a decent standard of living for its citizens is probably the primary motivation for this approach by the Lao leadership.[12] Even in the LPDR's period of strict adherence to socialist endeavour (the first decade after 1975), the LPRP leadership never attempted to construct a home-grown ideological framework — unlike neighbouring Vietnam and Cambodia. Nor has it yet sought to develop a cult around a home-grown revolutionary hero, such as Ho Chi Minh in Vietnam.

Civil Society and Human Rights

The character of Laos' civil society and the regime's regard for individual human rights is of a type one might expect in an authoritarian state led by a single party. Public criticism of the LPDR leadership, its policy and actions, is not tolerated. The *samana* re-education camps established after 1975 are no longer in operation, although a small number of political prisoners dating from the RLG regime may still remain in custody. The fledgling media and press are under the strict control of the leadership, and only disseminate news and views that concur with those of the LPRP. The LPRP's own newspaper is *Pasason* ("The People"), and the small number of other papers are published by bodies approved by the government. It should also be recognized that the "reach" of the media is quite limited in Laos. In 1995, according to the UNDP, Laos had on average just seven television sets for every thousand people. Domestic television is restricted to two channels, transmitting in the evenings only, and cannot be easily received beyond the Mekong lowland areas. Lao television must also compete with Thai broadcasts, which can be picked up on the Lao side of the Mekong River.

Even though Vientiane has come to accept the return of the Buddhist faith as the national religion — evidenced by the replacement of the hammer and sickle symbol by the Pha That Luang stupa on the national seal — the *sangha* in Laos remains under the watchful eye of the government's religious affairs department, and it is not permitted to contradict or challenge the policies of the LPRP. Only one officially approved sect of Theravada Buddhism is permitted to operate. Freedom of religious belief (and non-belief) is officially recognized under Article 30 of the Constitution. However, the Constitution forbids "fomenting division among religions and among the people", and has occasionally been employed by the leadership as a licence to act against those adopting evangelist techniques to gain new converts. In early 1998, five foreign nationals and 39 Lao citizens were arrested at what was claimed to be an extended bible study session in the capital. The foreigners were later expelled from Laos, and 13 of the Lao nationals received prison sentences for what the government alleged was a bogus religious meeting that "wrongly slandered the Lao government" and "disparaged other religions".[13]

MAJOR POLITICAL ISSUES

The LPRP Rules

It is evident that political power in contemporary Laos resides within a relatively small group of people that make up the senior ranks of the LPRP, and concurrently the senior ranks of the government and the military. As noted above, during the extended period of political and military struggle against the RLG regime, and since victory in 1975, the LPRP leadership has remained cohesive. This is particularly noteworthy, given an apparent dichotomy in the social origins of its founding leaders.

One element of the LPRP was sourced from the pro-communist elements within the earlier Lao Issara nationalist movement, led by Prince Souphanouvong. Derived from some of the élite families of Lao society, and well educated, this sub-group enjoyed a higher profile prior to 1975. Arguably employed by the LPRP as the "acceptable face" of the communist movement, these members tended to participate in the three coalition government attempts, along-side their contemporaries in the Lao social élite that represented neutralist or rightist parties. The best example of this grouping was Prince Souphanouvong who was half-brother of Prime Minister Souvanna Phouma. It was Souphanouvong's face, rather than that of LPRP general secretary Kaysome Phomvihane, that most Lao came to associate with the LPRP leadership up until 1975.

In contrast, the other element of the LPRP was not derived from the Lao social élite. Its members had less formal education, closer ties with Hanoi, and more hard-line communist convictions. This latter group kept a very low profile during the period of struggle, even in their "liberated" areas, and only really entered the public domain after attaining power in 1975, finally emerging from their military headquarters in Sam Neua.

After the establishment of the LPDR, the pre-1975 high profile group tended to be shunted into positions of less political clout, whilst the low profile and ideologically more radical, group assumed the reins of power. Nonetheless, a convincing appearance of LPRP leadership solidarity was — and continues to be — maintained. This cohesiveness within the LPRP leadership was perhaps only rivalled by its tendency for secrecy, which during its early years of struggle helped give it an exaggerated sense of omnipotence. Although the party leadership has gradually become more visible since attaining power in 1975, Laos' government remains a relatively opaque and shy entity.

Who Benefits?

The primary beneficiaries of the current regime and political power structure in Laos are members of the élite described above. The highest levels of the political and military leadership are still held by those cadres who rose in the ranks of the LPRP and Pathet Lao during the years of struggle prior to 1975. However, as the period since the founding of the LPDR in 1975 grows, these senior cadres are being succeeded by a younger generation of better educated party officials and state technocrats. Most founding fathers of the communist struggle — including Kaysone Phomvihane and Prince Souphanouvong — have now died. The succession process might provide an opportunity for further diluting the long-held ideological stance of the party, and/or a more pragmatic regard for non-LPRP groupings. It might also allow a more technocratic and administratively capable leadership to evolve. However, it is unlikely that the LPRP will willingly act in a manner that would dilute its monopoly on power, or pose problems for its own credibility. Any change in who controls the levers of power will be gradual. Current leaders continue to display loyalty to the ideological tenets still officially propounded by the LPRP.

The clannish characteristics of the social élite during the RLG regime may also be repeated among the leading families of the LPRP leadership. For example, observers have pointed to the close political alliance that is said to exist between LPRP general secretary and State President Khamtay Siphandon, and Prime Minister Sisavat Keobounphan, who are connected through the marriage of their children. Between the two of them, they hold the top three positions in the country. Given the small scale of the political élite in Laos, and the significant overlap between the top-most LPRP and executive posts, the emergence of such family links are perhaps inescapable.

Within the wider ranks of the LPRP, a proportion of cadres that joined the party after 1975 will have done so for reasons other than a strict sense of ideological or political conviction. Even some middle-ranking positions in the state bureaucracy and state sector are hard to attain without party membership, and the general pursuit of most business activity — whether it be wholly legitimate or within the parallel economy — is made much easier with the assistance of fellow party cadres able to help plough through the convoluted business environment in Laos. At this level, the LPRP can be harnessed as a social and professional ladder for those wishing to get ahead.

Beyond the political and military leadership in Laos, other major beneficiaries of the current regime include the more senior ranks of the state bureaucracy, particularly managers of state enterprises and various other state-owned commercial enterprises. Where such enterprises have been divested, the senior management has often been able to remain in situ, and enjoy the fruits that stem from privatization.

As economic reforms continue, managers from the state sector are being joined by, and in some cases facing increasing competition from, a small but growing number of successful local entrepreneurs who have been able to develop private companies within a more liberal commercial environment. There are also a small number of overseas Lao that have returned to the home country to take advantage of the recent economic liberalization. Although the profits to be derived from such a small and under-developed market remain modest, there is potential for future economic growth from such a low base point.

At present, most business activity in Laos still requires the indirect patronage of government officials to succeed, which results in an inevitable flow of illicit funds into the hands of some civil servants and senior party cadres. With official salaries for state functionaries so low (100,000 kip, or around US$25, per month for top state officials), it would be naïve to imagine otherwise. In this regard, some of the less savoury practices of the former RLG regime are being replicated by the current leadership.

Also somewhat inevitably, Laos' urbanites — almost all of whom reside in lowland Lao areas — have had far better access to the fruits of economic reform of the last decade than those in rural areas, the Lao Theung and Lao Sung. Although this trend tends to occur somewhat organically when a command economy opens up its market to foreign investment, external trade, and other aspects of economic liberalization, it has the potential to pose significant socio-political challenges for the government, particularly where it coincides with ethnic divisions. In the specific case of Laos, the resulting widening disparity in incomes between urban and rural areas can also be perceived as a widening disparity in incomes between the lowland Lao and the other ethnic minorities. Obviously, such a schism is unhelpful to a leadership seeking to govern an ethnically diverse populace, which less than 25 years ago was engaged in a civil war along uncomfortably similar dividing lines. It also makes the task of constructing a sense of shared nationhood (see below) more difficult to achieve.

Although the ethnic minorities, most notably the Lao Theung, provided the largest proportion of LPRP cadres and Pathet Lao troops that fought for the overthrow of the RLG regime prior to 1975, their share in the economic benefits of power have not been as great as they anticipated. Put another way, the lowland Lao that inhabited the areas governed by the RLG regime up until 1975, have ultimately not seen their economic dominance diminish under the LPDR regime. Due in part to their proximity to the Thai border, the urban and lowland areas along the eastern bank of the Mekong River have consistently been the more prosperous part of Laos, and the policies of the LPRP have tended not to reverse that well-established trend. In the three years after 1975, the lowland Lao underwent — and in some cases resisted — an ardent attempt by the LPRP leadership to make their economy conform with central planning and co-operativization. This failed, and in conjunction with the withdrawal of U.S. aid that had pay-rolled the lowland Lao economy for much of the previous twenty years, the economic fortunes of the lowland Lao deteriorated markedly after 1975, in tandem with the economic plight of the entire country. However, following the Seventh Resolution of 1979, and later the 1986 decision to embark on economic liberalization, the lowland Lao have been able to regain much of their general economic advantage over the other parts of Laos. Genuine attempts to increase the inclusion of ethnic minorities in the various political fora have not translated into markedly better economic prospects for the ethnic minorities.

The civil conflict prior to 1975 served to heighten previous levels of suspicion and distrust between those ethnic groups that found themselves on opposing sides in the conflict, and the leadership has made some strides to try and heal these rifts. Far from being an altruistic exercise by the LPRP, it is recognized that an inclusive policy towards minority groups is more likely to prevent any repeat of past ethnic hostility and potential future socio-political instability. Although lowland Lao are the most well-represented ethnic grouping within the ranks of the LPRP, the party has been careful to ensure that minorities are relatively well represented.

As noted, three of the four new members appointed to the LPRP's politburo in 1996 came from ethnic minority groups.[14] This apparent ethnic sensitivity on the part of the leadership dates back to before 1975, when the Pathet Lao was combating the RLG regime from territory dominated by non-ethnic Lao peoples, and the LPRP declared a desire to establish a socialist state that respected the ethnically diverse composition of the populace. Indeed, as one respected analyst has noted, "prior to 1975, tribal groups together probably provided a majority of both Party cadres and guerrillas" within the Pathet Lao movement.[15] One argument occasionally proffered to support the continuation of a single party state in Laos is that that any future attempt at political pluralism would inevitably lead to the creation of a series of political parties based solely on ethnic, regional or religious allegiances. Given the country's relatively recent history of conflict, this in turn could potentially result in the erosion of the Lao polity. Although such an argument can too easily be cited as a useful defence for the LPRP's continued monopoly on power (and its suppression of any challengers), there is probably some validity in the broad assertion.

Extent of Government Legitimacy

Initially at least, the current regime's primary pillar of legitimacy fundamentally stemmed from its victory over the RLG regime in 1975 — albeit with very considerable external assistance. However, increasingly a broader platform of legitimacy has been sought by the LPRP, with mixed success.

A degree of legitimacy may have come from economic gains. These were some time in gestation, as Stuart-Fox has noted:

> ... popular acceptance of the legitimacy of the [LPDR] regime was delayed by circumstances — some due to avoidable errors, others beyond the Party's control. Among these circumstances should be mentioned the economic collapse which followed withdrawal of Western — particularly American — aid, and the further deterioration in the economy due to the massive loss of skilled technicians and managers, largely through fear of forced political re-education.

> In addition, the disastrous decision to cooperativize agricultural production alienated many peasants, while forced resettlement of tribal people at lower altitudes in order to protect virgin forests did the same for some ethnic minority groups.[16]

However the reversal of such policies and economic liberalization from the mid-1980s did produce modest gains enjoyed particularly by urbanites among the lowland Lao.

As the regime's allegiance to socialism appears slowly to evaporate, several observers have suggested that a new-found sense of nationhood is being crafted by the leadership as an alternative form of legitimacy to fill the vacuum left by communism. But attempts to secure a convincing level of legitimacy through a stronger sense of Lao nationalism, and the identification of some historical continuity dating back to the kingdom of fourteenth century Lan Xang, is not an easy task. As noted above, the current territory of Laos is largely a product of French colonial rule, which at a stroke resulted in more ethnic Lao — and over half of the territory once "governed" by the Lan Xang kingdom — being placed outside the country's borders. And for those minorities outside the majority lowland Lao, it is understandable if they harbour some concern that the use of nationalism could mutate into policies that unfairly advantage the Lao Loum, to the detriment of their own interests and rights as full citizens of the LPDR. For others, there may be some concern that less emphasis on socialist ideology in favour of some form of nationalism will pose longer-term problems for the LPRP — particularly if it is not able to promote Laos further up the development ladder — and/or bring the role of the military into greater prominence.

Nationalist-oriented claims of legitimacy by the LPRP have not always been helped by the considerable input that North Vietnam, and later re-unified Vietnam, played in both the Pathet Lao's military campaign and ultimate victory, as well as during the first decade of the LPDR regime. During the late 1960s, a substantial Vietnamese force, including an estimated 34,000 combat troops provided support to the Pathet Lao. Until the mid-1980s approximately 40–50,000 Vietnamese troops were reported to be stationed in Laos. The LPDR has maintained close political ties with Vietnam, and some LPRP leaders have personal Vietnamese links by descent, marriage or education.[17] Although it is less influential today, the "Vietnam factor" remains something of an Achilles heel for the LPRP in any attempt to assume a more nationalist mantle.

The absence of any convincing political opposition within Laos may in part be a measure of the current regime's legitimacy. Overseas groupings opposed to the current regime — recruited primarily from exiles who fled Laos in 1975 and after — have also failed to establish any convincing form of opposition. Elements of the Hmong minority irregulars that had fought as part of America's "secret war" continued to resist Pathet Lao troops for almost two years after the founding of the LPDR, but were ultimately over-run. Although occasional incidents of insurgency are still reported in Laos, these tend to resemble acts of simple banditry, rather than politically motivated acts of armed opposition to the current regime. As such, they are more an irritant, rather than a genuine threat, to the security of the LPDR and the authority of the LPRP.

However, an aborted demonstration in Vientiane in October 1999, followed by a spate of bombings in the capital during 2000, suggests that opposition to the LPRP government is on the increase. While the former appears to have stemmed primarily from the sharp deterioration in economic conditions over recent years, the factors — and organization — behind the bombings are much less clear. They may be the work of domestic Hmong insurgents, although there has been some speculation of pro-RLG overseas Lao involvement. Others have opined that the bombings may stem from growing divisions within the LPRP itself, with rival sympathies towards China and Vietnam as the defining fault-line between the two sides. The varied locations of the bombings — the morning market, a bus station, the main post office, near cafes and foreign construction workers' accommodation, and near the Vietnamese Embassy — adds to the difficulty of drawing certain conclusions.

Despite changes in China and the socialist bloc over the last decade, no formal democracy movement has become apparent in Laos. Amongst reasons sometimes cited to explain this are the strong hold that the LPRP enjoys on the Lao populace, and its unforgiving treatment of the few who vehemently oppose it; a Buddhist sensibility that eschews direct confrontation; widespread political lethargy; or the fact that dissenters can easily opt to cross clandestinely into northern Thailand. It should also be noted that the last decade of economic reform has brought — for the urban lowland Lao at least — improved prosperity, which may act to deter some from rocking the boat. And for those in rural areas, perpetually engaged in a very immediate battle to adequately feed and support their families, the notion of political activity is probably an abstract one. The rural Lao interface with the state and ruling party is very limited, with personal horizons that do not extend far beyond the village or district.

Governance

Flush from its victory in 1975, the zeal with which the LPRP tried to implement its socialist ideological tenets in the new LPDR proved to be a major mistake. Both ill equipped to prepare the lowland populace for the changes ahead and to enact those changes sensibly, the first decade of the LPDR was marred by a massive exodus of Lao unwilling to tolerate the excessive actions of the new regime. It is estimated that about 10 per cent of the country's entire citizenry — including over 100,000 ethnic minority people from the mountain regions and 90 per cent of trained and educated Lao[18] — chose to exit the country. Most made a relatively easy crossing of the Mekong River, and sought initial refuge in neighbouring Thailand. The educated Lao, and the Chinese and Vietnamese business communities were precisely the people needed to re-build the country after decades of civil conflict. The effects were, in Stuart-Fox's words, "catastrophic, setting back development by at least a generation".[19] The exodus persisted into the 1980s, although by then the primary reason for departure had become economic disenchantment, rather than political persecution per se. It was only halted in 1985, when Thailand declared that all non-political refugees would be returned.

In retrospect, the leadership's initial, ambitious attempt to attain economic development for Laos through command economy techniques proved a dismal failure. The economic liberalization measures undertaken since 1986 have generated a fairly substantial improvement in economic conditions in Laos, and the enactment of economic reform has done much to improve the previously lacklustre track record of the Lao leadership in terms of governance. Since the introduction of economic reforms in the mid-1980s, the gradual improvement in the national economy has had a similarly restorative effect on living standards in the 1990s. According to the United Nations Development Programme, Laos' average per capita GDP in the period between 1984 and 1995 was at its lowest in 1988, and its highest in 1995. Between 1970 and 1995, the adult literacy rate increased from 32 per cent to 57 per cent. Similarly, between 1960 and 1995, average life expectancy rose from 40 to 52, and the infant mortality rate shrunk from 155 to 102 per 1,000 live births. However, the average daily supply of calories has actually declined, from 2,154 in 1970 to 2,105 in 1995.

Given the very limited human resources of the country, the leadership has been able to meet most of the basic needs of the populace, albeit with significant external assistance from bilateral donors and multilateral bodies. However, even when measured against standards set by the leadership itself, the Lao economy remains fairly weak, and its populace poor. To that extent, the leadership of Laos has found it difficult to meet even fairly humble expectations. The presence of good governance in Laos — as indicated by effective, honest, equitable, transparent and accountable government — remains a future ambition, rather than a current reality. Genuine respect by the leadership for rule of law, civil society, and some of the basic ideals cited in the constitution are not yet apparent. Regardless of ideological stance, question marks remain as to the competency of the leadership, its ability to deliver on stated policy initiatives, and its skill levels in managing an effective and honest bureaucracy. While many of the necessary state structures are in place, and official statements intimate the right way forward, evidence of the necessary volition, competence, and determination to deliver good governance is somewhat lacking.

Despite having a relatively undeveloped economy, and only rudimentary financial markets, Laos was certainly not immune from the economic turmoil that struck Asia in 1997–98.[20] Indeed, the non-convertible Lao currency (the kip) was probably the most heavily devalued currency in mainland Southeast Asia during 1997–98, due in large part to the ravages of the Asian Crisis. With the country so dependent on imports for much of its consumer and manufactured goods requirements, the devaluation has resulted in a high level of imported inflation, which in turn has put the salaries of some urbanites, including government employees, below acceptable levels. Foreign investment inflows have also suffered as a result of the Asian Crisis phenomenon, and some planned projects — most notably hydropower plants, which were to have generated electricity exports for Thailand (and much-needed hard currency earnings for Laos) — will undoubtedly be shelved. Judging by official statements, the Lao Government remains fully committed to the economic reform programme, despite the adverse effects of the Asian Crisis. But even prior to the onset of the regional downturn, the incremental manner by which economic reform was being implemented suggested that some concern persisted within the political élite as to the utility and socio-political perils of economic liberalization measures. Vientiane's efforts in this field will also have been hampered by vested interests that have benefited most from the socialist approach to economic planning methods, and who do not wish to see a fuller implementation of free market policies. Coming so soon after Vientiane made renewed strides to open its domestic economy to global markets, the unwelcome arrival of the Asian Crisis will have been a blow for pro-reform elements within the leadership seeking to liberalize the Lao economy further.

However, it remains too early to tell whether the Asian Crisis will have long-term consequences for economic policy and decision-making in Laos. Although the perils of exposure to the global market are now more starkly appreciated following the Asian Crisis, the Vientiane leadership is also aware that a return to the socialist planning methods of the late 1970s and early 1980s provides no answer to its economic problems. In terms of external economic relations, Vientiane's moves to comply with impending ASEAN Free Trade Area regulations on import tariffs, and efforts to gain entry to the WTO and NTR status from the United States, will continue.

The onset of the Asian Crisis seems to have brought a temporary halt in the trend towards a widening disparity in income between the lowland and highland areas, witnessed since the mid-1980s. For those engaged in semi-subsistence cultivation and barter trade in the highland areas, their exposure to the external economy and the adverse effects of the Asian Crisis have been relatively slight, if not wholly inconsequential. However, the urban areas of lowland Laos have been hit hard by some of the direct effects of the Thai and regional economic downturn, most notably with regard to a greatly devalued currency and a resulting high inflation rate in the large range of goods that Laos imports. With urban salaries not increasing to offset workers' reduced spending power since 1997, the lowland Lao have experienced a deterioration in their general standard of living. But once a degree of economic stability returns to the region, the long-term trend in favour of the lowland and urban areas is likely to resume.

As noted above, Laos' domestic economy is partly dependent on external assistance to function adequately. The government therefore needs external patrons able to provide not inconsiderable funds, at least relative to the size of its tiny economy. Since gaining independence in 1953, that patronage has been undertaken by a sequence of benefactors: the United States (prior to 1975), Vietnam and the Soviet Union (between 1975 and 1990), and most recently by various bilateral donors and multilateral agencies (since the mid-1980s). As a result, the current Lao Government can probably not overtly go against the wishes of its current benefactors, which desire to see economic liberalization persist and develop in Laos.[21] Therefore, even should Vientiane begin to have serious misgivings about the economic reforms underway since the mid-1980s, it has little choice but to at least *appear* to be still adhering to this path. Whether the current Lao political élite, the LPRP, is more genuinely convinced of the utility of economic liberalization is another issue, where current evidence seems decidedly mixed.

CONCLUSION

A number of factors combine to make the effective governance of contemporary Laos a challenging exercise. The current territorial and ethnic profile of Laos is, to a great extent, the product of a colonial power that failed to comprehend the inconsistency and divisiveness of its chosen borders. For much of the thirty years prior to 1975, Laos' post-colonial history was one of conflict and division, which only served to underline the ethnic complexity of its small populace. In physical terms, the country's topography is unforgiving, and the majority of its citizens have a standard of living that is associated with semi-subsistence agriculture in less developed countries. Communication within parts of the country is not easy, and infrastructure is minimal, exacerbating problems associated with provincial autonomy and regionalism. Human resources are in need of improvement, as is the capacity of most of the country's major institutions.

All the above factors pose significant challenges for the Lao leadership, and explain in part why the government has sought to find and forge a greater sense of national identity, as well as a platform of popular legitimacy for its own rule. Recent steps to dilute the vehemence of the government's adherence to communism have perhaps made this quest for a new central tenet of legitimacy even more pressing, although the lack of any opposing political force ensures that the search is not an extremely urgent one. One response has been to liberalize further and develop the economy of Laos, and thereby improve living standards, although this places new demands on the leadership to comprehend the factors that can promote economic prosperity, and how to regulate them.

After 1975, serious errors were made in the methods — and zealous implementation — chosen to attain economic progress, which only served to stymie the country's development, and resulted in a substantial proportion of the educated populace choosing to leave. Subsequent attempts to rectify past errors of economic planning have been relatively successful, but have been in operation for just a decade, and there is much more to be done. The Asian Crisis has also served to illustrate the perils — as well as the more well-known advantages — to be derived from greater exposure to the world economy. There are also some domestic perils associated with economic liberalization, most notably with regard to potential widening disparities in income between rural and urban areas, and therefore between ethnic groupings.

But even with the challenges cited above, Laos enjoys a relatively stable political environment. Partly because of Vientiane's zero tolerance for domestic opposition, there is apparently no significant threat posed to the current regime, the recent spate of bombings notwithstanding. With no immediate internal or external challenge the LPRP leadership arguably lacks a sense of urgency in finding and developing a tenable framework of legitimacy. Leaders are also able to adopt a relatively relaxed attitude towards effective governance, and some of its members are able to pursue more personal agendas. Perhaps the greatest challenge that faces the LPDR is that of creeping entropy. That in turn may prevent the country growing at a rate that permits Laos to climb up the development index and bring improved living standards for its populace in an equitable manner. Overcoming this fundamental challenge is likely to be the best guarantor of the LPDR's — and the LPRP leadership's — long-term survival.

The recent history of Laos has arguably been one of trying to create a viable economic entity from the limited resources — and particularly limited human and institutional resources — contained within its current territorial extent. The 1893 treaty that the French foisted on Siam, and which came broadly to define the present borders of Laos, reduced the former Lao kingdom to "... a remote colonial backwater, landlocked, underpopulated and underdeveloped".[22] Those same borders pertain today, and despite two markedly differing regimes since independence in 1953, Laos has still to attain a degree of economic viability. Throughout its recent history, the Lao state has been consistently influenced — and sometimes dictated — by the interests and actions of its more powerful neighbours. Most recently, the Vietnamese political and ideological hegemony of the period between 1975 and the late 1980s was gradually replaced by a degree of Thai economic and commercial influence.

Following the onset of the Asian Crisis, however, and the substantial downturn in the fortunes of Thailand's business community, Laos now finds itself entering a new period of flux with regard to its immediate neighbours, and its own political identity. Entry as a full member of ASEAN (in 1997) may provide a platform from which Laos can better balance the competing influences of stronger neighbours, and thereby attain a greater degree of autonomy. However, it seems that relations between Vientiane and Hanoi, which appeared to have slowly dissipated since the late 1980s, have picked up somewhat in recent years (as evidenced by the increased frequency of official visits), possibly as mutual anxiety over the effects of the Asian Crisis brings the two leaderships closer together. It is also apparent that China has been able to take some advantage of the vacuum created by the departure of Thai investors, and the mighty northern neighbour may have aspirations to assume a greater degree of influence over Laos. If so, Hanoi will ardently strive to keep such aspirations in check, but it remains to be seen what value added Vietnam can provide Laos, beyond a shared sense of anxiety over — and apparent indecisiveness in how to react to — the economic problems brought on by the Asian Crisis.

Notes

This chapter was penned prior to the Seventh Lao People's Revolutionary Party Congress, held in March 2001, and therefore does not contain details of changes made at that congress to the senior leadership line-up.

1 Martin Stuart-Fox, *Buddhist Kingdom, Marxist State: The Making of Modern Laos* (Bangkok: White Lotus, 1996), p. 18.
2 Ibid., p. 34.
3 For an illuminating depiction and assessment of Washington's low cost, low profile "secret war" in Laos, see Douglas Blaufarb, *Organizing and Managing Unconventional War in Laos, 1962–70* (Christiansburg VA: Dalley Book Service, 1972). Although primarily co-ordinated by the U.S. ambassador in Vientiane, and given logistical support from U.S. bases in Thailand, the focal point for the "secret war" effort by U.S. advisors and Hmong irregulars was the village of Long Tien, northeast of the capital.
4 As Stuart-Fox points out, the appointment of Souphanouvong as State President of the new LPDR helped mitigate in part the shock of abolishing the monarchy, as he was of royal blood and a half-brother of Souvanna Phouma. Stuart-Fox, op. cit., p. 79.
5 By the time the co-operativization programme was halted, about a quarter of all peasant families had been brought within approximately 2,800 co-operatives. Stuart-Fox, op. cit., p. 109.
6 For a detailed profile of the Hmong, see Jane Hamilton-Merritt, *Tragic Mountains: The Hmong, the Americans and the Secret Wars of Laos, 1942–1992* (Bloomington: Indiana Univ. Press, 1992).
7 Article 3 of the Constitution. See Program for Southeast Asian Studies, *New Laos, New Challenges* (Tempe: Arizona State University, 1998), p. 22.
8 See *Financial Times*, 6 June 1996.
9 For details of the most recent National Assembly elections, see *Vientiane Times*, 31 December to 2 January 1997, and 7–9 January 1998.
10 Stuart-Fox, op. cit., p. 75.
11 Ibid., p. 73.
12 The government's March 1998 decision to reduce the office hours for state employees from 42 to 35 hours per week, included a halt to Saturday working. This measure was intended to give state employees more time to supplement their meagre salaries (following the heavy devaluation in the local currency) with second incomes.
13 Economist Intelligence Unit, *Cambodia and Laos Country Report*, Second Quarter 1998, p. 29. Although worship or prayer within approved religious buildings is deemed acceptable, religious activities (particularly proselytizing) beyond such buildings is likely to prompt a reaction from the authorities. Vientiane also hosts a mosque, which serves the small community of Cambodian Muslims that sought shelter from Democratic Kampuchea in the latter half of the 1970s.

14   For details of the LPRP's Sixth Party Congress, see *Vientiane Times*, 22–28 March 1996.
15   Stuart-Fox, op. cit., p. 81. By 1975, over 60 per cent of the LPRP were Lao Theung. BKMS, p. 130. Most of the founding leaders of the LPRP were lowland Lao, although the precise ethnic profile of the LPRP today is not in the public domain.
16   Ibid., p. 85.
17   Ibid. For example, Kyasone Phomvihane's father was Vietnamese and he attended university in Hanoi, and both Souphanouvong and Nouhak married Vietnamese women.
18   Stuart-Fox, op. cit., pp. 166 and 177.
19   Stuart-Fox, op. cit., p. 168.
20   For an analysis of the effects of the Asian Crisis on Laos (and the other transitional countries of Southeast Asia), see Nick Freeman, "Greater Mekong Sub-Region and the 'Asian Crisis': Caught Between Scylla and Charybdis", in *Southeast Asian Affairs 1999*, edited by Daljit Singh and John Funston (Singapore: Institute of Southeast Asian Studies, 1999), pp.32–51.
21   Stuart-Fox, op. cit., p. 23. Also Douglas Blaufarb, *Organizing and Managing Unconventional War in Laos, 1962–70* (Christiansburg VA: Dalley Book Service, 1972), p. v. Observations of a similar vein can be found throughout the literature on Laos.
22   Stuart-Fox, op. cit., p. 24.

Further Reading

Blaufarb, Douglas. *Organizing and Managing Unconventional War in Laos, 1962–70*. Christiansburg VA: Dalley Book Service, 1972.
Brown, MacAlister and Joseph J. Zasloff. *Apprentice Revolutionaries: The Communist Movement in Laos, 1930–1985*. Stanford: Hoover Institution Press, 1986.
Evans, Grant. *Lao Peasants Under Socialism*. New Haven: Yale University Press, 1990.
Gunn, Geoffrey C. *Rebellion in Laos: Peasant and Politics in a Colonial Backwater*. Boulder Co: Westview Press, 1990.
Hamilton-Merritt, Jane. *Tragic Mountains: The Hmong, the Americans and the Secret Wars of Laos, 1942–1992*. Bloomington: Indiana Univ. Press, 1992.
International Monetary Fund. *Lao People's Democratic Republic: Recent Economic Developments*. Washington, D.C.: Staff Country Report, August 1998.
Kaysone Phomvihane. *Revolution in Laos*. Moscow: Progress Publishers, 1981.
Luther, Hans. *Socialism in a Subsistence Economy: The Laotian Way*. Bangkok: Chulalongkorn University, 1983.
Program for Southeast Asian Studies. *New Laos, New Challenges*. Tempe: Arizona State University, 1998.

Simms, Peter and Sanda. *The Kingdoms of Laos*. London: Curzon, 1999.

Stuart-Fox, Martin. *Buddhist Kingdom, Marxist State: The Making of Modern Laos*. Bangkok: White Lotus, 1996.

————. *A History of Laos*. Cambridge: Cambridge University Press, 1997.

———— and Mary Kooyman. *Historical Dictionary of Laos*. Metuchen: The Scarecrow Press, 1992.

Toye, Hugh. *Laos: Buffer State or Battleground*. London: Oxford University Press 1968.

Warner, Roger. *Back Fire: The CIA's Secret War in Laos and its Link to the War in Vietnam*. New York: Simon & Schuster, 1995.

Zasloff, Joseph and Leonard Unger. *Laos: Beyond the Revolution*. London: Macmillan, 1991.

5

MALAYSIA
Developmental State
Challenged

John Funston

INTRODUCTION

Malaysia stands out for having one of the most complex ethnic mixes in Southeast Asia, or indeed the world. It has, since independence, achieved a remarkable degree of political stability, along with economic and social progress, but has had many turbulent moments and now faces new challenges from the forces of *reformasi*.

Malaysia's golden age is the fifteenth century, when Malacca held sway over small sultanates that covered peninsular Malaysia, and similar entities in parts of Indonesia. Malacca was at that time one of the region's dominant powers, a major trading port, and a centre for spreading Islam. Its cosmopolitan city included traders from China, and traders and Islamic clerics from India and the Middle East. It had a sophisticated system of government, and well-developed laws (traditional — *adat* — and Islamic). The main historical document surviving this period, the *Sejarah Melayu* (Malay History), is still regarded as an important repository of Malay norms.

After Portugal conquered Malacca in 1511, the peninsula broke into a number of sultanates which retained a loose independence — sometimes falling under the influence of more powerful local neighbours or states in Thailand or Indonesia. British influence began to expand over the peninsula from the late eighteenth century, initially through trade and then with toeholds in Penang (1786), Singapore (1819) and Malacca (1824). Deeper colonial impact dates from 1874, when Britain signed the Pangkor Agreement with Perak, giving it the power to "advise" state authorities —

a misnomer really since British advice was seldom rejected. Such "indirect" rule, with the form of Malay sovereignty maintained, was progressively extended to all peninsular states (collectively know as Malaya) by 1915. In Borneo, British adventurer James Brooke (first of the "White Rajas") moved into Sarawak in 1843, and a commercial firm, the North Borneo Trading Company, took over Sabah in 1881.

Colonial rule lasted less than a century for most parts of Malaysia, but its influence was profound. Four legacies stand out. First, a change to Malaya's demography, entrenching a multi-ethnic society. Chinese and Indian labourers were brought into the country as labour for new tin and rubber industries, and support services, while Malays remained in traditional agriculture, or in a few cases manned lower and middle ranks in the bureaucracy. Occupational differences were reinforced by large religious and cultural divisions, creating what many observers saw as a classic "plural society". Secondly, within this society Britain reinforced the principle of Malay dominance, both by maintaining the Sultanates and providing a "special position" for Malays in areas such as employment in the bureaucracy, land ownership, and educational assistance. Thirdly, Britain provided the stability, infrastructure and business-friendly environment for developing a modern economy. Tin, and later rubber, brought wealth to the country as a whole — even if some sectors missed out, and colonial interests benefited disproportionately. Finally, Britain provided a strong but authoritarian bureaucratic foundation for independence. It educated an élite able to take over administration, and provide many of Malaysia's early political leaders. At the same time it bequeathed rules that greatly restricted political activity and left huge discretionary powers in bureaucratic (including police) hands. These included a catch-all Sedition Act, laws enforcing strict licensing requirements on societies, restrictions on freedom of the press, and a law permitting detention without trial (precursor to the Internal Security Act).

Nationalism began to emerge in the Malay community from the early twentieth century, a time that most Chinese and Indians looked to developments in their respective homelands. It surfaced dramatically in 1946 when, after a short Japanese interlude (1941–45), Britain attempted to introduce a Malayan Union. Objecting strongly to plans for abolishing powers of the Sultans, and extending citizenship to all, Malays came together in the United Malays Nationalist Organisation (UMNO), and forced Britain to back down.

For a brief period in the late 1940s the Malayan Communist Party also challenged for leadership of Malayan nationalism. It was,

FIGURE 5.1

Malaysia: Key Dates

1400	Malacca empire established. The pre-colonial golden age of Malay politics, economics and culture. Ended with conquest by Portugal in 1511.
1874	Beginning of British "indirect rule" over the nine Malay sultanates. Extended to all peninsular states by 1915. Sarawak incorporated into British influence by adventurer James Brooke in 1843, and Sabah by North Borneo Trading Company in 1881.
1946	Establishment of United Malays National Organisation (UMNO), to oppose British imposition of a Malayan Union.
1952	UMNO establishes alliance with Malayan Chinese Association in local elections, formalized as the Alliance in 1954. Expanded to include the Malayan Indian Congress in 1955, and parties from Sabah and Sarawak in 1963.
1955	Alliance wins 51 of 52 seats in elections for local rule.
1957	Independence for Federation of Malaya on 31 August. UMNO leader Tunku Abdul Rahman becomes Prime Minister.
1963	Federation of Malaysia established by addition of Sabah, Sarawak and Singapore (Singapore left two years later).
1969	Race riots begin on 13 May. Emergency rule imposed, and Parliament suspended for 21 months.
1970	Tun Abdul Razak becomes second Prime Minister, 22 September.
1971	Beginning of New Economic Policy featuring affirmative action for Malays. Constitution amended to limit political freedom and entrench Malay political pre-eminence.
1974	Establishment of Barisan Nasional (National Front) to succeed the Alliance. Initially, included Alliance members and four former opposition parties.
1976	Tun Razak dies in office in January, and is succeeded by Hussein Onn. Dr Mahathir Mohamad appointed Deputy.
1981	Hussein retires in July and is succeeded by Dr Mahathir.
1987	UMNO split. Dr Mahathir returned as president by 761 votes to 718. Escalating communal tensions followed by 119 arrests under the Internal Security Act (permitting detention without trial).
1988	UMNO declared illegal by court, and reconstituted as New UMNO. In apparently related actions the government sacked the country's chief judge, and two Supreme Court judges.
1993	Anwar Ibrahim becomes Deputy President of UMNO and Deputy Prime Minister.
1995	Barisan Nasional receives highest post-independence vote ever.
1998	In September, Anwar Ibrahim sacked as deputy government and party leader, expelled from UMNO, arrested under the ISA, assaulted by the Chief of Police while in jail, and charged with five counts of corruption (abuse of power) and five counts of sodomy. Unprecedented public protest against these actions.
1999	Anwar found guilty of four corruption charges and sentenced to six years jail. Government retains power in general elections, but Malay vote shifts away from UMNO.
2000	Anwar sentenced to an additional nine years jail on sodomy charges. Malay support for government continues to erode, despite harsher repression against the opposition and heightened command feeling. Chinese disenchanted by government's education policy and criticisms of alleged "extremists". Opposition unexpectedly wins by-election for the Kedah Assembly seat of Lunars in November.

however, handicapped by its predominantly Chinese membership, and close ideological allegiance to its Chinese counterpart. It was gradually sidelined after Britain declared Emergency rule in 1948, though the Emergency did not end until 1960, and the party only abandoned its struggle in 1989.

But it was UMNO, under Tunku Abdul Rahman, that headed the independence struggle. A chance electoral pact with the Malayan Chinese Association (MCA) for Kuala Lumpur municipal elections in 1952 proved successful, and became the Alliance in 1954. This was expanded by incorporating the Malayan Indian Congress (MIC) in 1955, then parties in Sabah and Sarawak after the formation of Malaysian in 1963. It lives on in an expanded form as the National Front (*Barisan Nasional* or BN), established 1974, which has remained in power to this day.

The Alliance won 51 of 52 seats in elections for home rule in 1955 — the remaining seat went to the *Persatuan Islam Sa Tanah Melayu* (PAS), a breakaway from UMNO's religious wing in 1951. With this mandate the UMNO-led Alliance was quickly able to negotiate independence (*merdeka*), and a new constitution. Both came into effect on 31 August 1957.

The early years of independence were turbulent. Both Malays and non-Malays were disappointed when expected benefits did not arrive immediately. The Alliance had no difficulty retaining power in the 1959 elections, winning 74 of 104 parliamentary seats, but it won only 52 per cent of the vote, and PAS took power in state assemblies in Kelantan and Terengganu. In 1961 the government began looking to expand by incorporating Sabah, Sarawak, Brunei and Singapore, eventually overcoming numerous obstacles and forming Malaysia (minus Brunei) on 16 September 1963. The initiative attracted armed *konfrontasi* from Indonesia, and strong opposition from the Philippines, but strengthened domestic support for the government in the 1964 elections.

From the mid-1960s communal tensions grew as Singapore leaders attempted to mobilize non-Malay support (leading to Singapore's expulsion in 1965) and Malays became increasingly convinced that their economic and cultural interests, particularly implementing Malay as the national language, were not being adequately recognized. Support for the Alliance plunged in the 1969 elections, giving it only 66 from 103 seats on the peninsula. On 13 May rioting started in Kuala Lumpur, and resulted in some 200 deaths. Emergency rule was imposed, and Parliament suspended for 21 months. In this time new policy initiatives were framed to restrict political liberties, entrench Malay pre-eminence, strengthen UMNO, and ensure stronger affirmative action for Malays under a New Economic Policy (NEP).

The reforms of 1969 led to a rejuvenation of UMNO, and the Alliance/BN, which sustained them into the mid-1980s, and through four Prime Ministers — Tunku Abdul Rahman (1957–1970), Tun Razak Dato Hussein (1970–75), Tun Hussein Onn (1975–1981) and Dato' Seri Dr Mahathir Mohamad (1981–). Then difficulties struck, as the economy went into recession. Intra-UMNO conflicts had become more intense in the 1970s, and in 1987 Dr Mahathir's leadership was challenged by former Finance, and Trade and Industry Minister, Tenkgu Razaleigh Hamzah — supported by Datuk Musa Hitam, who had fallen out with Dr Mahathir and resigned from his position of Deputy Prime Minister in 1986. Dr Mahathir survived by only 43 votes (761–718). Tengku Razaleigh then established *Parti Semangat '46* (Spirit of '46), and aligned with the opposition, before returning to the UMNO fold in 1996. In related developments, communal tensions flared in 1987, leading to 119 arrests under the Internal Security Act, and conflicts between Dr Mahathir and the judiciary climaxed in 1988 with the sacking of the top judge and two senior colleagues.

Aided by a booming economy, Dr Mahathir rebounded strongly from these set-backs, winning well in the 1990 elections, then achieving the best result ever for the governing party in 1995. UMNO also appeared stronger following the election of the young and charismatic Datuk Seri Anwar Ibrahim as deputy in 1993, and repeated assurances from Dr Mahathir that Anwar would be his successor.

Calm and optimism were again shaken when the Asian economic crisis arrived suddenly and unexpectedly in July 1997. Like other states in the region this initially prompted a critical reassessment of development strategies, with calls for *reformasi* and abolition of KKN (*korupsi, kronyisma, nepotisma*) in both the mainstream and alternative media. Dr Mahathir entertained this at first, but around the time of Indonesian President Soeharto's fall in May 1998 began to see the *reformasi* movement as a threat.[1] His conflicts with Anwar intensified from this time, though it was still a shock when he sacked Anwar from ministerial posts on 2 September 1998, then orchestrated his removal from all UMNO positions the following evening.

Since September 1998 Malaysian politics has been in a state of confrontation and upheaval, aggravated by the dramatic circumstances of Anwar's arrest, bashing by the Chief of Police, and controversial court cases on corruption and sodomy charges. Elections in November 1999 did not resolve matters, for although the BN won UMNO lost 22 seats. The emergence of a stronger opposition coalition, and the more prominent role played by civil society, were positive factors. But with UMNO no longer having clear Malay majority support, the basis of its political dominance hitherto, Malaysia is entering uncharted political waters.[2]

Geographic Determinants

Present-day Malaysia is a product of British decolonization. The peninsular states do share some historical experiences, and have similar ethnic and cultural backgrounds, though even here state loyalties sometimes outweigh national identification. Sabah and Sarawak, separated by the South China Sea, have different histories and ethnic mixes. Incorporating these states has been a major challenge of political integration.

Malaysia is centrally located in Southeast Asia. For years, when the Association of Southeast Asian Nations (ASEAN) numbered six, it was the only country to share boundaries with all members. Malaysia has had difficulties with all neighbours, particularly Singapore, which left the federation in acrimonious circumstances. Occasionally governments have used foreign threats to shore up domestic support, but foreign relations have seldom had a major impact on domestic issues — Indonesian *konfrontasi* being the major exception.

Malaysia has an abundance of natural resources. Mineral wealth in the form of tin and petroleum have provided large returns over many years, though both are now dwindling (tin because of declining demand, petroleum because of declining resources). Timber from natural forests has also been a major source of wealth, along with many forms of tropical agriculture (particularly rubber and palm oil). Such products dominated Malaysia's exports until the 1980s, when manufactured goods gradually began to take over.

Malaysia remains relatively underpopulated, particularly in Sabah and Sarawak. It has one of the few governments encouraging population growth, with a declared objective of 80 million towards the end of the twenty-first century. The peninsula has been urbanized since colonial times. Initially this was a non-Malay phenomenon, with Malays remaining in rural areas, but Malay urbanization has achieved great momentum in recent decades.

Unique Communal Society

Malaysia's multi-ethnic and multi-cultural identity is a starting point for understanding its complex society and politics. By late 1998 about 51 per cent of its 21 million citizens were Malay, 12 per cent other indigenes, 27 per cent Chinese, and 8 per cent Indian. This, however, masked significant regional variations. On the peninsula the division was 59 per cent Malay, 28 per cent Chinese and 9 per cent Indian, with over 90,000 "aborigines" (*orang asli*) accounting for a large part of the remainder. In Sabah 9 per cent were Malay, 63 per cent other indigenes (almost half Kadazandusun), and 15 per cent Chinese. Sarawak had 22 per cent Malay, 50 per cent other indigenes (almost two thirds Iban) and 28 per cent Chinese.[3] The communal breakdown is constantly changing, as birth rates of Malays and other indigenous groups are higher than Chinese and Indian. At independence in 1957, for example, only 50 per cent of the peninsular population was Malay, while Chinese numbered 37 per cent and Indians 11 per cent. Around 2 million non-citizens — 700,000 "legals" — also live in the country, most on short-term work contracts from Indonesia, the Philippines and Bangladesh.

Politics has mainly been articulated in communal terms. Most political parties have organized along ethnic lines, and have sought to maximize political power and economic benefits for a particular ethnic group, and promote group interests in areas such as language, education and culture. Conflicting demands have been mediated by leaders of the multi-ethnic governing coalition. Communal conflict has generally stopped short of open conflict, apart from the tragic riots of May 1969.

Malay-Chinese rivalry has been the main centre of conflict, but Malay relations with indigenous groups in Sabah and Sarawak have also been difficult. Kadazans and Ibans are culturally distinct from Malays (most are not Muslim), and suspicious of Malay efforts to extend federal power, though all have been known as *bumiputra* (sons of the soil) since Malaysia was established. Sabah was ruled by an opposition Kadazan leadership from 1985 until early 1994.

In practice, the effects of communalism have not been as detrimental as might have been expected. Malays and UMNO were never in a position to ride roughshod over others. Despite Malay electoral predominance, non-Malays did command a significant vote and had to be wooed. Government policies helped narrow the income gap between Malays and non-Malays, but the non-Malay economy also improved. Policies favouring Malays were also reduced from the mid-1980s as the government sought increasingly to tap non-Malay entrepreneurial skills.

Though studies continue to show that inter-ethnic socialization is limited, communalism has reduced in recent years as urbanization and rapid economic growth led to shared interests, particularly among a new middle class. These include, on the one hand, a high flying business and corporate élite enjoying conspicuous consumption — globe-trotting in private jets, high rolling at international casinos, and maintaining stables of luxury cars. Group members are generally grateful to, and dependent on, a pro-business government. Other middle-class members, however, have fulfilled the historically reformist role of this group, criticizing the government on issues such as democratic freedom, human rights, transparency and the environment. Such developments have led analyts to write of the "de-ethnicization" of politics. Nonetheless communal sensitivities can still be easily inflamed, as they were for non-Malays by BN campaigning in the 1999 elections.

Women have traditionally enjoyed a relatively high social status. They have played an active political role, though mainly through the women's sections of the major parties. They have provided some parliamentarians and ministers, but are considerably underrepresented in these areas.

Until recently all ethnic groups were seen as espousing so-called "Asian values", rejecting individualism in favour of the family, race and nation. Leaders were assumed to be benevolent, thus deserving deference, loyalty and gratitude. Traditionally, opposing the wishes of the Sultan (*menderhaka*) was a most serious offence, though *Sejarah Melayu* does make loyalty conditional — a ruler could be opposed if he were unjust, particularly if he should humiliate any of his subjects. Political party leaders have, over the years, often appealed to Asian values, and have seldom faced open opposition. But these values have become less tenable with expansion of the middle class. After Anwar's sacking, tens of thousands took to the streets or cyberspace to criticize government leaders. Conflict over such values has been exacerbated by a widespread perception that government actions against Anwar violated norms against humiliating an opponent, and by efforts of UMNO leaders to reinforce the loyalty principle at the expense of democracy within the party.

Islam, the constitutionally-required religion of Malays, also conflicted with feudal loyalty. Long at the centre of Malay social life and identity, Islam has undergone a notable revival since the 1970s, reflected outwardly in wider adoption of Islamic forms of clothing (such as head coverings for women), the mushrooming of *dakwah* organizations (missionary groups, but focused on self-improvement more than converting others), and an expansion of government institutions supporting the faith. Some *dakwah* groups, such as *Angkatan Belia Islam Malaysia* (ABIM), the youth movement established by Anwar Ibrahim in 1971, were at the forefront of those urging reforms in keeping with Islamic prescriptions for justice and democracy.

Besides such positive developments, others were worrying. Islamic revivalism has also been associated with a rise in fanaticism that has meant less tolerance for non-Muslims, even for less devout Muslims, and an attitude towards women that has distressed supporters of womens' rights.[4] Occasionally, fanaticism has led to violence. Incidents include the storming of a police station in Batu Pahat (Johor) in October 1980, with eight fatalities; a shootout with police at Memali (Kedah) in November 1985, in which four police and 14 Muslims were killed; and an arms heist in Grik (Perak) in July 2000, leading to three fatalities (two police).

Besides Islam there have been other pressures on Malay society. Tens of thousands of students have studied abroad. Globalization has brought Western music and TV programmes into Malaysian homes, and Western tourists flock to Malaysia. Middles class values have been determinedly modern. Rapid economic growth, and the urbanization of a once rural Malay community, have brought numerous social ills in its wake, including juvenile delinquency, a rapid increase in drug addiction, and the phenomenon of "hanging out" (*lepak*) at shopping centres instead of attending school or working.

Economy: From Primary Production to Industrialization

Economic change emerged gradually. At independence Malaya relied on primary products — tin, rubber, and later palm oil and timber. Primary products, plus oil, discovered in large quantities in the 1970s, made up some 70 per cent of exports until the early 1980s. Initial policy was laissez-faire, with foreign companies dominating a large part of the economy. Industrial development, to the extent that it existed at all, was for import substitution. State intervention was limited to providing infrastructure, such as roads and water supplies, schools and health clinics, and a major land resettlement project which was expensive but reached only two or three per cent of the rural population.

The riots of 1969 prompted a fundamental re-think. The two-pronged strategy of the NEP was to eliminate poverty irrespective of race, and restructure society so that race would not be identified with economic function. It also set a target of at least 30 per cent *bumiputra* ownership of commercial and business activities. Government intervention in the economy expanded enormously, with numerous bodies set up to pursue business opportunities "in trust" for *bumiputra*, and to plan and monitor policies and regulations to meet NEP goals. Existing foreign companies were urged to restructure in accordance with these guidelines, and in several cases were bought out by state-linked Malaysian companies. Malaysia also began to export light manufactured goods, setting up industrial estates in several cities and providing incentives for foreign investment there.

FIGURE 5.2

Malaysia : Key Statistics

Land area: 329,758 sq. kilometres

Population:[a] 23,260,000 (2000)

GNP:[b] Current exchange rate — US$98.2 bn (1997);
US$81.3 bn (1998)
Purchasing Power Parity — US$168 bn (1997);
US$171 bn (1998)

GNP Per Capita:[b] Current exchange rate — US$4,530 (1997);
US$3,670 (1998)
Purchasing Power Parity — US$7,730 (1997);
US$7,699 (1998)

Income Distribution (1981):[c]
Gini Index 48.5
% share of income or consumption:
Lowest 10% 1.8
Lowest 20% 4.5
2nd 20% 8.3
3rd 20% 13.0
4th 20% 20.4
Highest 20% 53.8
Highest 10% 37.9

Human Development Index (HDI) Ranking:[c]
World ranking 56 (1997); 61 (1998)
Value 0.768 (1997); 0.772 (1998)

Armed Forces:
Total no.[d] 105,000 (1999)
Expenditure[d] US$3.3 bn (1998)
% of GNP[b] 3.0% (1995)

Sources: [a] Official national sources.
[b] World Bank, *World Development Indicators* (Washington, D.C., 1999 & 2000).
[c] United Nations Development Programme (UNDP), *Human Development Report* (New York: Oxford University Press, 1999 & 2000).
[d] International Institute for Strategic Studies (IISS), *The Military Balance, 1999-2000* (London: Oxford University Press, 1999).

After Dr Mahathir became Prime Minister, policies changed once again. Adopting a "Look East" policy focused on Japan and South Korea, heavy industry became a priority, with the state-run Heavy Industries Corporation of Malaysia (Hicom), establishing joint ventures with foreign partners in areas such as steel, cement, motor-cycles and most famously the national car (Proton). In 1983 Mahathir also announced a commitment to "privatization", to give the private sector a role in areas hitherto confined to the state.

A global economic slow-down, and mounting public sector debts, pushed the economy into negative growth in 1985. The government responded by reducing direct assistance to Malays, speeding up privatization, deregulation and liberalization, and providing additional incentives for foreign and domestic private investors. The changes coincided with favourable international influences, and ushered in an unprecedented period of growth, registering over 8 per cent for a period of nine years before the Asian Crisis. Malaysia became the world's 17th largest exporter, and in just over a decade increased the proportion of manufactured exports, mainly electrical components, from around 30 per cent to over 70 per cent. A less communal National Development Policy followed the expiry of the NEP in 1990, and was reinforced by a 2020 Vision of an advanced industrial society, featuring the latest in technology, particularly for the futuristic Multimedia Super Corridor. Malaysia also became known for mega projects, building the world's tallest building, an ultra-modern international airport, multi-billion dollar hydroelectric schemes and the like.

The Malaysian bubble burst dramatically with the onset of the Asian Crisis. The ringgit soon fell to around 45 per cent of its previous value against the U.S. dollar, the stock market decreased 60 per cent, and growth in 1998 was –7.5 per cent. These developments had an enormous impact on the financial sector and the real economy, with several conglomerates — mostly NEP-created Malay businesses — amassing debts in the hundreds of million ringgit. At the time of writing such companies remain mired in debt, even though the economy rebounded to more than 5 per cent growth 1999 and 8 per cent in 2000. The future of Malaysia Inc remained uncertain.

THE POLITICAL SYSTEM

Malaysia is a constitutional monarchy with a federal parliamentary system of government. The formal state structure is set out in a written constitution. The *Yang DiPertuan Agong* (King, or *Agong*) is head of state. Administration is vested in a Cabinet headed by a Prime Minister. Cabinet is appointed by the Agong from Members of Parliament, and is collectively responsible to Parliament.

The 1957 Independence Constitution negotiated between the Alliance Party and British colonial authorities was a reasonably comprehensive document, but did not set the major features of the state in concrete. Most amendment required only a two-thirds majority in each house of Parliament. Up to 1996, 42 constitutional amendment acts had been passed, affecting numerous articles. Writing in 1970 Dr Mahathir declared that: "The manner, the frequency and the trivial reasons for altering the constitution reduced this supreme law of the nation to a useless scrap of paper".[5] Still, the frequency of constitutional change did not slacken after Dr Mahathir became Prime Minister.

The constitution sets out the structure of Malaysia's federal system of government, the separation of powers between executive, legislature and judiciary, emergency powers vested in the executive, mechanisms for the conduct of elections, and national policies in relation to issues such as language, citizenship, special assistance to indigenous Malaysians (*bumiputra*), and fundamental liberties for all.

Malaysia's federal system of government vests most powers in the national government — finance, foreign policy and defence, internal security, education and social welfare. The only areas of substantial importance under control of the states are land (including, importantly, forests and logging), water and Islam. Sabah and Sarawak have additional powers, including over immigration and education, but these have been diluted over time, and seldom allowed more independence in practice. The system of government at state level in many ways mirrors that at the national, though government leaders are known as Chief Ministers (*Mentri Besar* in the sultanates, and *Ketua Mentri* elsewhere), while legislatures are unicameral Assemblies. At the lower municipality level officials are appointed by state governments. They were elected up until 1964, but elections were suspended during Indonesia's Confrontation. These were never resumed, ostensibly because elected local governments were open to corruption and abuse of power.

A unique feature of the Constitution is that — following colonial practice — it acknowledges the Malay character of the country, and recognizes the special needs of the Malay community. The 1957 Constitution installed Malay sultans as the heads of most states and the federation. Malay became the national language. Islam was "the" religion of the country, though freedom of worship was guaranteed and Islamic law applied only to personal law of Muslims. Land reserves were set aside for Malays. And under Section 153 the government was empowered to "safeguard the special position of the Malays" by fixing quotas for Malays in the public service, schools and universities, and in the allocation of scholarships and commercial licenses. When Sabah and Sarawak joined the federation in 1963 the land and quota arrangements were extended to natives of these states. Changes to the Sedition Act in 1970 and the Constitution in 1971 made it illegal to question these provisions, and sought to limit the possibility of amendment by making this subject to approval from the Conference of Rulers, rather than simply the Agong.

Nonetheless, there are countervailing assurances for non-Malays. Section 153 also includes several sections designed to safeguard "the legitimate interests of other communities". The inclusion of citizenship in the entrenched constitutional provisions of 1971 was to protect non-Malays, as most had only gained this in the late 1950s and their entitlement had sometimes been questioned.

Head of State

At the apex of Malaysia's political structure is the *Agong* (King). He is the Supreme Head of the Federation, the repository of executive, legislative and judicial authority, the Supreme Commander of the Armed Forces, and the Head of Islam in the Federal Territories (Kuala Lumpur and Labuan) and the states of Malacca, Penang, Sabah and Sarawak. Under a unique system he is elected every 5 years on a rotational basis from among the nine traditional state sultans. These rulers, together with appointed Governors from the four other states, make up the Conference of Rulers. On most issues the *Agong* acts on the advice of Cabinet, or "a Minister acting under the general authority of Cabinet" (Article 40.[1]) — meaning in practice, the Prime Minister. In other words, he reigns but does not rule. He has some discretionary powers over whom he appoints as Prime Minister — but must ensure that the nominee commands majority support in Parliament — and dissolution of Parliament. And the Conference of Rulers must also be consulted before any changes are made to racially sensitive constitutional issues, such as Article 153.

In 1983 the government sought to define the powers of the *Agong* more explicitly. Parliament enacted legislation removing the necessity of the *Agong*'s signature for an act to become law, and extending full power to the Prime Minister to declare a state of emergency (rather than the *Agong* acting on the Prime Minister's advice). A crisis ensued when the then *Agong* refused to sign the legislation. Government leaders then launched an offensive, criticizing the Rulers at mass rallies, and allowing open season for the media to expose royal indiscretions. By early 1984 a compromise had been reached that gave the government the substance of their demands, though in some respects it actually strengthened the monarchy: the *Agong* was given powers to delay legislation by referring it back to Parliament, a right which under the Westminster system he was not expected to have.[6] The *Agong's* power to declare a state of emergency was not changed, but the rulers gave informal assurances that they would always follow advice. Further constitutional changes in 1993 removed the *Agong's* and sultans' immunity from prosecution, through a specially constituted court, and reduced their power to bestow royal pardons except on advice.

These changes left the Rulers as continuing symbols of Malay political dominance, while reducing their ability to play active political roles. Still, in many cases the sultans continue to be viewed as "protectors" of Malay society in their own states, buttressed by perceived mystical powers (*daulat*). And they have regained some importance since the political crisis that followed Dr Mahathir's sacking of Anwar Ibrahim in September 1998. Opposition groups have frequently called on the rulers to intervene on their behalf. In September 1999 thousands marched to state palaces, and then the *Agong's* palace, and presented petitions calling for a Royal Commission into allegations that the government had attempted to poison Anwar. There were no signs that the Rulers acted on these, or other requests, but the opposition drew consolation from the fact that their petitions were received. The government also sought royal support. In March 2000 Dr Mahathir called on the Rulers to use their status as religious heads to help unite the country. This was, in effect, an indirect call for endorsement of the government, as Dr Mahathir had blamed the opposition for causing division by spreading false Islamic teachings.

The Executive

The *Agong* is the chief executive, but effective executive power rests with a Cabinet, collectively responsible to Parliament. It meets weekly, on Wednesday, and most important issues go before it. It comprises ministers heading all portfolios (see Figure 5.3), plus the Deputy Prime Minister and other ministers (currently four) in the Office of the Prime Minister (OPM — also referred to as the Prime Minister's Department).[7] Members are appointed and dismissed by the *Agong*, on the advice of the Prime Minister. They must be Members of Parliament, and by tradition most are from the Lower House.

The Prime Minister must be a citizen by birth, the only minister for whom this is required. He is appointed by the Agong, but as noted must come from the largest party represented in the Lower House. His customary power to appoint other Cabinet Members makes him unquestionably *primus*

FIGURE 5.3

Malaysia: Government Ministries

Office of the Prime Minister (OPM)
Including:
  Anti-Corruption Agency
  Attorney-General
  Economic Planning Unit
  Election Commission
  Islamic Development Department
  National Oil Corporation (Petronas)
  Public Service Commission
Ministry of Agriculture
Ministry of Culture, Arts and Tourism
Ministry of Defence
Ministry of Domestic Trade and Consumer Affairs
Ministry of Education
Ministry of Energy, Communications and Multimedia
Ministry of Entrepreneur Development
Ministry of Finance (Treasury Malaysia)
Ministry of Foreign Affairs
Ministry of Health
Ministry of Home Affairs
Ministry of Housing and Local Government
Ministry of Human Resources
Ministry of Information
Ministry of International Trade and Industry
Ministry of Land and Co-operative Development
Ministry of National Unity and Social Development
Ministry of Primary Industries
Ministry of Rural Development
Ministry of Science, Technology and Environment
Ministry of Transport
Ministry of Works
Ministry of Women and Family Development
Ministry of Youth and Sports

inter pares, though he does have to ensure a broadly equitable share for parties included in the ruling coalition, and balance between the different states. He is assisted by a Deputy Prime Minister, a position not mentioned in the Constitution. While the deputy shares some of the perquisites of office — the honorific *Yang Amat Berhormat* (Most Excellent), rather than *Yang Berhormat* (Excellency) for other politicians, police outriders, and an official residence — he does not have any of the powers held by the Prime Minister.

Besides ministers there are also deputy ministers (currently 29) who are not part of the Cabinet. They have administrative roles in their respective ministries, as assigned by the minister. Below deputy ministers some portfolios have parliamentary secretaries (currently 15). Their duties are defined in the same way as deputy ministers.

Under Cabinet are the OPM, and 24 ministries. These in turn are sub-divided into departments and agencies,[8] and are manned by permanent officials. Although not readily apparent from the Constitution, the public service is expected to follow the Westminster tradition of an apolitical institution. A small number of officials at about department head level are appointed by Cabinet, but otherwise departments and agencies are autonomously run, under guidelines set by the Public Service Department. Senior and middle-ranking officials are precluded from holding political office.

In practice, Malaysia's bureaucracy has never been sharply separated from politics. Particularly in the early years of independence most political leaders came from a bureaucratic background, inclining them to look directly to the bureaucracy for advice. Senior bureaucrats were expected to be sympathetic to UMNO objectives, and the prohibition on political party activism was not rigidly enforced. More importantly, several parts of the bureaucracy have served transparently as virtual adjuncts of the ruling BN party, including: Radio and Television Malaysia, and a Special Section, both under the Information Ministry; the 14,000 strong *Kemas (Jabatan Kemajuan Masyarakat*, or Social Development Department) under the Rural Development Ministry; and the BTN (*Biro Tata Negara*, or National Civics Bureau) under the OPM. The bureaucracy is overwhelmingly Malay, with a legal preferment of 4:1 in the élite Administrative and Diplomatic Service.

The OPM is far more influential than other ministries. Apart from the benefits of having the Prime Minister as its head, several important agencies come under it, including: the Public Service Commission; the Election Commission; the Malaysian Islamic Development Department (for co-ordinating the activities of state Islamic councils); the Attorney-General's Department; the Anti-Corruption Agency; the National Oil Corporation (Petronas) and the Economic Planning Unit (EPU).

The most important ministries and agencies on economic matters are Finance, which has responsibility for fiscal policy, and the National Bank (*Bank Negara*) which falls under the Finance portfolio and looks after monetary policy. Also important are the Ministry of International Trade and Industry (MITI), which handles international trade and foreign investment, and also oversees special share allocations to *bumiputra* entrepreneurs; the EPU, which formulates medium- and long-term plans, prepares the budget for development programmes and projects, and plans and co-ordinates the privatization programme; and the Securities Commission (again under Finance) which manages the Kuala Lumpur Stock Exchange. In November 1997 a National Economic Affairs Council (NEAC) was announced, comprising senior political, bureaucratic and business representatives, with broad responsibilities for monitoring and taking immediate measures to improve the economy. Described as a body that would address economic problems then afflicting the country in a similar way to Emergency rule, it was, however, theoretically subordinate to Cabinet.[9]

Outside the economy there are a small number of additional "heavyweight" portfolios. Home Affairs is much sought after because it controls the police, and implements various laws that restrict political activities, such as the Internal Security Act (ISA) and the Printing Presses and Publications Act (see below). The Prime Minister or his deputy have generally held this post, Dr Mahathir from 1986–99. Education, and to a lesser extent Agriculture, have traditionally been important to Malay politicians, providing opportunities to build support among the masses, though growing urbanization and commercialization have reduced their significance. Defence and Foreign Affairs are high profile ministries, but provide only limited opportunities for developing a home base. Prime Ministers have frequently taken a personal interest in these areas, or the National Security Council under the OPM has been influential.

The executive's role increased dramatically from the launch of the NEP in 1971, with the bureaucracy given major responsibilities to support the growth of a new *bumiputra* commercial and professional class, and to intervene directly in business activities as a proxy for *bumiputra*.[10] Increased emphasis on privatization in the mid-1980s may have led to some decline in public sector employment, but the executive (especially the EPU) played a key role in determining privatization arrangements. The awarding of privatization contracts without open tendering, or any other form of transparent arrangements, enhanced executive power.[11]

The executive has also been strengthened by an ever-expanding array of legislation giving it discretionary power. Among the most important is the right to declare a state of Emergency — effectively in the Prime Minister's hands — and to rule by decree. This has been invoked on four occasions — in 1964 because of confrontation with Indonesia, in 1966 and 1977 to address state-level political problems in Sarawak and Kelantan, and in 1969 after racial riots in the national capital. The most important period of Emergency rule was in 1969, when Parliament was suspended for twenty-one months, and the government ruled by decree through a National Operations Council (NOC).

Any decrees issued during Emergency rule are exempt from judicial review. Since a constitutional amendment in 1960, an Emergency remains in force until annulled by Parliament; none of those declared thus far have been revoked. The government can, therefore, exercise its powers under Emergency regulations any time it chooses to do so.

The ISA has also been used extensively for executive political purposes. Passed in 1960 with the ending of the communist Emergency, this gives police the right to detain for two months without trial anyone suspected of endangering Malaysia's security or essential services. The Minister of Home Affairs may then extend this indefinitely in two-year packages. Courts have no jurisdiction over these detainees. Until 1993 a cumulative total of 9,542 people had been detained under this legislation.[12]

The original justification for the ISA was anti-communist, but from the outset its net was cast more widely, and in particular targeted perceived threats to communal stability. The largest uses ever made of the ISA were after racial riots in 1969 (117 arrested), and when racial disturbances threatened in 1987 (119). On a number of occasions the arrests had a clear political intention, including the detention of several student leaders in 1974 (among them later Deputy Prime Minister, Anwar Ibrahim), two UMNO deputy ministers and an editor of the influential Malay newspaper *Berita Harian* in 1976, PAS leaders in 1984, and several opposition politicians, some out-of-favour members of the ruling coalition, and leaders of non-governmental organizations (NGOs) in 1987. Religious dissidents have often been targeted, including leaders of the Islamic organization, *Darul Arqam* in 1994. One of Dr Mahathir's first acts on coming to power was to release several high profile ISA detainees, and to announce the number under detention (470), encouraging expectations that he might use it sparingly if at all. However, he subsequently conducted the largest ISA round up ever in 1987, and continued to use it in controversial ways against sacked deputy Anwar Ibrahim and supporters in September 1998.

Besides the ISA there are numerous other laws allowing the executive to impose its will on the public. These include:

- The Emergency (Public Order and Prevention of Crime) Ordinance 1969 and Dangerous Drugs (Special Preventive Measures) Act 1985, allowing preventive detention without trial where there is insufficient evidence to prosecute in court.
- The Official Secrets Act (1972 and amended 1986) restricting the right to any classified government information.
- The Police Act (1967), making it necessary to apply for a police permit for any meeting of four or more people 14 days in advance, and giving full powers to the police to approve or reject.
- The Sedition Act, first passed in 1948 to prohibit virtually all activities causing disaffection against the government or the administration of justice, and widened in 1970 to address acts that might cause communal ill will — in particular by questioning constitutional provisions that were "entrenched" the following year.
- The Printing Presses and Publications Act, originally passed in 1948 to require all newspapers and printing presses to obtain a licence annually. In 1987 amendments made licences more difficult to obtain, and any rejection by the Minister for Home Affairs beyond the scope of judicial review. Political party publications were freely sold for many years, but in 1991 annual licences were amended so that they could only be sold to party members. The PAS newspaper *Harakah* defied this for some years, but was forced to comply in early 2000.
- The Societies Act (1966), requiring all organizations to be registered, provides an annual report to the Registrar of Societies. Under 1981 amendments, any action by the Registrar to refuse or de-register societies is not subject to judicial review.
- The Universities and University Colleges Act passed in 1971 forbade student clubs and societies affiliating with organizations such as political parties. Amendments in 1975 gave the Minister for Education direct control over universities — including appointment of Vice-Chancellors — and in turn gave Vice-Chancellors direct authority over all student activities.
- The Trade Unions Ordinance in 1959, that stopped office bearers of political parties holding office in trade unions. Amendments in 1969 and 1980 banned the use of union funds for political purposes. And to prevent the emergence of large organizations, unions had to be from

similar (in the eyes of the government's Trade Union Department) trades, occupations or industries.

Political Role of Military and Police

The military and police have never had a direct political role in Malaysia, except for the period of NOC rule. (The ten-member NOC initially contained the heads of the military and police, and a senior army officer was appointed Executive Secretary.) Civilian dominance over the military is firmly established, and all Defence Ministers have been civilians. Nonetheless the military do play a silent political role. Malaysian governments have taken the view that a strong military serves to enhance the credibility of government. Military expenditure jumped sharply after riots in 1969, with the number of battalions increasing from 14 to 20 that year, then steadily to 34 by 1980. Total numbers now are about 80,000 for the army, 12,500 for the airforce and 12,500 for the navy. There is also a part time Territorial Army (*Wataniah*) with 43,000 members, and a People's Volunteer Unit (*Rela*) numbering around 200,000. Military intelligence organizations directly assist the ruling BN in various ways, not least in conducting ground surveys of political sentiment in the lead-up to elections. The military is overwhelmingly Malay, constituting another important reassurance of Malay political dominance. In 1981, 75 per cent of officers and 85 per cent other ranks were Malay,[13] a figure that is likely to have increased since then.

The police force, which plays a similar role of reinforcing government authority, comes under the Home Affairs Ministry. It includes a 20,000 strong paramilitary Field Force, and a 2,500 strong Federal Reserve Unit specially trained for dealing with demonstrations, strikes and riots. The Special Branch looks after subversion, and political intelligence. Again, the police is a predominantly Malay institution. In 1989 60–70 per cent of officers were Malay, and the percentage for other ranks was much higher.[14]

The Legislature

Soon after independence parliamentarians moved into an imposing, futuristic building, sited on a hill overlooking Kuala Lumpur's scenic Lake Gardens — a strong symbolic affirmation of commitment to parliamentary government. Following the Westminster tradition parliament was meant to have a monopoly on legislation, control of the purse strings, and be able to call the executive to account.

Malaysia has a bicameral parliament, consisting of a 193-member *Dewan Rakyat* (House of Representatives), and a 69-member *Dewan Negara* (Senate) — also known, respectively, as the lower and upper houses. The *Dewan Rakyat* is by far the most important. It provides the Prime Minister and most of the cabinet, initiates all bills, and has exclusive powers over finance.

The *Dewan Negara* is intended to act as a house of review, and to protect state interests. In 1957 a majority of senators were elected by state assemblies, but constitutional change in 1963 left state appointees as a minority, effectively removing the state representational role (see section on Elections below). From the constitution it appears that the chamber's powers are much the same as the *Dewan Rakyat*, except for financial matters, but in practice it does not initiate legislation, and has no power to delay any bill. It does have power to block amendment of the constitution, but has never exercised this, and its predominantly appointed character makes it unlikely ever to do so.

In a formal sense parliament has exercised control over legislation and the nation's purse strings, except when parliament was suspended during the NOC period. However, the legislature sometimes handed these powers to the executive, through "its tendency to confer wide powers on ministers to enact delegated legislation".[15] Moreover, a large amount of government revenue is off budget, since large state enterprises (such as the cash-rich oil company Petronas) are not accountable to parliament. The existence of a ruling party that has always commanded over two thirds of parliamentary seats has also meant that much of the legislative and financial oversight has been pro-forma, and that parliament has not acted as a check on the executive.[16]

There are additional reasons for parliamentary weakness. Unlike many of its counterparts the Malaysian parliament has few committees to probe government performance, and does not have research support staff. It also lacks basic information technology capabilities. The parliamentary web site — once touted as having the potential to provide comprehensive details on parliamentary activities and parliamentarians — provides only the most basic information, and is not updated on a timely basis.[17]

Nonetheless, parliament has had other uses. It has provided a training ground for younger politicians, giving them an opportunity to attract public attention. Dr Mahathir is among those who have benefited from an effective performance during his first parliamentary term (1964–69). Parliament has also forced the government to answer some questions put to them by the opposition that they might otherwise have ignored —

ministers have proved reasonably forthcoming in responding to questions put on notice. And it provided at least limited opportunities for the opposition to gain media attention.

Elections

A five-member Election Commission is formally in charge of Malaysian elections. Its members are appointed by the *Agong* (the king), on the advice of cabinet. Members must be capable of attracting public confidence, a criterion generally addressed by appointing senior public servants, ensuring representation from the three major racial groups, and including a representative of Sabah and Sarawak. Although it is administratively under the OPM the Commission is expected to be independent, and in its early years was.

All Malaysian citizens have the right to vote for the *Dewan Raykat* and state Assemblies. Registration and voting are not compulsory. Around 80 per cent do register, and some 70 to 80 per cent of these cast ballots on election day. Candidates compete in single member constituencies, with results decided on a first-past-the-post basis. They are elected for a 5-year term, calculated from the date of parliament's first meeting. (Parliament must be convened within 120 days; once five years have expired the EC may allow up to 60 days before elections.) The Prime Minister may, of course, choose to call elections ahead of schedule. There are no limits on the number of terms a candidate may stand. National and state elections are synchronized for peninsular states, but Sabah and Sarawak hold state elections at times of their choosing.

The number and delineation of constituencies changes after periodic Election Commission reassessments. Today's 193 seats has been approached gradually from 52 in the first peninsular elections (1955). Twenty-eight of these seats are in Sarawak, and 20 in Sabah, giving them around 25 per cent of parliamentary seats with a population of only 18 per cent — a price paid to entice the Borneo states into federation.

The 1957 constitution made no specific recommendation for delineating constituencies, leaving this to the Commission. However, constitutional amendments in 1962 required that recommendations on delineation had to be submitted to the Prime Minister — who was free to make such amendments as he saw fit — then approved by parliament. Also, rural constituencies could be half the size of urban constituencies. A further constitutional change in 1973 removed any limitation on the variation of electorate sizes, leading to some cases where some urban electorates were more than five times the size of rural electorates. These changes weakened the Commission and gave the government a strong say over constituency delineation, and — because of the concentration of Malays in rural areas — were a critical factor in entrenching Malay political dominance over the political system.

One other feature of Malaysian elections that has worked to the government's advantage is the short time limit for campaigning. Elections may be held within 11 days of parliament's dissolution (four days up to nomination day, and seven days for campaigning).[18] Apart from this minimum period the Commission supposedly decides on how long the campaign should be. National elections in 1986, 1990, 1995 and 1999 were all completed in under three weeks, justified by the Commission on the grounds that prolonged campaigns generated high tension and unrest. This obviously gave the government considerable advantage, as the Prime Minister alone decided when elections would be held.

TABLE 5.1

Election Results for the Dewan Rakyat, 1959–99

(By seats and percentage of votes won)

Election Year	Government*			Opposition			Total
	Number of Seats	Per cent of Seats	Per cent of Votes	Number of Seats	Per cent of Seats	Per cent of Votes	Number of Seats
1959**	74	71.15	51.7	30	28.85	48.3	104
1964**	89	85.58	58.5	15	14.42	41.5	104
1969	95	66.00	49.3	49	34.00	50.7	144
1974	135	87.66	60.7	19	12.34	39.3	154
1978	130	84.42	57.2	24	15.58	42.8	154
1982	132	85.71	60.5	22	14.29	39.5	154
1986	148	83.62	55.8	29	16.38	41.5	177
1990	127	70.55	53.4	53	29.45	46.6	180
1995	162	84.38	65.2	30	15.62	34.8	192
1999	148	76.68	56.5	45	23.32	43.5	193

* Government means the Alliance for 1959 and 1964, the Alliance and coalition partner the Sarawak United People's Party for 1969, and the Barisan Nasional from 1974.
** 1959 figures are for Malaya. Similarly, 1964 figures are only for Peninsular Malaysia as parliamentary elections were not held in Sabah and Sarawak.
Sources: Zakaria Haji Ahmad, "The 1999 General Elections: A Preliminary Overview", Table 1, in "Trends in Malaysia: Election Assessment". Trends in Southeast Asia series, (Singapore: Institute of Southeast Asian Studies, January 2000). This reference provides a full citation, but all sources ultimately are based on statistics provided by the Malaysian Election Commission.

Senators are elected on a quite different basis. Two members from each state are elected by state Assemblies. Two representing the Federal Territory of Kuala Lumpur, and one the Federal Territory of Labuan, and 40 others, are appointed by the *Agong*, on the advice of Cabinet. They serve an initial three-year term, and may be renewed only once.

Malaysian elections have generally been regarded as free in terms of providing the necessary conditions for voting freely, and accurately counting the outcome. However, this has increasingly been questioned during recent elections, with NGOs claiming widespread used "phanton voters", suspect postal voters, and other malpractices.[19] There is, moreover, no secret voting; ballots are numbered and marked off against the voter. Opposition parties have, at various times, succeeded in coming to power at state level in four states (Kelantan, Terengganu, Penang and Sabah). But the advantages provided to the government by its influence over the Electoral Commission noted above, and other factors related to the strength of the BN and its control over government machinery and the media have ensured the ruling coalition has always commanded a two-thirds majority in the federal parliament. It did fall just shot in the 1969 election, but by the time parliament reconvened after a period of Emergency rule several former opposition parties had agreed to support the government (See Table 5.1.). The nature of the first-past-the-post system has also played a part. The support of 56.5 per cent of voters in 1999 provided 77 per cent of *Dewan Rakyat* seats.

Judiciary

The judiciary was established as an independent arm of government, with primary responsibility for defending and interpreting the constitution. The court system is made up of Superior Courts (High Court, Court of Appeal and Federal Court) and Subordinate Courts (Sessions, Magistrates and Native Courts). A right of appeal to the British Privy Council existed until 1985. Members are appointed by the *Agong* on the advice of the Prime Minister. However, the *Agong* is further required to consult with the Conference of Rulers, and the Prime Minister with senior judges, before appointments are made.

In the early years of independence the judiciary maintained a high reputation for independence and integrity, though analysts saw it as adopting very literal interpretations of constitutional provisions relating to civil liberties, and consistently upholding parliamentary acts even when these made substantial inroads on fundamental liberties.[20] No act of parliament has ever been held unconstitutional. Relations between the senior judiciary and the political leadership remained cordial under Malaysia's first three prime ministers, all of whom had legal training.

Government relations with the judiciary changed dramatically under Dr Mahathir, the first Prime Minister not to come from a legal background. Tensions peaked in 1988 after the High Court, on 4 February, declared UMNO an illegal organization for allowing 30 unregistered branches at its 1987 Assembly. The decision in itself was not a problem — though often cited by UMNO leaders as "proof" that the courts are independent, or even anti-government, this was precisely the outcome party leaders had sought, to ensure that Tengku Razaleigh's faction could not gain control. But by some accounts, the possibility of a successful appeal did cause anxiety. Whether linked to this issue or not, constitutional amendments in March sought to weaken the courts. Instead of "judicial power" being vested in the courts, it became subject to parliament — in effect removing recourse to common law principles such as natural justice. Legal circles expressed strong opposition, and the nation's top judge, Tun Mohamed Salleh Abas, wrote to the *Agong* expressing concern. The dispute then escalated and came to include the *Agong* and Dr Mahathir in opposition to Tun Salleh. In a complicated and controversial series of moves Tun Salleh was suspended from office in late May, then had his case brought before a tribunal in June. He refused to attend, after unsuccessfully challenging its composition, and was dismissed on the tribunal's recommendations in August. Five other judges who became involved in legal manoeuvres relating to the case were also suspended, two later being dismissed. Rais Yatim, a prominent Malaysian legal and political figure (currently defacto Law Minister in the OPM) makes the following judgement: "The decision to remove Salleh and his two colleagues was a political one, although the *modus operandi* might seem to have followed constititutional arrangement .... The whole episode ... was based on the desire of the executive to have an untrammelled say in the direction the judiciary should take in future."[21]

Since the Tun Salleh case there have been large questions about judicial independence. This, and related issues about the administration of justice — particularly the extent of independence enjoyed by the Attorney-General — have intensified since the sacking of former Deputy Prime Minister Anwar in September 1998. Ther report, *Justice in Jeopardy: Malaysia 2000,* issued by four high profile international legal groups in April 2000, provides a detailed look at Malaysia's legal system, arguing that "there are well founded grounds for concern as to the proper administration of justice in Malaysia in cases which are of particular interest, for whatever reason, to the government".[22]

The scope of Malaysian civil courts is generally thought not to extend to aspects of Muslim personal law. For many years the two overlapped, but a 1988 constitutional amendment was believed to give Syariah courts exclusive jurisdiction over this area. However, in Anwar's and related court cases, legal arguments that sodomy is an offence under Syariah law failed to persuade judges that the charges belonged exclusively under the Syariah's jurisdiction.

Political Parties

One party — UMNO — has been at the forefront of Malaysian politics since 1946, though Malaysia is not a one-party state. It has maintained support by focusing on specifically Malay, communal interests. Initially it did this through the targeted dispersion of government funds, but since the 1970s its activities have been broadened to encompass a direct role in economic activities. It is now a mass party with a claimed 2.7 million members, and has consistently garnered a majority of peninsular Malay votes (except, probably, in 1969 and 1999). It remained confined to the peninsula until expanding to Sabah in 1991, and still has no presence in Sarawak. It has, as noted, faced and overcome several crises over the years, but events associated with the September 1998 sacking of Anwar Ibrahim pose the greatest threat yet.

UMNO has always held the main posts in cabinet. Its electoral clout has meant that after elections its President automatically becomes the Prime Minister. Traditionally, also, the Deputy President is regarded as the heir apparent to the top job. That nexus has only been broken once, when Musa Hitam resigned from the Deputy Prime Minister post in 1986 and retained his party post until elections the following year. Even the path to the Deputy Presidency has so far followed an ordered procedure. All Deputy Presidents — including those initially appointed in an acting capacity — have come from the three Vice-Presidents elected at triennial Assemblies. When Prime Minister Hussein Onn appeared inclined to depart from this tradition in 1975, the Vice-Presidents presented a joint ultimatum demanding that the choice be limited to one of them. The highest vote-getter is traditionally regarded as the senior Vice-President, but has no absolute right of advancement.

Still, UMNO has never ruled alone. It has done so through the Alliance, then the BN after 1974. The BN initially included the former Alliance members, and four former opposition parties. Membership has fluctuated, and at the time of writing numbers fourteen. Emphasizing the complexity of this arrangement, parties that are part of the BN at the federal level have not always been so in the states — the *Parti Bansa Dayak Sarawak* (Sarawak Dayak Party), for example, was for many years part of the federal coalition while excluded at the state level.

UMNO, or more accurately UMNO's leader, has always dominated these coalitions. Decisions within the Alliance and BN have been by unanimity, not majority vote. This meant, in practice, that deals were worked out behind the scenes, then formally endorsed by the coalition. UMNO's leadership derived from its critical role in securing independence and subsequent electoral dominance.

Nonetheless UMNO did provide opportunities to other parties to participate in government. Political scientists have described such communally-based co-operation as consociationalism. Rather than ethnic groups competing directly against one another — potentially dangerous — communal interests are resolved in the framework of a grand coalition.

The MCA, formed in 1949, has always been the second leading party in Malaysia. During most of the Alliance period its importance was reflected in its control of Finance, and Commerce and Industry portfolios, but under the BN these have gone to UMNO. The party is led by an English-educated business élite, and has always found difficulty attracting majority Chinese support, relying on UMNO Malays in many of its seats. MCA parliamentary representation has been subject to wild swings, but it has defied repeated predictions of its demise.

Gerakan (Movement) is a major MCA rival for Chinese support, but also an ally in the BN. It burst onto the scene in the 1969 elections, as a bold attempt to offer Malaysians a non-communal alternative to existing race-based parties. *Gerakan* gained few Malay votes, but attracted strong support from Chinese in the Penang area, and has headed state governments there ever since.

Indian interests in the BN are represented by the MIC, and East Malaysian interests by ever-changing coalitions and parties. With Indians comprising less that 10 per cent of the electorate, and no constituency with an Indian majority, the MIC has always relied heavily on UMNO benevolence.

Opposition parties have waxed and waned, but two have become permanent features. *Persatuan Islam Sa Tanah Melayu* (PAS), as noted earlier, was established in 1951 when the Islamic wing split from UMNO, and won the only non-Alliance seat in the 1955 election. It went on to win state government in Kelantan and Terengganu at the 1959 elections. Though it lost power through defections in Terengganu two years later, PAS has retained leadership of Kelantan (except for a period between

1977 and 1990), and regained Terengganu in 1999. It has maintained strong support from Malays in these northern states, plus Kedah and Perlis, on a political platform that has emphasized Islam and Malay rights, and has consistently polled 30 to 50 per cent of the peninsular Malay vote. In 1973 it was renamed *Parti Islam SeMalaysia* (retaining the acronym PAS, based on *jawi* characters).[23] A younger, more Islamic leadership took over in the early 1980s, but Malay nationalism has never been completely sidelined. The 1999 elections were its most successful ever. Benefiting from its identification with the cause of *reformasi*, it won 27 parliamentary seats, double its previous best performance, and emerged as the new opposition leader.

The Democratic Action Party (DAP) was established in 1966 as a successor to the People's Action Party of Singapore, a year after Singapore's expulsion from Malaysia. The DAP espoused a non-communal approach to Malaysian politics, but in the absence of significant Malay support directed most of its attention to non-Malays. In its early years it identified particularly with the defence of Chinese culture, language and education, attracting majority Chinese support on the peninsula until the overwhelming BN victory in 1995, and gaining a small foothold in Sabah and Sarawak. In recent years the DAP image has moderated, but it made only small electoral gains in the 1999 elections, and long-running leader Lim Kit Siang lost his parliamentary seat.

The predominantly Malay socialist party, *Parti Rakyat Malaysia* (PRM), has captured only a handful of parliamentary and assembly seats since its establishment in 1955. However some party leaders — including current head, retired academic Dr Syed Husin Ali — have been highly respected figures in Malay society, and independently exerted considerable political influence.

In the wake of Anwar's sacking the *Pergerakan Keadilan Social* (Social Justice Movement) or ADIL, led by Anwar's wife Wan Azizah, was launched in December 1998 as a specific vehicle for pro-Anwar reformists. Its leadership was mainly drawn from NGOs, particularly but by no means exclusively Malay Islamic groups such as ABIM. This transformed itself into the *Parti keADILan Nasional* (National Justice Party, or keADILan) in April 1999. It won five parliamentary and four state seats in the 1999 elections — Wan Azizah held Anwar's former seat with a majority of over 9,000 — a reasonable performance for a party barely eight months old.

Opposition parties have often co-operated during elections so that the anti-government vote would not be split. In 1999, however, four parties —

PAS, DAP, keADILan and PRM — formed a *Barisan Alternatif* (Alternative Front, or BA) and contested elections on a common platform. The BA has stayed together since, perhaps institutionalising a two coalition system in Malaysia.

State Ideology

Malaysia proclaimed the *Rukunegara* its official ideology on 31 August 1970, the thirteenth anniversary of independence. It was drawn up during Emergency rule, after deliberation by a 66-member National Consultative Council, established to address sensitive communal issues in the wake of the 1969 racial riots. Bearing an obvious indebtedness to Indonesia's *Pancasila* state ideology, it comprises: Belief in God; Loyalty to King and Country; Upholding the Constitution; Rule of Law; and Good Behaviour and Morality. In practice *Rukunegara* has not played a major role in Malaysian politics. It is taught in schools, its principles are not disputed, but its generality seems to have curtailed active use in public life.[24]

Outcomes of a National Cultural Congress in August 1971, convened by the government as a step towards defining a new national identity, also come close to representing an official ideology, though like the *Rukunegara* they have not been embedded in legislation. The three basic conclusions were that: national culture should be based on the original inhabitants (meaning Malays); Islam should be an important element of this culture; and other "suitable and appropriate cultural elements could also be accepted".[25] This left a great deal open in terms of the specifics of national culture, but it has been drawn on from time to time to reinforce the legitimacy of an essentially Malay national identity.

In popular form the slogan "*Bangsa, Agama, Negara*" (race, religion, nation) approximates a national ideology. UMNO leaders have used the slogan since the early days of the party, and political leaders instinctively resort to it whenever they wish to assert sincerity and selflessness. Though initially a purely Malay slogan, and still often used in this way, in recent years it has also been invoked before multi-ethnic audiences.

Civil Society and Human Rights

Malaysia has an array of institutions and organizations essential to the development of civil society, including a developed media, business organisations, trade unions, farmers, language and youth organisations. From the outset many of these were owned or controlled by the government.

Nonetheless, in the early years of independence civil society sometimes did play a significant role. The Malay and Chinese press were often critical of the government, at least until the main Malay newspaper, *Utusan Melayu*, was taken over by UMNO in 1961. Trade unions led occasional strikes. Chinese language and Malay language organizations campaigned actively on behalf of their respective causes. Student organizations centred at the University of Malaya — particularly the Malay Language Society (*Persatuan Bahasa Melayu Universiti Malaya*) and the National Union of Islamic Students (*Persatuan Kebangsaan Pelajar-pelajar Islam Malaysia*) — began to flex muscles after Anwar Ibrahim began studies in 1967.

Some of this activism heightened communal tension, and thus contributed to the increase in laws that curtailed civil society after the 1969 riots. Media freedom was also restricted by UMNO's take-over of the other major Malay paper, *Berita Harian*, and its English-language parent, the *New Straits Times*, in 1972. The remaining English and Chinese newspapers also came under control of UMNO allies around this period.

Nonetheless the 1970s also saw the establishment of several new organizations, and expanded activities by others established earlier. Among the more important were ABIM, which built a mass following under Anwar Ibrahim's leadership, *Aliran* (*Aliran Kesedaran Negara*, or National Consciousness Movement), the Penang Consumer's Society, Women's Aid Organisation, and the Environment Protection Society. Such organizations began to campaign strongly on issues such as corruption, protection of the poor, care for the environment, and the expansion of democracy. This provoked a strong government reaction, including the arrest and 22-month detention of Anwar under the ISA in late 1974. Even stronger government action followed in 1987, when a wide range of NGO leaders were amongst those detained under the ISA.

NGOs were intimidated by the 1987 actions, but did not fade away. *Suaram* (Suara Rakyat Malaysia, or Voice of the Malaysian People) was established in direct response to these developments. The Bar Council of Malaysia emerged as a strong government critic in the wake of the judicial sackings in 1988. Others, such as the International Movement for a Just World (JUST) and *Hakam* (*Persatuan Kebangsaan Hak Asasi Manusia*, or National Human Rights Society), were established in the 1990s. The 1990s also saw the expansion of newspapers, new editorially independent intellectual journals, and greater daring among the existing papers and television channels, particularly in the immediate aftermath of the economic crisis.

This *glasnost* was only allowed for a short while. The mainstream media was brought into line just before Anwar Ibrahim's dismissal. The government did legislate to establish ostensibly independent watchdogs in charge of consumer protection and human rights (Human Rights Commission), but without first seeking public views. NGOs immediately expressed scepticism over their independence and effectiveness, though the appointment of former Deputy Prime Minister Musa Hitam as head of the Commission was welcomed. NGOs have, however, continued to play a major role in support of Anwar's position, many making their views know through the Internet as other avenues were closed.

The rights of Malaysians to participate in civil society, and protection of basic civil liberties, are spelt out at length under the second part of the Constitution, headed Fundamental Liberties. But virtually all of these freedoms are qualified by an overriding right of the government to decide otherwise if it wishes, in the interests of national security or public order. The steady expansion of executive power since independence has, in practice, left very few guarantees of individual liberties.

MAJOR POLITICAL ISSUES

Centralized Power Structure

Malaysian leaders frequently assert that Malaysia is a democracy, and power rests with the people, because elections are held at least every five years. While democracy obviously involves more than elections, there is some substance to these claims.

All Malaysian governments have sought to enhance legitimacy by maximizing their vote. Moreover, governments must get a two thirds majority in the *Dewan Rakyat* — this is necessary for the practical reason of amending the constitution, but is also a psychological measuring stick of government performance. The last four elections, particularly in 1999 when UMNO was weakened by the "Anwar affair", were all widely seen as providing opportunities to deprive the BN of its two thirds majority. A divided Malay electorate — with over 30 per cent always voting for PAS or parties such as Semangat '46 — has forced the BN to offer incentives to all, and prevented any complacency. At the state level the electorate has even been able to change governments, a frequently cited measuring stick of democracy.

Besides elections, Malaysia's civil society has, as noted above, asserted some influence over government decisions. Notwithstanding official hostility, NGOs continue to make their views known and have gained sufficient backing to ensure that the government takes some notice.

Malaysian leaders have also defined their approach to development as involving a partnership between three sides: the government (political leaders and bureaucrats), private entrepreneurs, and labour. This implies that for major decisions in areas such as infrastructure development, power is shared between the three partners. Malaysia has offered its expertise on "smart partnerships", or Malaysia Inc, to the world.[26]

The idea of Malaysia Inc has also attracted the critical attention of many writers who argue that it reflects not partnership but "cronyism".[27] Labour certainly has no significant say in decision-making; its role is essentially confined to ensuring minimum standards of employment and industrial harmony. Business leaders may be influential at times, but they are so heavily dependent on state favours for privatization awards, other government contracts, and government and banking loans, that the relationship is an asymmetrical one. And in many cases businessmen cannot be seen as independent since they hold high office in government parties.

In a broad sense it is obviously true that political power rests largely with Malays. As noted, since independence, and particularly after 1969, they were able to use their numbers and indigenous status to entrench their political power. Since Malay dominance is exercized largely through UMNO, it is important to ask where power is located in this party.

UMNO's rank and file do have some influence. Triennial party elections have traditionally been keenly contested, and are often regarded as more significant than national elections in determining Malaysia's political course. Once the party head (President) has been chosen he is seldom challenged, though as noted Dr Mahathir was in 1987 and survived narrowly. The Deputy President position — which provides the assumed heir apparent — has been contested more frequently, and the three directly elected Vice President posts are always contested.

Nonetheless, the powers enjoyed by the UMNO President are extensive. Since 1960 UMNO's constitution has been amended several times, on each occasion concentrating more power in the hands of the executive (Supreme Council) and particularly the party head.[28] Amendments added in December 1998 included giving the Supreme Council powers to suspend party elections for up to 18 months — a right that was quickly invoked — and making the president's position more secure by requiring that nominations come from at least 30 per cent of the party's 165 Divisions.

The President has enormous powers of patronage. He approves all candidates for national elections. He appoints fifteen of the 47 Supreme Council members, and state party leaders. He has influence over his deputy's post, either through indicating support for a particular candidate, or making an "acting" appointment when the post has become vacant (by death, or in Anwar Ibrahim's case, through expulsion) between Assemblies. Tun Razak appointed Hussein Onn acting deputy, Hussein Onn did the same for Dr Mahathir, and Dr Mahathir appointed Abdullah Badawi to "carry out" deputy president functions (without a formal title) — though these acting appointments were later approved by the Assembly.

The President, wearing his other hat as Prime Minister, selects State leaders (Mentri Besar and Chief Ministers) and the Cabinet. Once a top party position was a guarantee of ministerial preferment, but Dr Mahathir has set aside this aspect of party tradition. As Prime Minister he also presides over an extensive and ever growing array of powers to take action against individuals or organizations. He maximized his powers in this regard by holding the Home Affairs Ministry from 1986 to January 1999. In addition, as the top figure in Malaysia Inc he is in a critical position to facilitate business opportunities. After the 1987 split, and again in 1998, the losing side soon found credit facilities and business opportunities drying up.

Finally, the UMNO leader and other leaders, benefit from the cult of loyalty deeply embedded in Malay society. While subtle indications of dissent are permitted, open defiance of UMNO leaders has been rare. Dr Mahathir has invoked this tradition within UMNO since the sacking of Anwar, though broad public opposition suggests that future leaders may face a more critical grassroots.

In recent years Dr Mahathir has used all available advantages to restrict opportunities for the rank and file. UMNO Assemblies have been increasingly managed so as to preclude contests and campaigning, with no contests for the top two positions at the last two meetings (1996 and 2000). Proceedings have done little more endorse the President's leadership.

Authoritarianism in Malaysia pre-dates Dr Mahathir, but he has carried the process forward substantially. Dr Mahathir maintains that he had tried to be liberal until 1987 — when he was challenged in UMNO, and faced resurgent social unrest — but was therafter forced to take a tougher approach. He has continued to amend the Constitution, and add to the collection of laws that enhance executive power and reduce individual rights. And since sacking Anwar he has used state power more transparently than ever to resist the opposition.

Who Benefits?

From the discussion thus far it is apparent that in many respects Malays have been major beneficiaries of the Malaysian political system. Malays dominate politics. And prominent symbols of a Malay state, along with the Malay/*bumiputra* "special position", are enshrined in the Constitution. Nonetheless, the question of who benefits is more complex than these facts might suggest.

In the period before the racial clashes of 1969 non-Malay (and foreign) interests were well taken care of by the close relations top members of the MCA and MIC had with Prime Minister Tunku Abdul Rahman. Business and educational opportunities were largely unrestricted. The state funded Chinese-medium schools at the primary level, English remained an important language of education and government, and government attempts to address problems of Malay economic backwardness made limited headway.

Post-May 1969 changes, including the introduction of the NEP in 1971 changed this, reinforcing Malay political dominance and giving a strong impetus to Malay participation in business and the professions. Still, growth benefited all communities. Per capita GNP went from RM1,142 in 1970 to RM12,102 in 1997. Absolute poverty in the same period declined from around 50 per cent of the population to 6.8 per cent, along with improvements in a wide range of social indicators such as infant mortality, life expectancy, and school enrolments. Subsidies on basic food items kept the cost of living low. Income distribution also improved, with the Gini index over the same period going from 51.3 to 44.6. Inequality between races also declined. The 1970 monthly mean income for Malay households in peninsula Malaysia was 44 per cent that of Chinese and 56 per cent that of Indians; by 1987 the respective percentages were 61 and 80.[29]

Making use of education and commercial opportunities under the NEP, *bumiputra* participation expanded rapidly in the professions and the business sector — though they remain under-represented. For the period 1970–1990 *bumiputra* accountants increased from 7 to 14 per cent, engineers from 7 to 35 per cent, doctors from 4 per cent to 28 per cent and architects from 4 to 24 per cent.[30] *Bumiputra* participation in the share market — often misleadingly cited as a measurement of overall community wealth — reportedly rose from around 2 to 20 per cent, while non *bumiputra* (mainly Chinese) went from 37 per cent to 46 per cent and the foreign sector declined.[31]

For the UMNO leadership a major apparent success was the creation of a Malay entrepreneurial class able to compete with Chinese counterparts. Initially state institutions were set up to invest in private companies as trustees for Malays. Then UMNO-linked companies began to assume a more direct business role, starting with the purchase of the *New Straits Times* newspaper group in 1972. This process was accelerated by the intensification of privatization from the mid-1980s, signalled particularly by the awarding of a US$1.3 billion contract to build the North-South highway to UMNO-linked United Engineers in 1987. By the end of the 1980s the accepted truism that the Chinese dominated the economy no longer held. Benefits trickled down to smaller Malay companies through the UMNO network, and UMNO became an organization based to a large extent on its powers of patronage. The provision of special funding arrangements, and guaranteed income, appeared to make such projects fail-safe. The down-sides to such policies — including the development of a class dependent on state patronage and unable to stand alone — became apparent after the crisis of July 1997, but were seldom perceived before then.

Many non-Malays also welcomed these changes. They too benefited from privatization projects, and in a variety of other ways. In particular they welcomed expanded opportunities for English-medium education in private schools, the establishment of twinning arrangements with foreign universities that substantially reduced the costs of overseas education, and the expansion of English-medium courses in local universities. These changes were formalized in the passage of five education-related bills in 1996.

While the benefits were widespread there remained pockets of "hardcore poor", particularly among "aborigines" (*orang asli*), and *bumiputra* in Sabah and Sarawak. And many paid a price for the turbo-charged speed of development. As noted, the rapid urbanization of the Malay community brought numerous social ills in its wake. The environment suffered at the hands of developers, loggers and others, causing outrage when deforestation led to flash floods that cut roads and collapsed large apartment blocks. Corruption in the bureaucracy and money politics in UMNO escalated. A tearful Dr Mahathir warned the UMNO Assembly in 1996 that such activities could ruin the country. And the income distribution gains made earlier, together with the narrowing of the racial gap, began to reverse in the 1990s. The Gini index went from 44.6 in 1990 to 46.4 in 1995 (or higher, see Figure 5.2). Intra-ethnic income differences broadened rapidly, particularly amongst Malays. The gap between Chinese and Malays also rose, and by 1997 Chinese family incomes were rising twice as fast as their Malay counterparts.[32]

The 1997–98 economic crisis affected particularly the corporate sector, which ran up massive debts, and government services. It also had important implications for areas such as education and health in the long run. But the population was largely shielded from major difficulties. Wages were generally maintained, and unemployment and inflation did not exceed 5 per cent.

Extent of Legitimacy?

The Malaysian political system has faced two major challenges to its legitimacy, the first with the election and subsequent racial riots of 1969, and the second in the wake of Anwar Ibrahim's sacking. At most other times strong electoral support for the governing coalition, and the absence of social unrest, has indicated a high degree of public support.

Events in 1969 reflected a challenge from both non-Malays and Malays. Non-Malays voted against the governing coalition to demand a greater say in government, and more concessions on issues such as Chinese language and education. Malays sought government adherence to constitutional provisions upholding the Malay nature of the country — in particular Malay as the official language — and greater assistance in areas such as education and the economy.

After 13 May a more Malay-oriented system was established, which satisfied most Malays, but initially left many non-Malays unhappy. However in practice these policies, particularly the NEP, improved Malay opportunities without, generally, depriving non-Malays — the happy result of a rapidly expanding economic pie. This, along with changes in language and educational policies noted above, changed non-Malay attitudes. The 1995 election victory was a strong endorsement of the legitimacy of the political system and the ruling BN. For the first time ever, a majority of non-Malays voted for the governing coalition.

After the economic crisis began in July 1997 Malaysia's political system again came under intense scrutiny in the media, particularly the Malay press. Analysts broadly agreed that some changes would have to be made. Cronyism should end, and good bureaucratic and corporate governance, along with civil society, be promoted. Many writers echoed Indonesian calls for *reformasi*, for transparency (*ketelusan*), and an end to KKN.

Anwar's sacking strengthened such concerns, and gave rise to an unprecedented outpouring of public protest. In the closing months of 1998, and in 1999, tens, perhaps hundreds of thousands took part in protests across the country. Mass arrests, and increasingly strong police measures to control protests — including tear gas and chemically-laced water sprays — limited opposition, but never looked like stopping it, as similar measures had in the past. An alternative media, represented by the PAS newspaper *Harakah*, independent weekly/monthly broadsheets, and several pro-*reformasi* sites on the Internet, maintained a stream of critical analysis of government policies and actions. From detention, Anwar maintained a blistering attack on government leaders through articles posted on the Internet, interviews, court statements and five police reports, with supporting documentation alleging corruption by Dr Mahathir and close associates. The various court cases involving Anwar, the Royal Commission into his bashing while under police custody, and a host of new police reports, statutory declarations and mega-dollar law suits added to tensions. The 1999 elections — the worst ever for UMNO, and the best ever for PAS and its allies — confirmed the obvious, that the government had lost much legitimacy in the eyes of Malays. Many non-Malays in urban areas also supported *reformasi* candidates, though overall non-Malays continued to support the government.

Three factors made this crisis quite different to others in the past. The economic decline in 1998 was more severe than any previously experienced, and laid bare shortcomings in the Malaysia Inc model. Secondly, it marked the coming out of a new middle-class, particularly Malays, who were critical of the excesses and autocratic ways of older leaders. Many were influenced in earlier years by idealistic organizations such as ABIM. Thirdly the government mishandled its case against Anwar — no former leader was ever publicly shamed as he has been, contravening entrenched Malay values against such behaviour — and Anwar surprised by the strength of his counterattack.

Governance

Until July 1997 Malaysia was generally credited with a long history of sound, conservative economic management, reinforced by a decade of outstanding growth rates. The World Bank, and others, held it up as an exemplar of the "Asian Miracle". Planners had drawn up numerous economic plans — including various five-year plans, the NEP and National Development Policy — and had implemented them successfully. Prime Minister Mahathir had proclaimed a widely applauded Vision 2020 seeking to propel Malaysia to the status of an industrialized country.

Critics now claim that Malaysian achievements were a mirage, and that fundamental weaknesses in the nature of its "crony capitalism" explain why it succumbed to the regional crisis. Dr Mahathir and his supporters respond that cronyism had nothing to do with it, and that international speculators caused the crash by forcing down the Malaysian currency and stock market. The truth probably lies somewhere in between.

Malaysia Inc did have shortcomings, as many Malaysians have come to acknowledge. There was a lack of transparency in deals between the government and private sector, and in the activities of the stock market. Too many businesses were highly leveraged, with debt as a proportion of GDP around 150 per cent. Loans were often based more on political connections than strict economic criteria, and were used for less productive investment in areas such as prestigious shopping centres, housing and the stock market. Corruption had also become deeply entrenched among both political leaders and sections of the bureaucracy. A lack of transparency caused worries about this. Cabinet ministers were required to declare assets to Dr Mahathir from 1986, but details were never publicly released.

Still, the 1997 mass exodus of investors out of the Malaysian currency and stock market in a herd-like manner was unrelated to fundamentals or the ills listed above — as a rapid return of investors in 1999 demonstrated. And the exodus did contribute substantially to the economic plunge in 1998.

Malaysia's corporate sector remains deeply mired in debt, and this will limit attempts to reform both the private and public sectors. Some reforms are going ahead, such as in consolidating the financial sector, and improving regulatory control over the Kuala Lumpur Stock Exchange, but progress is slow and apparently constrained by political considerations. Similarly, corruption appears to be an issue that is responded to quickly when government critics are involved, but the Anti Corruption Agency moves cautiously when government supporters are the target.

Little immediate progress is likely in the area of participation. Despite initiatives to establish institutions such as the Human Rights Commission, the government remains fundamentally wary of NGOs, and committed to top-down planning. However civil society has grown stronger, and may be able to exert more influence over future leaders.

Malaysia generally measures well on other indices of governance. Personal security is high, with crime rates moderate, and the probability of disruptive social unrest low. Even at the height of the economic crisis, and the Anwar affair, communal tensions were not inflamed. Basic needs in such areas as education, housing, health and transport have been a focus of successive governments. The record is not perfect, but it registers favourably on any international comparison.

MALAYSIA INC UNDER CHALLENGE

In 1957 Malaya began independence as a relatively liberal democracy, though with a constitution and electoral arrangements that gave a "special position" to Malays. In the first decade conflict revolved largely around a range of communal issues — Malay-Chinese rivalry over political influence, and issues such as education, national language and economic opportunities — particularly after Singapore joined Malaysia in 1963. Most accounts at this time used concepts such as "communalism" or "consociationalism" to explain politics,[33] and these factors have remained important through to the present day. Two qualifications to this consensus should however be noted. First, class factors were also at play — the ruling Alliance was led by an élite from each of the three major communities, and the split between UMNO and PAS in part reflected social divisions in the Malay polity. Secondly, liberal forms did not run as deep as many accounts assumed. Prime Minister Tunku Abdul Rahman exercised strong dominance over both the state and UMNO, and executive power was enhanced by passage of the ISA, and developments such as erosion of the Election Commission's independence.

The 1969 riots marked a watershed in Malaysian politics. UMNO emerged from this as a rejuvenated and much stronger organization, though party leaders could still impose their will with relative ease if they wanted to. UMNO insisted that others recognize Malay preeminence, introduced affirmative action for Malays through the NEP, broadened state participation in the economy, and began to go into business ventures of its own. Communalism and consociationalism remained the favoured analytical concepts, but took on an entirely new meaning in the face of overwhelming UMNO dominance, and a dramatic expansion in the role of the executive.

After Dr Mahathir came to power in 1981 these developments were taken even further with a shift towards a developmental state in the Northeast Asian mould. The political leadership, the bureaucracy and the private sector were merged in a seamless way to ensure co-operation in achieving manufacturing-led economic growth, and political hegemony for UMNO and Dr Mahathir. Malaysia Inc perhaps went even further than these states in using privatization for this purpose, and UMNO direct involvement in business was also greater, with the possible exception of the Kuomintang in Taiwan. This model faltered briefly during recession in the mid-1980s, but after narrowly fending off a challenge to his leadership in 1987, and jousting with the judiciary in 1988, Dr Mahathir and UMNO emerged with even tighter political control. Analytical works at this time began to give less emphasis to communalism, and focus on the workings of Malaysia Inc (particularly the business activities of UMNO), the political philosophy and practice of Dr Mahathir, and the nature of Malaysia's "semi democracy".[34]

In the early 1990s Malaysia Inc appeared immutable, particularly after a record government win in the 1995 general elections. The economic crisis, and fallout from the sacking of Anwar Ibrahim have, however, led to profound changes, the implications of which are still being analysed and debated. Opposition to the government and to Dr Mahathir personally has been mobilised as never before. Traditional measures of repression have not been effective, and new developments such as the Internet make it possible for anti-government groups to sustain opposition in ways that were not previously available. In the 1999 general elections Malays deserted the government, depriving UMNO of the traditional source of its political preeminence, and leaving much uncertainty about the future.

Notes

1 The dispute between Dr Mahathir and Anwar is examined in detail in John Funston, "Malaysia: A Fateful September", *Southeast Asian Affairs 1999*, edited by Daljit Singh and John Funston (Singapore: ISEAS, 1999), pp. 165–84.

2 For further details see John Funston, "Malaysia's Tenth Election: Status Quo, *Reformasi* or Islamisation?" *Contemporary Southeast Asia* 22, no.1 (April 2000): 23–59.

3 Percentages are calculated from Department of Statistics, *Monthly Statistical Bulletin, Malaysia*, October 1998.

4 See Zainah Anwar, *Islamic Revivalism in Malaysia* (Petaling Jaya: Pelanduk Publications, 1987).

5 Mahathir bin Mohamad, *The Malay Dilemma* (Singapore: Asia Pacific Press, 1970), p. 11.

6 The *Agong* had 30 days to give assent, failing which he would be deemed to have done so. If, however, in this time he returned the bill for reconsideration, his assent was required within 30 days once parliament had returned the bill a second time. See, Harold Crouch, *Government and Society in Malaysia* (St. Leonards: Allen & Unwin, and Ithaca: Cornell University, 1996), pp. 144–46.

7 The full cabinet can be found on the Internet at <http://www.smpke.jpm.my/govern/federal.html>.

8 For details on the Internet see <http://www.smpke.jpm.my/about2.htm>.

9   *Straits Times*, 22 November 1997.

10 John Funston, *Malay Politics in Malaysia. A Study of UMNO and Party Islam* (Kuala Lumpur: Heinemann Educational Books [Asia] Ltd, 1980), pp. 255–56.

11 Privatization was generally conducted on a "first come, first served" basis. This policy gave companies the opportunity to come up with initiatives of their own. If these were accepted the company then had a special opportunity to negotiate detailed arrangements with the government.

12 Reported by Reuters, citing a parliamentary report, in *Sydney Morning Herald*, 22 September 1998.

13 Harold Crouch, *Government and Society in Malaysia*, p. 135.

14 Ibid, p. 137.

15 Andrew Harding, *Law, Government and the Constitution in Malaysia* (London: Kluwer Law International, 1996), p. 248.

16 The current Prime Minister had such facts in mind three decades ago when he wrote: "In the main, Parliamentary sittings were regarded as a pleasant formality which afforded members opportunities to be heard and quoted, but which would have absolutely no effect on the course of the Government .... The sittings were a concession to a superfluous democratic practice. Its main value lay in the opportunity to flaunt Government strength". Mahathir Mohamad, *The Malay Dilemma*, p. 11.

17 See <http://www.parlimen.gov.my/bi.htm>. The site was launched in 1996; by early 1999 its most recent update was February 1997.

18 S. Sothi Rachagan, *Law and the Electoral Process in Malaysia* (Kuala Lumpur: University of Malaya Press, 1993), p. 39.

19 John Funston, "Malaysia's Tenth Elections", p. 48.

20 See, for example, Tommy Thomas, "The Role of the Judiciary", in *Reflections on the Malaysian Constitution*, published by the Persatuan Aliran Kesedaran Negara (Aliran: Penang, 1987), pp. 97–100.

21 Rais Yatim, *Freedom Under Executive Power in Malaysia* (Kuala Lumpur: Endowment Publications, 1995), p. 355.

22 *Justice in Jeopardy: Malaysia 2000*. Report of a mission on behalf of the International Bar Association, ICJ Centre for the Independence of Judges and Lawyers, Commonwealth Lawyers Association, Union Internationale. (Released on 5 April 2000), p. 77. On Anwar's prosecution, the report expresses concern over the appointment of a very junior judge in the first case, and eight different rulings made by that judge (p. 48).

23 Many accounts say that the acronym PAS started in the 1970s, and the party was previously known as the Pan Malayan/sian Islamic Party on PMIP. This is incorrect. PMIP is indeed an acronym for the English translation of the various party titles, but in Malay PAS and its extensions have always been used. English usage eventually caught up with Malay practice.

24 For a more detailed discussion, see John Funston, *Malay Politics in Malaysia* pp. 219–21.

25 Ibid, p.265.

26 The Langkawi International Dialogue has been held annually since 1995, attracting up to 350 participants from international business and government. The 1997 meeting had 11 heads of government. *Straits Times*, 28 July 1997.

27 See Edmund Gomez and Jomo K.S., *Malaysia's Political Economy. Politics, Patronage and Profits* (Cambridge: Cambridge University Press, 1997). Both authors have numerous other works on related topics.

28 UMNO's organization structure and changes through to the mid-1970s are discussed in John Funston, *Malay Politics in Malaysia*, pp. 168–72, 235–36.

28 See Zainal Aznam Yusof, "Income Distribution in Malaysia", Paper presented to the Australia-Malaysia Conference, 19–21 November 1997, Canberra, Australia; and Harold Crouch, *Government and Society in Malaysia*, pp. 189–91.

30 From *Laporan Majlis Perundingan Ekonomi Negara*, Kerajaan Malaysia, Kuala Lumpur, 1991, and quoted in a Working Paper by Zainal Abidin Abdul Wahid, "Perkembangan Pendidikan Dan Masa Depan Malaysia" (seminar and date not cited).

31 Harold Crouch, *Government and Society in Malaysia*, chapter 11. However, many assumptions behind these calculations are questionable, and at best they can be accepted as broad indicators. (On the 1970 figures, see John Funston, *Malay Politics in Malaysia*, p. 260.) Figures released by the Kuala Lumpur Stock Exchange in 1998 claim *bumiputra* share ownership of 28.6 per cent in 1990 and 36.7 per cent in 1996, with non-*bumiputra* holding 46.2 per cent and 44.1 per cent. *Business Times* (Singapore), 28 February–1 March 1998.

32 See Zainal Aznam Yusof, "Income Distribution in Malaysia", pp. 7–10.

33 The classic account on communalism is K.J. Ratnam, *Comunalism and the Political Process in Malaya* (Singapore: University of Malaya Press, 1965). On consociationalism, see particularly Diane K. Mauzy, *Barisan Nasional: Coalition Government in Malaysia* (Kuala Lumpur: Maricans, 1983).

34 See, for instance, Edmund Gomez and Jomo K.S., *Malaysia's Political Economy. Politics, Patronage and Profits;* Khoo Boo Teik, *Paradoxes of Mahathirism. An Intellectual Biography of Mahathir Mohamad* (Kuala Lumpur: Oxford University Press, 1995); Peter Searle, *The Riddle of Malaysian Capitalism. Rent Seekers or Real Capitalists?* (St. Leonards: Allen & Unwin, 1999); R.S. Milne and Diane K. Mauzy, *Malaysian Politics Under Mahathir.* (London: Routlege, 1999); Harold Crouch, *Government and Society in Malaysia.*

Further Reading

Crouch, Harold. *Government and Society in Malaysia.* St. Leonards: Allen & Unwin, and Ithaca: Cornell University, 1996.

Funston, John. *Malay Politics in Malaysia. A Study of UMNO and Party Islam.* Kuala Lumpur: Heinemann Educational Books [Asia] Ltd, 1980.

Gomez, Edmund and Jomo K.S. *Malaysia's Political Economy. Politics, Patronage and Profits.* Cambridge: Cambridge University Press, 1997.

Harding, Andrew. *Law, Government and the Constitution in Malaysia.* London: Kluwer Law International, 1996.

Kahn, Joel S. & Francis Loh Kok Wah. *Fragmented Vision. Culture and Politics in Contemporary Malaysia* St. Leonards: Allen & Unwin, 1992.

Khoo Boo Teik. *Paradoxes of Mahathirism. An Intellectual Biography of Mahathir Mohamad.* Kuala Lumpur: Oxford University Press, 1995.

Milne, R.S. and Diane K. Mauzy. *Malaysian Politics Under Mahathir.* London: Routledge, 1999.

Searle, Peter. *The Riddle of Malaysian Capitalism. Rent Seekers or Real Capitalists?* St. Leonards: Allen & Unwin, 1999.

Rachagan, S. Sothi. *Law and the Electoral Process in Malaysia.* Kuala Lumpur: University of Malaya Press, 1993.

Ratnam, K.J. *Commundism and the Political Process in Malaya.* Singapore: University of Malaya Press, 1965.

Zainah, Anwar. *Islamic Revivalism in Malaysia.* Petaling Jaya: Pelanduk Publications, 1987.

6

MYANMAR
Military in Charge

Tin Maung Maung Than

INTRODUCTION

Myanmar is perhaps the most controversial country in Southeast Asia. The legitimacy and the authority of the ruling junta have been contested since its inception in 1988, not only by the legally constituted political opposition and a constellation of illegal or unlawful organizations, insurgents and expatriate groups, but also by some Western states and non-governmental organizations as well. Even its name is in dispute — many foreigners and expatriates prefer Burma, the accepted designation from colonial times until changed by the junta in June 1989.

Myanmar nation-building began around the 11th century with the establishment of Bamar (formerly known as Burman) hegemony over other indigenous "nations", but was interrupted by British conquest, completed in 1885. The traditional concept of dynastic rule and legitimate authority goes back much further in time and was influenced by Buddhist and Hinduistic concepts of leadership. Despite personalized rule, a tradition of righteous kingship guided by moral and ethical codes of conduct served as a counterbalance to despotic tendencies of absolutist rule.

When the country was governed as a province of British India "Burma proper" was separated from the "frontier areas" (half the country comprising the Arakan hill tracts to the West and the hill areas bordering China, Laos and Thailand in the North and East) by the colonial administration. The latter came under indirect rule, whereby local ethnic chieftains were allowed to maintain their power and status. Thus an opportunity for the indigenous nationalities to develop a sense of belonging and bonding culminating in an "imagined community"[1] that could forge a modern nation-state out of disparate ethnic nations was lost.

The society in colonial Myanmar developed into a "three-tiered pyramid" with "a small British group of civil servants, soldiers and businessmen" at the apex.[2] The middle class "was composed of Burmese, Indians, and Anglo-Burmans, as well as a few Chinese and Europeans" while the "worker and peasant class, approximately 95 per cent of the population ... was racially divided between Burmese, mostly peasants ... and Indians, mostly coolies and industrial workers".[3] The influx of Indian migrant labour, following the opening of the rice frontier in the Ayeyarwady (Irrawaddy) delta during the second half of the nineteenth century, was a significant feature of the economic re-organization carried out by the colonial government. Even after separation from India in 1937, the economic role of Indians remained a source of resentment reinforcing nationalist sentiments up to the 1960s.

Most members of the Myanmar élite remained unexposed to the philosophical and conceptual foundations of Western political thought (democratic or otherwise) until well into the twentieth century, when many anti-colonialists became influenced by socialist ideas. World War II brought Japanese militarism and fascist practices into Myanmar. The subsequent anti-Japanese resistance and the successful confrontation with the British bestowed fame and glory to the new politico-military élite (mainly Bamars) and legitimated them as the saviours of independent Myanmar. In July 1947, Myanmar's independence movement suffered a most traumatic tragedy when Bogyoke Aung San, regarded as the prime mover of the movement and national hero, was gunned down with members of his legislative assembly by political assassins. The experience under fascist rule and the assassination of Aung San together with the influence of "leftist" ideology over the nationalist élite, who became the major protagonists in post-independent Myanmar, created a historical legacy which introduced considerable tensions into the post-independence political process.

After independence in 1948, the state was established as a parliamentary democracy under the Constitution adopted the previous year. It was a union comprising the central government and state (provincial) governments in a bicameral legislature in which states inhabited by non-Bamar ethnic groups were given some local autonomy. The Anti-Fascist People's Freedom League (AFPFL) — the national front that was formed as a clandestine resistance movement against Japanese occupation — dominated the Myanmar political arena for a decade and formed successive governments after winning elections in 1947, 1951 and 1956.

In the first three years of independence the AFPFL government, and its outnumbered armed forces, had to overcome overwhelming odds to survive the onslaught of Communist and ethnic rebellions that erupted soon after independence. Once the danger of civil war had subsided, differences amongst the leaders of the AFPFL became more accentuated and an internecine power struggle within the AFPFL led to its break-up into two factions in 1958, and attempts to draw the military into the fray. In September, as the danger of violent conflict between the contenders for state power loomed large, the prime minister invited (albeit under pressure) the head of the armed forces to form a non-partisan caretaker government mandated with the task of holding free and fair elections.

The overwhelming election victory of the so-called "clean faction" over the rival "stable faction" of the AFPFL in the elections of February 1960 did not bring about political stability, as the winner was beset by an intra-party feuding within a year. Meanwhile, ethnic-based politicians demanded more autonomy for their states, and some threatened to secede (allowed by the constitution after a period of ten years following independence) if they could not secure substantial concessions form the central government. In March 1962, the armed forces leader General Ne Win staged a coup and established the ruling Revolutionary Council (RC), justifying the take-over as a pre-emptive measure to avoid national disintegration.

The RC formed a cadre party called the Burma Socialist Programme Party (BSPP) and restructured state and society into a socialist mould guided by an eclectic approach known as the Burmese Way to Socialism (BWS); a blend of Buddhism, nationalism and Marxist philosophy. Public political activities were banned. The depoliticization of the citizens and reassertion of the state was deemed necessary to start afresh with an ideology true to the goals and aspirations of the pre-independence progenitors of national socialist ideals.

In 1974, the junta handed over power to an elected government in accordance with a new constitution that established a one-party socialist unitary state. The state was led by the BSPP, transformed into a mass party in 1971. Representation was based on a four-tier hierarchy, elected on a quadrennial basis, for the People's Councils (ward/village, township, and state/division) and the unicameral *Pyithu Hluttaw* (people's assembly). However, given the BSPP's prerogative of nominating "official" candidates, elections implied confirmation rather than competition. All central organs of state power operated under the leadership and guidance of the BSPP. Similarly, the territorial hierarchy of People's Councils were led and guided by the party organizations at the corresponding level. This system lasted for 14 years, and atrophied before it was toppled by a popular upheaval that swept through urban Myanmar during August and September 1988.[4]

FIGURE 6.1

Myanmar: Key Dates

900	Bagan, the first Bamar kingdom was established.
1824	First war with Britain. Rakhine (Arakan) and Tanintharyi (Tenasserim) were ceded to Britain. The rest of Myanmar annexed after further wars in 1852 and 1885.
1941	The Burma Independence Army (BIA), precursor of the present *Tatmadaw* was established in Bangkok under Japanese tutelage. Japan invaded Myanmar together with the BIA in 1942.
1945	The Myanmar armed forces led by General Aung San revolt against the Japanese occupiers.
1947	General Aung San and six members of the government Executive Council assassinated. New constitution adopted, establishing parliamentary democracy.
1948	Myanmar granted independence by Britain. Anti-Fascist People's Freedom League (AFPFL) leader U Nu becomes the first prime minister. Ethnic and communist insurgencies becomes the main focus of government attention for next decade.
1958	Following splits in the AFPFL, U Nu agrees to hand over power to a caretaker government led by the *Tatmadaw* (military) commander-in-chief General Ne Win.
1960	U Nu's Union Party wins the elections.
1962	General Ne Win stages a coup, forming the military Revolutionary Council (RC). The Burmese Way to Socialism announced as the national ideology. The Burma Socialist Programme Party (BSPP) established as a cadre party.
1971	Burma Socialist Programme Party (BSPP) transformed into a mass party at the First Party Congress.
1974	New constitution instituting a one-party socialist state adopted after overwhelming endorsement in a national referendum. Retired General Ne Win becomes first president of the new regime.
1981	U Ne Win relinquishes the presidency, but retains the BSPP Chairmanship.
1987	Demonetization of the majority of bank notes in circulation creating resentment amongst the polity.
1988	Tea-shop brawl in March leads to rioting and demonstrations in Yagon by tertiary students. Security forces repel violently. Student-led demonstrations resume in the capital Yangon in June, and extend throughout the country in July and August. General Saw Maung, the *Tatmadaw* commander-in-chief takes power in the name of the State Law and Order Restoration Council (SLORC) in September. The National League for Democracy (NLD) founded by Daw Aung San Suu Kyi and associates the same month.
1989	Daw Aung San Suu Ky placed under house arrest in July.
1990	General elections on 27 May. NLD wins 80 per cent of seats and 60 per cent of votes. In July, SLORC Declaration No. 1/90 spells out steps towards civilian rule that precluded transfer of power to the NLD. The National Coalition Government of the Union of Burma (NCGUB), led by dissident NLD members, formed in exile at a rebel camp on the Thai-Myanmar border.
1991	Daw Aung San Suu Kyi awarded the Nobel Peace Prize.
1992	Junta Chairman General Saw Maung replaced by Gen. Than Shwe.
1993	SLORC convenes the National Convention (NC) in January to draw up the principles for a new constitution.
1995	Daw Aung San Suu Kyi released from house arrest in July.
1996	NC begins indefinite recess in April. Major universities and colleges closed after December student demonstrations.
1997	Myanmar admitted into ASEAN (July). In November, the State Peace and Development Council (SPDC) replaces the SLORC.
1998	Ten-member Committee Representing the People's Parliament (CRPP) formed by the NLD in lieu of the parliament never allowed to convene.
2000	Daw Aung San Suu Kyi confined to home in September after attempts to travel outside Yangon. The International Labor Organization decided in November to impose sanctions for Myanmar's failure to eliminate forced labour. Secret meetings between secretary - 1 of jumta and Daw Aung San Suu Kyi initiated in October

The collapse of BSPP rule heralded a new contentious era in Myanmar's politics. The armed forces seized power in September 1988, setting up the State Law and Order Restoration Council (SLORC) and ruling by decree. Opposition groups led by Daw Aung San Suu Kyi established the National League for Democracy (NLD) in the same month. In 1990 the SLORC permitted elections, in which the NLD won 80 per cent of seats. However, the SLORC did not allow parliament to convene after these elections, establishing instead a National Convention representing diverse groups towards the end of 1992, to draw up the principles of a new Constitution. Since then the NLD and junta, reorganised as the State Peace and Development Council (SPDC) in 1997, have been locked in confict. Progress on a new constitution has been glacid, and junta actions have attracted much adverse comment from both inside and outside the country. There were signs of thaw in the impasse by early 2001, with the junta releasing some NLD detainess and stopping media attacks on Daw Aung San Suu Kyi, after revelation that secret talks between the latter and Secretary-1, Lt. Sen Khim Nyunt, were initiated in October.

Geography and Demography

With a land area of more than 676,000 square kilometres, Myanmar shares over 6,000 kilometres of contiguous land frontiers with five states — India, China, Bangladesh, Thailand and Laos — and possesses a coastline stretching over 2,200 kilometres. Hemmed in between the two most populous states on earth Myanmar's 50 million inhabitants are outnumbered by all its neighbours except Laos. Its frontiers have prominent natural barriers in the form of mountain ranges in the north-west, north, and east and rivers in the west and south-east, but these did not prevent determined military excursions across some of them in the past. For the last five decades, the frontier zones have been, more often than not, contested areas where drug-traffickers, warlords, and insurgent groups challenged the authority of the central state. Thus, Myanmar leaders had purportedly "given priority to the pursuit of a frontier diplomacy aimed at achieving solid, secure, and recognized borders".[5] In terms of geopolitics, Myanmar stayed out of all blocs and regional groupings during the Cold War period observing strict neutrality. It initially remained outside the Association of Southeast Asian Nations (ASEAN), but joined in July 1997.

Myanmar is a multi-cultural, multi-racial and multi-religious society. Officially, there are 135 national (racial) groups constituting eight broad ethnic categories. According to the 1983 Census, Bamar constituted some

FIGURE 6.2

Myanmar: Key Statistics

Land area: 676,578 sq kilometres

Population:[a]   49,130,000 (2000)

GNP:[b]   Current exchange rate — US$14.2 bn (1998)

GNP Per Capita:[b]   Current exchange rate — US$300 (1998)

Income Distribution:
            Gini Index[c]   56.0 (urban); 41.0 (rural)
            % share of income or consumption: [d]
            Lowest 20%   8.0
            Highest 20%   40.0

Human Development Index (HDI) Ranking:[e]
            World ranking   128 (1997); 125 (1998)
            Value   0.58 (1997); 0.585 (1998)

Armed Forces: [f]
            Total no.   429,000 (1999)
            Expenditure   US$2.1 bn (1998)

Sources: [a] Official national sources.
     [b] International Monetary Fund Staff Country Report No. 99/134, November 1999.
     [c] Unpublished paper by Mya Than, "A Basic Needs Approach to Development: The Burmese Experience". Nd. Based on surveys for North Okkalapa Township, Yangoon (urban, 1981) and Thanatpyin village (rural, 1982).
     [d] World Bank, *Burma: Policies and Prospects for Economic Adjustment and Growth* (Washington, D.C: World Bank, 1985).
     [e] United Nations Development Programme (UNDP), *Human Development Report* (New York: Oxford University Press, 1999 & 2000).
     [f] International Institute for Strategic Studies (IISS), *The Military Balance, 1999–2000* (London: Oxford University Press, 1999).

69 per cent of the country's inhabitants. The Shan was the largest ethnic minority group with 8.5 per cent of the population, others including: Kayin, 6.2 per cent, and Rakhine, 4.5 per cent. In terms of religious denomination, the census records Buddhists comprising 89.4 per cent, Christians, 4.9 per cent and Muslims, 3.9 per cent.[6] There is freedom of religion in Myanmar, which has no professed *de jure* state religion, though Buddhism appears to have enjoyed considerable personal support from the military leadership.[7]

Population grew at around 2 per cent annually throughout the 1990s. The percentage of urban population grew from 13.5 per cent in 1953 to nearly 25 per cent in 1983 (the year of the last census) and further increased to over 26 per cent in the mid-1990s.

Economy

More than a century ago, a *laissez-faire* economy was established and the mercantilist policies of the colonial state led to an exploitation of the natural and human resources of Myanmar with most of the benefits accruing to the metropolis and an alien business class. This exploitative arrangement created an emotionally-charged prejudice against capitalism in general and foreign investment in particular among nationalist leaders of Myanmar's independence movement, whose generation led the country for forty odd years after 1948.

Myanmar's political leadership embarked on an unsuccessful attempt at import-substituting industrialization (ISI) soon after independence, based on nationalization and state intervention. The *dirigisme* intensified during the RC rule where autarkic practices stifled growth. Thereafter, under the guidance of the ruling BSPP, the state pursued a resource-based ISI strategy with heavy dependence on official development assistance (ODA), while practically shutting its doors to foreign direct investment (FDI). This led to a near-bankruptcy of the state and the socialist economy all but collapsed in 1988. Only then the new post-independence generation of military leaders who constituted SLORC decided to break away from the socialist proclivities of the past and discard the latter's historical baggage, announcing an "open door" economic policy that was meant to attract FDI and transform the socialist command economy into a more outward-oriented economy.

Myanmar is an agriculture-based transitional economy where a mixture of state-owned enterprises (SOEs), private firms, and a small co-operative sector operate under a plethora of rules and regulations.[8] In 1997, nearly 63 per cent of the working population was in the agriculture sector with only

9 per cent in processing and manufacturing. The contribution to the gross domestic product (GDP) for fiscal year 1999/2000 (in constant prices) by the private sector was 75.8 per cent, followed by the state sector with 22.3 per cent and the cooperative sector with a marginal 1.9 per cent. Goods account for around 60 per cent of GDP, trade and services 20 per cent each.

Since the mid-1990s, Myanmar's economy has been facing difficulties in the form of increasing trade deficits, high inflation, falling currency value, a drastic reduction in FDI, balance of payments problems and an energy shortage. The much-needed FDI inflow was drastically curtailed by the East Asian Financial Crisis as the major investors were from affected countries. Attempts to boost economic development are constrained by domestic political conditions which, in turn, have been linked to sanctions on trade, investment and aid imposed by Western Europe and the United States.

THE POLITICAL SYSTEM

Myanmar is currently under direct military rule by the junta called the State Peace and Development Council (SPDC). The military has been ruling by decree after abrogating the 1974 Constitution. Initially the junta imposed martial law in some regions, but progressively rescinded this over two years as the security situation improved. It has promised to establish a multi-party democratic political system and is sponsoring the formulation of the basic principles for a new constitution through a national convention.

Administratively, Myanmar is divided into 14 regions, comprising seven states (named after the major national group that inhabits the region) and seven divisions (generally areas with Bamar majority).[9] They overlap with the 12 military regional commands. Apart from the national capital Yangon, each state and division has a designated regional capital. In a descending order of administrative hierarchy, there were 64 districts, 324 townships, and 2471 wards as well as 13747 village tracts (grouping of villages) in 1997.

Today's debate over a new constitution has been shaped by historical experience. The Constitution of the "Union of Burma" formulated by the Constituent Assembly (with the assistance of Myanmar lawyers and jurists) in 1947 delineated a quasi-federal union with a centralized Union Government and constituent (ethnic-based) States supervised by State Councils. Some States (Shan and Kayah) enjoyed the right to secede after ten years.[10] The hereditary ruling élites of the Shan State were allowed some local autonomy in the form of traditional administrative and legal authority that undermined the central government's legitimacy and authority.

In a sense, this Constitution attempted to ensure national unity among the indigenous national races by employing both electoral and territorial solutions. However, neither the institution of the Chamber of Nationalities (upper house) with limited powers and the incorporation of ministerial portfolios for heads of constituent States in the Cabinet, nor the creation of such States for territorially distinct ethnic communities (Shans, Kachins, Kayins, Kayahs and a special Division for the Chins), appeased the exponents of greater ethnic autonomy. Attempts by Shan leaders in the late 1950s to demand greater autonomy, and transform the "Union" into a more "Federal" arrangement, unsettled many Bamar politicians and antagonized the military leadership. The Constitution was abrogated by the military when it took power on 2 March 1962. The present junta has been propounding the view that the 1947 Constitution "had to be written poste-haste within one year as desired by imperialists" and was "full of flaws".[11]

The most obvious shortcoming of the 1974 Constitution, in the present context, was its prescription of a socialist one-party state with a unicameral parliament called the *Pyithu Hluttaw* (people's assembly). First initiated in mid-1971 through the formation of a 97-member constitution drafting commission (appointed by the BSPP and comprising junta members, and other sectoral interests), it took three drafts and over two years of deliberations and feedback sessions organized by the ruling BSPP to complete. It was overwhelmingly endorsed by a national referendum in January 1974. It is a very detailed document that enshrined the leading role of the BSPP and stipulated the instituting of single-party quadrennial elections for people's representatives at the central, state/division level, township level, and ward/village tract levels.[12] This Constitution was abolished when SLORC (State Law and Order Restoration Council) took state power on 18 September 1988.

According to the military junta, a firm constitution which avoided the pitfalls of both the 1947 and 1974 constitutions was necessary for a stable political environment in which indigenized rules of "multi-party democracy" could be "formulated".[13] SLORC envisaged a political configuration which would institutionalize the military's role in "national politics" as a solution to the problem of dysfunctional "party politics".[14] Towards this goal SLORC convened a National Convention (NC) in 1993. Representation in the NC was classified according to eight categories — nominees of political parties (numbering 50), representative-elects (successful candidates in the

1990 elections) (99), nationalities (215), peasants (93), workers (48), intellectuals and intelligentsia (41), service personnel (civil servants) (92), and other invited delegates (57). A complex selection procedure ensured most delegates were sympathetic to the SLORC, and able to contribute to the junta's objective of managed transition.[15]

The deliberations of the NC commenced on 9 January 1993 with much fanfare. The Convention objectives were enunciated earlier by an 18-member National Convention Convening Commission (NCCC) comprising high ranking military officers and senior judicial and administrative officials. These called for a "genuine multiparty democracy" that would promote "justice, liberty and equality"; instituting the military "to participate in the national political leadership role of the future state"; and the upholding of the trinity of "main national causes" that had been enunciated by SLORC, namely "Non-disintegration of the Union", "Non-disintegration of the National Solidarity", and "Consolidation of Sovereignty". The NC's proceedings were guided by a SLORC-appointed 27-member steering committee called the National Convention Convening Work Committee (NCCWC), comprising government officials and the chief justice as chairman.

Principles underlying state structure, administrative configuration, and political representation were subsequently formulated by the NCCWC, taking into consideration the various proposals put forward by convention delegates during the proceedings. By September 1993, a detailed set of 104 "basic principles", endorsed by NCCC had been established as a basis for future deliberations. These presumably represent the broad outline of future political arrangements. The essential points were:[16]

State Structure

- a secular republic based on seven "regions" and seven "states" having equal status
- territorial structure for administrative purposes would include the "Union" territories (under direct presidential administration) as well as a hierarchy consisting of region/state, district, township, and village/ward levels
- contingent local autonomy for "national races" in the form of "self administered areas"
- no part of the country's territory allowed to secede under any circumstances

The Legislature

- a bicameral parliament with a five-years tenure in the form of *Pyithu Hluttaw* (House of Representatives) and *Amyotha Hluttaw* (House of Nationalities) which together constitute the *Pyidaungsu Hluttaw* (Union Parliament)
- a *hluttaw* (provincial parliament) in each state or region
- one-quarter of the seats reserved for military representatives nominated by the armed forces Commander-in-Chief (C-in-C)

The Executive

- an executive president, elected by electroal college
- cabinet and the attorney-general appointed by the president. Ministers need not be elected representatives. Any elected representative appointed must forego party affiliation
- the chief minister of region/state governments would be a presidential appointee
- establishment of "leading bodies" to govern the self-administered areas

The Military

- military would enjoy complete autonomy with its C-in-C designated as the supreme commander.
- provision for the supreme commander to assume state power in a national emergency, i.e., force, disturbances and violence are used to usurp state power or there is danger of disintegration of the union and national solidarity as well as the loss of national sovereignty.

Under these proposals the president and the armed forces C-in-C, between them, would wield considerable powers. All significant executive positions at the national and provincial level are ultimately responsible to the president. Political parties that win national and regional elections face a situation whereby executive positions may be filled with personnel who are not elected and do not belong to any party. When elected representatives are chosen to serve in the government they have to forego their party affiliations. Thus, the political system under the new Constitution effectively de-links state power from political parties and representation of voting constituencies.

The NC has been in recess since April 1996, though the NCCC continues to sit frequently for deliberations. No official explanation has been given for this, but there have been hints that the NC's inability to reach a consensus on the issue of autonomy for national races is the main reason. Chief Justice U Aung Toe, Chairman of the NCCWC, said that the NC would be reconvened once the discussions, at the steering committee, on basic detailed guidelines regarding separation of powers between the legislative, executive, and judiciary at different levels were completed.[17]

Head of State

Since April 1992, Myanmar's Head of State has been Senior General Than Shwe who is the Chairman of the State Peace and Development Council (SPDC) and concurrently the prime minister, the defence minister, as well as the Commander-in Chief (C-in-C) of the Myanmar Defence Services. Thus, the head of state is not a titular position but a position of ultimate authority in the public domain. Under the present system, the head of state is at the apex of a hierarchical governing structure operating at the central, state/division, district, township, and ward/village levels throughout the country.

Looking forward, under "basic principles" of the new Constitution the head of state would be an executive president and head of government. The future head of state must have a minimum of 20 years continuous domicile in Myanmar, and also satisfy the condition that the "President of the Union himself, parents, spouse, children and their spouses" must not "owe allegiance to" or "be a subject of foreign power". The President must not be a "citizen of a foreign country ... [and] not be ... entitled to the right and privileges of a subject or citizen of a foreign country." Another condition that the person be at least 45 years old and "well acquainted with the affairs of State such as political administrative, economics and military affairs" would rule out most political activists of the younger generation and seem to square mostly with establishment figures.[18]

The presidential electoral college consists of three groups from the *Pyidaungsu Hluttaw*, comprising elected representatives from the *Amyotha Hluttaw* and *Pyithu Hluttaw*, and nominated military representatives. Each group shall elect one vice-president who need not be an elected *hluttaw* representative. The president will then be chosen by the entire electoral college from among these three nominees, after vetting by a body composed of leaders and deputy leaders of the two *hluttaw*. The unsuccessful candidates will assume the vice-presidencies for the five-year term of office.

The wide-ranging powers accorded the future president allow unprecedented control over the executive branch. At the central level, the

President could designate ministries and appoint or dismiss ministers, deputy ministers, the attorney-general, the auditor-general, as well as members of the Union Civil Service Board (the equivalent of the CSSTB) — positions that would not be confined to elected *hluttaw* representatives only. The President could prescribe the ministries and the number of ministers in region or state governments and nominate the chief ministers who will lead the region or state governments. All such actions must be endorsed by the relevant *hluttaw* but the latter could not eject the President's nominee unless that person does not conform to the qualifications stipulated by law. In a state of emergency, the President could exercise executive and legislative power in any region, state, or a self-administered area in accord with provisions to be stipulated in the Constitution. However, minister/deputy-minister posts for defence, security/home affairs and border affairs are reserved for military personnel nominated by the armed forces C-in-C. The President would have to co-ordinate with the C-in-C in appointing them. Co-ordination with the armed forces C-in-C is also required to appoint military personnel to any minister/deputy-minister post.

The Executive

Under current military rule the highest executive authority rests with the military junta. The Cabinet of ministers, presided by the Prime Minister who is also the Chairman of the junta, is subordinate to the junta and is entrusted with the day-to-day conduct of governing Myanmar. The General Administration Department of the Ministry of Home Affairs exercises the public administration functions through a hierarchy of local offices down to the township level. There is also a parallel hierarchy of peace and development councils, organized along territorial lines, subordinate to regional authorities at the State and Division level who are accountable to the junta.

Military Junta

When the military took over state power on 18 September 1988, the 19-member State Law and Order Restoration Council (SLORC) was formed with the Chief of Staff of Defence Services as the Chairman and the Director of Defence Services Intelligence (DDSI) as the Secretary-1 and Colonel (General Staff) as Secretary-2. The other members were the three Vice-Chiefs of Staff (VCS) of the army, navy, and air force, the Adjutant-General, the Quartermaster-General, the two Chiefs of the Bureau of

Special Operations (Office of the Chief of Staff), and the nine regional commanders. Eventually, all SLORC members, except the Vice-Chairman and two Secretaries, were appointed to Cabinet. Army VCS General Than Shwe was appointed Vice-Chairman of SLORC soon after the junta was formed. In January 1992, SLORC inducted three new members who were later appointed as ministers in addition to being SLORC members. In April 1992 General Than Shwe became the Chairman of SLORC when the junta decided to retire General Saw Maung on medical grounds.

In November 1997, the junta dissolved SLORC and reconstituted itself as the State Peace and Development Council (SPDC). Only the Chairman, Vice-Chairman, and the two Secretaries retained their positions in the reconstituted junta. The remaining members lost their places in the junta, and 14 of them were removed from their ministerial positions as well. Subsequently, except for the Chairman, SPDC members have not been a part of Cabinet. In a minor reorganization the position of Secretary-3 — assumed by Adjutant-General Lt. General Win Myint — was added to the junta. Other new members included the two C-in-C for navy and airforce, and all commanders of the 12 military regional commands.

Though SPDC members other than the Chair are not included in the government that operates under the Cabinet system, the five top leaders of the SPDC are very much involved in executive affairs. The Vice-Chairman is believed to be the Chairman of the Trade Council and have a hand in formulating important economic policies. Secretary-1, Lt. Gen. Khin Nyunt, who is the Director of the Directorate of Defence Services Intelligence (DDSI) and the Head of the Office of Strategic Studies (OSS) at the Ministry of Defence, is believed to supervise socio-cultural and political affairs of the state. Secretary-2, Lt. Gen. Tin Oo (deceased; February 2001), who was Chief of Staff (Army) and Chief of the Bureau of Special Operations at the Ministry of Defence, was involved in overseeing infrastructure development and economic affairs. Secretary-3, Lt. Gen. Win Myint, appears to be looking after economic matters as well. SPDC Secretaries are also in charge of various ministerial committees. The Foreign Affairs Policy Committee is chaired by Secretary-1. The Central Supervisory Committee for Ensuring Smooth and Secure Transport was chaired by Secretary-2. And the committee (formed in December 1999) aimed at reducing commodity prices is chaired by Secretary-3.

There are also two "ministers" attached to the SPDC Chairman's Office (all military officers) and another three (two active and one retired military officers) attached to the Prime Minister's Office (PMO). Although ministers attached to the junta Chairman's office and the PMO hold no portfolio, they do carry out specific tasks assigned by the SPDC Chairman that entail supra-ministerial functions, mainly to promote production and tackle bottlenecks in the economy. One minister at the PMO chairs the Extended Prawn Breeding Committee. Another at the Chairman's office is reported to be in charge of external economic affairs that covers functions previously assigned to line ministries such as planning and economic development and commerce. A third is in charge of a committee to alleviate congestion in the Port of Yangon.

In exercising its absolute power and authority, the junta also issues laws, rules, orders, and declarations. SPDC meetings are infrequent (normally three times a year), but anecdotal evidence suggests the junta Chairman regularly holds informal meetings with the top executives of the SPDC and Cabinet members, where important decisions are made. Staff support is provided by the SPDC Chairman's office, headed by a director-general.

The regional military commanders (major-general rank) who are members of the ruling junta have considerable latitude in managing areas under their jurisdiction. They not only have control over their territorial military commands but also are in charge of public affairs as chairmen of their respective State or Division Peace and Development Councils (PDCs). Their status is higher than that of line ministers and, perhaps, even deputy prime-ministers.

FIGURE 6.3

Committees and Organizations under the Junta's Purview

Special Projects Implementation Committee (SPIC)
Central Committee for the Development of Border Areas and National Races
Union Solidarity and Development Association (USDA)
Myanmar Central Committee for Drug Abuse Control (CCDAC)
Myanmar Naing-Ngan Education Committee
National Health Committee
National Commission for Environmental Affairs (NCEA)
The Information Dissemination Policy Committee
Committee for Activating and Disseminating Patriotism among the People
National Mottos Writing Supervision Committee
Civil Service Selection and Training Board (CSSTB)
Myanma Cultural Heritage Preservation and Protection Central Committee
Privatization Commission
Myanma Industrial Development Committee

The SLORC established 14 committees and organizations, which have been continued under the SPDC. (see Figure 6.3). They are organized along the lines of a task force or an institution to accomplish stated objectives (reflected in their names) and act as supra-ministerial steering bodies cutting across ministerial portfolios. They also co-ordinate and supervise the relevant line ministries, government agencies, private sector organizations, and NGOs in tackling problems and issues within their purview. Two of them are chaired by the junta Chairman himself, while five are chaired by Secretary-1. In addition, the Mayor of Yangon who is concurrently the Chairman of the Yangon City Development Committee (YCDC; the municipal authority) was conferred ministerial rank in June 1995 and is accountable to the SPDC Chairman as YCDC had been placed under the latter's purview.

The Cabinet

The cabinet institution has long been part of government in Myanmar. The current cabinet meets regularly and is an integral part of the continuing administration.

When SLORC took power it formed a Cabinet of nine members including the prime minister (the junta chairman). There were 18 portfolios. In the twelve years that followed, the number of members as well as portfolios expanded to 39 and 32 respectively (see Figure 6.4.) Two deputy-prime ministers posts were introduced in September 1992 by the SLORC, and a third by the SPDC in 1997. The SPDC appoints the Cabinet members, though as noted only the SPDC chair is a member (prime minister and minister of defence).

In the line ministries, nearly two-thirds have senior military officers (colonel and above) as ministers and the majority of the remainder are manned by retired military officers. There are no female ministers. Although the ministerial functions are well defined at the central level, the regional authorities exercise significant control over local resources and substantial influence in the operation of government agencies. Moreover ministers are lower in the protocol order than regional military commanders who are SPDC members — even though, more often than not, they were once subordinates of those ministers in the military hierarchy. Complicating matters further are the SLORC-established task forces mentioned above (Figure 6.3) that cut across ministerial and regional boundaries, as well as instructions by the SPDC Chairman, Vice Chairman, and the three Secretaries during their tours and field trips to the countryside.

FIGURE 6.4
Myanmar: State Organization

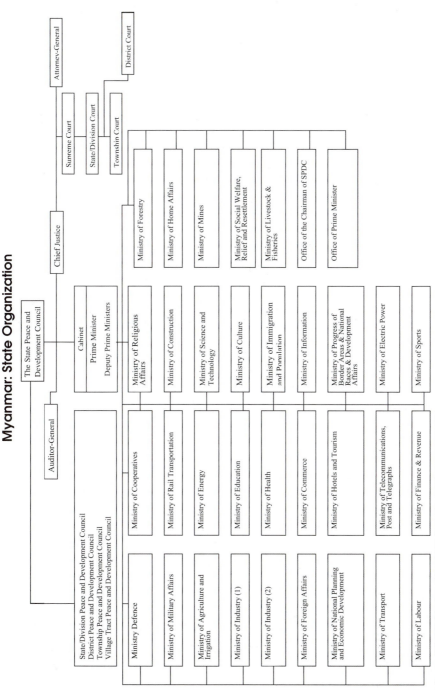

Sources: IDE-JETRO Institute of Developing Economics and Myanmar government.

Consequently, the ministries operate under constraints regarding resource allocation and prioritization of tasks. The ministers also are in charge of various ministerial committees and are members of inter-ministerial bodies that focus on specific policy issues.

All these cross interactions must pose a heavy demand for close co-operation amongst the relevant government agencies and their regional counterparts in peace and development councils (PDCs). This, in turn, would require the Cabinet as well as the individual ministers to monitor all these activities, over and above the task of coordinating the routine functions of line ministries.[19] This is a tall order which is further complicated by the lack of timely and comprehensive data inputs due to the absence of an efficient information infrastructure.

Other Executive Members

Deputy ministers are also appointed by the SPDC, and their functions are similar to those of a minister of state or junior minister or under secretary in other political systems. There are nearly 40 deputies in the present Government, the majority active or retired senior military officers. Some ministries (e.g., co-operatives, sports, and telecommunications, post and telegraphs) do not have any deputy minister but others (e.g., education, forestry, health, and information) have two deputy ministers each. Their duties include assisting the minister and are usually assigned to be responsible for a cluster of agencies under their respective ministries.

The highest authority on legal matters resides in the Attorney-General's Office.[20] The Attorney General and Deputy Attorney-General are appointed by the military junta. The Office is responsible for scrutinizing, formulating, and translating all the drafts of laws and rules, giving legal opinions to government agencies, and functioning as state prosecutor or defence attorney.

The Office of the Auditor General (AG) is responsible for inspecting and auditing the accounts of all government ministries, state economic enterprises and other government departments.[21] It has also given advice on the privatization process, and produces manuals and guidelines for accounting and budgetary control. The AG and the Deputy AG are appointed by the SPDC, and are *ex-officio* Chairman and Vice-Chairman of the Myanmar Accountancy Council, responsible for maintaining accounting standards and training certified public accountants and certified auditors.

As the government's regulatory body the AG has had some success in establishing autonomy and maintaining its standards as a watchdog over government financial transactions. This is despite challenges posed by the absence of a parliament and the inherent commandism of a military government to which the imperatives of national security overrides other concerns over due process.

A hierarchy of regional and local peace and development councils (PDCs), known as law and order restoration councils (LORCs) under SLORC, are responsible for public affairs throughout the country. There is a four-tier structure of PDCs below the junta covering division or state level, district level, township level, and the ward or village tract level. Military leaders dominate at the higher levels. The PDCs are supposed to oversee, supervise, and coordinate all security and administrative matters, except those within the purview of the military and the judiciary.

Civil Service

The civil service may be classified as comprising government employees who are in the General Administration Department (GAD) and those in the social, cultural and economic fields. Active and retired military officers are seconded to or appointed as executives and staff officers in ministries as well as the departments, corporations and state economic enterprises (SEEs). More than one-third of the chief executives of government agencies are senior military officers, and many deputies are also. The chief executives of government agencies are appointed by the Cabinet with the approval of the junta.

During the upheaval of 1988, large numbers of civil servants in cities and towns abandoned their posts and many of them joined in the demonstrations. Since then the junta has exerted strong pressure to keep them in line. 2,972 service personnel were dismissed or retired and another 1,573 persons were reprimanded, transferred, or demoted for their "malpractice[s]" during the 1988 "disturbances".[22] In April 1991, the junta issued an order prohibiting service personnel from engaging in party politics or assisting a political party in any way, or participating in any political or other organization whose formation does not conform to the rules prescribed by the government. Further, all service personnel must prevent their dependants and those under their guardianship from directly or indirectly participating in any anti-government activity.

There is no official figure for the total number of civil servants in government employ, but by collating staff-strength figures for various government ministries and departments a "lower bound" figure of slightly over one million, as at March 1991, could be arrived at. There are apparently two streams in the classification of civil service positions, management and professional/technical. Nevertheless, there is ample crossover of personnel between these two at the top echelons.[23] In terms of salary scales and corresponding grades, there exist two bands of service personnel (*wundan* in Myanmar language), officers (*ayardan*) and junior staff (*ahmudun*). Direct entry into the upper band is via nation-wide competitive examinations, conducted by the Civil Service Selection and Training Board (CSSTB)[24] and usually requires a university degree. Except for the lowest level general labour and factory worker, the minimum formal educational level is a pass at secondary/high school level.

Anecdotal evidence suggests that the majority of service personal are competent but lack initiative and motivation. They are underpaid when compared to the private sector despite a five-fold salary increase in early 2000. There seems to be endemic small-scale corruption and moonlighting in the lower ranks, primarily due to inadequate income and new opportunities offered by the market economy. However, most agency heads now find themselves entrusted with more authority and administrative space than before as the economy opens up and modern management practices are introduced. On balance, the civil service has the potential to develop into a crucial instrument for development of the country in a democratic setting especially if there are wide-ranging reforms to enhance the integrity, boost the morale and improve the welfare of service personnel across the board.

Political Role of Military and Police

From September 1988 onwards Myanmar's military leadership has controlled the state executive, and often the government-controlled media refers to a "*Tatmadaw* Government". The *Tatmadaw* (literally, the royal military) has portrayed itself as the most disciplined, cohesive and enduring institution in Myanmar. The popular refrain, that it is neither a mercenary outfit nor a conscript armed force but a unique patriotic volunteer organization born out of a historic struggle for national independence, has been reiterated continuously for the last five decades. Many civilian politicians who took part in the national struggle for independence endorse this view. The military has, all along, been a volunteer force. Though an act for conscription was legislated (in March 1959), it was never used, except for doctors, selected to do national service for three years.

Since Myanmar's independence, the armed forces has continually engaged in military operations against ideological and ethnic insurgencies.

In the 1950s it had to mount costly campaigns against remnants of the Kuomintang army that had fled to the Thai-Myanmar border after losing control of China to the Chinese Communist Party. Given the continual military threat posed by domestic rebellions, Myanmar armed forces had been, until the 1990s, largely geared towards counter-insurgency operations. The result was an infantry-heavy army dominating the force structure.

The post-independence defence services were established initially as a tri-service force, under the War Office, with the naval and air arms given equal status despite the army's dominance in terms of sheer manpower and capability. The reorganization of the military in the mid-1950s with the creation of the Ministry of Defence reduced the status of the navy and air force chiefs to that of Vice-Chiefs of Staff under an army Chief of Staff. In May 1989, the designation of each of the three service chiefs (army, navy and air force) was changed from "Vice Chief-of-Staff" to "Commander-in-Chief" of the respective service while the overall (supreme) commander's designation was changed from "Chief of Staff, Defence Services" to "Commander-in-Chief of Defence Services". This basic structure has remained since then, though many positions have been upgraded with the Chairman of the ruling junta assuming the unprecedented rank of Senior General (perhaps equivalent to a five-star general in the U.S. military) in May 1990.[25]

There is no evidence of inter-service rivalry as the army's pre-eminence by virtue of the command structure as well as its vanguard role in overcoming the security challenges posed by multiple insurgencies has been accepted by all concerned parties. The limited nature of counter-insurgency warfare as well as resource constraints — that has precluded the acquisition of expensive weapon systems — relegated the other services to a supporting role for the army in an overwhelmingly inward-oriented military force commanded by a succession of army generals. In addition, since the advent of the RC, the defence portfolio has been held either concurrently by Army Generals, the Chief of Staff or (in the 1985–88 period) the retired Chief of Staff.

Since the 1962 coup military officers have frequently intervened in government affairs. During the RC period (1962–74) the supreme state authority was a military junta, with the Revolutionary Government (Council of Ministers) essentially a military cabal. In the 1974–88 period, serving or retired senior military officers in the ruling party's Central Executive Committee, the party Central Committee, and the Cabinet wielded considerable influence. The SLORC and SPDC are unquestionably pure military organizations. As such, the autonomy of the military and the pervasive influence of the military establishment in politics have been the rule rather than the exception.

The order of battle of the Myanmar armed forces has never been revealed but estimates put the authorized strength at around 430,000. The army has over 90 per cent of the total personnel and is a highly proficient battle-tested force.[26] It is organized into 12 regional army commands with garrison battalions, 10 mobile light infantry divisions (brigade strength), and supporting regiments of armour, artillery, signals, engineering and constructions, supply and transport, ordnance, and air defence. The Directorate of Defence Services intelligence is an important organization within the defence establishment in that it is widely seen as an agency that keeps tabs on the military personnel as well as political dissenters.

A paramount concern of the military leadership since the coup of 1988 has been the perpetuation of corporate solidarity within its ranks. Dire warnings concerning the catastrophic consequences of disunity in the military have been repeatedly issued by the leadership. The rank and file are constantly reminded of the internal and external threats posed by communists, ethnic insurgents, neo-colonialists and neo-imperialists, the Western media, self-serving expatriates and NGOs, hypocritical proponents of human rights and democracy, and a hostile superpower.[27] The reification of the *tatmadaw* as the "parent" of its individual members zeroes in on Myanmar values and culture and serves as a constant reminder to maintain corporate loyalty and group solidarity within the armed forces.

The police have a different historical background, being initially viewed with disdain as a lackey of the colonial power. After independence, the AFPFL Government was accused by the opposition of using the police against them. The public generally subscribed to this view, and believed that the police force was fraught with corruption and partisanship towards local political bosses. The RC attempted to polish the tarnished image of the police by reorganizing it along military lines, staffing it with military personnel, and renaming it the "People's Police Force". Nevertheless, doubts about the integrity of its personnel lingered on and the public confidence in the police remained moderate throughout the BSPP era.

In the upheaval of 1988, anti-riot police units bore the brunt of the public abuse and violent reprisals by the militant mobs. By September, the police command authority had collapsed, and an isolated, outnumbered, and demoralized force stopped functioning. Many individual police professed solidarity with the demonstrators, some even joining the protest marches. After the military coup, the junta purged the top ranks of the force and revamped it into an armed organization not only responsible for maintaining law and order but also for supporting and supplementing the military's role in preserving national security, but still under the home ministry. It was renamed the Myanmar Police Force (MPF) in September 1995.[28] The MPF is tightly controlled by the military, and most top positions are now held by military officials. Its image appeared to have improved in the last decade, but whether the public perception of the police as a reliable and impartial guarantor of the people's life, home, and possessions (according to a Myanmar adage) can be unequivocally established remains to be seen.

The main force of the MPF, at present, comprises around 50,000 personnel[29] in a three-tier regional hierarchy of command organized along the lines of the GAD structure and virtually subordinated to the corresponding PDCs. There are also specialized agencies, such as the Criminal Investigations Department (CID), and police battalions (anti-riot duty).

The Legislature

The country has no legislature at present, all laws being issued as decrees through the junta. For the future, according to the basic principles adopted by the NC for the new Constitution, there will be a bicameral parliament comprising a 440-seat *Pyithu Hluttaw* or Chamber of Deputies and a 224-seat *Amyotha Hluttaw* or Chamber of Nationalities. In the former constituencies would be based on population-size within a township. In the latter each of the seven Regions and seven States would be allocated twelve seats to be contested within the Region or State. For both chambers the military would be entitled to one-quarter of the seats through nominations by the C-in-C of the Defence Services. *Hluttaws* or provincial parliaments will also be established at the region and State level.

The modalities of the proposed legislature and its relationship with the executive have yet to be spelt out in detail. From what has been revealed about the power of the executive presidency (see above section on head of state) the legislature will play a subordinate role. However, the President could be impeached by the *hluttaw* under specific provisions. Voters would also have a right to recall an elected representative under certain yet-to-be specified conditions.

Elections

Elections have been regularly held for most of Myanmar's independent history. The last was in May 1990, under the *Pyithu Hluttaw* Election Law promulgated by SLORC, dated 31 May1989. (Earlier elections are discussed in the introduction and following section on Legitimacy.) The Election Commission established 11 September 1988 by the parliament of the BSPP era was retained by SLORC to oversee the promised "multi-party democracy general elections".[30]

Between 12 March and 21 April 1990, the 93 political parties that contested the elections were allowed to use the national radio (15 minutes) and television (10 minutes) for a series of campaign broadcasts. Each party selected a symbol to represent it from a list of symbols provided by the election authorities. Although 492 single seat constituencies were established only 485 were contested because of logistical difficulties in the seven remaining constituencies. Voting was on a first past the post basis. Altogether, 2,209 candidates were fielded by the political parties and 87 stood as independents. The voting turnout was 72.6 per cent, but 12.3 per cent of the total votes became null and void due to various irregularities. Independents won six seats while 27 parties won 479 seats in what was seen to be a free and fair elections. The National League for Democracy (NLD) won 392 seats and claimed victory. The NLD won 80.8 per cent of the total seats with 59.9 per cent of the total votes cast, whereas the National Unity Party (a reincarnation of the BSPP) won only 10 seats (2.1 per cent) but garnered 25.1 per cent of the votes. The Shan National League for Democracy (SNLD, an ethnic-based party allied to NLD) which won 23 seats in the Shan region, managed to capture only 1.7 per cent of the votes.[31]

In the aftermath of the elections the NLD pressed for a transfer of power based on the 1947 Constitution and called for talks with the junta on the modalities of such a transfer. SLORC refused to meet with any party and cited many unsettled issues regarding the elections, such as the submission of complete financial accounts of the political parties and pending complaints against successful candidates as well as balloting irregularities.

Finally, in the face of mounting calls for the speedy transfer of power by the winning parties and their Western sympathizers, the junta issued the Declaration No. 1/90 that spelt out the path to be followed by all parties concerned in the process of eventual transfer of power to an elected government. In essence, the junta's declaration meant that there would be no transfer of power until and unless a proper constitution were drafted and ratified. The role of the successful election candidates was not to form a government but to participate in a convention that would draft an "enduring" constitution. As such, the 1990 elections did not lead to the formation of a government by the winning party, and that has become a bone of contention between the junta and its political detractors. Deliberations by the NC have not yet provided any indications of whether current electoral arrangements will be entrenched, or a new system introduced.

Judiciary

Myanmar's judiciary has passed through three phases since independence. The first phase lasted for 14 years under the parliamentary democracy system of government, saw an independent judiciary comprising central (Supreme Court and High Court) and regional courts (State/Division, District, and Township). During the RC era, the central courts were abolished and replaced by a Chief Court under the Ministry of Judicial Affairs. The regional courts were retained but the executive branch oversaw the judiciary in practise and the former's autonomy was lost. Special Courts were also created to try economic crimes, political subversion and crimes against the state. The BSPP Socialist State instituted the system of People's Courts in which elected People's Council representatives replaced the professional judges at all levels in the regional hierarchy. The Supreme Court was replaced by the Council of People's Judges staffed by elected *Pyithu* Hluttaw representatives. Special Tribunals were also convened from time to time to try serious crimes against the state. During periods of emergency rule, such as in 1974 and 1975 when anti-government demonstrations led to rioting in the capital, martial law was declared and military tribunals were authorized to pass judgements. Though accountable to the legislature in theory the People's Courts system was overshadowed by the leading role of the BSPP that virtually controlled all three branches of government.

When SLORC came to power and imposed martial law in selected parts of the country (164 townships out of 324), military tribunals were instituted to adjudicate any serious offences related to subversive and anti-government activities. The organizational structure of the judiciary reverted back to the pre-1962 structure of central and regional courts by a law promulgated on 26 September 1988, and the courts were allowed to exercise authority in ordinary criminal and civil cases. The martial law ordinances were gradually withdrawn as the law and order situation improved, and by mid-1990 they were no longer in force.

The current Supreme Court is presided over by the Chief Justice and five Justices who are appointed by the junta. It is the highest judicial body in the land. The Office of the Chief Justice also oversees the advocates and lawyers and supervise their registration for law practise as well. There are State/Division Courts as well as branches of the former functioning as

District Courts and Township Courts throughout Myanmar. There are also separate functional courts such as the Juvenile Court (Yangon), Township Courts (Municipal), and Township Courts (Traffic) as well. All these courts professed impartiality and autonomy based on "seven principles of judiciary": administering justice independently according to law; protecting and safeguarding the interests of the people and aiding in the restoration of law and peace and tranquillity; educating the people to understand and abide by the law and cultivating in the people the habit of abiding by the law; working within the framework of law for settlement of cases; dispensing justice in open court unless otherwise prohibited by law; guaranteeing in all cases the right of defence and the right of appeal under the law; and aiming at reforming moral character in meting out punishment to offenders.

Given the frequent exhortations by the Secretary-1 and Chief Justice on the need to stamp out graft and corruption, and evidence that nearly 150 judicial "officials" were subject to disciplinary action in recent years (from April 1995 to November 1997), one may infer that there could have been cases of corruption among individuals at the lower levels of the judiciary. On the whole, the system appears to be as autonomous as can be expected under direct military rule and seems to be geared towards a judiciary that conforms with the universal principles of justice and liberty.[32]

Few details regarding the future judiciary under the new Constitution have emerged, but the basic principles indicated that there would be a *Pyidaungsu Taya Hluttaw* (literally Union Judicial Assembly) at the national level whose authority and function would be similar to the present Supreme Court. Each of the seven Regions and States would have a *Taya Hluttaw* or High Court as well as lower courts of law at different levels down to the township. The aims and objectives of the envisaged judiciary would be similar to those enunciated by the junta for the present system and the independence of the judiciary would be assured by constitutional guarantees.

Political Parties

Political parties have played a central role in much of Myanmar's recent history. In the early post-independence years the AFPFL dominated political activity in a multi-party setting. From the 1960s until 1988 the BSPP was the sole party allowed. Since then government leaders have again supported the adoption of a multi-party system.

Prior to the 1990 elections the Election Commission allowed the registration of political parties. Out of 235 parties, 102 subsequently dissolved voluntarily, and three were de-registered because they were found out to be front organizations for rebel groups. Another 31 were de-registered in February 1990 for failing to contest the elections and six more were de-registered for their inability to contest the stipulated minimum of three constituencies in the elections. The 93 parties that contested the elections were soon reduced further. Fifteen parties disbanded voluntarily, 5 were de-registered for involvement in treasonous activities, 7 became void after breaching regulations that required a minimum of five members in a central executive committee, and 56 were de-registered due to the absence of organizational structure or lack of grass-roots membership. That has left only 10 legal political parties at present, nine of which have accepted the *status quo* and devote their political activities to participation in the NC.[33]

The National Unity Party (NUP), officially registered on 12 October 1988, is the most important of the nine pro-regime parties. It is, in effect, an offshoot of the disgraced and disbanded BSPP. That is probably the main reason why it gained only 10 seats in the May 1990 elections, despite formidable resources inherited from the BSPP. However, it did manage to secure over 25 per cent of the votes, illustrating its potential as a serious contender for future elections, especially with the continuing decimation of NLD's grass roots. The main drawback of the NUP, aside from its BSPP lineage, is its leadership, comprising ageing second echelon leaders (many retired senior military officers) of the former BSPP, who might be perceived as mediocre and too conservative.

The NUP's platform is based on a procedural interpretation of democracy with local characteristics and a market economy. It favours continuity and a communitarian ideology, envisaging a unitary state model with some regional autonomy and a strong central executive.[34]

The Union Solidarity and Development Association (USDA), formed on 15 September 1993, is a unique organization registered as a social organization, yet it more resembles a quasi-political arm of the junta. With "morale, discipline, solidarity, and unity" as its motto, the USDA rapidly expanded to some 12 million members under the patronage of the junta chairman and senior military commanders. USDA's Central Executive Committee comprises Cabinet members, and it has a hierarchical network of central, state/division, district, township, and ward/village-tract level organizations. It has penetrated the society throughout the country and is especially active in organizing youth to engage in sports, hobbies, cultural and other extra-curricular activities. It has played a significant role in all mass rallies that have been held to commemorate significant national events and achievements, as well as to denounce the NLD and its leadership or Western interference of internal affairs. Most observes believe the junta is preparing the USDA to perform a function not dissimilar to that of Golkar in Suharto's Indonesia.

Only the NLD has taken on the regime and continues to play politics outside the parameters prescribed by the Government. Although the Government has declared itself a neutral entity in the political arena, the NLD has assumed a role as an "opposition" party against the regime.

The party was founded on 24 September 1988 with Daw Aung San Suu Kyi as General Secretary, and leading figure. Under her influence the party has portrayed itself as in the vanguard for the popular democracy movement and the epitome of institutionalized opposition to authoritarian rule. From the outset the NLD was a coalition of individuals and groups advocating different means towards the same end. Though many were moderate "centrists" as regards strategy and tactics there were also elements, especially within the student echelon, which harboured radical impulses and were confrontational. Party members agreed, however, on Western notions of liberal democracy and a market economy with an independent monetary authority. They emphasised liberty, individual rights, freedom of the press, rule of law, equal opportunity for all, social justice, and leaned towards a federalist state system.[35]

Throughout the period leading to the elections, political tensions remained high as the NLD, together with its affiliates, incessantly defied martial law restrictions and challenged SLORC's legitimacy in general and its laws, rules, and regulations in particular. SLORC's response was to apply the full force of existing laws, especially Martial Law provisions, and to enact more of them for controlling information flows and registering organizations. Daw Aung San Suu Kyi was placed under house arrest with effect from 20 July 1989, and in December party chairman U Tin U was imprisoned by a military tribunal for subversion and anti-military activities.

Denied the right to call parliament and form a government after its victory in the May 1990 elections, the NLD met on 29 July and called, *inter alia*, for convening parliament in September 1990, and a meeting between SLORC representatives and NLD representatives. The junta did not move on a transfer of power, but several NLD leaders were arrested in September for breaking existing laws such as those related to publications and printing, and official secrets.

Subsequently, some elected NLD representatives and party activists in Mandalay (the second largest city) got together during September and October of 1990, and attempted to form a parallel government. The government arrested many of those involved, and the rest fled to the Thai-Myanmar border. On 18 December 1990, a parallel government called the National Coalition Government of the Union of Burma (NCGUB) was established under the aegis of the DAB (Democratic Alliance of Burma) based at Manerplaw (Kayin insurgents' headquarters).[36] Thus, the NLD was split into a legal main faction inside Myanmar, and an illegal rump named NLD-LA (liberated areas) abroad that was eventually disowned by the former.

The NLD took part in the NC, and played a low key conciliatory role until resuscitated by Daw Aung San Suu Kyi, after her release from house arrest on 10 July 1995. The NLD delegates walked out of the NC in November 1995, ostensibly due to dissatisfaction with the conduct of the proceedings, and were subsequently expelled for breach of discipline. Thereafter, relations between the Government and the NLD's leadership became fraught with difficulties, resulting in a political impasse that remains until the present day. In the next two years, the NLD and its leadership appeared somewhat marginalized and moribund. Daw Aung San Suu Kyi's movements continued to be restricted, and visitors to her residence were screened by the security forces. Party activities were severely compromised as prior permission from local authorities was required for all public activities, and this was seldom granted.

The NLD picked up momentum in 1998. In May it set 21 August as the deadline for convening the Parliament with elected representatives who had won in 1990. The deadline passed without any major incident, but party leaders publicly expressed their determination to continue their challenge by convening a people's parliament in the near future. Thereafter, the government stepped up the psychological warfare against the NLD and its supporters at home and abroad by allowing a deluge of op-ed pieces in newspapers that ridiculed, belittled, berated, and condemned Daw Aung San Suu Kyi and the NLD leadership. The government warned that the illegal convening of a "national parliament" in the absence of a "national constitution" would be tantamount to the NLD assuming the role of a parallel government "which no government in the world could accept".[37] In September, scores of NLD elected representatives and hundreds of party activists were temporarily taken away for prolonged "discussions" with local authorities. Subsequently, the government announced a cascading series of voluntary resignations by NLD members, and dissolution of local party branches continued until the end of the year.

The NLD raised the stakes again by announcing the formation of the "Committee Representing the People's Parliament" (CRPP), chaired by

NLD Chairman U Aung Shwe, on 16 September, to act "on behalf of the Parliament until a parliamentary session attended by all the elected representatives is convened". The CRPP, comprising ten members (mainly from the NLD Central Executive Committee), passed resolutions claiming the right to exercise political activities, affirming parliamentary immunity for elected representatives from prosecution over their discharge of duties, and calling for the immediate and unconditional release of all political prisoners (whose existence is denied by the government). The CRPP also proclaimed that all laws, rules, procedural laws, orders and notifications passed after the military coup of 18 September 1988, except for those specifically endorsed by the CRPP, as well as some allegedly "repressive" laws dating from the parliamentary era, were deemed to have no legal authority. Daw Aung San Suu Kyi's appeal to elected parliaments of the world to recognize the CRPP, however, did not elicit any response.

Since September 1998, many of the NLD township organizing committees and branches had publicly declared their dissolution. Tens of thousands had resigned from the party, ostensibly over the confrontational stance and intransigent attitude of the party leadership. By mid-2000, the organizational network of the NLD, which claimed to have two million members in early 1990, had all but collapsed. It was left with only 110 elected representatives due to attrition during the decade following the elections. Still, as the party entered the thirteenth year of existence, the top leadership of the NLD remained uncompromising in its challenge to the ruling SPDC.

State Ideology

During the parliamentary period (1948–62) governments adhered to a quasi-official ideology of democratic socialism, combined with an economic nationalism biased against foreign economic interests. However, the Burmese Way to Socialism (BWS), espoused by the RC and adopted by the BSPP, was the country's only formally articulated state ideology. The one-party Socialist State established by the 1974 Constitution also subscribed to the BWS as the guiding principle in so much as the BWS had been the ideology of the BSPP that led the state and its citizens.

The BWS (*Myanma Hsoshelit Lanzin*), was announced in a policy declaration on 30 April 1962. Inspired by the *Do Bama* (We Burman) socialist tradition of the pre-independence nationalists, the BWS denounced bureaucratic practices, repudiated parliamentary democracy as the means to Myanmar's socialist goals, and promised to develop a non-exploitative planned socialist economy and institute a socialist democracy appropriate to Myanmar conditions.[38] In fact, the *Myanma Hsoshelit Lanzin Parti* or BSPP was established to operationalize the BWS into political practice. This was followed by publication of the theoretical treatise representing the BSPP's world view in January 1963, grandiously entitled "The System of Correlation of Man and His Environment". It was an eclectic mixture of Buddhist tradition and Marxist dialectics couched in general terms, open to various interpretations depending on the context. The upheaval of 1988 could be interpreted as an ideological repudiation of the BWS for its perceived failure to bring prosperity and social justice.

The post-1988 military junta (both SLORC and SPDC) has not formulated any state ideology as such but it has articulated a set of official "main causes" that can be taken as representing a quasi-official ideology. They are: Non-disintegration of the Union; Non-disintegration of the National Solidarity; and Consolidation of Sovereignty. These serve the purpose of guiding and justifying the junta's actions and responses against the NLD and its Western supporters as well as all its detractors at home and abroad.

Civil Society and Human Rights

During the first few years after independence Myanmar was engulfed in civil war, with states of emergency proclaimed in many parts of the country. Conditions were not conducive to the development of civil society. Civil liberties were, more often than not, suspended and the issue of human rights never articulated. In the decade leading to the 1962 coup, there was a relatively free press (which was nevertheless partial to various political parties) and a plethora of civic groups — mainly based on ethnic, regional, and religious affinity — business organizations, peasant, trade, and student unions (often linked to political parties), and self-help groups. Civil society, though weak and fragmented, was starting to take root by around 1960, with the ruling party's encouragement, but was cut short by the 1962 military coup. Rights and freedoms over the same period were marred by sporadic political violence, and the government of the day often exercised its prerogatives under the Sedition Act, the Public Order Preservation Act, the Official Secrets Act, and the Unlawful Association Act, to the detriment of its detractors.[39]

During the RC era, trade unions and student unions were abolished and private business organizations became dormant under the autarkic economy. The junta's restrictions on formation of associations and organizations resulted in the virtual disappearance of civil society groups except those dedicated to purely religious activities, old students associations and fraternal associations based on geographical roots (mainly commonality of birthplace).

Under the provisions of the 1974 Constitution, Myanmar citizens enjoyed the fundamental rights in the form of cultural freedom, religious freedom, security of possessions and wealth, freedom of expression, freedom of association, and the freedom to lodge complaints over grievances. Nevertheless, these rights were constrained by the higher social needs to preserve state security and sovereignty, the essence of socialism, racial harmony and national unity, public order, and public morality. During the era of the one-party Socialist State, the BSPP and its affiliated organizations dominated the society in all spheres of activities, leaving virtually no space for an autonomous civil society to develop. At that time, however, international attention was not focused on Myanmar, and little attention was given to it by human rights organizations, the Western media and governments, or the United Nations.

Ironically, it was only after SLORC decided to open up the economy and allow some pluralism in the political arena, giving sustenance to some emerging civil society elements, that human rights and civil liberties came to the fore in the relationship between state and society in Myanmar.[40] Compared to the BSPP era there is more space for civil society to develop under SPDC rule, despite the absence of Constitutional guarantees. Apart from the traditional socio-cultural and religious groups, the new constellation of non-governmental organizations (NGOs), business groups and the emerging middle class adds diversity and dynamism into Myanmar society, making it less dependent on the state.

On the other hand, NGOs in Myanmar are either professional associations or functional organizations that aim to foster and enhance national and sectoral goals of the state, or are adjunct to government agencies in performing specific tasks. There is no issue-based NGO in a socio-political sense that is autonomous from the state.

The junta's detractors including the NLD, human rights groups, pro-democracy lobbies, and armed ethnic opposition groups, as well as the United States and its Western allies have persistently accused SLORC and the SPDC of condoning human rights violations and suppression of democracy activists. In particular, Amnesty International and Humans Rights Watch claim to have documented numerous violation of human rights, and the International Labour Organization (ILO) has also condemned the junta for alleged employment of forced labour. Other allegations from international organisations are that hundreds of thousands have been internally displaced, in addition to a huge number that have fled to neighbouring countries due to ethnic conflict, and that high-profile promotion of the Buddhist faith has led to discrimination against other faiths and coercive proselytization. As punitive measures, the United States, some Western countries and the European Union (EU) have imposed arms embargoes, removals of trade privileges, a ban on new investments (by the United States President's executive order of 20 May 1997) and visa restrictions (by the EU) on Myanmar officials. The UN Human Rights Commission (UNHRC) has repeatedly called for the cessation of the alleged human right violation in Myanmar. UN Secretary General Kofi Annan has also deplored the human rights situation and sent his special envoy to Myanmar on several occasions in the last few years to mediate between the junta and the political opposition.

The Myanmar Government has consistently and persistently rebutted all such allegations and refused to acknowledge any wrong-doing, while claiming the right of a sovereign nation to conduct its internal affairs without interference. From the junta's view, the UN's increasing attention on human rights and democracy in Myanmar is deemed unwarranted.

MAJOR POLITICAL ISSUES

Who Has Power?

All governments and political leaders of Myanmar have claimed that power belongs to its citizens and they are there to serve the people. The term *mi-pha pyithu* or "people who are our parents" is frequently used, especially during elections and in times of crisis.

Up to 1956, the ruling party dominated the political landscape of Myanmar and power at the centre was concentrated at the top of the AFPFL hierarchy. However, in the countryside, local "bosses" (most of them allied to the ruling party's top personalities), many of whom had private armed followers, held sway over their domains. In the Shan State and other areas under emergency rule, the local military commander practically ran the place. Despite the quasi-federal structure of the state and government, the majority Bamars dominated the political arena and the ethnic representatives could only get into the corridors of power by being co-opted by the ruling party.

When the AFPFL leaders split into contending factions in the second half of the 1950s, power became more fragmented at the political centre and leftist and ethnic-based parties, factions, and even individual representatives became significant in the shifting coalitions. In the countryside, the local bosses also figured prominently depending on their ability to "deliver" resources and votes and "fix problems" for their mentors in the capital. Despite winning an overwhelming victory in the 1960 elections, Prime Minister U Nu's government suffered from a diffusion of power due to internecine struggle within the ruling party. The increasing isolation of U Nu, whose authoritarian temperament became more evident during the short tenure of this government, led to a drift, in a government that faced increasing challenges from ethnic leaders. Business leaders and prominent entrepreneurs, many ethnic Indians, wielded some influence on powerful politicians, and enjoyed their patronage as well.

The 1962 coup made the military the centre of power in Myanmar. For the next 26 years the authoritarian military remained the most powerful political institution. Its supreme commander General Ne Win (who formally retired from the military in 1971) acquired an unprecedented personal authority and an awesome reputation, despite the absence of a personality cult and the norm of collective decision-making advocated by himself and the BSPP. The No. 1, as he was referred to by his subordinates, admirers, and detractors wielded considerable power both during the RC period of direct military rule as well as in the subsequent BSPP socialist one-party rule in which the military indirectly controlled state and society. Many still believe, despite persistent denials by both parties, that the retired general has had a hand in decisions on major issues of concern to the current junta. During that period ethnic groups were accorded some local autonomy and their leaders were co-opted by the regime in a supporting role. The ruling party and the government took great pains to portray its magnanimity towards the minorities in providing them with opportunities for social and political advancement, but suspicions of a glass ceiling for the latter were never allayed. Because of the inward-looking and nationalistic economic policies the role of the business community in the power relationship was negligible.

Under SPDC rule, there is no doubt that the Bamar-dominated military as a corporate body holds the power and exercises it resolutely. The ultimate decision-making power probably belongs to the junta chairman whose seniority within the junta is almost a generation ahead of other senior junta members. However, for all practical purposes, the quinquepartite of top five junta leaders (chairman, vice-chairman and the three secretaries) is the focus of national power. The power and authority of the regional military commanders over their respective territories, that appeared to have been increasing over the last few decades, seems to have reached a high point with their induction into the junta. In a similar vein, senior military officers who are PDC chairmen at the state/division and district level hold local power. Though not directly involved in public affairs, military base commanders and station (cantonment) chiefs (brigadier rank) as well as those in charge of regional operation commands and military operation commands (brigadier rank) probably share power and privileges with their counterparts in the PDCs.

In the border areas, the leaders of armed groups (officially 17 by mid-2000) that had made peace with the junta have maintained their authority as leaders of the respective national races, and are allowed to keep their armed troops. They enjoyed close working relations with junta members and are tacitly recognized by the government as members of an influential local power elite. Some of them lead quasi-political organizations, while others have become very successful entrepreneurs at the national level, thereby further enhancing their clout.

The civil service wields very little power on its own but it has relatively more authority than in the BSPP era and in some agencies, with important functional responsibilities, bureaucrats manage to exercise local power over the populace.

After the opening of the economy in late 1988, a small coterie of local business tycoons has emerged who have been co-opted by powerful personalities in the military and government. The patronage network of this (mostly *nouveau riche*) class is still small and probably comprises a few dozen in the inner circle. They appear to have some inputs into the power holders' decision-making calculus at the central and/or regional level in economic issues related to their line of business or the relevant branch of an economic sector. At the local level, the business lobby also has some influence through close rapport with local authorities.

Currently, there are few institutional checks and balances to the power holders in Myanmar. On their part, they claim to be sincere and patriotic individuals who are not going to hold on to the power longer than necessary. In this context, it has been stated that the "the military government regards itself as a transitional or caretaker government exacting a step-by-step transformation to democracy [that] it cherishes for the entire nation".[41]

Under the new Constitution, the executive presidency will be the locus of power. The legislature and the judiciary would provide a certain degree of check and balance against presidential power but the central executive appears to have an edge in the power relationship among institutions that will govern the envisaged unitary state. Some power will be vested in the Region and States (of the Union) and in the case of the latter the ethnic nationalities will have some say in their locality. Nevertheless, the centre is likely to prevail in all critical and national issues.

Who Benefits?

The favourite refrain of all Myanmar leaders is that the people are the ultimate beneficiaries of the political system of the day.[42] It is customary to speak of delivering the three essential needs, viz., "food, clothing and shelter" to the masses. In reality, the differential impacts of successive governments since independence on different sections of society have resulted in a series of winners and losers in the relative sense, as well as a wide variation in benefits.

During the first decade of independence the civil war severely disrupted the lives of the populace, especially in the rural areas. Compounded by the devastation suffered during World War II, the rural population of peasant farmers were impoverished. The land nationalization and reform programme of the AFPFL government succeeded in abolishing an absentee landlord class but, by and large, failed to emancipate the farmers. Landlessness remained a critical problem, and rural-urban migration, driven by security and economic conditions in the countryside, was very much evident. Underemployment and unemployment was prevalent in the mid-1950s as the state's drive to foster import-substituting industrialization fizzled out. Security conditions improved substantially with the institution of the military caretaker government in 1958. Meanwhile, the retreat of the state from direct intervention in the economy fostered a budding private industrial sector (mainly urban) and a viable commercial sector (both rural and urban) in the second half of the parliamentary period. Consequently, the fulfilment of the three essential needs for the general populace seemed to be within reach in the next decade.

The main beneficiaries of the AFPFL rule in the urban economy were traders and industrialists close to the ruling elite, including non-citizens (Indian and some Chinese). Political patronage allowed some in the business community to reap windfall profits from a national economy closed to foreign direct investment (FDI). Though abject poverty and starvation were not apparent, workers and the peasants did not benefit substantially from the little that trickled down, since GDP growth in the 1950s was a modest 5 per cent from a very low base. Statistics on income distribution are not available, but anecdotal evidence suggests that inequality was high. In the urban sector this was probably accentuated by government policies on trade and industry that favoured the local business elite.

In the decade that followed, the military junta instituted an autarkic economy and nationalized most private business concerns. As a result, the incipient business class was almost wiped out but for the black market economy that expanded steadily and provided a niche for the more audacious business people. The junta professed to uplift the well being of peasants and workers, but its autarkic policies, restrictions on land ownership, cropping and marketing, fixed pricing, and compulsory procurement of crops, negatively affected the farmers' income and livelihood in such a way that the much-vaunted abolition of the exploitative capitalist class could not make up for the farmer's disadvantaged position *vis-a-vis* urban state employees who had access to subsidized (but rationed) staples and benefited from government price controls on commodities and services. On the whole, one could say that the income distribution became more equitable under the RC rule due to the levelling affect of the autarkic economy. The winners seemed to be those who had cornered the thriving underground market. Moreover, the multiplier affect of the informal sector enabled many people to find means of livelihood despite limited employment opportunities. Underemployment was the order of the day in the public sector. The (mainly private) service sector, which had latched on to the informal economy, grew at the expense of the productive sector and provided some relief to the unemployed and underemployed.

The BSPP era saw some economic growth in the middle of its 14 year period, due to a relatively high infusion of official development assistance, relaxation of restrictive regulations on trade and agriculture, and the success of high-yielding rice varieties in paddy farming (the mainstay of the agriculture sector). Sections of rural farmers who cultivated paddy and de-controlled crops benefited most from these developments but the business environment in the urban areas remained stagnant. The rapid expansion of the BSPP and the state apparatus provided some employment. However, educated unemployment increased with the huge expansion of educational facilities that outstripped job opportunities. The urban workers with fixed salaries fell behind the successful farmers in terms of income and standard of living. In the last stages of the one-party socialist era, the economy faltered and the whole country was affected. Government attempts to curb inflation and punish the lucrative business of blackmarketeering by demonetizing currency notes hurt the population more than the intended targets.

Throughout the entire BSPP period, the party *nomenklatura* and those in the military and the state apparatus enjoyed perks and privileges which, though modest by capitalist standards, put them a cut above the rest in terms of material benefits. Though the provision of the three essential needs by the BSPP regime was more successful than its predecessor, the relative deprivation in relation to the ruling class was perceived to be greater than before and the gap between the ruling elite and the masses was seen as widening steadily. This was one of the probable causes of the 1988 upheaval.

Under the SLORC and SPDC regimes employment opportunities in the private sector have grown substantially due to the opening up of the economy to both FDI and private initiatives. The corporate interests of the military remain satisfied by ventures in areas such as mining, industry, agriculture, finance and banking, trade, and services. Nationally, the agriculture sector seems to be reaping most of the benefits of the marketization process. Moreover, the incessant building of transport infrastructure by the military government, though not without opportunity costs, clearly benefits the rural sector. Rural incomes of farmers cultivating cash crops and rice have risen substantially. These peasants are generally better off than urban workers, the majority of whom have to endure double-digit inflation and rapid escalation of housing costs in the 1990s. The continued existence of a flourishing informal sector — despite market-oriented reforms in the formal sector — enabled many people to find a niche for their livelihood in the turbulent market economy.

A struggling middle class comprising small-scale private entrepreneurs and professionals has taken root in the last decade. At the apex of the business community lies a small group of local "tycoons" (see the previous section) who enjoyed state support in their entrepreneurial activities and have amassed fortunes from near-monopolies and oligopolies in the earlier phase of market expansion. Some of them still enjoyed similar advantages and continued expanding while other are stretched thin by ventures that are either caught in the wrong phase of the business cycle (the real estate boom collapsed in the late 1990s) or by too rapid an expansion. Apart from those in the umbra of state patronage there is a much larger group in the penumbra who are exploiting opportunities offered by the new business environment. Numbering perhaps tens of thousands, these entrepreneurs enjoy a rapport with local authorities and live a comfortable life, owning property, cars and modern amenities.

The ethnic groups that have maintained cease-fires with the government are also benefiting from the latter's border areas development programme that provides health, welfare, education and infrastructure facilities (to which a dedicated ministry is assigned), and business opportunities in local resource extraction and border trade, as well as a number of government concessions on imports/exports and taxation.

In the business community, non-Bamar citizens of Chinese and Indian origin appear to be enjoying the same opportunities as their Bamar counterparts. In fact, they probably enjoyed some advantages over their Bamar counterparts by reviving their connections with the overseas ethnic network that was disrupted over three decades ago. The so-called *guanxi* (personal connections) factor may have contributed significantly for their success, especially in the border trade business.

Another small but growing group that benefits from economic openness is made up of Bamar expatriate workers, mainly skilled labour and professionals. No figures are available but there are likely to be tens of thousands of such expatriates who are earning hard currency abroad, mainly in East Asia but spread all over the world. Though their numbers are relatively small in relation to the work force, they are significant in that their return would strengthen the middle class due to their international exposure and accumulated savings.

Extent of Legitimacy?

The legitimacy of the AFPFL parliamentary regime was challenged by a variety of ethnic and communist rebellions throughout its decade-long rule. If elections are taken as indicators of legitimacy in a democratic political system, the AFPFL's appeared to decline steadily in the first decade of independence. The party enjoyed an overwhelming electoral mandate in the pre-independence constituent assembly elections in 1947, and was returned in the 1951 elections with a majority (in the parliament winning some 60 per cent of the seats as well as votes cast). That election was held under very difficult security conditions in the middle of the civil war making its fairness questionable. In the 1956 elections, seen as relatively free and fair, the AFPFL still won control of the parliament with around 58 per cent of the seats but its share of the popular vote shrunk to about 48 per cent. After the party's split, U Nu's faction, renamed the *Pyidaungsu* (Union) Party won the 1960 elections convincingly by winning 81 per cent of the seats and two-thirds of the popular votes. Observers opined that this victory was more of a personalized endorsement of the charismatic U Nu and a protest vote against his rivals, than a resounding endorsement for the winning party. Despite the vitriolic campaigning and some reports about coercion, vote-buying, and cheating by both sides, analysts deemed it as free and fair as possible under the circumstances.

The caretaker military government that assumed power in the 1958-60 period enjoyed widespread legitimacy at the outset but its strict and regimented style of governing rankled many in later stages. The lingering resentment against this regime, perceived as close to U Nu's rivals, probably contributed to U Nu's victory in the elections that followed. The RC was initially welcomed with some relief by the populace after experiencing uncertainty and a sense of drift in U Nu's government afflicted with internecine power struggle and besieged by increasing demands for autonomy by ethnic politicians. The harsh revolutionary measures and the autarkic economic policies rapidly eroded support, but faced with the might of a military junta people accepted the rule fatalistically.

The BSPP regime held four elections in which the voters had to choose whether to vote for or against a single candidate, usually endorsed by the BSPP. There were very high turnouts, and virtually all candidates were elected to the parliament and the regional/local peoples councils with overwhelming majority of votes. However, as pointed out by one specialist, in the BSPP era, "elections are means of socializing individuals into the norms of the state" and "of legitimizing its activities" and served to affirm existing power rather than to redistribute power.[43] As such, people had developed the capacity to accept the status quo with resignation. The challenge to the BSPP regime's legitimacy by multiple insurgencies continued unabated and the number of rebel groups as well as their strength appeared to have increased during the period concerned.

The overwhelming election victory of the NLD in the May 1990 elections was interpreted by some observers as a repudiation of SLORC by the public at large — similar to U Nu's victory in 1960. Both the SPDC and SLORC (its predecessor) have been actively seeking performance legitimacy through various economic reforms and development programmes in general, and much-publicized infrastructure projects in particular. This is being supplemented by attempts to utilize the symbolic dimension of legitimacy by reviving Myanmar traditions in language, literature, culture, and religion and appealing to the people's nationalist sentiments. Huge public turnouts in commemorative events and mass rallies organized to denounce opposition actions and foreign interference, could be taken an indicator of mass support for the regime but similar behaviour during the deposed BSPP regime did not translate into mass support when the crunch came.

The SPDC's legitimacy and authority have been challenged by domestic and external elements. The political awakening of the masses triggered by the 1988 upheaval liberated a huge amount of pent-up emotions and energy sympathetic to the opponents of the regime who used democracy as a catch-all term to challenge SLORC's legitimacy and authority. The mobilization of masses by aspiring politicians and the tremendous surge of political activities following the liberalization of the political domain was accompanied by sharp criticisms of the military's conduct in the 1988 upheaval as well its subsequent role in administering the state. The junta, however, claimed *de facto* legitimacy by portraying itself as the restorer of law and order (SLORC) after the apparent chaos and anarchy of 1988, and the provider of peace and development (SPDC) in the next phase.

The Western press, NGOs, expatriate dissident groups, and even some governments almost continuously condemn and criticize the military over a wide spectrum of issues ranging from logging to human rights while praising and lionizing the democratic opposition. However, there is scant evidence that such denunciations and vilification have any significant impact on the legitimacy of the regime as perceived by the people. It could even provoke nationalist sentiments and indignant reaction among the people leading to a pro-government stance. It is highly likely that peoples' perceptions on the regime's legitimacy are more influenced by economic considerations and the sense of physical well-being rather than international condemnation based on human rights and democratic norms.

Headway has been made against the ethnic insurgencies. The government has secured peace agreements with 17 major insurgent groups, and those remaining are no match for the overwhelming power of the Myanmar armed forces.

Governance

The successive governments of Myanmar from 1948 to 1988 had performed unsatisfactorily in fostering economic development. The parliamentary governments pursued a failed strategy of self-reliant ISI and economic nationalism, while the RC government impoverished the country through autarkic policies. The BSPP socialist regime tried to mimic a developmental state with the help of ODA funds, but failed to achieve sustained growth due to its inward-looking economic policies and discrimination against the private sector.

The SPDC's economic policies appear to be *ad hoc* at times, especially those concerning trade and commerce. It is banking on agriculture as the leading sector in its push for growth. However, lack of transparency in policy-making as well as in implementation and monitoring of progress makes it very difficult to assess their success or failure. Official statistics are inadequate, and lack timeliness. In fact, most macroeconomic data are now considered classified, making them unavailable in open literature and inaccessible to independent analysts. The government does not tolerate criticism of its economic policies and practices; the deputy minister of national planning, a brigadier general, was dismissed in mid-2000 for doing so. Myanmar has not received any significant ODA or loans from multilateral financial institutions since the military's power seizure in 1988, so issues of accountability in economic governance have not been subject to as much international scrutiny as in other regional countries affected by the recent Asian financial crisis.

Domestically, the issue of accountability has been obviated by very nature of the power structure whereby the junta is not accountable to anyone or any organization but itself. Nevertheless, graft and corruption appears to be the issue most representative of the problem of accountability in Myanmar.

Rumours of high level corruption surfaced from time to time during the later years of SLORC rule. Several ministers cum SLORC members in charge of commercially-active ministries were suspected to have been involved in corrupt practices, and were replaced in the Cabinet reshuffle following the transformation of SLORC into SPDC in November 1997. In 1998, dozens of their personal assistants, staff officers, and executives closely associated with these ministers lost their jobs and many of them were detained or given long prison sentences. Subsequently, occasional announcement of resignation or replacement of ministers, deputy ministers, or heads of government agencies led to speculation and rumours about corruption and collusion. Anecdotal evidence suggests that endemic corruption exist in the low-level bureaucracy and corruption, collusion and cronyism may be on the rise at higher levels from a low base.

The central bank is not autonomous to the finance ministry and there has always been a soft budget constraint. Fiscal prudence is far from being satisfactory according to international standards and monetary policies tend to accommodate deficit spending and are constrained by persistent balance of payments problems.

In general, policy-making in Myanmar has been opaque and centralized since the 1950s. This top-down approach is still much evident under the SPDC. Participation by civil society is virtually non-existence and there are no countervailing elements to the domineering state in the process of governance.

CONCLUSION

Four major political objectives enunciated by SLORC, and maintained by the SPDC refer to:

- stability of the state, community peace and tranquillity, prevalence of law and order;
- national reconsolidation;
- emergence of a new enduring state constitution;
- building of a new modern developed nation in accordance with the new constitution.

The realization of the fourth objective appears to have been premised upon the attainment of the first three goals. Thus, as far as the government is concerned the political practice and the dynamics of political participation at the present phase should be subordinate to these four political objectives which represent higher "national politics" in contrast what it perceived as narrow self-serving "party politics" that characterized political parties.

The military asserted that it "represents no political ideology whatsoever" nor "any particular class of people", and "does not represent any national group" or "any particular territory". Citing its considerable political experience, purportedly "much greater" than that of political parties, it has staked a claim for itself in national politics to permit the Tatmadaw a role in the future political leadership of Myanmar.[44]

The political space in Myanmar has been significantly circumscribed by perceived imperatives of national security since the upheaval of 1988. From the national security perspective the identities of the state, the regime, and the military all appear to have been amalgamated to form a seamless web in which the security interests of one institution cannot be considered apart from those of another.

As such, political challenges and attempts to extend the political space by political parties, groups, or individuals are regarded as security challenges endangering the unitary state. Dissent is given little latitude, and loyalty is highly valued. Law and order and maintenance of peace in the country takes precedence over all other issues be they inequity, or social justice or the environment. The government has time and again come up with alleged expose' of conspiracies and plots against the state perpetrated by domestic and external enemies. These, more often than not, seem to have entailed NLD involvement in one way or the other.

Indeed, the most persistent challenge to the government has come from the NLD. The NLD leaders have constantly tried to organize public gatherings, meetings, conferences and excursions. They have publicized speeches, distributed party pamphlets, issued statements, and contacted the foreign media without seeking permission from relevant authorities or not bothering to wait for a reply to its request.

In response, the government has been enacting and amending laws and acts related to printing and publishing, audio and video material and computers and electronic media. In this context, with the advent of the Internet (which the NLD and the expatriate dissidents and NGOs have been utilizing with significant impact abroad) control, management, and dissemination of information is likely to become more important in future contests for the hearts and minds of the public between the government and its detractors.

If the SPDC gets its way, it is eminently clear that the nature of government and constitutional politics in future Myanmar will not emulate the orthodoxy suggested by liberal democratic traditions. It is ostensibly tailored for Myanmar conditions, as perceived by the military leaders who are not prepared to leave the fate of the future Myanmar state in the hands of political parties. A strong state led by an autonomous national leader is deemed not only desirable but also essential for national unity as well as economic development. It follows that the military must play a leading role in national politics. This could lead to an institutional symbiosis with the state. Although societal aspirations for participation and representation may be satisfied by a multi-party electoral process, the military's institutionalized dual function will prevent the dominance of political parties in defining the national interest and setting the policy agenda. This could ultimately lead to the de-linking of state power from political power.

The timing of the current military attempt to control the political process has both advantages and disadvantages. Overt challenges to national security posed by armed insurrections have declined substantially. The Communist threat has disappeared and most armed ethnic groups had been accommodated through separate accords with the government. This releases more resources for the military's national political undertaking. However, the recent regional economic crisis has made it more difficult to obtain needed foreign investment, and upheaval in Indonesia has complicated apparent efforts to move towards an Indonesian-style political arrangement. Growing international support for intervention in the international affairs of other countries for perceived human rights violations has been an added obstacle.

The military's search for an enduring formula to ensure national unity, territorial integrity, accountability, and socio-economic well-being for the polity is a complex and demanding task which requires finesse, sensitivity and magnanimity as well. Its envisaged pivotal role in the state-society nexus entails not mere acquiescence but whole-hearted cooperation by the public at large. Moreover, the type of legitimacy conferred to those associated with the independence movement is no longer available to current military leaders, who would have to rely on the "performance legitimacy" contingent upon the delivery of political and economic goods. In this context the political system and practice envisaged by the SPDC is likely to emulate an illiberal democracy, whereby concepts such as equality, freedom, pluralism are reinterpreted and fused with indigenous values as perceived by the military and refashioned into what the military has identified as "discipline flourishing democracy". The procedural component of this democracy centred around periodic elections may not be different from its liberal counterpart. Nevertheless, it is likely to be of a different spirit and character.

Notes

1 See, e.g., Benedict Anderson, *Imagined Communities: Reflection on the Origin and Spread of Nationalism*, revised edition (London: Verso, 1993).

2 Robert H. Taylor, "The Relationship between Burmese Social Classes and British Indian Policy on the Behavior of the Burmese Political Elite, 1937–1942". Ph.D. dissertation, Cornell University, 1974, p. 663.

3 Ibid., p. 664.

4 See Tin Maung Maung Than, "Myanmar Democratization: Punctuated Equilibrium of Retrograde Motion?". In *Democratization in Southeast and East Asia*, edited by Anek Laothamatas (Singapore: Institute of Southeast Asian Studies, 1997), pp. 181–87.

5 Daw Than Han, "Common Vision: Burma's Regional Outlook". Occasional Paper (Washington, D.C: Institute for the Study of Diplomacy, 1988), p. 11.

6 Government of Burma, *Burma 1983: Population Census* (Rangoon: Immigration and Manpower Department, 1986), p. 21-22. Ethnic activists opposing the military regime contended that these figures underestimated the proportions of the minority groups. The 135 sub-nationalities comprised: 12 for Kachin; 9 for Kayah; 11 for Kayin; 53 for Chin; 9 for Bamar; one for Mon; 7 for Rakhine; and 33 for Shan (*Lokethar Pyithu Neizin* [Myanmar language daily], 26 September 1990).

7 The state continues to support the organized hierarchy of the Order of Buddhist monks instituted in 1980. Newspapers, which are invariably state-owned, have carried front-page news of military leaders visiting Buddhist monuments and paying respects to senior monks on their field trips. The state sponsored the bringing of the sacred Tooth Relic of Buddha from Beijing twice during the 1990s and also took the lead in the building (with privately

donated funds) of two commemorative pagodas (housing replicas of the Tooth Relic) in Yangon and Mandalay. Celebrations of Buddhist festivals and consecrations of religious artifacts as well as generous donations to Pagodas, monasteries and Buddhist organizations are also much publicized, notwithstanding the fact that the government assiduously extends support for other major religions such as Christianity and Islam as well.

8 The government has imposed licensing requirements for both imports and exports. Foreign currency is strictly controlled and the local currency (the kyat) is not convertible under normal circumstances. There is believed to be a large informal sector that escapes the tax net and reputedly involving illegal transactions as well (*Myanview*, October 1997; ibid., July 1998; and personal communications).

9 The seven States are Chin, Kachin, Kayah, Kayin (Karen), Mon, Rakhine (Arakan), and Shan. The seven Divisions are Ayeyawady (Irrawaddy), Bago (Pegu), Magway (Magwe), Mandalay, Sagaing, Tanintharyi (Tenasserim), and Yangon (Rangoon).

10 This is the most objectionable point from the military's current perspective. It is seen as a source for the eventual disintegration of the Union See, e.g., Nawrahta, *Destiny of the Nation* (Yangon: The News and Periodicals Enterprise, 1995), p. 90.

11 Ibid., p. 50.

12 Those elected "people's representatives" would then be appointed as state executives, legislators, and members of the judicial, legal, and inspection authorities, all under the guidance and supervision of the corresponding BSPP hierarchy .

13 The address by the Chairman of the National Convention Convening Commission, Lt. Gen, Myo Nyunt at the Convention's plenary session on 7 June 1993 (*New Light of Myanmar* [hereafter *NLM*], 8 June 1993).

14 Ibid.

15 See, *NLM*, 12 January 1994.There was no separate group for military personnel who were included in the service personnel group. The ratio of the former in the latter was not revealed. It appeared that under this allocation scheme, the ostensibly apolitical delegates selected by the authorities outnumbered the political representatives by more than three to one.

16 Chairman of the NCCWC, Chief Justice U Aung Toe's address to the National Convention on 16 September 1993 and on 2 September 1994 (*NLM*, various issues). Those points on military participation in governance and the executive presidency were not endorsed by some political parties including the National League for Democracy (NLD) and its affiliates.

17 *NLM*, 1 September 1998.

18 Ibid.

19 These routine functions can be quite overwhelming because there still is a lot of central control over the operations of the agencies under line ministries.

Internal administrative and service affairs are put up to the minister's office and often times require Cabinet or Sub-Cabinet approval. Some examples are: awarding state scholarship; official travel abroad; meeting with foreigners; procurement of capital equipment; and resignations of officers. Anecdotal evidence suggests that most ministers, deputy ministers and agency heads spend long hours at offices and many stayed overnight at headquarters.

20 See for example, *Government of Myanmar, Nation-Building Endeavours, Volume Three: Historic Records of Endeavours Made by the State Law and Order Restoration Council (From 1 April 1995 to 14 November 1997)*, (Yangon: Printing and Publishing Sub-Committee, Government of Myanmar, 1999), pp. 105–10.

21 Ibid., pp. 111–16.

22 Speech given by Secretary-1, Major-General Khin Nyunt on 4 October 1991 to heads of government agencies.

23 The highest-ranking post in a SEE is usually the managing director, while the corresponding one in non-commercial agencies is director-general.

24 The CSSTB was formed in 1977 by an act of parliament and is the successor to the Public Service Commission. It is responsible for recruiting and training civil servants at the entry level for the upper band (popularly known as gazetted officers; a colonial legacy) and the universities and colleges. It also scrutinizes and endorses proposals made by government agencies regarding internal promotions to and within the upper band. It is also in charge of the training institutes for civil servants.

25 See *Working People's Daily*, 11 May 1990. The regional commanders were given two-stars rank, while those commanding the light infantry divisions and regional naval headquarters were upgraded to Brigadier (one star) rank.

26 The number of infantry battalions reportedly increased from 168 to 422 in the decade since 1988. See, Maung Aung Myoe, "Building the Tatmadaw; The Organisational Development of the Armed Forces in Myanmar, 1948–98", SDSC Working Paper No. 327 (Canberra: ANU, 1998, pp. 24, 27).

27 This theme is present in almost all speeches made by military leaders in their addresses at graduation ceremonies for military cadets, commemorative speeches on Independence Day, Armed Forces Day and other national commemorative events as well as in addresses to military commands and units during tours and field trips.

28 The rank structure of the police was changed to conform to the army with the Chief of MPF designated as a police major general.

29 The figure is from International Institute for Strategic Studies, *The Military Balance 1999–2000* (Oxford: Oxford University Press, 1999).

30 The Chairman was a retired financial commissioner and the members were: a retired ambassador; a retired commissioner of savings and securities; a retired ethnic Kayin Brigadier; and an AFPFL era politician who was also a respected Muslim community leader. All were septuagenarians and

octogenarians on appointment and three of them including the Chairman had since passed away.

31 See, Robert Taylor, "Myanmar 1990: New Era or Old?", in *Southeast Asian Affairs 1991* (Singapore: Institute of Southeast Asian Studies, 1991), p. 204.

32 Detractors of the regime usually point out that harsh sentences have been given to "political prisoners" without "proper" proceedings. The government's answer to such allegations is that all the accused were tried and sentenced according to "existing laws", many of which have existed since the colonial days.

33 The ten parties are: Kokang Democracy and Unity Party; National Unity Party; Union Karen League; Union Pa-O National Organization; Mro or Khami National Solidarity Organization; Shan Nationalities League for Democracy; Shan State Kokang Democratic Party; Lahu National Development Party; Wa National Development Party; and the well-known National League for Democracy.

34 This observation is based on the NUP's election campaign broadcast and its stand in the NC deliberations.

35 This observation is based on numerous speeches by Daw Aung San Suu Kyi and various postings on the Internet attributed to the NLD headquarters.

36 Dr Sein Win, first cousin of Daw Aung San Suu Kyi and an elected representative, became the Prime Minister of the NCGUB which never managed to secure official recognition by any foreign government. The DAB was formed in November 1988 as a united front of 21 insurgent groups against SLORC.

37 Myanmar Information Committee, Government of Myanmar, "Information Sheet No. A 0589 (I)", 2 September 1998 (Internet edition).

38 See "Burmese Way to Socialism", in *The System of Correlation of Man and His Environment*, 3d ed. (Rangoon: BSPP, 1964), pp. 43–52.

39 See for example, chapter 4 of Maung Maung Gyi, *Burmese Political Values: The Socio-Political Roots of Authoritarianism* (New York: Praeger, 1983).

40 This has been partly due to the unprecedented (for Myanmar) media exposure of the 1988 upheaval, and partly to the inclusion of liberal democratic norms in the foreign policy agenda of the United States and other Western countries, as well as the changing priorities and issues in the agenda of United Nations and multi-lateral international organizations.

41 Hla Min, Lt. Col. *Political Situation of Myanmar and its Role in the Region*, 17th ed. (Yangon: n.p., July 1999), p. 58.

42 This section is based on the following sources: Robert H Taylor, *State in Burma* (London: C. Hurst, 1987); and various issues of (Myanmar language magazine) *Dana* (Wealth), *Myanma Dana* (Myanmar's Wealth), and *Kyawnyar Hnint Zeiwei Lanhnyun* (Advertising and Buying Guide).

43 Taylor, *State in Burma*, p. 327.

44 Nawrahta, op. cit., pp. 10, 108,110.

Further Reading

Furnivall, J.S. *The Governance of Modern Burma,* 2d. edition. New York: Institute of Pacific Relations, 1960.

Government of Myanmar. *Taingkyo Pyipyu* [Nation-Building Endeavours], Volume III, 1995–1997. Yangon: Printing and Publishing Sub-Committee on the Historical Records of Endeavours made by the State Law and Order Restoration Council from 1 April 1995 to 14 November 1997, 1999.

Hla Min, Lt. Col. *Political Situation of Myanmar and its Role in the Region.* Internet edition, <www.myanmar-information.net/political/politic.htm>.

Nawrahta. *Destiny of the Nation.* Yangon: The News and Periodicals Enterprise, 1995.

Pederson, Morten B., Emily Rudland and Ronald J. May. *Burma Myanmar: Strong Regime Weak State.* Adelaide: Crawford House, 1999.

Silverstein, Josef, ed. *Independent Burma at Forty Years: Six Assessments.* Ithaca: Cornell University Southeast Asia Program, 1989.

Taylor, Robert H. *The State in Burma.* London: C. Hurst, 1987.

Weller, Marc, ed. *Democracy and Politics in Burma: A Collection of Documents.* Manerplaw: National Coalition Government of the Union of Burma, 1993.

7

PHILIPPINES
Continuing People Power

Joaquin L. Gonzalez III

INTRODUCTION

On 12 June 1998, the Philippines celebrated 100 years of independence
from Spanish colonialism. It was a century since the country declared
itself a nation-state, an independent republic after 333 years under Spanish
colonial rule. Though the first country in Asia that gained its independence
through a bloody revolution the Philippines immediately had to accept
American hegemony for another 46 years and Japanese rule for a brief
three years. The birth of the Philippine nation-state in 1898 and granting
of political independence by the Americans in 1946 are historical milestones
in the country's history that reflect the Filipinos resolve to self-govern and
determine their future as one country sans foreign colonizers.

Characteristic of a vibrant democracy, internal divisiveness and conflict
between and among classes, ideologies, and ethnicities, replaced the national
solidarity exhibited by the people in their anti-colonial struggles
immediately after America shifted the reins of government to Filipinos.
Philippine history has been characterized by the dualisms of colonialism
and neocolonialism, revolution and counter-revolution, and dictatorship
and democracy. The difficult but exciting process of making and unmaking
of a liberal democratic nation-state remains a continuing one. The country
is shaped by its past, in defining its vision, national goals and objectives,
policies, institutions, structures, and processes. Achieving national unity
in diversity continuous to be a daunting task in the post-colonial era.

Archeological and anthropological evidences show that a thriving
civilization already existed in the islands before the arrival of the first
European explorers. Beginning about 1000 BC, these original inhabitants
of what became the Philippine nation were joined by migrating Malays,

Negritos, and Indonesians. Some of them managed to pass through "land bridges" that once connected the Philippine islands with the Malay peninsula and the Indonesian archipelago. But many dared cross the treacherous seas in rough weather to get to the Philippines. These initial migrants came to the islands and joined *barangay* or village settlements. In the south, powerful Muslim sultanates controlled trade as early as the 14th century, and retained a degree of independence even during colonial rule. These initial settlers of the country hunted, fished, and planted as well as exchanged goods among themselves. By the 1400s, the local political leaders also allowed the trading of goods with "foreigners" who came in their wooden ships from — China, India, and as far away as the Middle East. Marriages among the native inhabitants and these foreign traders contributed to the cultural mix of the population.

Intrigued by tales of adventure and rich opportunities in the Far East, European explorer Ferdinand Magellan launched an expedition that claimed the islands in March 1521. As tribute to his benefactor King Philip of Spain, Magellan named the archipelago "the Philippines". Magellan was slain in a battle by Lapu-Lapu, a fierce local chieftain, and was never able to return to complete his voyage back home. Undeterred by his death, Spanish authorities decided that the country would be an ideal place for a permanent trading position. Over the next decades, Spain united and controlled the islands under a central government located in Manila. "Divide and conquer" became the motto that gave rise to the country's first western inspired politico-administrative units at the local level — provinces and towns. Aside from commercial interests, the Spaniards introduced Christianity to the native inhabitants. The Spanish government and Catholic Church in the Philippines became very powerful political institutions. Nonetheless, unequal treatment of Filipinos and abuse of their power and authority made the Spanish *conquistadores* (conquerors) and religious orders very unpopular with a majority of the local population. This led to peaceful calls for serious reforms from prominent Filipino intellectuals, the best known being Jose P. Rizal, executed by Spain in 1896. Spain's lack of attention and the Filipinos' boiling frustration transformed into an armed revolution against Spain.

Despite the declaration of Philippine independence on 12 June 1898, freedom from foreign rule was short-lived. In April 1898, war had started between Spain and the United States after the sinking of the American warship *USS Maine* in Havana, Cuba. Spain was not only fighting a losing battle with the Filipinos but was also being destroyed by the powerful armed forces of the United States. So as not to accept defeat from its non-

European subjects, Spanish authorities ceded the Philippines to the Americans for US$20 million and continued trade access, under the Treaty of Paris signed on 10 December 1898. After approval by the United States Congress, the treaty formally converted the status of the Philippines from a Spanish possession to an American colony. Serious fighting erupted between the Filipinos and Americans as a result of this political switchover. But the fighting did not last long due to the sheer superiority of the American military units.

Under their new colonizer, the Filipinos made significant gains in the areas of government and education. Unlike the Spaniards, who never allowed the Filipinos to get involved in public administration, American officials allowed limited self rule under a presidential form of government similar to the United States, and trained Filipino civil servants. They also improved the educational system, opening English medium schools to all Filipinos.

The Japanese occupied the Philippines from 1942–45. They supposedly wanted to liberate the country from western control and create a "Greater East Asia Co-Prosperity Sphere." But their puppet Filipino government left Japanese military officials firmly in control of the country. During the war period, Japanese and American forces fought many naval, air, and land battles around the Philippines. In 1945, the Americans regained possession after the liberation of Manila and the surrender of Japan. They in turn finally ended more than four centuries of foreign domination after turning over control of the government to Filipinos on 4 July 1946. A series of post-independence administrations tried very hard to wean the country from its heavy reliance on the United States. However, the economic devastation during the war led the young nation's leaders to continue seeking U.S. economic assistance and political support.

Democratic rule, however, did not necessarily follow freedom from foreign control. On 21 September 1972, President Ferdinand Marcos, using emergency powers granted to him as Chief Executive, declared martial law. Under his 21-year rule, Marcos was accused of being a dictator after he abolished the elected legislature and replaced it with a Parliament that was loyal to him. He asked the military to arrest anybody opposed to him on charges of being Communist agents. And he silenced all labor unions, media groups and student organizations, while confiscating power, water, and other vital industries owned by his political opponents. Corruption in government and human rights violations peaked under his regime.

The Marcos dictatorship ended with the bloodless People Power Revolution in February 1986. When Marcos refused to step down after disputed elections returns, civil society and the united opposition mobilized

FIGURE 7.1

Philippines: Key Dates

1521	European explorer Ferdinand Magellan sets foot on Philippine soil and claims the country for Spain.
1896	Spanish officials execute national hero Jose Rizal by firing squad in Manila.
1898	Philippine independence from Spain and the start of American occupation.
1942–45	Japanese occupation of the Philippines.
1946	United States of America grants independence to the Philippines.
1972	Martial law declared by Ferdinand Marcos.
1983	Marcos nemesis, Benigno Aquino, Jr. is murdered at the Manila International Airport.
1986	People Power revolution leads to the ouster of Ferdinand Marcos in February. Corazon Aquino becomes president.
1991	Philippines senate votes against US military bases in the country.
1992	Fidel Ramos elected president.
1998	Actor-politician Joseph "Erap" Estrada win election by the highest margin in Philippine presidential contests.
2000	Estrada becomes first president to face impeachment.
2001	Gloria Macapagal Arroyo succeeds Estrada after his ouster in a repeat of the 1986 People Power revolution.

against him, led by Corazon C. Aquino, the widow of his assassinated political nemesis Benigno Aquino, Jr. Critical religious "blessing" and military intervention were provided by Manila Archbishop Jaime Cardinal Sin, then-Armed Forces Vice Chief-of-Staff General Fidel V. Ramos, and Marcos' long-time Defense Minister Juan Ponce Enrile. Confronted by hundreds of thousands in the streets of Manila, Marcos fled to exile in Hawaii with strong encouragement from the United States.

Aquino's presidency was a trying time and a great challenge as the country was in transition from authoritarian rule to liberal democracy. Despite seven coup attempts, she persevered in setting up a new pro-people 1987 Constitution, in de-Marcosifying the governmental bureaucracy, and in re-establishing a popularly elected Congress and local government positions. After serving her six-year term, President Aquino endorsed West Point educated Fidel V. Ramos as her successor.

In a seven-candidate field Ramos won the 1992 election, with a mere 24 per cent of the vote. He continued to liberalize the country both political and economically. After decades of stagnation or decline, the country's economy started to show significant growth. The Asian economic crisis of 1997 put a damper on these gains, though the Philippines managed better than many of its neighbours.

In 1998, Ramos' Vice President and former actor Joseph E. Estrada won the Philippine presidency by the highest margin in Philippine elections. President Estrada pledged to better the achievements of the Aquino and Ramos administrations with a pro-poor agenda. But since the beginning of his term in office Estada had been accused of not living up to his pro-poor campaign promises, promoting a return to cronyism, restarting the age-old political conflict in Mindanao, and protecting and benefiting from illegal gambling activities. In November 2000 he was impeached on gambling charges, the first president to face such actions. The public, however, was convinced the Senata impeachment trial was partial, and he was forced out of office by a second people power revolution. Vice President Arroyo was sworn in as successor on 20 January 2001.

Geography

The Philippines is an archipelago of over 7,100 islands. It has a breadth of 700 miles and is surrounded by large bodies of water — the Pacific Ocean in the east, the South China Sea in the west, the Bashi Channel in the north, and the Sulu Sea and the Celebes Sea in the south. These seas are breeding grounds for tropical weather disturbances, and the Philippines is visited by an average of 20 typhoons a year. It is also the home of more than 200 volcanoes, though only around 21 are active. Typhoons and volcanoes are much a part of a Filipino's daily life, wreaking devastation but also the rain and fertile lands needed for crop farming and livestock raising.

The Philippines occupies an important geostrategic location, close to major trade routes to Northeast Asia, and adjacent to several contested islands or islets, including in the Spratlys. The country's strategic importance was highlighted by powerful American naval and airbases at Subic Bay, Olongapo and Clark Airfield, Angeles, until a nationalistic senate decided to eject the United States in 1991.

Society

As in most Asian countries, personalism is strong in Philippine society and politics, oftentimes eclipsing the political institutions where power is constitutionally vested. This is largely a consequence of the imbalance and uneven development of the country's political and economic systems. The erection of a modern state apparatus on generally agriculture-based and pre-liberal social foundations augmented the persistence of pre-capitalist forms of social exchange such as kinship, clanship, and clientelism (or patron-client links), which are regularly invoked in transactions with public bureaucracies. These conditions, together with an ethos which expressed itself in what has been appropriately termed an "extractive" approach to politics, gravely impedes the development of administrative stability and renders the public sphere as a whole (not simply its upper reaches) highly susceptible to appropriation for private purposes.[1]

Networks of patron-client ties permeate Philippine society, starting with immediate family members, to extended blood and marital relatives, landlord and tenant, boss and subordinate, as well as into the community at large. This sense of concentric circles has always been especially important in regard to the obligations of social interaction. The notion of debt of gratitude or reciprocity of obligation (*utang na loob*) and the burden of paying back those favours done for one by others are salient characteristics of Filipino's life. The relationship extends socially and politically to dominant patrons for whom resources such as lands, jobs, loans, and legal and physical protection may be exchanged for loyalty, deference, information, and even violence against competitors. Election into political office and maintaining oneself in power are greatly facilitated by these cultural practices especially the patron-client system.

A small group of élite Filipino families (including Filipino-Chinese and Filipino-Spanish) continue to dominate the political, economic, and social landscape of the Philippines. Over the years, many of these rich families have become integral parts of larger clans. Intermarriages among them have created an ever more complex web of social, economic, and political interrelationships. They not only operate domestically but also have social and financial links to the larger international market. Due to their enormous wealth, some élite families have been able to perpetuate themselves in local and national politics for generations, forming seemingly invincible political and economic dynasties.

As the only predominantly Christian nation in Asia, the church also has an important influence on society — and in some respects quite different to that of clans and dynasties. The Roman Catholic Church, subscribed to by 85 per cent of the population, rivals state institutions in terms of nationwide reach, and its ability to permeate and affect the lives of all social strata, even the most marginalized. Aside from homilies, the Catholic Church exerts power through the issuance of pastoral letters read in every pulpit in the country that discloses the stand of the Church on varied political, economic, and social issues and policies of the government. Through these letters Catholics are enjoined to support the Church and mobilize them in concerted action — including demonstrations, prayer rallies and vigils — either in adherence with or in contravention of government's policies and actions. Acting often against the elite in support of the dispossessed, sometimes in co-operation with other participants in the Philippines' burgeoning civil society, the Catholic Church and other religious denominations have played an important role in leveling the playing field on which political contest occurs.

Ethnically, Filipinos come from a mix of over 100 linguistic, cultural, and racial groupings. These wide-ranging ethnic backgrounds are represented in various aspects of Philippines politics. There are more than 70 dialects and 11 native languages spoken. The Constitution states that the national language is Filipino, which is actually dominated by Tagalog, the dialect spoken in Metropolitan Manila and its environs as well as parts of the Southern Luzon region. Under the 1987 Constitution, English, Spanish, and Arabic are also recognized languages in the Philippines. There are also the various types of mestizos (mixed ethnicity) who have ethnic backgrounds from Europe, America, and other parts of Asia (e.g., China and India). Ethnic Chinese make up approximately 1.5 per cent of the population. Generally, people from the Philippines will call themselves Filipino, but most will also identify themselves as Cebuano, Ilocano, Kapampangan, Bulakeño, Maranao, or Tausog. To accommodate two cultural minorities, the 1987 Philippine Constitution created autonomous administrative regions for the Cordilleras in Northern Luzon (for indigenous Igorots, distinguished from most Filipinos by the fact that their cultures did not undergo Hispanization) and in Muslim dominated areas of Mindanao and the Sulu archipelago. Filipino Muslims make up around 5 per cent of the total population.

Economy

The Philippines is blessed with rich natural resources, a large portion of which still remains unexploited. The country is flourishing with abundant flora and fauna, marine resources as well as mineral and energy sources.

The economy of the Philippines is primarily dependent on agriculture, with 43 per cent of the working class involved in this area. The farmlands and plantations in the Philippines yield crops such as rice, corn, cassava, sweet potatoes, sugar, copra, tobacco, abaca, fruits and nuts. The Philippines ranks first in world in the production of coconut and hemp products, which are used in making ropes, clothes, and hats. It is second in world sugar and fifth in tobacco production.

The benefits of this rich bounty have, however, been unequally distributed, with most rural workers deeply entrenched in debt and exploited by unhelpful legal, market and social conditions. The Philippines is a signatory to many international agreements and conventions on the protection of the environment. However, the overall environmental record has been poor, with vast forested areas laid waste by unsustainable logging, rivers poisoned by mining operations, and marine resources devastated by extensive use of dynamite and chemicals.

The Philippines' manufacturing sector has greatly expanded since the 1950s, with the largest concentration in processed food, clothing materials, medicine, chemicals, wood products, electronic assembly, and oil refining. In dollar terms, the Philippine generally imports more than it exports. Its leading imports are petroleum, machinery, transportation equipment and parts, and metal ores. The country also depends on other countries for electrical and electronic components, clothing, and other products. The two major trading partners for both imports and exports are the United States and Japan. Other important trading partners are its regional ASEAN neighbours.

In the late 1970s and into the 1980s, while Asian neighbours were creating an export-oriented and market-friendly environment, encouraging domestic and foreign private sector investments into the economy, and increasing their savings rates, the Philippines was going in the opposite direction. President Marcos embarked on a state-oriented development programme dominated by crony capitalists close to him. Loyal friends and relatives were given choice monopolies in many critical sectors of the economy, ranging from agriculture to construction. Even the banking and credit sectors were not spared.

The net result was devastating. From a position next to Japan at the top of Asia in the mid-1960s, the country declined rapidly to almost the bottom by the early 1980s. The Philippines' external debt ballooned, with foreign borrowings mostly owed by an inefficient and ineffective public enterprise sector. The country's administrative system had become bloated and corruption-infested. Already serious income inequalities continued to

---

FIGURE 7.2

Philippines: Key Statistics

Land area:	300,176 sq. kilometres
Population:[a]	76,348,000 (2000)

GNP:[b]   Current exchange rate   — US$88.4 bn (1997);
                                         US$78.9 bn (1998)
           Purchasing Power Parity — US$270 bn (1997);
                                         US$280 bn (1998)

GNP Per Capita:[b] Current exchange rate   — US$1,200 (1997);
                                         US$1,050 (1998)
           Purchasing Power Parity — US$3,670 (1997);
                                        US$3,725 (1998)

Income Distribution (1997):[b]

Gini Index	46.2
% share of income or consumption:	
Lowest 10%	2.3
Lowest 20%	5.4
2nd 20%	8.8
3rd 20%	13.2
4th 20%	20.3
Highest 20%	52.3
Highest 10%	36.6

HDI Ranking:[c]

World ranking	77 (1997); 77 (1998)
Value	0.74 (1997); 0.744 (1998)

Armed Forces:

Total no.[d]	110,000 (1999)
Expenditure[d]	US$1.4 bn (1999)
% of GNP[b]	1.5% (1995)

Sources: [a] Official national sources.
        [b] World Bank, *World Development Indicators* (Washington, D.C. 1999 & 2000).
        [c] United Nations Development Programme (UNDP), *Human Development Report* (New York: Oxford University Press, 1999 & 2000).
        [d] International Institute for Strategic Studies (IISS), *The Military Balance, 1999–2000* (London: Oxford University Press, 1999).

widen. The overall situation was so bad the country was labeled the "sick man of Asia". Many workers sought employment abroad. Today some two million Filipinos work overseas, mainly in Asia and the Middle East, in occupations ranging from domestic servants, to construction labourers and professionals. Another four million contribute to the economies of the United States, Canada, Australia, and other countries, as immigrants or permanent residents.

Major economic restructuring was started as soon as Corazon Aquino took over, after the 1986 ouster of Marcos. Although hampered by political instability, she began the task of liberalizing the economy, with privatization of more than 250 government-owned or -controlled enterprises (GOCCs) a top priority. President Ramos built upon these foundations, pushing strongly for the implementation of market-based economic reforms. During the Ramos period, lawmakers enacted bills that liberalised the country's trade and investment regime, restructured the tax system, and improved debt management. Additionally, in an under appreciated but highly significant step, the government also removed restrictions on foreign exchange transactions. Despite fears to the contrary, this bold move produced a net inflow of foreign exchange earnings from old and new sources. Economic reform continued under President Estrada, though the process was muddied by serious allegations of a return to cronyism. After Estrada's ouster, high hopes have been pinned on his successor, Gloria Arroya, who is a trained economist.

THE POLITICAL SYSTEM

The Philippines is a republican state with a presidential form and unitary structure of government. The President is both the head of state and head of government. The government has three branches: the Executive, headed by the President; the bicameral Legislature or Philippine Congress with the Senate and House of Representatives (HOR) headed by the Senate President and Speaker of the House respectively; and the Judiciary with the Chief Justice of the Supreme Court at the helm. These branches are in theory co-equal and reflect a system of separation of powers and checks and balances between and among them. The concept of co-equality and separation of powers forestalls the dominance of any of the branches and enhances a democratic arrangement of power. The 1987 Philippine Constitution sets effective limits upon the power that it confers to each branch of government.

The first fundamental law of the Philippines, the 1935 Constitution, heavily reflected the ideals of both American liberal democracy and market-based capitalism. Filipinos had no choice but to adopt this constitution since the country was then a U.S. Commonwealth. The 1935 Constitution helped preserve preferential treatment to American goods and services in the Philippines. Even after independence in 1945 the United States government felt it had a legal document that protected American landholdings and other vital business interests in the former colony. One of Marcos' promises, which won him two terms as president, was to change this biased scenario and make the country's economy more "pro-Filipino." The 1973 Constitution, passed under Marcos' martial law conditionalities and approved by the electorate through Marcos' "peoples' assemblies," was supposed to accomplish this. It did eliminate many of the pro-American provisions. However, Marcos replaced these with sections that gave him virtual dictatorial powers, which he used to transform the economy to one that was dominated by his anointed relatives, cronies, and technocrats. The monopolies that were created for his close associates scared away many foreign investors from the country.[2]

After the ouster of Marcos, President Corazon Aquino, issued Proclamation No. 9 immediately creating and convening a Constitutional Commission (Concom). President Aquino received many nominations and in the end selected 47 national, regional, and sectoral representatives. The Concom drafted a fundamental law that sought to re-democratize the country and make it a more business friendly place, and is the basis for the Philippines' current liberal democracy. It contains many provisions on people participation, sectoral representation, agrarian reform, social justice, private sector liberalization, administrative decentralization, and human rights, which were introduced by the Concom members to prevent the emergence of another dictatorial regime, and the abuses as well as excesses that come with it. A proposal to amend the Constitution can be implemented by: a three-fourths vote of Congress members; a constitutional convention; or a petition of at least 12 per cent of the total number of registered voters, of which every legislative district must be represented by at least 3 per cent of the registered votes therein.

The importance of regional autonomy is emphasized in the 1987 Constitution, and local governmental units (LGUs) are one of the main beneficiaries of post-Marcos Philippine political and economic democratization processes. The local government system can be sub-divided into provinces, cities, municipalities and *barangays*. At the provincial level are governors, vice governors, and provincial board members. At the city level are mayors, vice mayors, and city council members. At the municipal level are municipal mayors, vice mayors, and municipal council members. At the *barangay* level are *barangay* captains and *barangay* council members. All local government officials, from governors to *barangay* captains, are elected by the people. Based on this constitutional mandate, the Congress passed the Local Government Code (LGC) of 1991 which is generally perceived as a "magna carta" of local government autonomy especially after experiencing centuries of centralized colonial rule and decades of central government control and supervision.

With enhanced political freedom and administrative autonomy, LGUs now have a larger share of tax collections from the national government. They also have the authority to levy additional local taxes as they deem necessary. This financial base allows them to budget and spend independently for the delivery of health care, social welfare, natural resources and environment, agricultural extension, and public works services directly to their political constituents. The Code also provides guidelines for the creation of consultative and deliberative fora such as school boards, health boards, development councils, and peace and order councils, and strongly encourages private sector and civil society participation in local governance.[3]

In line with drive to promote administrative autonomy, the Philippine government created autonomous regions in Muslim Mindanao and in the Cordilleras. Republic Act 6766 (1989) devolved a high degree of political and administrative responsibility to these areas. Within the autonomous region, the indigenous peoples of the Cordillera and Mindanao can exercise legislative, executive and judicial functions that are in keeping with their needs and particularities. More importantly, they will have the right to maintain and develop their indigenous cultures, including their own economic, social and political institutions.

Head of State

As with republican systems generally, the Philippine President is head of state, with both symbolic and executive powers. The President is directly elected by the people to serve a single six-year term in office. Article VII, Section 2, of the Constitution decrees that: "No person may be elected President unless he is a natural-born citizen of the Philippines, a registered voter, able to read and write, at least forty years of age on the day of the election, and a resident of the Philippines for at least ten years immediately preceding such election."

The President is the highest symbol of the country's sovereignty, meeting with foreign counterparts, receiving credentials from foreign ambassadors, and certifying the eligibility and approving appointments of Philippine ambassadors. Yearly, he or she addresses the opening session of Congress to give a State of the Nation Address (SONA), where major policy issues, accomplishments, and administration plans are highlighted. As the head of state, the President is also expected to lead the country in the observance of major national holidays like New Year's Day (1 January), Holy Week (March or April), Labor Day (1 May), Independence Day (12 June), All Saints and All Souls Days (November 1st and 2nd), Christmas Day (25 December), and Rizal Day (30 December). Official greetings and statements are published in all major newspapers and television and radio coverage of all ceremonies associated with these events are broadcast nationally.

The President is assisted by the Vice-President who is separately elected for a six-year term but is allowed to serve for two successive terms. It is possible for the President and Vice-President to come from two different political parties, as in the case of the Ramos and Estrada administrations. The Vice President may also be appointed to hold a Cabinet position and is normally an active participant in Cabinet meetings. Presidential succession is spelled out in Article VII, Section 8 of the Constitution, which states that: "In case of death, permanent disability, removal from office, or resignation of the President, the Vice-President shall become the President to serve the unexpired term. In case of death, permanent disability, removal from office, or resignation of both the President and Vice-President, the President of the Senate or, in case of his inability, the Speaker of the House of Representatives, shall then act as President until the President or Vice-President shall have been elected and qualified."

The Executive

As head of the executive branch of government the President bears the main responsibility for policy enforcement and administration. The President has the power to appoint (or remove) Cabinet members, who are responsible to and aid him or her in managing the affairs of government. Cabinet appointees can come from political parties, the business community, the government bureaucracy, or the NGO sector. Philippine Presidents try hard to diversify Cabinet representation in terms of gender, ethnic background, region of origin, professional occupation, religious affiliation, and political ideology. Each Presidential appointee must undergo rigorous scrutiny and be confirmed by the legislature, acting through the Congressional Commission on Appointments (CA). The President is allowed to appoint a member of the Cabinet twice, but is obligated to change if the CA denies confirmation after the President's second endorsement. The number of cabinet positions is not set by law, hence changes with every new president. (The list of members in President Arroyo's Cabinet is included in Figure 7.3).

Apart from Cabinet members (holding an official title of Secretary), the President is also mandated to appoint members of the Judicial Bar Council, diplomatic representatives, and officers of the armed forces from the rank of colonel or naval captain, all with the concurrence of the CA. Just like in the United States presidential system, the Philippine President has been known to appoint officials at the upper echelon of the public service from Secretaries, Undersecretaries, Assistant Secretaries, Commissioners, to Directors, sometimes bypassing career civil servants. The President's high-ranking political appointees (e.g. Secretaries and Undersecretaries) also have the capacity to appoint whomever they want at the middle to lower ranks. This practice of political rewards is a mix of the American-inspired political "spoils system" and what was earlier described as Filipino-style "patron-client system."

As chief administrator and head of government, the President is vested with heavy fiscal and budgetary responsibilities, and powers to organize and re-organize the government. He or she has various means of lobbying the legislature into passing bills, including through the State of the Nation Address at the opening of each legislative session. Although technically no bill originates from the executive branch, the President may course his or her proposed legislation through a Senator or Representative. Every congressional bill passed has to be signed by the President before it becomes a law. A bill that remains unsigned for 30 days automatically becomes a law unless the President registers his/her objection, through the exercise of a veto. Vetoed bills need to be reviewed and reconsidered by the legislative body for possible amendments as indicated by the President. However, Congress can override the President's veto power by a two-thirds vote of its members.

As Commander-in-Chief of the Republic's armed forces, the President decides when conditions warrant the suspension of the *writ of habeas corpus* and the declaration of martial law. Given the abuses of power committed by Marcos during martial rule, the 1987 Constitution places limitations on the use of these powers. For instance, the suspension of the *writ of habeas corpus* and declaration of martial cannot be imposed for more than 60 days; any extensions need the concurrence of the Philippine Congress voting jointly by simple majority of all its members. If Congress is not in session, it must convene within 24 hours. Should Congress revoke

---

FIGURE 7.3

Members of President Gloria Arroyo's Cabinet

Vice-President

Executive Secretary

Agrarian Reform Secretary

Agriculture Secretary

Budget Secretary

Education, Culture and Sports Secretary

Energy Secretary

Environment and Natural Resources Secretary

Finance Secretary

Foreign Affairs Secretary

Health Secretary

Interior and Local Government Secretary

Justice Secretary

Labor Secretary

National Defense Secretary

National Economic and Development Authority Director-General

Public Works Secretary

Science Secretary

Social Welfare Secretary

Tourism Secretary

Trade and Industry Secretary

Transportation and Communications Secretary

National Security Adviser

Press Secretary

martial law, the President cannot overrule nor dissolve Congress. Further, the state of martial law will not suspend the operation of the Constitution, nor supplant the functions of civil courts or legislative assemblies, nor authorize the conferment of jurisdiction on military courts and agencies over civilians were civil courts are able to function.

The President is the country's top diplomatic and foreign policy maker. Besides ceremonial roles as head of state, he or she has overall responsibility for the conduct of foreign policy, including reaching agreement on treaties and international agreements (with consent from two-thirds of the Senate).

Cabinet portfolios in the Philippine presidential system are supposed to be treated with equal importance. However, depending on who is in power, certain departments are given more attention and priority than others. For example, it seems that departments handling "economic, security, finance issues" such as the Department of Budget, the Department of Foreign Affairs, Department of National Defense, and the Department of Finance are always on top of the agenda while departments tacking "social issues" such as the Department of Education, Culture, and Sports, the Department of Social Welfare and Development, and the Department of Health are accorded lesser priority. There are also certain Cabinet members who are closer to the President than others, creating special attention to their respective concerns. For instance, the Executive Secretary, who also holds Cabinet rank but no department portfolio under him or her, is a critical gatekeeper and a presidential confidante earning whoever holds this office the nickname —"Little President".

The personnel component of the executive, the bureaucracy, is managed by the Civil Service Commission (CSC). It is tasked with establishing a career service, strengthening merit and reward systems, institutionalizing a management climate conducive to public accountability, and adopting measures that promote morale, efficiency, integrity, responsiveness, progressiveness, and courtesy in the civil service. As of 2000, there were approximately 1.4 million Filipino civil servants, though a large majority work as public school teachers and law enforcement officers. The devolution and privatization of government has contributed to an increase in local government employees and a corresponding decline in the number of civil servants in national government agencies and government owned or controlled corporations (GOCCs). The CSC's Chairperson has a term of seven years and is assisted by two Commissioners with terms of five and three years respectively. Theoretically speaking, as an independent Constitutional body, the CSC, is not supposed to be influenced by the other three branches. It enjoys relative fiscal autonomy, with annual appropriations released automatically. However, in reality, interference and intervention in its work exists through a complex system of patronage and clientelism that is imbedded in Philippine political culture. Appointments and approval into these bodies are still at the discretion of the President and his or her political advisers, and the CSC is powerless to stop persons who have not taken the Civil Service Examinations if they are given political or contractual appointments especially those originating from Malacañang Palace, the Presidential office.

Another important constitutional body that works closely with the executive branch is the Commission on Audit (COA). This commission is mandated to examine, audit, and settle all accounts relating to the revenue and receipts of, and expenditures or uses of funds and property, owned or held in trust by or pertaining to, the government, or any of its subdivisions, agencies or instrumentalities, including government-owned and controlled corporations. A Chairperson with a term of office of seven years heads it. Two other Commissioners with five and three year-term respectively aid him/her. All of them are appointed by the President.

Political Role of Military and Police

Although a part of the executive branch, the Armed Forces of the Philippines (AFP) has been likened by many political scientists to another branch of the Philippine government. The AFP reached its peak during the martial law years, when it experienced a significant growth spurt from 60,000 to close to 200,000.[4] The police and the Philippine Constabulary (a military unit with special police powers created by U.S. General Douglas MacArthur) became integral parts of the AFP. According to then President Marcos, the AFP's consolidation and expansion were needed to counter the growing Communist and Muslim insurgencies. But the AFP was also utilized by Marcos to quell streets protests, arrest and intimidate opposition leaders, and suppress civil society including the media, the church, labour, women, ethnic groups, farmers, fishermen, students, and academia.

This large armed services bureaucracy, composed of the Army, Navy, Marines, and Air Force, was conceived primarily for internal security purposes. Battle-tested within the country, the Philippine armed forces lacks the modern equipment that its neighboring countries' military services have to combat external threats. External defence of the country was for years heavily subsidized by the presence of United States Armed Forces in Clark Air Base and Subic Naval Base under the Military Bases Agreement (MBA). However, in 1991 the Philippine Senate rejected a new MBA, forcing the U.S. military to withdraw. Despite this, the military alliance remains under the Mutual Defense Treaty of 1951, and the 1999 Visiting Forces Agreement (VFA) provides the framework for joint military exercises between the two countries.

Under the current AFP Modernization Plan the Philippines is beefing up its external defense capability with purchases of more modern weapons systems, naval vessels, and tactical aircraft. In times of peace, the AFP is also an active partner in the nation's countryside development programs. Military servicemen and civilian personnel also help build and maintain roads, bridges, schools, playgrounds, as well as provide disaster assistance and coordination.

Following exposure to civilian politics and administration during the Marcos martial law years, some elements in the military have sought a more direct political role. President Aquino faced several coup attempts, but all were eventually repulsed — the Philippines never has experienced a successful military coup. The military played an important role in the downfalls of Marcos and Estrada, but in each case did so in support of a popular mass uprising. Many officers now pursue a different political path. Retired generals and admirals have become ambassadors, cabinet members, and commissioners. Some former military officers have also run for elections and become mayors, governors, representatives, and senators. General Ramos even became President!

In December 1990, President Aquino signed into law Republic Act No. 6975 establishing the Philippine National Police under the reorganized Department of the Interior and Local Government. This formally segregated police and military powers. With the devolution of powers to local government units, the police must now report to local officials. However, the police are also supervised by the Philippine National Police (PNP) which is an office under the Department of the Interior and Local Government (DILG) while the Armed Forces of the Philippines is guided by the Department of National Defense (DND).

The Legislature

Legislative authority is vested in the bicameral Philippine Congress consisting of the Senate (Upper House) and the House of Representatives (Lower House). The Senate has only 24 members, elected for six-year terms, but prohibited from serving more than two consecutive terms. Thus, a politician can resume a senate career after "sitting off" one term in office. According to the 1987 Constitution, a person qualifies to be elected as Senator if he or she is a natural-born citizen of the Philippines, at least 35 years old, able to read and write, a registered voter, and a resident of the country for not less than two years immediately preceding the day of the election.

The House of Representatives has not more than 250 members. Of these 208 are elected from legislative districts apportioned countrywide in accordance with the number of inhabitants. A person is qualified to run as a Representative if he or she is a natural-born citizen of the Philippines, at least 25 years old, able to read and write, a registered voter, and a resident of the country for not less than one year immediately preceding the day of the election. They serve terms of three years, but are prohibited from more than three consecutive terms. In some cases, this becomes an opportunity for an anointed successor (most of the time a family member) to take over the reigns of power. The Constitution also provides that 20 per cent are elected through a party-list system (PLS) for non-governmental organisations (NGOs) and disadvantaged sectors.

The Congress has, as noted earlier, power to amend the constitution. Declaration of war can only be carried out through a two-thirds vote during a joint session of the Senate and House of Representatives. It also has the power to impeachment the President, the Vice President, the members of the Supreme Court, the members of the Constitutional Commissions, and the Ombudsman for violation of the Constitution, treason, bribery, graft and corruption, other high crimes, or betrayal of public trust. The House of Representatives has the exclusive power to initiate cases of impeachment. Power to try and decide on impeachment cases is solely vested in the Senate. When the President is on trial, the Chief Justice of the Supreme Court shall preside, but shall not vote. The system of checks and balances between Houses is further manifested by the Senate's exclusive right to approve treaties, while the Representatives has privileged power to appropriate funds through the enactment of the annual General Appropriations Act, which defines the national budget.

Congress operates through a committee system whereby bills and resolutions introduced are referred to an appropriate committee for study and action. The Senate President and the House Speaker, each elected by the respective chamber, determine committee membership. Both Houses have counterpart committees that are charged with the function of sifting or screening bills — deciding which are worthy of study and further consideration and those that are not. In the interest of enjoining wider participation in the formulation of bills, public hearings are conducted to solicit views of experts and interested parties on the proposed measure. Each bill must pass through three readings in both Houses. This normally gives rise to two versions — Senate and HOR. Any discrepancies and differences between the two are reconciled in the Bicameral Conference Committee that is tasked to prepare a consolidated bill for the President's signature before it becomes a law. In all congressional committees, both majority and minority parties are represented.

The principle of checks and balances also pertains to the Office of the President and Congress. Although the President can impose sanctions on Congress by virtue of his/her authority to release or withhold funds already appropriated, Congress can set the parameters for resource allocation or change established patterns. Moreover, the bicameral Commission on Appointments (CA) serves as a tool in ensuring executive appointees conform to the standards and requirements of their respective duties and functions as seen by the legislature. The CA is composed of the Senate President as *ex officio* Chairman and 24 members, half from each house, chosen on the basis of proportional representation of parties in Congress.

Aside from Congress, the Constitution also empowers the people to directly propose laws, or reject any law passed by Congress or local legislative bodies, through a system of initiative and referendum. In order to start this process at the national level, at least 10 per cent of the total number of registered voters, including at least three per cent of every legislative district, must petition for the enactment or repeal of a particular law. A national referendum follows which approves or rejects the proposed law. Since the passage of the 1987 Constitution a national referendum has yet to be held.

Elections

A constitutionally-mandated body like the CSC and COA, the independent Commission on Elections (COMELEC) has primary responsibility to organise elections at national and local levels. It is empowered to deputize (with the concurrence of the President), law enforcement agencies and instrumentalities of government, including the Armed Forces of the Philippines, for the purpose of ensuring free, orderly, honest, peaceful, and credible elections. In addition, it is tasked to recommend to Congress effective measures to minimize election spending and prevent or penalize all forms of election frauds, offenses, malpractices, and nuisance candidacies. The Commission has seven members with the Chairperson having a term of seven years, three of the six Commissioners seven years, two five years, and one with one year. Like the CSC and COA, COMELEC Chairpersons and Commissioners are all appointed by the President.

The right of suffrage of all citizens (natural-born or naturalized) of the Philippines is guaranteed under the Constitution. Qualifications are as follows: 18 years of age, resident of the country for at least one year and in the place wherein they propose to vote for at least six months immediately preceding the elections. No literacy level, property ownership, or physical ability requirement is imposed on the exercise to vote. Voting is not compulsory. Nevertheless, as shown by past elections, more than 85 per cent of eligible voters exercise this right.

Elections are held on a regular basis whereby qualified electorates exercise the right of suffrage at large. The people elect the President, Vice-President, and Senators every six years (their term is six years, but half the senate is elected every three years), and members of House of Representatives every three years. The election campaign period mandated by the constitution must commence 90 days before the day of election, and end 30 days thereafter except in special cases as determined by COMELEC. Normally, national and local elections take place on second Monday of May, unless provided otherwise by law, and elected representatives assume office on 30 June.

The President, Vice-President and Senators are elected on a nation-wide basis. The highest vote pollers win. (There is no run-off where a president elect, for example, secures less than a majority.) For the lower house, as noted, voting is split between representatives of 208 legislative districts elected on a first-past-the-post basis by their respective constituents, and sectoral representatives chosen nationally under the Party List System (PLS). The presidential and vice presidential victors are proclaimed at a joint session of Congress. Others are announced by COMELEC.

The PLS is an important feature of Philippine representative democracy, allowing the election of registered national and regional parties, or organizations, representing "labour, peasant, urban poor, indigenous communities, women, youth, and such other sectors as may be provided by law". Party-list representatives (PLR) constitute 20 per cent of the total members of the House of Representatives, meaning (currently) 42 congressional seats. The aforesaid constitutional provision was further bolstered by the Party-List System Act (PLSA or Republic Act 7941) by adding the following sectors: fisherfolk, elderly, handicapped, overseas Filipino workers, veterans, and professional sectors. Thus, a total of 12 sectors are to be represented in the House.

Local officials are elected directly by their local constituencies every three years. The executive arm comprises Governors and Vice-Governors for Provinces and Autonomous Regions, Mayors and Vice-Mayors for city and municipalities, and Chairpersons and Vice-Chairpersons for *barangay* (village government or the lowest political unit). There are also legislative bodies (assemblies) at the same levels.

In case of a contested result involving the President or Vice-President, the Supreme Court, sitting *en banc*, has the sole power to judge. For the legislature, the Electoral Tribunals of either the Senate or HOR are mandated to decide on issues relating to election, returns, and qualifications of their respective members. The Tribunal is composed of nine members: three from Justices of the Supreme Court designated by the Chief Justice and six from members of the Senate or HOR chosen on the basis of proportional representation from the political parties and the parties or organizations registered under the PLS. The senior Justice in the Tribunal acts as the Chairperson. For disputes involving local officials, courts have the sole responsibility.

As a corollary to elections, the constitution provides a system of initiative and recall against elected local officials perceived by constituents to be unsatisfactory in performing his/her functions. The 1991 Local Government Code (LGC) stipulates that upon the petition of at least 25 per cent of the total number of registered voters in the LGU concerned proceedings for recall have been validly initiated and an election has to be called and administered by COMELEC. However, recall can be initiated only once during the official's term and cannot take place within one year from their assumption of office, or one year preceding a regular local election.

Relative to electoral exercises in some parts of the world, Philippine elections are peaceful. However, the use of "guns, goons, and gold" (coercion, terrorism, and money) exists especially in hotly contested areas where political feuds have been in existence for decades. During the campaign period, persons who want to win an election must illustrate their being a "good patron" by distributing goods, services (infrastructure, health and medical, and welfare), and cash. As election day draws near, pressure mounts, and some candidates and their followers turns to violence — harassing and threatening their opponents and supporters as well as terrorizing citizens and election officials. COMELEC, and civil society groups, have reduced such practices in recent years.

Judiciary

The Judicial branch of government is engaged in settling disputes regarding the appropriate application of a law, interpretation or clarification of the true meaning or scope of an indeterminate statute, and adjudication upon claimed violations of a rule. Judicial power is vested in the Philippine Supreme Court (SC) and other lower courts. In discharging judicial power, courts determine what is law. Any act of the legislature or of the executive that conflicts with the constitution, transgresses the proper limits of their power, or infringes upon guaranteed human rights, is considered as unlawful and void.

The Judiciary enjoys relative fiscal autonomy as appropriations cannot be reduced by the legislature below the amount appropriated for the previous year and, after approval, has to be automatically and regularly released. The SC, the highest Court of the land otherwise known as the "court of last appeal," is composed of a Chief Justice and 14 Associate Justices and exercises administrative supervision over all other courts and their personnel. The Chief Justice and SC members as well as judges of lower courts are all appointed by the President and require no confirmation from the legislature's CA. Judicial appointees serve until the age of 70 or become incapacitated to discharge the duties of their office.

Nominees to the SC are chosen by the Judicial Bar Council (JBC), a body created under the constitution. JBC's regular members are the SC's Chief Justice as *ex officio* Chairman, the Secretary of Justice, and a representative of the Congress as *ex officio* members. These members are free from CA's confirmation. Other members — a representative of the Integrated Bar of the Philippines (IBP), a professor of law, a retired member of the SC, and a representative of the private sector — have to be confirmed by the CA. The JBC prepares a list of three nominees, from which the President chooses one.

The SC sits *en banc* and renders final judgement in cases relating to: the validity or constitutionality of a treaty, executive agreement, law, presidential decree, proclamation, order, and other regulations; criminal cases in which the death penalty is imposed; cases heard by a division which could not be decided with the concurrence of five justices; cases in which a doctrine or principle of law laid down by the Court *en banc* or in division may be modified of reversed; and in all other cases which under its rules are required to be heard *en banc*.

Other courts under the administrative supervision of the Supreme Court include the Court of Appeals, Regional Trial Courts (RTC), Metropolitan Trial Courts (MTC), Municipal Trial Courts (MTC), and Municipal Circuit Trial Court (MCTC). There are also autonomous special courts, namely the *Sandiganbayan*, (anti-graft court), Sharia'a Court (Muslim courts in Muslim areas of Mindanao) under the Code of Muslim Personal Laws of the Philippines, and the Court of Tax Appeals.

In general, the credibility of the Philippine judiciary, especially at the highest levels, has been held in high esteem. Just like other high-ranking public officials, lower and higher court judges are highly respected by the citizenry. Overseas, some former Philippine Supreme Court justices have even served in the prestigious International Court of Justice (ICJ). Nevertheless, the judicial branch has also had its share of accusations of corruption, red tape, and inefficiencies. Cases literally used to pile along the halls of justice, taking many years to resolve. Guided by the post-Marcos era 1987 Constitution, serious attempts at judicial reforms and administrative reorganizations have been introduced to address these concerns and streamline operations. For instance, Article VIII, Section 15 (1) of the 1987 Constitution tried to rectify the caseload problem by requiring that "All cases or matters filed after the effectivity of the Constitution must be decided or resolved within twenty-four months from date of submission for the Supreme Court, and, unless reduced by the Supreme Court, twelve months for all lower collegiate courts, and three months for all other lower courts."

People Power II, clearly illustrated that the Judiciary remains an important check and balance on the powers of the executive and legislative branches. With the Presidency and Congress both paralized, an independent and credible Juciciary needed to act quickly to pave the way for a transfer of power from Estrada to Arroyo. On the morning of 20 January 2001 the Supreme Court en banc invoked a time-honoured principle — "the welfare and will of the people is the supreme law" — to approve Arroyo's installation. This powerful decision provided the legal basis for the Chief Justice to swear in the new president a few hours later, averting both bloody civilian strife and a military takeover.

Political Parties

Political parties came together with elections at the turn of the 20th century. As in the American model, two parties were initially established, the *Partido Federal* (Federal Party) and the *Partido Conservador* (Conservative Party). Their platforms had to be approved by U.S. authorities. The passage of the 1901 Sedition Law, which imposed the death penalty on any political party endorsing independence from the United States, even by peaceful means, enabled *Partido Federal*, effectively to dominate the political landscape during those early years. With heavy support from the land-owning class, it was able to popularize its agenda of stronger political, economic, and social ties with America. After independence in 1946 until 1972, two parties — the Nationalista Party and the Liberal Party — became the prominent political organizations in the country. The two parties controlled a majority of the elective positions in government. Generally speaking, personalities rather than platforms distinguished the Nationalista and the Liberal since they both advocated policies that would help the country achieve economic independence and social equity. Persons jumped party affiliation when they were not chosen to run for that elective office. This is what Ferdinand Marcos did when not selected as the presidential candidate of the Liberal Party; he simply switched to the Nationalista Party and was made its standard bearer.[5]

During martial law (1972–81), the Philippines entered an era of one-party politics, with Marcos' *Kilusang Bagong Lipunan* (KBL or New Society Movement) as the only party in power. Even after the lifting of martial law in 1981 and the revival of other political entities, the KBL used its government links to ensure a majority of votes in national and local elections. Accusations of massive election fraud, vote buying, terrorism, and irregularities were widespread. In order to defeat Marcos and his KBL machinery in the 1986 snap presidential elections, the Pilipino Democratic Party (PDP), Lakas ng Bayan (LABAN), and United Democratic Opposition (UNIDO) formed an opposition coalition. Inheriting the mantle of the Nationalista and Liberal parties, these groups coalesced around powerful leaders, but were united by opposition to Marcos.

The ouster of Marcos in 1986 ushered a new era in party politics, which has encouraged a free and an open multi-party system. There is currently a broad spectrum of parties, from leftist, centrist, to rightist. On the extreme left the Communist Party of the Philippines is legal — a rare exception to the norm in non-communist Southeast Asia — even though a small number of communists remain in armed opposition to the state. The party has not openly contested elections, but close affiliates have. All political parties, organizations, or coalitions with platforms or programme of governments have to be registered with the COMELEC.

Aside from re-invented versions of the old, many new parties find it wise to form coalitions, alliances, or merge to increase their chances of winning. For instance, President Aquino formed Lakas ng Bayan (LAKAS) another coalition of parties to contest the 1987 national and local elections. Aside from the original PDP-LABAN-UNIDO partners, LAKAS also included the Liberal Party (Salonga faction), the National Union of Christian Democrats (NUCD), and other minor regional parties. In the 1992 presidential election, President Fidel Ramos was supported by a LAKAS-NUCD-UMDP (United Muslim Democrats of the Philippines) coalition. For the 1998 national elections, President Estrada's Partido ng Masang

Pilipino (PMP) allied with the Nationalist People Coalition (NPC) and the LABAN to increase its capacity to win multi-sectoral and multi-class support. This became the nucleus of Estrada's winning Lapian ng Masang Pilipino (LAMP). Other "progressive" political organizations in the post-people power revolution era are Promdi (Provincial), Sanlakas (One Strength), Reporma (Reform), and Aksyon Demokratiko (Democratic Action), all of which are founded on principles set by certain charismatic personalities. In late 2000, together with LAKAS, they formed a political alliance seeking the resignation of President Estrada over "juetengate" (gambling scandal).

As in many parts of the region, major Philippine political parties are viewed as basically "élite clubs", vehicles for political and economic élites to perpetuate themselves in power. They form around powerful individuals, and disintegrate quickly when such people lose influence. Non-élites join because of patron-client ties as opposed to ideological links. A client's debt of gratitude determines whom he or she will support politically. Political parties then tap into this complex web of inter-relationships spread across society to harness grassroots' support in the urban and rural areas.

State Ideology

The Philippines has no official state ideology, but leaders espouse strong liberal-democratic values in accordance with the country's Constitution. Article II of the Constitution, provides the "Declaration of Principles and State Policies" of the country. It affirms that: "The Philippines is a democratic and republican State. Sovereignty resides in the people and all government authority emanates from them." The succeeding principles and policies elaborate on this fundamental theme. Civilian authority is supreme over the military, whose role is confined to protecting the people and defending of the country's sovereignty. Church and state are separate. Government must serve and protect the people, maintain peace and order, secure life, liberty, and property, and promote the general welfare.

The national anthem, *Bayang Magiliw*, and an oath of allegiance to the country (*Panatang Makabayan*) are sung and recited regularly by school children in both public and private schools. Belief in democratic ideals, justice, equality, freedom, and patriotism are inculcated to all Filipinos through the study of social studies and current events, Philippine history, Philippine government, the Philippine Constitution, as well as the life and works of Jose Rizal (national hero). There are mandatory subjects on these areas in elementary and secondary schools, as well as colleges nationwide. State principles and ideals are also shared through the country's vibrant media and publishing industries. In the public sector, many government offices have flag-raising ceremonies and the singing of the national anthem as part of their weekly routine.

Civil Society and Human Rights

Civil society in Philippines had tentative beginnings in the second half of the nineteenth century, as an emerging élite came together first in charity and cultural pursuits, than in political groups and trade unions. These activities developed slowly during the twentieth century, gathering momentum for the 1960s as the Catholic Church gave more attention to social action programmes and contact with the grassroots.

NGOs played a major role in the two and half years of unrest from August 1983 (assassination of Corazon Aquino's husband, Benigno) that led to the "People Power" revolt of February 1986. In recognition of their contribution, the framers of the 1987 Constitution assigned them an important political role (Articles 2 and 13, Sections 23 and 15–16 respectively). The 1991 Local Government Code (LGC) institutionalized this further by requiring the participation of NGOs in the government of local affairs. The restoration of democratic rights in 1986, also created "democratic space" in which NGOs could proliferate. In 10 years (1986–95), NGOs mushroomed by 160 per cent — from 27,100 to 70,200 — making the Philippine civil society community one of the largest in the developing world.[6]

In an attempt to forge a strategic alliance between the state and NGOs, the Aquino government appointed a number of NGO leaders to cabinet and to Presidential committees, and created NGO Liaison Desks in 18 government departments and five specialized government agencies. Moreover, NGO representatives participated in the formulation and implementation of the Medium Term Philippine Development Plan for 1987–1992, which outlined a comprehensive programme of collaboration between state agencies and NGOs. In 1992, President Fidel Ramos continued his predecessor's policy by drawing more NGOs into the orbit of government. In launching his "Philippines 2000" development strategy, aimed at achieving the status of a Newly Industrializing Country by the year 2000, he promised "to forge a strategic alliance" with business, labour and NGOs.[7] President Gloria Arroyo, in her political agenda, also encourages partnerships among the public, private, and people sectors.

In certain instances, however, state-society partnership in the Philippines is threatened by political leaders' (national and local government officials and the military) initiatives to set up grassroots organizations, otherwise known as GRINGOs (government-initiated NGOs). In most cases, the political motives of GRINGOs are self-interested: the maintenance of control over allocation of resources dispersed to the local or national level by national or international sources; and recourse to a traditional élite strategy of co-opting popular institutional initiatives that endangered the existing socio-economic and political order.[8] In 1991 Congress established the Countryside Development Fund (CDF), a new "pork barrel" programme that allowed members to channel development funds in their respective constituent areas through their own or "favorite" NGOs or GRINGOs, either as a reward for electoral support or simply a conduit for their personal fund.[9]

Media groups, investigative journalists' and artists' circles, social weather stations, academic think-tanks, trade unions, migrant worker's alliances, women's organizations, development institutes, business groups, religious organizations, student councils, farmers and fishermen's associations, have all emerged as critical components of Philippine civil society. They act as lobbyists, fiscalizers, advocates, alternative delivery systems, discussion forums, mouthpieces, for a plethora or social, economic, political, social, environmental, and other issues. For the Catholic Church, their most influential mouthpiece is the Catholic Bishops Conference of the Philippines (CBCP). On the private sector side, the Makati Business Club (MBC), Management Association of the Philippines (MAP), Bankers Association of the Philippines (BAP), Philippine Chamber of Commerce and Industry (PCCI), and other allied organizations provides a forum for businesspersons — with interests that often go beyond mere commercial benefit and include reforms in the direction of good goverance. Aside from their respective student councils and organizations, students also have the League of Filipino Students (LFS), fraternities and sororities, among others campus-based groups. Meanwhile, the Trade Union Congress of the Philippines (TUCP), Kilusang Mayo Uno (May First Movement), and a broad spectrum of labor groups highlight worker's views. From the press side, the Philippine Center for Investigative Journalism (PCIJ), newspapers, TV and radio reporters, and other independent media groups play the critical roles of "watchdogs" and "whistleblowers".

Complementing the role of NGOs and other civil society groups, an independent and influential Commission on Human Rights (CHR) was created as an investigative body under the Executive branch of government.

Created under Article XIII of the 1987 Constitution, the President appoints its Chairman and four members. Its salient powers and functions include investigating on its own or on complaint by any party, all forms of human rights violations involving civil and political rights; providing appropriate legal measures for the protection of human rights of all Filipinos including those residing overseas; recommending to Congress effective measures to promote human rights and provide compensation to victims of violation of human rights, or their families; and monitoring the government's compliance with international treaties and obligations on the advancement of human rights. The CHR seeks to ensure that human rights violations will never reach martial law proportions. It has moved successfully to investigate many reports and actual cases since its inception.

MAJOR POLITICAL ISSUES

Who Has Power?

The 1987 Constitution formally sets a framework for an equal relationship between and among the executive, the legislative, and judicial branches. Especially after experiencing Marcos' abuse of power before 1986, the constitutional framers wanted to ensure that there were enough checks on executive power. However, in practice, although the degree of executive power is no longer what it used to be, and the capacity of the other branches to check and balance have increased, the Presidency is still a major force when it comes to leveraging support and influencing decisions of state institutions and even civil society. It is undoubtedly the focal point of political power in the Philippines.[10]

One of the pillars of strength of the President is the control he or she has over the gargantuan Philippine government bureaucracy, the largest employer in the country. Tasked with the implementation of public policies, the public bureaucracy is a massive source of human, material, and financial resources — all at the disposal of the President. The President does not need to co-opt civil servants in the various Departments since they serve whoever is elected into power. Moreover, the President has the power to appoint persons who he or she trusts to manage the financial and material resources allocated to the various executive offices. She or he also has the power to reward, through promotions and perks, civil servants who have shown loyalty and service to his or her administration. Presidential power and influence does not end at the national level. Even after the passage of the Local Government Code, which devolved fiscal power to local government units, governors, mayors, other local officials still kowtow to the President in order to expedite disbursement of resources or to receive more funds than what are due to them.

Another pillar of strength is the power and influence the President has over Congress — the forum for legislative agenda setting and law formulation. The Philippine Congress is also the "home" of Filipino traditional politicians (tradpols). Historically and biologically, Philippine Presidents and tradpols are the products of the same entrenched political clans and dynasties. Although, theoretically, an independent branch, every President moves swiftly to capture the support of Congress. The Presidents knows very well that the leaderships in both houses must be aligned to him or her to ensure that legislative members are "friendly" to his or her policy initiatives. Thus, even though the President has no direct hand in the selection of the Senate President or House Speaker, he or she makes sure that his or her preferred candidates win. If the President party has the majority in both houses, then securing the Senate Presidency or the House Speakership is not a problem. However, if this is not the case then alliances with other parties need to be forged. As the titular head of his or her party, the President uses political charisma, diplomatic savvy, and negotiation skills in leveraging the support of other party leaders represented in Congress. The President must appeal to a wide range of interests and demands. In exchange for Congressional loyalty and support, the President pledges to help senators and representatives in their numerous development projects and programs, at times, over and above their standard "pork barrel" allocations. Of course, not all Congressional members show support for the President. There are still ruling party members who will occasionally play "devil's advocate," or sectoral and regional representatives who will act independently to protect their narrow interests, or opposition stalwarts who will vote against the President's wishes. But at the end of the day, with successful alliances with other parties, the President's legislative agenda passes through the democratic process of "majority wins".

The President's influence is, however, moderated by civil society — a "fourth branch" of government, which, as noted earlier, emerged during the people power revolution. State-society partnerships, the privatization of state institutions, and the devolution of authority mandated in the 1987 Constitution have reduced the relative dominance and diffused the power of the state, most notably the national government. This post-martial law trend has allowed non-state actors in society, including business, media, academe, NGOs, church, women, labour, community-based organizations, ethnic communities, private voluntary groups, among others, to assert their influence in the public policy process. Hence, aside from the traditional politicians the President must listen to civil society groups' solicited and unsolicited advice and recommendations and act on them. In the past, presidential appointments to political positions, commissions, and statutory boards were reserved for his or her political supporters especially traditional politicians. However, post-Marcos presidents have moved away from this norm by selecting respected individuals from the business community and civil society groups to serve in advisory and policy-making positions in state bodies like economic, social, and human rights committees and commissions. On the one hand, multi-sectoral representation is empowering and democratic. However, on the other hand, multi-stakeholder bodies can also help legitimize the President's agenda. Just as they can be a forum for independent views, they can also be used for cooptation, under the Philippines' patronage dominated system. Whether in the halls of Congress, which is dominated by traditional politicians, or the "parliament of the streets", which is dominated by people power, the President plays an important role as mediator and facilitator.

Who Benefits?

Philippine development efforts can only be considered to be successful if post-Marcos attempts to harness the energies of government, business, and civil society, are able to facilitate not only power-sharing but also wealth-sharing among the members of the larger society. More importantly, the fruits of development need to reach the economically disadvantaged and the poverty-striken. The Philippines, which seeks to join the ranks of its fast-growing East Asian neighbors, ultimately needs to catch up with these countries not only in terms of maintaining a robust economy but also reducing income inequality and reducing poverty.

A perennial challenge to Philippine politicians is creating enough social and economic rewards for all Filipinos in a nation with a population growth rate that is one of the highest in the Southeast Asian region. From 1965 to 1974, the Philippines' population grew at a rate of 3.1 per cent annually, and although now declining it remains over 2 per cent. More than half the rural population of the Philippines is still considered poor by international standards and critically needs government, business, and civil society intervention to facilitate economic and social development projects, including genuine land reform, that would help change their age-old tenurial status. Many village communities are still unable to sustain even basic human needs like access to potable water, sanitary toilets, and immunization services. Some households in the poorest provinces still do not have access to sanitary toilet facilities and close to some households in these same poor provinces do not have access to a safe water supply. High rates of malnutrition, especially among children, still exist in a number of depressed areas even in Metropolitan Manila. Ironically, some of these provinces are the most resource rich in the country. For instance, National Economic Development Board statistics show that some Muslim areas in Mindanao, which accounts for a significant part of the country's GNP, are still some of the most backward in the nation.[11] No wonder lasting peace between the Philippine government and Muslims has remained elusive.[12]

A small group of élite Filipino families (including Filipino-Chinese and Filipino-Spanish mestizos) continue to benefit more than the rest of the population politically, economically, and socially. Over the years, many of these rich families have become integral parts of larger clans. Intermarriages among them have created an even more complex web of interrelationships. They not only operate domestically but also have links to the larger international market. Due to their enormous wealth, as noted earlier, some political élite families have been able to perpetuate themselves in local and national politics for generations forming political dynasties with solid control of congressional districts, provinces, and towns. Amongst the better known are the Marcoses of Ilocos Norte, the Sumulongs of Rizal, the Laurels and Rectos of Batangas, the Aquinos and the Cojuangcos of Tarlac, the Magsaysays of Zambales, the Duranos and the Osmeñas of Cebu, the Lopezes of Iloilo, the Yulos of Negros Occidental, the Roxases and the Villareals of Capiz, the Sarmientos of Davao del Norte, the Alemendras of Davao del Sur, and the Amatongs of Zamboanga del Norte. Not to be outdone are Filipino Muslim families —the Candaos, Datumanongs, Masturas, and Matalams of Maguindanao and the Alontos, Lantos, and Dimaporos, of Lanao del Sur and Lanao del Norte.[13]

A number of familiar names also dominate and extract benefits from the Philippine business sector. There are the Filipino-Chinese clans who control a large segment of the lucrative banking, logging, retail and wholesale sectors of the country; for instance, the Tys who own Metrobank, the Sys who own Shoemart, and the Gokongweis who own Robinsons, Manila Times, and Robina Farms. Aside from putting up "megamalls," Filipino-Chinese families are into real estate, banking, shipping, agriculture, mining, and other industries. Filipino-Spanish mestizo clans like the Zobels, Ayalas, and Sorianos control large corporations such as Ayala and Anscor. There are also traditionally landed families like the Lopezes, Aranetas, Yulos,

Cojuangcos, and Osmeñas who are now into diversified business interests which go beyond agriculture. In Mindanao, some Muslim royal families have successfully held on to their business concessions and trade monopolies for centuries. Although family feuds occur at times, these Filipino elites are generally highly supportive of clan members.

The terms technocrats and cronies became popular during the Marcos years. These two labels were used interchangeably to describe the private sector oligarchy he developed made up of loyal relatives and friends. Marcos used his group of cronies and technocrats as a counter weight against the wealth and power of the traditional elite families like the Lopezes and Osmeñas. This grand coalition of new elites were notoriously called Marcos' cronies — Disini, Cuenca, Silverio, Benedicto, Floriendo, Tan, Cojuangco, etc. Marcos recruited these key allies from the First Family's former classmates, friends and relatives, fraternity brothers, golf buddies, and province mates. Every Presidential administration, before and after Marcos, has also had their share of accusations of cronyism. But the intensity of allegations increased again under Estrada after his buddies — also former Marcos cronies — Eduardo Cojuangco regained San Miguel (one of the country's top corporations) and Lucio Tan was allowed to buy the controlling interests in Philippine Airlines and the Philippine National Bank (two privatized government corporations).

Although there is some trickle down of political, economic, and social benefits, the obvious divide between these "haves" and the "have nots" in the Philippines continues from generation to generation. Ironically, in the urban areas, one can see the posh mansions and fancy cars in areas where street beggars, urban slums, and squatter settlements are also a common sight. In the rural countryside, poor disbursement of funds due to political squabbling is hampering the implementation of land redistribution and rural infrastructure that are critical activities of the country's land reform programme.

Extent of Legitimacy

As a constitutional democracy, Filipinos are socialized to believe that regime legitimacy in the Philippines is gained through the ballot box. Voting is not compulsory but to encourage everyone to exercise their right of suffrage, a national holiday is declared on every election day. People go out of their way to travel long distances to get to the province or municipality where they have registered as a voter. The unique workings of the Filipino patron-client system are manifested in each electoral exercise. As a political client, many take leaves of absences from their work to help in the election or re-election campaign of their political patrons. All-out support is given to the patron no matter what party he or she comes from. Clients believe that it is the person and not the party that counts. This gracious deed is done to pay back a political debt or to gain a political favour. Voter turnouts during election days are very high.

To illustrate the relative importance of elections to legitimacy, Filipino political scientists point out that despite having enormous powers unchecked by a legislature or citizenry, Marcos still relied on electoral exercises to perpetuate his martial law rule. Both military and civilian authorities have always relied on electoral results as a key justification for regime change and maintenance. Even the leaders of the People Power revolution, which ousted Marcos, argued that massive electoral fraud caused the numbers to go in Marcos' favor. In other words, without the vote padding and coercion, the ballots would have shown that Aquino won. Whenever they are disgruntled with an administration, they would immediately call for "snap elections." This just goes to show that Filipinos firmly believe that people power should emanate from electoral power and vice versa.

In what seems like a paradox, however, Filipinos have shown the world that despite their belief in the electoral process they will resort to use "people power" to de-legitimize and overthrow an unpopular regime. Hence, although not written into the Constitution, many Filipinos feel that they have the right to reject a President or any elected official before his or her term and demand his or her immediate resignation. In late 2000, this was the main justification former President Aquino, former President Ramos Cardinal Sin and others used against President Estrada after allegations surfaced on his direct involvement in illegal gambling.

Interestingly, people power has also acquired a legitimizing force of its own since 1986, and continues through the work of civil society groups before, during, and after elections. During elections it is manifested in the participation of numerous unpaid volunteers. The National Movement for Free Elections (NAMFREL), one of the largest non-partisan electoral watchdog group in the Southeast Asian region, mobilizes an army of volunteers to assist COMELEC ensure that elections are free and fair. Groups representing civil society reinforce the legitimizing process by taking stands aligned with certain candidates and parties. Before election day, the Catholic Church makes it usual spiel about "voting your conscience" to encourage people to vote for candidates who exemplify "upright moral values". Other Christian groups and NGOs use the ballot box to reflect their preferences for political candidates who have been supportive to their cause or promise to be once elected. After elections, civil society then plays an important role as a "watchdog", making sure that elected officials are held accountable to their promises and actions after the elections. The section on governance below will elaborate on people power through state-society partnerships.

In spite of this widespread "faith" in elections and people power as legitimizing forces, there are groups within Filipino society who question regime legitimacy based on these political processes. These groups include: Muslim rebels in Mindanao like the Moro Islamic Liberation Front and their sympathisers, some ethnic communities in the Cordilleras, the National Democratic Front (NDF) and the New People's Army (NPA), including some militant labour and student organizations. They argue that these "democratic" processes are captured by elite interests and will never really lead to political change that will be meaningful to them. Hence, to these groups, the only legitimate way to effect meaningful regime change is through armed struggle.

Governance

Over the past two decades, sweeping political, economic, and social changes have occurred in the Philippines that have affected the relationship between the public (government), the private (business), and the people (civil society) sectors. The 1986 People Power revolution and the meteoric rise of Philippine civil society, the passage of the pro-people 1987 Constitution, as well as the implementation of the landmark Local Government Code of 1991 and number of development plans are events that created a new system of national and local governance encouraging partnerships among groups representing government, business, and civil society. As a result, transparency, predictability, and accountability have improved.

Before his overthrow, Ferdinand Marcos, the cronies he pampered, and the state-oriented development regime they created suppressed many segments of civil society, including the church, media, labour, peasants, women's groups, student organizations, among others. Mass support for the political uprising against Marcos came from these same societal groups marginalized under his authoritarian regime.

The rebirth of a flourishing Philippine nongovernmental organization (NGO) community was an interesting post-Marcos phenomenon to watch. Advocates of issues pertaining to health, religion, labour, environment, women, urban poor, overseas workers, etc., came forward and started lobbying the executive and legislative branches and even holding mass rallies and demonstrations to argue their causes. Post-Marcos administrations have acknowledged their important role in nation-building especially as an alternative service delivery system to the government. Many NGOs operate relatively free from government influence and control. As mentioned earlier, the Philippines has become an NGO haven of Southeast Asia, with NGOs numbering in the thousands operating freely everywhere in the country. The government has successfully reached out to these groups and made them partners for progress.

The role of the market and the corporate community in national development has been transformed after the departure of Marcos. Crony and government monopolies were dismantled — Estrado's attempt to resurrect them led to his downfall. The business community as a whole welcomed the privatization of inefficient government-owned and -controlled corporations, which had enjoyed competitive advantages *vis-à-vis* private enterprises. The Build-Operate-Transfer Law of 1993 — enabling private enterprise to build infrastructure then operate it for a number of years before returning to public ownership — has led to closer cooperation between business and government. Public-private partnerships and co-financing schemes have been introduced to develop transportation, communications, tourism, and the industrial sectors. This emerging governance arrangement has made government more accountable, transparent, and participatory. Sharing power with civil society has strengthened the effectiveness of the Philippine state.

As stated earlier, the 1987 Philippine Constitution contains many provisions, concerning social justice and human rights, which were civil society's reactions to the excesses of Marcos. In addition, although Marcos promised he would decentralize development administration down to the *barangay* level, he never fulfilled it. Indeed, during martial law local government units became highly dependent on the national government in terms of policies, finances, and manpower. This changed significantly under the post-Marcos administrations. People's representatives in Constitutional Commission introduced into the 1987 Philippine Constitution provisions that expressed the wish for democratic development and decentralization.

There are still deep-seated barriers that need to be overcome despite a prevailing environment that promotes a new governance system, involving genuine cooperation between government, business, and civil society, to address effectively the country's social and economic concerns. Most compelling among these issues is the inherent lack of trust between and among individuals and organizations from representing the government, business, and civil society sectors. Deeply ingrained attitudes of blaming the central government for its inefficiency, criticizing civil society for its narrow and biased interests and viewing business as interested only in its own bottom line do not auger well for strong, supportive relationships among these groups. A desire for power and control by many Filipino bureaucrats and politicians are additional barriers to successful partnership. Finally, in some cases, it continues to be a daunting challenge to change national and local governance relationships that have been institutionalized for decades under authoritarian rule, to ones that are more participatory and inclusive of multiple groups. As highlighted by the media, a resulting dysfunction from the lack of transparency and participatory mechanisms is corruption in various forms, from influence peddling to rigged public biddings.

Conclusion

Historically, government and politics in the Philippines have been marked by powerful continuities and discontinuities, with periods of alternating advancement and regression. The country had four centuries of colonial government, which had a significant influence on its politico-administrative culture. The Philippines inherited both good and bad features from these models. For instance, subdividing the country into administrative and political units was a positive legacy from Spanish rule while democratic institutions introduced by the Americans created popular representation through elections. However, colonialism also brought some negatives like a patron-client structure, which came with the hacienda system (large holdings tilled by tenant farmers) under the Spanish regime, and the "spoils system", which is a classic dysfunction of the American model. Although the general results were good, mixing the two negatives produced some problems for the evolving administrative culture. Captured by elite interests and tainted with inefficiencies, Filipinos turned to bribery and other corrupt acts to get things done within the political system.

Nevertheless, after World War II, the Philippines moved forward and even joined Japan on top of Asia in the 1960s in terms of economic progress. But, democracy and development both declined sharply during two decades of authoritarian rule under President Marcos. In 1986, President Aquino and the people power revolution restored democratic institutions, including a popularly elected Congress and a pro-people Constitution. Moreover, a new governance system has been born with attempts to form government, business, and civil society partnerships. The new arrangement also promises to increase transparency, accountability, responsiveness, and people participation in development governance. Improved governance precipitated economic liberalization and growth under President Fidel Ramos. Internal security improved, with a peace accord was finally signed with the new Muslim organization in Mindanao after centuries of strife.

However, just as the country seemed to be heading for a much-awaited economic renaissance, President Joseph Estrada took over the helm at the turn of the century, and was soon beset with serious economic and political problems. Internationally, globalization and the Asian economic crisis did not help Estrada's cause, contributing to a declining peso and shaky stock market. Domestically, kidnappings resumed, fighting in Mindanao escalated, and Estrada faced allegations of receiving millions of pesos from illegal gambling. There are obvious parallels with earlier Philippine political disasters, and the awesome power of globalisation to punish states that fail to maintain political stability makes the current situation particularly worrisome. But no reversion to Marcos style politics seems likely. This was illustrated by Estrada's ouster in People Power II. Government institutions and policies have made advances since and enjoy widespread popular support. In the final analysis, the quest for democracy and development advances through continuing and resilient "people power".

Notes

1   Robin Theobald , *Corruption, Development and Underdevelopment* (Durham: Duke University Press, 1990), p. 163.
2   Joaquin L. Gonzalez III and Luis R. Calingo, *Success Secrets to Maximize Business in the Philippines* (Singapore: Times Publishing, 2000).
3   Joaquin L. Gonzalez III, "Political Economy of Philippine Development: Past Issues and Current Reforms", *Humboldt Journal of Social Relations*, 23, nos. 1&2.
4   Charles C. McDonald, *The Marcos File* (San Francisco: San Francisco Publishers, 1987), p. 159.
5   Rommel C. Banlaoi and Clarita R. Carlos, *Political Parties in the Philippines: From 1900 to the Present* (Manila: Konrad-Adenauer-Stiftung, 1997), pp. 102–105.
6   Gerard Clarke, *The Politics of NGO in South-East Asia: Participation and Protest in the Philippines* (London: Routledge, 1998), pp. 70, 93.
7   Fidel V. Ramos, "Philippines 2000: Our Development Strategy", *Multi-Sectoral Reform Secretariat* (Manila, 1993), p. 23.

8   Gerard Clarke, *The Politics of NGOs in South-East Asia: Participation and Protest in the Philippines* (London: Routledge, 1998), pp. 71, 80.
9   Alvin Capino, "Scrutinize Recipient Foundations of Congressional Pork Barrel," *Today* (Manila), 31 July 1996 as cited in Clarke, ibid, p. 80.
10 See Alex B. Brillantes, Jr. and Bienvenida M. Amarles-Ilago, *1898–1992: The Philippine Presidency* (Quezon City: University of the Philippines, 1994).
11 National Economic Development Authority, *Philippine National Development Plan: Directions for the 21ˢᵗ Century* (Manila: NEDA, 1998).
12 See Rosalita Tolibas-Nunez, *Roots of Conflict: Muslims, Christians, and the Mindanao Struggle* (Makati: Asian Institute of Management, 1997).
13 See Eric Gutierrez, *The Ties that Bind: A Guide to Family, Business and Other Interests in the Ninth House of Representatives* (Pasig: Philippine Center for Investigative Journalism, 1994) and Alfred W. McCoy, *An Anarchy of Families: State and Family in the Philippines* (Madison: University of Wisconsin, 1993).

Further Reading

Abueva, Jose V. *Filipino Politics, Nationalism and Emerging Ideologies.* Manila: Modern Book Co., 1972.

Agoncillo, Teodoro. *History of the Filipino People.* Quezon City: Garotech, 1990.

Brillantes, Alex B. *Dictatorship and Martial Law.* Quezon City: University of the Philipines, 1988.

Clarke, Gerard. *The Politics of NGOs in South-East Asia: Participation and Protest in the Philippines.* London: Routledge, 1998.

Coronel, Shiela, ed. *Pork and Other Perks: Corruption and Governance in the Philippines.* Manila: Philippine Center for Investigative Journalism, 1998.

De Guzman, Raul P. and Mila A. Reforma, eds. *Government and Politics of the Philippines.* New York: Oxford University Press, 1988.

Feder, James F. and Robert Youngblood. *Patterns of Power and Politics in the Philippines: Implications for Development.* Arizona: Arizona State University, 1994.

Gutierrez, Eric. *Ties that Bind: A Guide to Family, Business and Other Interests in the Ninth House of Representative.* Pasig: Philippine Center for Investigative Journalism, 1994.

Lande, Carl. *Leaders, Factions, and Parties: The Structure of Philippine Politics.* New Haven: Yale University, Southeast Asian Studies, 1966.

Padilla, Efren N. *The New Filipino Story.* Dubuque: Kendall/Hunt, 1998.

Varela, Amelia P. *Administrative Culture and Political Change.* Quezon City: University of the Philippines, 1996.

Wurfel, David. *Filipino Politics: Development and Decay.* Ithaca: Cornell University Press, 1991.

8

SINGAPORE
Meritocratic City-State

Jon S.T. Quah

INTRODUCTION

Singapore was governed by the British for nearly 140 years, from its founding by Stamford Raffles in January 1819 until its attainment of self-government in June 1959. In July 1926, Singapore became part of the Straits Settlements together with Malacca and Penang. The pre-colony phase ended in 1867 when control of the Straits Settlements passed from the India Office to the Colonial Office. British colonial rule was briefly interrupted by the Japanese occupation (February 1942–August 1945). Singapore became a crown colony in 1946 and its constitutional status was changed to a ministerial form of government under the Rendel Constitution in 1955.

The first general election held in April 1955 resulted in the formation of the Labour Front coalition government under the leadership of David Marshall. The People's Action Party (PAP) government assumed office in June 1959 after winning 43 of the 51 seats in the May 1959 general election and capturing 54.1 per cent of the valid votes. On 16 September 1963, Singapore achieved independence from Britain by becoming one of the 14 states of the Federation of Malaysia. However, Singapore's sojourn in the Federation was brief as after 23 months, it separated from Malaysia on 9 August 1965, and became the 117th member of the United Nations on 21 September 1965.

Even though Singapore has been independent for the past 35 years, there has been no change in government during this period as the PAP government was re-elected nine times. Lee Kuan Yew served as Prime Minister from June 1959 until November 1990, when he became Senior Minister and was succeeded by Goh Chok Tong. This change in political leadership has also been accompanied by a shift from a paternalistic to a more consultative leadership style.

When Singapore attained self-government in June 1959, it was a Third World country. Its economy was dependent on entrepot trade and its per capita Gross Domestic Product (GDP) in 1960 was S$1,330 (or US$443). The population of 1.58 million was growing by 4 per cent, and the unemployment rate was 5 per cent. Housing was a serious problem as half of the population was living in squatter huts and only 9 per cent were provided with public housing. Corruption was rampant and the crime rate was also rising. Under such circumstances, it was not surprising that Albert Winsemius, the Dutch economist leading the United Nations study mission to Singapore in 1960, was pessimistic about Singapore's future when he said, "Singapore is going down the drain, it is a poor little market in a dark corner of Asia."[1]

Today, four decades later, Singapore has been transformed into "an advanced developing country", with an affluent and competitive economy. According to the *World Development Report 1998/99*, Singapore was the fourth richest country in the world in 1997, with its per capita GNP of US$32,940 below only Switzerland (US$44,320), Japan (US$37,850) and Norway (US$36,090).[2] Government expenditure on education has increased by 90 times. The housing shortage was solved by the Housing and Development Board's (HDB) showcase public housing programme, which caters for 86 per cent of the population. Corruption is no longer a serious problem because of the PAP government's effective anti-corruption strategy. Similarly, other problems like crime and traffic congestion have been tackled effectively by the PAP government. .

However, in spite of Singapore's tremendous progress during the past four decades, there are three contextual factors which have remained constant viz., its small, heterogeneous population, its small size, and its strategic location. First, the resident population of 3,217,500 is multi-racial (76.9 per cent Chinese; 14.0 per cent Malays; 7.7 per cent Indians; and 1.4 per cent other ethnic groups); multi-lingual (with four official languages — English, Mandarin, Malay and Tamil — and many dialects among the Chinese and Indians); and multi-religious (53.8 per cent Buddhists and Taoists; 14.9 per cent Muslims; 14.5 per cent with no religion; 12.9 per cent Christians; and 3.3 per cent Hindus).[3] This diversity requires the incumbent government to formulate and implement policies for nurturing racial harmony. Both public and private organizations should also be fair and impartial in the treatment of their clients, regardless of their ethnicity, language or religion. There are two presidential councils to protect minority rights and ensure religious harmony in Singapore.

FIGURE 8.1

Singapore: Key Dates

1819	Stamford Raffles founded Singapore.
1824	Singapore was ceded in perpetuity to the English East India Company by the Sultan of Johor.
1826	Singapore became part of the Straits Settlements with Malacca and Penang.
1942	The Japanese occupied Singapore in February.
1945	The Japanese surrendered to the British in August.
1946	Singapore became a Crown Colony of Britain.
1951	Public Service Commission was established for the recruitment and promotion of civil servants.
1955	A new constitution was introduced and provided for a Legislative Assembly of 32 members, of which 25 members were elected.
1959	The People's Action Party (PAP) won the 30 May general election and formed the government on 3 June, with the attainment of self-government from the British.
1961	Tunku Abdul Rahman, Prime Minister of the Federation of Malaya, proposed the formation of Malaysia, which would include the Federation of Malaya, Singapore, Sarawak, Sabah and Brunei.
1963	Singapore became independent and part of Malaysia on 16 September. On 21 September, the PAP was re-elected in the general election as it won 37 of the 51 seats.
1965	Singapore separated from Malaysia on 9 August.
1966	The 13 Barisan Sosialis Members of Parliament boycotted Parliament, resulting in a *de facto* one party dominant system.
1968	The PAP won all the 58 seats in the 13 April general election.
1972	The PAP was returned to power for the fourth time when it won all the seats in the September general election.
1976	The PAP captured all the 69 seats in the December general election.
1980	The PAP won all the 75 seats in the December general election.
1981	J.B. Jeyaratnam of the Workers' Party won the Anson by-election on 31 October and broke the PAP's 15-year monopoly of Parliament.
1984	The Non-Constituency Member of Parliament scheme was introduced in July to ensure the election of three opposition members in Parliament even if the PAP had won all the seats in a general election. The PAP won 77 seats and lost two seats to the opposition in the December general election. There was a decline in 12.6 per cent in votes for the PAP. M.P.D. Nair of the Workers' Party was offered a seat as a NCMP but he declined as his party opposed the NCMP scheme.
1985	The Feedback Unit was formed in March.
1988	The Constitution was amended in May to establish 13 Group Representation Constituencies in the September general election, which the PAP won, capturing 80 of the 89 seats.
1990	Parliament approved the Nominated Member of Parliament Bill on 29 March. The first two NMPs were appointed on 22 November. Lee Kuan Yew stepped down as Prime Minister on 28 November, and was succeeded by Goh Chok Tong.
1991	The PAP won 77 seats and the opposition parties won four seats in the August general election. Six NMPs were appointed to Parliament.
1993	Ong Teng Cheong was elected as the President for six years on 28 August.
1997	The PAP won 81 of the 83 parliamentary seats in the January general election. Nine NMPs were appointed to Parliament.
1999	S.R. Nathan was returned unopposed as Singapore's second Elected President on 18 August. He assumed office on 1 September after Ong Teng Cheong's term of office ended on 31 August.

TABLE 8.1

Singapore in 1959 and 1999

Indicator	1959	1999
Size of Population	1.58 million	3.21 million
Per capita GNP	US$443*	US$32,810
Unemployment Rate	5%	3.3%
% people in public housing	9%	86%
Govt spending on education	S$63.39 million	S$5,718.32 million
Extent of Corruption	Rampant	Minimized

* 1960 figure.

Sources: *Singapore Facts and Pictures 2000* (Singapore: Ministry of Information and the Arts, 1998), p. 9; *Economic and Social Statistics Singapore 1960–82* (Singapore: Department of Statistics, 1983), pp. 7 and 12; *Yearbook of Statistics Singapore 2000* (Singapore: Department of Statistics, 2000), p. 239; *Pocket World in Figures 2000 Edition* (London: Economist, 1999), p. 206.

The other contextual constraints are Singapore's small size and geographic location. As a city-state with a total land area of 659.9 sq. km., smallness is a mixed blessing. While compactness has enhanced the implementation of public policies, it also means the absence of natural resources, as there is no rural hinterland for the cultivation of crops or the mining of minerals; and limited land for housing and the construction of roads. To compensate for the lack of resources, the PAP government adopted a two-pronged strategy: industrialization to promote economic growth through foreign investment; and heavy investment in education to upgrade the city-state's human resources. The scarcity of land dictates the need for the public housing programme and explains the government's drive to curb traffic congestion by increasing exorbitantly the cost of car ownership.

Finally, proximity to both Malaysia and Indonesia has forced the government to consider the reactions of these countries to some of its public policies, especially those dealing with minority issues and the increasing problem of illegal immigrants. The visit of Israeli President Chaim Herzog to Singapore in November 1986, for example led to Malaysian protests that Singapore had been insensitive to Malay/Islamic concerns over Israel.[4] In February 1999, Indonesian President, B.J. Habibie, made a *faux pas* when he wrongly accused the Singapore Armed Forces of discriminating against Singaporean Malays.[5] Indeed, according to Michael Leifer, relations with Malaysia and Indonesia "have always been handled at the highest political level" as "the tyranny of geography means that

FIGURE 8.2

Singapore: Key Statistics

Land area: 659.9 sq kilometres

Population:[a]   3,893,600 (1999)

GNP:[b]   Current exchange rate   — US$101.8 bn (1997);
                                               US$95.5 bn (1998)
                    Purchasing Power Parity — US$91 bn (1997);
                                               US$80 bn (1998)

GNP Per Capita:[b] Current exchange rate   — US$32,810 (1997);
                                               US$30,170 (1998)
                    Purchasing Power Parity — US$29,230 (1997);
                                               US$25,295 (1998)

Income Distribution (1999):[d]
                    Gini Index   0.467
                    % share of income or consumption:
                    Lowest 20%   2.8
                    Middle 60%   47.4
                    Highest 20%   49.9

Human Development Index (HDI) Ranking:[c]
                    World ranking   22 (1997); 24 (1998)
                    Value   0.888 (1997); 0.881 (1998)

Armed Forces:
                    Total no.[d]   73,000 (1999)
                    Expenditure[d]   US$4.2 bn (1999)
                    % of GNP[b]   4.7% (1995)

Sources: [a] Official national sources.
           [b] World Bank, *World Development Indicators* (Washington, D.C.,
               1999 & 2000).
           [c] United Nations Development Programme (UNDP), *Human
               Development Report* (New York: Oxford University Press, 1999 &
               2000).
           [d] International Institute for Strategic Studies (IISS), *The Military
               Balance, 1999-2000* (London: Oxford University Press, 1999).

Singapore cannot escape a locale in which problematic relations with close neighbours are permanent facts of political life".[6]

THE POLITICAL SYSTEM

Singapore's political system can be described as a "controlled democracy", that is "a republic with a parliamentary system of government based on the British Westminster model, but which has been adapted to suit the local conditions".[7] There are three important differences between the Singaporean and British parliamentary systems. First, Singapore has a written constitution while the United Kingdom has an unwritten one. The second difference is the unicameral legislature, which was originally recommended by the Rendel Commission in 1954 as Singapore is a city state.[8] The size of this unicameral legislature has grown from the original 32-member Legislative Assembly in 1955 to 83-member Parliament in 1997.[9]

The third key difference with the United Kingdom is that Singapore is not a monarchy. Its head of state is a President, who was originally appointed for a term of four years and did not have political power. Parliament has a maximum term of five years, unless it is dissolved earlier by the President, who also appoints the Prime Minister as the head of government on the basis of a majority vote in Parliament. The Prime Minister and his 15 ministers constitute the Cabinet, which is the supreme policy-making body of the government.[10] However, the Cabinet is collectively responsible to Parliament, which is the supreme legislative authority in Singapore.

In his comparative study of political systems, Douglas V. Verney has observed that parliamentary government is concerned with *efficient* government, while presidential government emphasizes *limited* government.[11] This observation certainly applies to Singapore, where the focus during the first 25 years of PAP rule from 1959 to 1984 was on making government more efficient rather than limiting its powers. However, Singapore's success in economic development has resulted, *inter alia*, in a hugh increase in its foreign reserves, which amounted to S$22.8 billion in 1984.[12] In April 1984, Prime Minister Lee Kuan Yew revealed that his government was considering amending the Constitution so that the foreign reserves could only be spent with the agreement of the President and a special committee.

Accordingly, a White Paper on the need for an elected President was presented in Parliament in July 1988. After two and a half years of discussion of the proposal both within and outside Parliament, the

Constitution was amended in January 1991 and the presidency was transformed in two ways. First, the President is now elected by the citizens of Singapore for a term of six years. Second, the elected President is no longer a symbolic figure as he is "empowered to veto government budgets and appointments to public office, and to examine the government's exercise of its powers under the Internal Security Act and religious harmony laws and in investigations into cases of corruption".[13] In short, an important political consequence of Singapore's rapid economic growth was the transformation of the Presidency from a ceremonial role to an elected President with veto powers.

FIGURE 8.3

Singapore: Government Ministries 2000

Prime Minister's Office
Ministry of Communications and Information Technology
Ministry of Community Development and Sports
Ministry of Defence
Ministry of Education
Ministry of the Environment
Ministry of Finance
Ministry of Foreign Affairs
Ministry of Health
Ministry of Home Affairs
Ministry of Information and the Arts
Ministry of Law
Ministry of Manpower
Ministry of National Development
Ministry of Trade and Industry

The Electoral System

Compulsory Voting

Singapore adopted the British electoral system of "first past the post". Voting was not compulsory during the first election held in April 1955 to implement the Rendel Constitution.[14] In July 1957, Lee Kuan Yew complained about corrupt practices during the June 1957 by-election. A Commission of Inquiry convened to investigate the extent of corrupt practices during elections found that current election practices facilitated bribery and the exercise of undue influence by members of secret societies and by candidates' supporters "working in aggressive groups, particularly on polling day". To overcome the problem of an apathetic electorate and to prevent the occurrence of corrupt practices at elections, the Commission recommended the introduction of compulsory voting.[15] The Labour Front government accepted this recommendation and voting became compulsory during the May 1959 general election and all subsequent general elections.[16]

Non-Constituency Member of Parliament Scheme

Feedback from its party branches, the various grass-roots organizations, and the ministerial walkabouts made the PAP realize in 1984 that the population wanted an opposition in Parliament. Thus, on 24 July 1984, Prime Minister Lee Kuan Yew introduced the Non-Constituency Member of Parliament (NCMP) scheme to allow for the seating in Parliament of three opposition candidates who had received the highest percentage of votes (exceeding 15 per cent) in their constituencies. The aim of this scheme was to ensure that there would be at least three opposition members in Parliament even if the PAP had won all 79 seats. The NCMPs differ from the elected MPs in that they would not be able to vote in Parliament on Bills to amend the Constitution, a Supply Bill or Supplementary Supply Bill, a Money Bill, or a vote of no confidence in the government.[17]

Lee provided three reasons for the NCMP scheme: (1) to educate younger voters (who make up 60 per cent of the electorate) on the myths on the opposition's role in Parliament since they had missed the political conflicts of the !950s and 1960s; (2) to sharpen the debating skills of the younger ministers and MPs in Parliament; and (3) to provide a means of giving "vent to any allegation of malfeasance or corruption or nepotism" in order to "dispel suspicions of cover-ups of alleged wrongdoings".[18] However, the NCMP scheme was not welcomed by both the public and opposition parties because the restrictions imposed on the NCMPs made them "second-class" MPs.[19]

Since Chiam See Tong and J.B. Jeyaretnam won the Potong Pasir and Anson constituencies respectively in the December 1984 general election, only M.P.D. Nair from the Workers' Party (WP) was offered a seat as a NCMP as he had obtained the most votes as an opposition candidate after Chiam and Jeyaretnam. However, Nair did not accept the offer as his party did not support the NCMP scheme. The WP has, since then reversed its stand on this issue as Jeyaretnam became a NCMP after the January 1997 general election.

Group Representation Constituency Scheme

The Group Representation Constituency (GRC) scheme was first announced by the MP for Kebun Baru, Lim Boon Heng, in January 1987, when he proposed that instead of voting for an MP in each constituency, voters in three adjacent constituencies forming a town council (TC) would vote for a team of three candidates from the teams fielded by the political parties contesting a general election. The team that obtains the highest number of votes would win the election, and its three members would become MPs and be held collectively responsible for administering their TC.[20] Lim gave two reasons for introducing the GRC scheme. First, in view of the 12.6 per cent swing of votes against the PAP during the 1984 general election, he reminded voters to "vote wisely because they have to live with their choices".[21] Second, the GRC scheme would help to enhance the calibre of candidates standing for election, especially those from the opposition political parties, as those elected must have administrative ability to run the TC.

The initial public reaction to Lim's proposal was negative as there was a widespread public perception that this proposal was an attempt by the PAP government to handicap the electoral participation of the opposition political parties.[22] For example, an administrative assistant contended that the GRC scheme was "another way of making sure that the PAP stays in power" by making "it more difficult for opposition parties to get in".[23]

Responding to public criticism of the proposal, Goh Chok Tong argued on 27 February 1987 that the GRC scheme was politically neutral since it did not favour any political party. He added that "if it benefits the People's Action Party, it will be because the party offers better candidates".[24] The initial negative public response to the scheme forced the PAP government to reveal its real, though unstated, goal and to modify the original aim of linking the scheme with the TCs. Indeed, Goh was the first PAP leader to hint at the *raison d'être* for the scheme when he spoke to members of the Singapore Malay Teachers Union on 11 April 1987. After referring to the Sri Lankan situation, which "contains one important lesson for all multiracial societies: that an ethnic minority must feel alienated when" its members are discriminated against and deprived of the benefits of national progress, he posed these questions to them:

> To be specific, how do we ensure that all the major races will be adequately represented in Parliament and in the Cabinet? ... How do we ensure ... that Parliament will always have multiracial representation? ... Is it important that our legislature reflects

multiracial Singapore? If so, how do we ensure that the major communities continue to be adequately represented in the Government?[25]

In his National Day Rally speech on 16 August 1987, Prime Minister Lee Kuan Yew contended that the GRC scheme would ensure the "continued representation of minority races, particularly the Malays, in Parliament". He revealed that the 1980 and 1984 general elections had shown that voters would vote for capable candidates who could speak dialect or Mandarin, thus making it increasingly difficult for Malay candidates to be elected. Indeed, my analysis of the racial composition of the Singapore legislature from 1959 to 1984 shows that the Malays have been under-represented in Parliament since 1972.[26] Lee suggested that a solution should be found before the backlash occurred: "Some way must be found, don't wait for these problems to mount up".[27]

The Constitution of the Republic of Singapore (Amendment No. 2) Bill and the Parliamentary Elections (Amendment) Bill, which provided for the formation of GRCs, were passed on 30 November, 1987. Each team of three MPs must include at least one MP who is a Malay, Indian, or a member of any other minority group. The new Parliament after the 1988 general election consisted of 39 MPs from the 13 GRCs and 40 MPs from the single-member constituencies. The number of GRCs increased to 15 in the 1997 general election with teams of between four to six MPs. The number of single member constituencies was correspondingly reduced to nine.

Nominated Members of Parliament

Since the NCMP scheme did not satisfy the electorate's desire for more parliamentary opposition, the PAP government introduced the nominated MPs (NMPs) scheme in 1989. Goh Chok Tong, then the First Deputy Prime Minister, identified the two objectives of the NMP scheme:

> to further strengthen our political system by offering Singaporeans more opportunity for political participation and to evolve a more consensual style of government where alternative views are heard and constructive dissent accommodated.[28]

To qualify as a NMP, a person must be a Singapore citizen of at least 21 years of age, who is living in Singapore, and is a qualified voter. The candidate must also be able to speak, read and write in one of the four official languages so that he can participate in the parliamentary proceedings. An NMP is appointed for a term of two years and has the same voting rights as a NCMP i.e., he can vote on all bills except money and constitutional bills, and motions of no confidence.[29]

Parliament approved the NMP Bill on 29 March 1990. The first two NMPs appointed on 22 November 1990 served for only eight months as Parliament was dissolved in August 1991 for the general election. Six NMPs were appointed in the Eighth Parliament after the 1991 general election.[30] In 1997, the Constitution was amended to increase the number of NMPs to nine.

PAP's Predominance

Five months after its formation on 21 November 1954, the PAP fielded four candidates in the April 1955 Legislative Assembly election and won three seats, obtaining 8.7 per cent of the total valid votes. The next political contest was the 1957 City Council election, when the PAP fielded 14 candidates and won 13 seats. Even though the PAP did not have an absolute majority in the 32-seat City Council, one of its members, Ong Eng Guan, was elected Mayor at the Council's first meeting.[31]

The PAP's landslide victory in the May 1959 general election led to its assumption of political office and the beginning of its long and durable rule. Table 8.2 below shows the PAP's electoral performance during 1959 to 1997. The party system in Singapore has been transformed from a competitive

TABLE 8.2

PAP's Electoral Performance, 1959–97

General Election	No. of Seats Contested	No. of Seats Won by PAP	Valid Votes Won(%)	No. of Seats Won by Opposition
May 1959	51	43	54.08	8
September 1963	51	37	46.93	14
April 1968	7 (51)*	58	86.72	0
September 1972	57 (8)	65	70.43	0
December 1976	53 (16)	69	74.09	0
December 1980	38 (37)	75	77.66	0
December 1984	49 (30)	77	64.83	2
September 1988	70 (11)	80	63.17	1
August 1991	40 (41)	77	60.97	4
January 1997	36 (47)	81	64.98	2

* Uncontested seats are indicated in brackets.

Sources: *Singapore 1998* (Singapore: Ministry of Information and the Arts, 1988), p. 338.

one (May 1959–September 1966) to a *de facto* one party dominant system in October 1966, when the 13 Barisan Sosialis MPs boycotted Parliament, and to a *de jure* one party dominant system after the April 1968 general election, when the PAP won all the 58 parliamentary seats. The PAP repeated its feat of winning all the parliamentary seats in the 1972, 1976 and 1980 general elections. However, its monopoly of Parliament was broken in October 1981, when J.B. Jeyaratnam of the Worker's Party defeated the PAP candidate, Pang Kim Hin, in the Anson by-election.

According to the Registry of Societies, there are 23 registered political parties in Singapore.[32] However, not all of them are active as only six political parties participated in the 1991 and 1997 general elections. Table 8.2 above also shows that the number of opposition MPs had initially increased from eight to 14 during 1959–63, the era of the competitive party system. There was no parliamentary opposition in Singapore for 15 years (from October 1966 to October 1981) and the number of opposition MPs fluctuated between one and four since the 1984 general election. The four reasons responsible for the PAP's dominance in Singapore politics are discussed below.

Ensuring Singapore's Survival

The PAP leaders, especially Lee Kuan Yew, fought for merger with Malaysia because they believed that Singapore could not survive on its own. However, after Singapore's separation from Malaysia in August 1965, they were forced to ensure Singapore's survival as failure would mean "crawling back" to rejoin the federation on "Malaysia's terms".[33] Thus, to ensure Singapore's survival, the PAP government had two urgent tasks: to continue its policy of industrialization initiated in 1961 to promote economic growth; and to build-up its armed forces through the introduction of compulsory military service in 1967 and the acquisition of military hardware.

The British government announced in 1968 that it would withdraw its military forces based in Singapore by December 1971. This move threatened Singapore's survival as the British naval base employed about 40,000 workers and contributed to 15 per cent of the GDP. Accordingly, the PAP government initiated several measures to minimize the economic effects of the withdrawal of the British forces, beginning with the formation of a Bases Reconversion Unit to convert the naval base into a commercial shipyard. More importantly, the 1968 amendment of the Employment Act prevented workers from striking so that labour unrest would not discourage foreign investors.

In short, the PAP government's success in encouraging foreign investment and minimizing the effects of the British withdrawal has promoted economic growth and the population's acceptance of national service has contributed to the creation of a credible defence force.

Fighting the Communists and Communalists

The PAP government acquired legitimacy among the population because of its effective response to communism and communalism, which were two important threats to Singapore's survival during the 1950s and 1960s because the communists wanted to destroy democracy and overthrow the incumbent government by force; and the communalists fomented racial riots to erode the multi-racial harmony in the country. However, communism and communalism are no longer serious threats to Singapore's survival today as a result of the effective measures employed by the PAP government.

The PAP government relied on such positive measures as promoting economic development, five instruments of nation-building (education, national service, public housing, national campaigns, and grass-roots organizations) and the provision of relevant information to increase the people's awareness of the dangers of communism and communalism and to prevent them from being influenced by these threats. In addition, such coercive measures as the Internal Security Act and the Newspaper and Printing Press Act were also employed to deal with those involved in pro-communist and pro-communalist activities, which endangered the security and survival of Singapore.[34]

In 1976, then Minister of Home Affairs, Chua Sian Chin, warned that while the communist threat was under control, this did not mean that the communists would not try to exploit or create issues.[35] This warning came true 11 years later, on 21 May 1987, when 16 individuals were arrested by the Internal Security Department (ISD) for their involvement in a Marxist conspiracy to overthrow the PAP government and establish a communist state in Singapore. During the first phase of subversion in the 1950s and 1960s, the communists mobilized students and workers in their struggle against the British colonial and PAP governments. The second phase of communist subversion was revealed by the ISD in May 1976 when it indicated that the Communist Party of Malaya (CPM) had initiated a new recruitment strategy for attracting all Singaporeans, including those with a middle-class background, to participate in its cause of overthrowing the PAP government by force. The Marxist conspiracy represented the third phase of communist subversion, which was characterized by the CPM's cultivation and infiltration of Christian groups, student organizations, the Workers' Party, and an English-language drama group. Unlike the poor Chinese-educated CPM cadres in the 1950s and 1960s, the 16 persons arrested were "comfortably well-off English-educated graduates and professionals". Thus, the Marxist conspiracy demonstrates the need for the ISD to be continually vigilant as a preventive measure to nip in the bud any attempts by the communists to create trouble for the incumbent government.[36]

Improvement in Living Standards

As indicated in Table 8.1 above, Singapore's per capita GDP improved by 74 times and transformed Singapore from a poor Third World country in 1959 to the fourth richest country in the world in 1997. The serious housing shortage experienced in 1959 was resolved by the HDB's successful public housing programme as 86 per cent of the population live in HDB flats, "with 9 in 10 residents owning their homes".[37]

According to the Department of Statistics, the average monthly household income of Singaporeans increased from S$3,076 in 1990 to S$4,716 in 1997. Table 8.3 below shows that the proportion of households earning

TABLE 8.3

Average Monthly Household Incomes of Singaporeans, 1990 and 1997

(S$)

Category	Average Monthly Household Income 1990	Average Monthly Household Income 1997	Average Annual Change (%)
Top 10%	S$9,670	S$14,801	2.9%
Next 10%	S$5,152	S$7,915	2.9%
Next 10%	S$3,897	S$6,054	4.1%
Next 10%	S$3,116	S$4,909	4.3%
Next 10%	S$2,541	S$3,997	4.3%
Next 10%	S$2,075	S$3,237	4.2%
Next 10%	S$1,686	S$2,598	4.0%
Next 10%	S$1,321	S$1,988	3.7%
Next 10%	S$934	S$1,341	3.2%
Bottom 10%	S$370	S$325	–3.8%

Source: Leong Ching, "S'poreans better off than in 1990", *Straits Times*, 29 December 1998, p. 3.

more than S$3,000 a month rose from 37 per cent in 1990 to nearly 60 per cent in 1997. The average household income for the top 10 per cent of Singaporeans increased from S$9,670 to S$14,801 a month during 1990–97. However, the poor Singaporeans became poorer as their average monthly household income fell by 12 per cent from S$370 in 1990 to S$325 in 1997. Thus, in spite of Singapore's affluence, there are still 11 per cent of Singaporeans or 340,000 persons who earn less than S$500 a month.[38]

Weak and Ineffective Opposition Political Parties

Finally, the PAP has been predominant in Singapore politics because the weak and ineffective opposition political parties do not provide a credible alternative to it. As mentioned earlier, there are 22 other registered political parties in Singapore apart from the PAP. However, usually only a handful of these parties participate in general elections. For example, in the 1991 general election, 45 candidates were fielded by five opposition parties; and 36 candidates were fielded by five opposition parties in the 1997 general election.

There were 14 opposition MPs after the September 1963 general election: 13 belonging to the Barisan Sosialis and one to the United People's Party. The 1963 figure of 14 opposition MPs has not been surpassed because of the severe limitations facing the opposition political parties. According to an observer, their internal weaknesses are "gaps in leadership, ideology and programmes, how their lack of funds made for a weak party machinery, and how they all, without exception, have at one time or other been wracked with intra-party and inter-party dissensions and cleavages".[39]

More specifically, opposition political parties in Singapore are deficient in four respects. First, they are weak organisationally, do not have adequate funds, and have difficulty in recruiting professionals as members. For example, the 75 opposition candidates contesting the 1988 general election spent an average of S$3,097 each, which was nearly one-third of the PAP candidates' average of S$8,333.[40]

Second, they do not have any rigorous selection system because they lack the means nor are they able to recruit candidates of sufficient calibre because of the PAP's cooptation of talented civil servants and professionals. Consequently, they found it extremely difficult to attract capable and well-qualified men and women to join their ranks. Indeed, there were few professionals among the opposition candidates fielded in the recent general elections. This problem is not surprising because if the PAP with all its resources found it difficult to recruit professionals, the obstacles facing the opposition parties in their search for capable candidates must appear to be insurmountable. In Singapore, few professionals are prepared to enter politics, let alone join the opposition political parties because of their perceived fear that such a move would jeopardize their career prospects. In view of this, it is understandable why the opposition parties cannot afford to be too demanding in their choice of candidates.

Third, no opposition political party has succeeded so far in providing a creditable alternative programme to compete with the PAP government's comprehensive array of policies. Above all, opposition political parties have fared badly in general elections because they, with a few exceptions, have not learned from their mistakes in previous general elections. Unlike the PAP's election campaign which begins from the day of its election, the opposition parties' most serious mistake is their continued inactivity during the interim period between general elections. Indeed, most of the opposition parties "hibernate" and do not have an active programme of activities to involve their members and potential supporters during the interim period between elections and are therefore unable to garner support or win seats in a general election. Indeed, the success of the Singapore Democratic Party (SDP) in securing three parliamentary seats and the Workers' Party victory in Hougang constituency during the 1991 general election demonstrate the need for opposition parties to be active during the interim period between general elections.

Finally, the introduction of the GRC scheme in 1988 has adversely affected the opposition political parties in two ways. First, the number of single member constituencies (SMCs) has been reduced from 79 in 1984 to 21 in 1988 and to nine in 1997. As the current two opposition MPs are in SMCs, this means that the maximum number of opposition MPs cannot exceed nine if the opposition parties field their candidates only in the SMCs. Second, the opposition parties because of their difficulty in recruiting credible candidates, have difficulty in forming teams of candidates as the electoral deposit required for each candidate is S$6,000. This means that opposition parties must be able to pay between S$24,000 for a GRC of four MPs to S$36,000 for a mega-GRC of six MPs if they wish to field teams in a general election.

Civilian Control over the Military

In her 1985 analysis of military-civilian relations in Singapore, Chan Heng Chee observed that "the most striking feature of the Singapore scene is the undisputed predominance of the civilian sector over the military".[41] Indeed, in spite of the introduction of compulsory military service in 1967 for male citizens on reaching the age of 18, and the huge amount spent annually on defence (7 per cent of the GDP), the military does not play an active role in Singapore politics as it is subservient to the political leadership.

Given the high cost of maintaining a large army, the PAP government decided on the establishment of a citizen army with a small corps of regular professional soldiers. The Israeli model was chosen because Israel had an impressive citizen army and its compressed system of training enabled Singapore to produce its citizen army in a few years.[42] To enhance the status of the military, the PAP government provides scholarships for outstanding students to study abroad at prestigious universities. On graduation, these scholar-officers are required to serve in the Singapore Armed Forces (SAF).[43]

As the SAF is a young peacetime defence force, with no experience of war or revolution, it does not have a strong political ideology. In 1967, the Minister of Defence, Goh Keng Swee, "suggested that the political leadership was concerned to innoculate the armed forces against 'imported ideas' (read coup-making) and to prescribe the proper relations between armed forces and society." In fact, the SAF Code of Conduct "emphasizes a strictly professional role for the armed forces as an instrument of the state in defence and security" and its members are reminded "not to allow party politics to interfere with their loyalty to the government at any time".[44]

While civilian control over the military will continue in Singapore, two important trends must be noted. The first trend is the appointment of senior SAF officers to head public organizations. In the view of Yong Mun Cheong, "the ultimate link that can be developed to bridge the Armed Forces and society is of course the movement of personnel between the military and non-military sectors". He further contends that this sharing of personnel has two benefits: "managerial expertise learnt in the Armed Forces could be deployed for non-military functions"; and "an extended career path" has been created for top military officers.[45] Two examples of such transfers are the appointment of Brigadier-General Lee Hsien Yang as President and Chief Executive Officer (CEO) of Singapore Telecommunications Ltd; and Major-General Han Eng Juan was appointed Chief Executive of the Land Transport Authority.

The second and more important trend is the selection of cabinet ministers from individuals with military or naval backgrounds. Lee Hsien Loong was the only minister with a military background in the 1989 Cabinet. He was joined by Brigadier-General George Yeo in 1992 and Rear-Admiral Teo Chee Hean in 1997.[46]

The Judiciary

The Judiciary in Singapore consists of the Supreme Court and the Subordinate Courts. It is independent constitutionally and functions as the chief guardian of the Constitution through its judicial review of the constitutionality of laws. The independence and integrity of the judiciary are ensured by laws providing for the inviolability of judges in the exercise of their duties and for safeguards on tenure and compensation relating to judges. The organization, jurisdiction and procedures of the courts are governed by the Supreme Court of Judicature Act, 1969, the Subordinate Courts Act, 1970, and the Criminal Procedure Code.

The Supreme Court is made up of the High Court and the Court of Appeal, which comprises the Chief Justice and two Judges of Appeal. The 14 judges of the Supreme Court are appointed by the President on the advice of the Prime Minister. The Subordinate Courts consist of the District Courts, Magistrates' Courts, Juvenile Courts, Coroners' Courts, and Small Claims Tribunals. There is also a Family Court to deal with family matters. For the Muslim community in Singapore, there is a separate system of courts and judicial officers to administer Muslim law in religious, matrimonial and related matters.[47]

In 1959, trial by jury except for capital offences was abolished, and in 1969, trial by jury was completely abolished through an amendment of the Criminal Procedure Code. Trial by jury was abolished because Lee Kuan Yew "had no faith in a system that allowed the superstition, ignorance, biases, prejudices and fears of seven jurymen to determine guilt or innocence".[48] Amnesty International has also criticized the PAP government for retaining the colonial practice of detention without trial and using it against "suspected Communists, left-wing trade unionists, students, 'Chinese chauvinists', gangsters, and drug traffickers". Lee Kuan Yew defended the practice of detention without trial by referring to the "difficulty of getting witnesses to testify in court because of the fear of reprisals".[49]

The judiciary in Singapore has been "criticized for its pro-PAP leanings, although such allegations are difficult to substantiate".[50] In recent years, PAP leaders have resorted to bringing defamation suits against members of opposition parties for making libellous statements in their electoral campaigns. These defamation suits direct "the most public international attention to the Singapore style of government and the use of the legal process in the practice of politics." Indeed, criticism by international organizations are "directed not so much at Singapore's legal system per se as against the PAP government's use — and alleged misuse — of the court process".[51] Prime Minister Goh Chok Tong justified the reliance on defamation suits to protect the reputation and integrity of Singapore's political leaders thus:

> In Singapore, we believe that leaders must be honourable men, gentlemen or *Junzi* (a Confucian gentleman), and if our integrity is attacked, we defend it. … If leaders and politicians do not defend their integrity, they are finished. … So, each time our integrity is impugned, we come out strongly and go to the courts to defend it. If you do not do that, over time, politics in Singapore is going to degenerate into politics like some other countries where leaders are called liars and cheats and nothing is done.[52]

State Ideology: Shared Values

The notion of a national ideology was first raised by Goh Chok Tong in October 1988 when he warned members of the PAP Youth Wing that the values of younger Singaporeans were being transformed from communitarianism to individualism as a result of their daily exposure to external influences. He suggested that the core values of Singaporeans be formalized as a national ideology and taught in schools, homes, and work-places to immunize Singaporeans from the undesirable effects of alien influences and to bind them together as a nation.[53]

A ministerial committee chaired by Lee Hsien Loong, then Minister for Trade and Industry, was appointed to examine the issue on 5 November 1988. President Wee Kim Wee identified these four core values in his opening address at the Seventh Parliament on 9 January 1989 as:

> placing society above self, upholding the family as the basic block of society, resolving major issues through consensus instead of contention, and stressing racial and religious tolerance and harmony.[54]

The Institute of Policy Studies (IPS) was then commissioned by the government to conduct a study to identify those national values that would unify all Singaporeans. The IPS Study Group on National Values completed its study within 10 months (August 1989–May 1990) and its report was published in September 1990.[55]

On 2 January 1991, the PAP government presented a White Paper on *Shared Values* in Parliament after taking into account the IPS report and extensive discussion on the topic both within and outside Parliament after President Wee's parliamentary speech. The White Paper identified the following five shared values, which are refinements of the original four core values:

1. Nation before community and society above self.
2. Family as the basic unit of society.
3. Regard and community support for the individual.
4. Consensus instead of contention.
5. Racial and religious harmony.[56]

The White Paper on *Shared Values* was debated in Parliament on 14–15 January 1991 and it was adopted with two amendments. First, the third shared value of "regard and community support for the individual" was changed to "community support and respect for the individual". The second amendment concerned the fourth shared value of "consensus instead of contention," which was revised to "consensus, not conflict".[57]

Major Political Issues

Who Rules: The Power Elite

C. Wright Mills defined the power elite in terms of "men [and women] whose positions enable them to transcend the ordinary environments of ordinary men and women; they are in positions to make decisions having major consequences" and "are in command of the major hierarchies and organizations of modern society".[58] Who fulfils this role in Singapore?

In 1975, Peter S.J. Chen contended that the power élite in Singapore consisted of the political élite, the civil bureaucrats, and the "select professional élite." The political élite referred to the political leaders of both the PAP and the opposition political parties, and included professionals, intellectuals and trade union leaders. The civil bureaucrats were the permanent secretaries, and chairmen of statutory boards and other top civil servants. The "select professional élite" included the intellectuals. However, Chen excluded the military and business élites from the power élite in Singapore.[59] How useful is Chen's analysis today, 25 years later?

In their study of "Who runs Singapore?" Cherian George and Jason Leow identified 107 individuals "holding full-time office in the executive, the civil service, the uniformed services, statutory boards, and government-owned corporations on January 1, 1998". However, PS100 provides "an insight into the anatomy of the public sector elite" but "is not meant to be a ranking of Singapore's most powerful individuals".[60] Table 8.4 below provides details of "PS100" by category. Indeed, PS100 is not equivalent to the power élite in Singapore as two important categories are excluded: the other 58 MPs who are not ministers or ministers of state, and the business élite. In other words, the power élite in Singapore today consists of the political élite (which includes the select professional élite), the civil bureaucrats, the military élite, and the business élite. Table 8.5 below provides details of Singapore's power élite in 1998 by category.

In sum, the power élite in Singapore as indicated in Table 8.5 below is made up of 226 individuals with 42 per cent from the bureaucratic élite, 41.6 per cent from the political élite, and 16.4 per cent from the business élite. However, this list is not exhaustive as complete data on the business élite and the chief executive officers of the Government-Linked Companies are not available.

The Beneficiaries and Non-Beneficiaries

Who has benefitted and who has suffered during the past four decades of PAP rule? Obviously, members of the power élite identified above have

TABLE 8.4

PS100: The Public Sector Elite in Singapore by Category, 1998

Category	Number
President	1
Ministers	16
Ministers-of-State	8
Permanent Secretaries	18
Supreme Court Judges	13
Key Appointment Holders*	2
Uniformed Services Chiefs	7
Envoys	12
Statutory Boards and GLCs**	30
Total	107

* These refer to the Speaker of Parliament and the Attorney-General.
** Government-Linked-Companies
Source: Cherian George and Jason Leow, "Who runs Singapore?" *Sunday Times*, 26 April 1998, p. 36.

benefited from the various policies of the PAP government. As shown in Table 8.3 above, the average monthly household income of the top 10 per cent of the population has increased from S$9,670 to S$14,801 during 1990–97. It should be noted that the PS 100 list is dominated by those bureaucrats and military officers who received scholarships for overseas study from the government on the basis of their academic excellence. These scholar-bureaucrats and scholar-officers are the major beneficiaries of PAP rule as they are members of the power élite and are well-paid and rewarded with accelerated promotion if they are high flyers.[61]

TABLE 8.5

Singapore's Power Elite in 1999 by Category

Category	Number
Political Elite	**94**
President	1
PAP Members of Parliament	81
Opposition Members of Parliament	2 + 1*
Nominated Members of Parliament	9
Bureaucratic Elite	**95**
Permanent Secretaries	17
Supreme Court Judges	14
Uniformed Services Chiefs	7
Envoys and Ambassadors	18
CEOs of Major Statutory Boards	39
Business Elite	**37**
Tee's List**	32
George and Leow's List***	5
TOTAL	**226**

*   Non-Constituency Member of Parliament
**   This refers to the 32 of the 35 persons listed in Tee Ming San, *The Singapore Successful Business Elites* translated by Huang ShengFa (Singapore: Cross Century Creative City, 1995). Of the three persons excluded, one was from Indonesia, another was a senior civil servant who resigned in 1997, and the third person had died.
*** These are the five "reservists" not on the PS100 list as they are corporate chiefs with two of them being former Cabinet ministers.
Source: Singapore Government Directory January 1999 (Singapore: Ministry of Information and the Arts, 1999); Tee Ming San, *The Singapore Successful Business Elites;* and Cherian George and Jason Leow, "Not on the list, but..." *Straits Times*, 26 April 1998, p. 37.

The PAP government's liberal policy of granting permanent residence to foreigners with the required skills or talent means that these permanent residents "enjoy the same benefits as Singapore citizens without being required to perform such obligations of citizenship as national service". These permanent residents, especially those from Malaysia and Hong Kong, are reluctant or unlikely to take up citizenship when there are no added advantages for doing so. Moreover, if citizens are treated similarly as permanent residents, they will question the value of their citizenship. Ironically, the two members of the Singapore expedition that reached the summit of Mount Everest in 1998 were not citizens but permanent residents. The fact that citizenship was not a criterion for joining the national expedition to Mount Everest "was a symbolic demonstration to Singaporeans that citizenship did not matter". If citizens are treated in the same manner as permanent residents, they will question the value of their citizenship and think twice about fulfilling such obligations as military service.[62]

On the other hand, which groups have suffered or not gained from the policies of the PAP government? The fact that opposition political parties have won more than 30 per cent of the valid votes during the last four general elections since 1984 shows that not all Singaporeans are happy or satisfied with PAP rule. Perhaps, the group that has benefited the least are the bottom 10 per cent income earners, who have become poorer in recent years in spite of the country's affluence and economic progress. Indeed, the 340,000 Singaporeans (11 per cent of the population) who earn less than S$500 a month have clearly not benefited from the PAP government's policies. In September 1993, the *Report of the Cost Review Committee* found that even though "the lowest 20 per cent of households have seen an improvement in their material well-being", these households also "do have a sense of being left behind" because their members "are still disappointed to find that they have not improved their position relative to others".[63]

Another method of identifying the poor or "underclass" in Singapore, is to check the list of those recipients of public assistance from the Ministry of Community Development.[64] Table 8.6 shows that the majority of these recipients during 1986–96 were the aged destitutes, followed by the handicapped and disabled, those medically unfit for work, abandoned/distressed wives and orphans, and widows with young children. These five groups of Singaporeans have certainly suffered under PAP rule. The plight of the handicapped and disabled in Singapore has been neglected mainly because of this group's powerlessness. For example, all the existing Mass Rapid Transit stations are not user-friendly to handicapped or disabled commuters.

Finally, while the scholar-bureaucrats and scholar-officers have benefited from the PAP government's policy of accelerated promotion and competitive pay for high-flyers, this has also resulted in serious morale problems for those civil servants and military officers who have been denied such rewards because they are non-scholars and low-flyers. While it is necessary to attract, motivate and retain the high-flyers and scholars in the civil and military bureaucracy, it is equally important to ensure that the rest of the civil servants and military officers are not alienated by the great disparity in salaries, fringe benefits and promotion prospects.[65] Indeed,

TABLE 8.6

Number of Public Assistance Recipients, Ministry of Community Development, Singapore, 1986–96

Category	1986	1991	1992	1993	1994	1995	1996
Aged destitutes	2736	2030	1954	1915	1852	1695	1701
Medically unfit	79	89	90	87	76	86	106
Wives & Orphans	53	75	70	73	61	57	58
Handicapped and disabled	155	95	102	104	101	98	115
Widows with young children	52	43	39	41	42	22	22
Total	3075	2332	2255	2220	2132	1958	2002

Source: Ministry of Community Development, Singapore; quoted in Linda Low and Ngiam Tee Liang, "An Underclass among the Overclass", in Singapore: Towards a Developed Status, ed. Linda Low (Singapore: Oxford University 1999), pp. 235–36, Table 11.1.

a great deal needs to be done to improve the morale of the low-flyers and non-scholars in the civil service and SAF.

Legitimacy of the PAP Government

In her 1976 study of PAP's dominance at the grass-roots level, Chan Heng Chee observed that the "record of tangible achievements and effectiveness" during the first decade of PAP rule (1959–69) "provides the solid economic basis of support for the ruling party".[66] During the May 1959 general election, the PAP promised to solve the housing shortage and provide more jobs to reduce the unemployment problem if it were elected to public office. Accordingly, when the PAP government succeeded in solving the housing shortage through the construction of 833,814 apartments by the

HDB for 86 per cent of the population during 1960–97[67] and increased the country's per capita GDP by 74 times between 1959 and 1997, its legitimacy among the population was enhanced as it fulfilled its election promises.

According to Christine A. Genzberger et al., "Lee's rule has enjoyed strong support from Singaporeans" because the "government and its people formed an unwritten social contract: soft authoritarianism in exchange for economic prosperity". In return for participating in the unwritten social contract, Singaporeans enjoy "rapid economic growth, low inflation, full employment, political stability, an 80 percent rate of home ownership, an average life-expectancy of 76 years, and a mere 0.3 percent poverty rate".[68] This means that if there is no economic growth, Singaporeans might no longer accept or adhere to the unwritten social contract if they no longer benefit from a system that requires them to sacrifice some of their personal freedoms. In other words, the legitimacy of the PAP government might be eroded if it fails to deliver the economic goods to Singaporeans.

On the other hand, Simon Tay contends that the "Lee Kuan Yew hypothesis" or "trade-off" hypothesis of Singapore's trading human rights for economic prosperity is "an over-simplification". According to him:

> The assessment of Singapore's example does not show a blanket barter of rights for prosperity. Rather, both social and economic rights and civil and political rights have grown over the last twenty years. The PAP government provided equitable distribution of economic goods and social justice while consistently maintaining the popular vote.[69]

As Singaporeans become more affluent, better educated and informed, widely travelled, and have higher expectations in the 1990s, the need for enhancing political participation becomes much more obvious. As their basic survival needs have been met, Singaporeans are now more concerned with higher-level needs, such as the need for greater control over decisions involving their personal lives. In this connection, Stella Quah has observed that:

> One by-product of higher levels of education is a keener awareness of the negative effects of an over-regulated society where policies may determine the children's career path and the relations between family members. People would like to see the institutional channels of participation in decision-making

being expanded beyond elections in order to arrive at policies that reflect faithfully the common will, particularly in matters of an intrinsic and higher-level nature.[70]

The PAP government responded to the electorate's call in the 1984 general election for more consultation and participation by creating the Feedback Unit in March 1985 and launching the National Agenda in February 1987. Furthermore, unlike his predecessor, Goh Chok Tong has relied on the Select Committee as a mechanism to obtain public feedback on proposed legislation. Thus, there has been a clear shift from a paternalistic or authoritarian style of government during 1959–84 to a consultative style of government after 1984.

Concomitant with the economic affluence and rising expectations among Singaporeans, there has also emerged a growing demand by them for political opposition to serve as a check on the PAP government and for increased political participation to provide them with opportunities for giving feedback on public policies and to recommend appropriate solutions. If this demand for political participation is not satisfied or ignored, those affected might resort to violent means or opt out of the system by emigrating to other countries. Albert Hirschman has contended that individuals will use the exit option if they are not given sufficient voice to improve their system.[71] If talented Singaporeans leave Singapore because of the limited channels for political participation, the country will be the poorer for it.

Governance Singapore-Style

Accountability, transparency, predictability and participation are the basic elements of good governance. There is a high degree of accountability, transparency and predictability in Singapore, but the level of political participation is low. Singapore was the least affected in Southeast Asia by the regional financial crisis because of the strict regulations imposed on financial institutions by the Monetary Authority of Singapore (MAS). Singapore was the only country that did not allow the Bank of Credit and Commerce International (BCCI) to operate in Singapore because the MAS investigated BCCI and "concluded that it was a poorly regulated institution". According to Peter Truell and Larry Gurwin, "Tiny Singapore did something that the United States, Great Britain, France, Japan, and other major countries had failed to do so. It said no to BCCI."[72]

Governance Singapore-style is characterized by four major features. First, the PAP government continued the British colonial government's policy of meritocracy in recruiting and promoting civil servants but rejected the emphasis on seniority in favour of efficiency as the basis for promotion. Lee Kuan Yew has reiterated the importance of meritocracy in his keynote address to African leaders in November 1993 when he said: "A strong political leadership needs a neutral, efficient, honest Civil Service. Officers must be recruited and promoted completely on merit. ... Appointments, awards of scholarships must be made to the best candidates."[73] Ezra F. Vogel has used the term "macho-meritocracy" to describe the PAP leaders' belief that meritocracy applies "not only for bureaucrats but also for politicians". He contends that "for the first generation of Singapore leaders, the pillar of good government was not a separation of powers but a strong central meritocracy."[74]

Second, governance in Singapore is characterized by the PAP government's concern with clean government as reflected in its reliance on both the Prevention of Corruption Act (POCA) and the Corrupt Practices Investigation Bureau (CPIB) to minimize corruption by reducing the opportunities for corruption and by increasing the penalty for corrupt behaviour if one is caught as it could not afford then to raise the salaries of civil servants. However, the government was only able to improve the salaries and working conditions of public officials to reduce their vulnerability to corruption from 1972 onwards with the payment of the 13 month bonus and periodic revision of salaries.[75] In March 1985, Prime Minister Lee Kuan Yew warned in Parliament: "Pay political leaders the top salaries that they deserve and get honest, clean government or underpay them and risk the Third World disease of corruption." He concluded that the best way of tackling corruption was "moving with the market", which is "an honest, open, defensible and workable system" instead of hypocrisy, which results in "duplicity and corruption".[76]

Thirdly, a good government is a pragmatic one in the Singapore context. In November 1993, Senior Minister Lee Kuan Yew had advised visiting African leaders to adopt a pragmatic approach in formulating economic policy rather than a dogmatic one. Instead of following the then politically correct approach of being anti-American and anti-multinational corporations in the 1960s and 1970s, Singapore went against the grain and "assiduously courted MNCs" because "they had the technology, know-how, techniques, expertise, and the markets" and "it was a fast way of learning on the job working for them and with them". This strategy of relying on the MNCs paid off as "they have been a powerful factor in Singapore's growth".

The fourth feature of governance Singapore-style is its reliance on policy diffusion, that is, the "emulation and borrowing of policy ideas and solutions from other nations".[77] Thus, instead of "reinventing the wheel", which is unnecessary and expensive, the PAP leaders and senior civil servants will consider what has been done elsewhere to identify suitable solutions for resolving policy problems in Singapore. The policy solutions selected will usually be adapted and modified to suit the local context. Initially, Singapore looked toward Israel and Switzerland as role models during the post-independent period to provide inspiration for devising relevant public policies for defence and other areas. Later, other countries like West Germany (for technical education), the Netherlands (Schiphol Airport was the model for Changi International Airport) and Japan (for quality control circles and crime prevention) were added to the list. In short, the important lesson in these learning experiences is the adoption by Singapore of ideas which have worked elsewhere (with suitable modification to consider the local context if necessary) as well as the rejection of unsuccessful schemes in other countries.

Major Political Developments

What are the political milestones in Singapore during the past four decades of PAP rule? The first milestone was obviously the 31 May 1959 general election which resulted in the PAP's victory and its assumption of political office. The next three major political events were Singapore's joining the Federation of Malaysia on 16 September 1963; the July and September 1964 racial riots, and Singapore's subsequent expulsion 23 months later on 9 August 1965, when it attained independence.

After independence, the competitive party system was transformed into a *de facto* one party dominant system in October 1966, when the 13 Barisan Sosialis MPs boycotted Parliament. With the withdrawal of the Barisan Sosialis from competing in the April 1968 general election, the PAP won all the 58 seats and the party system became a *de jure* one party dominant system. The "clean sweep" phenomenon was repeated three times as the PAP won all the seats in the 1972, 1976 and 1980 general elections. On 31 October 1981, the Workers' Party candidate, J.B. Jeyaratnam, obtained 51.9 per cent of the valid votes and broke the PAP's 15-year monopoly of Parliament by winning the Anson by-election.

The December 1984 general election is perhaps the most important election in Singapore's history because even though the PAP won 77 of the 79 seats, it was astounded by its 12.8 per cent drop in valid votes, from 77.6 per cent in the 1980 general election to 64.8 per cent in 1984.[78] The most important consequence of the 1984 general election was the transformation of the PAP's paternalistic leadership style into a more consultative one with the establishment of the Feedback Unit in March 1985, the launching of the National Agenda in February 1987, the formation of the Institute of Policy Studies in December 1987, and the creation of six advisory councils in February 1988.

The Constitution was amended in May 1988 to allow for the creation of 13 GRCs in the September 1988 general election. Thus, the country's electoral system was changed from one consisting entirely of 79 SMCs in the 1984 general election to 42 SMCs and 13 GRCs of three constituencies each in the 1988 general election. The number of SMCs has been reduced to nine and the number of GRCs increased to 15 in the 1997 general election.

In November 1990, Lee Kuan Yew stepped down as Prime Minister after serving for nearly 32 years and became the Senior Minister. The First Deputy Prime Minister, Goh Chok Tong succeeded Lee as Prime Minister and was responsible for moving towards a more consultative style of leadership. Indeed, unlike Lee, Goh's reliance on the Select Committee as a mechanism for obtaining public feedback on proposed legislation represents a clear shift from a paternalistic style of government during 1959–84 to a consultative style of government after 1984.

Perhaps, the most important change to Singapore's political system was the transformation of the presidency into an elected one in January 1991 and the election of Ong Teng Cheong as President in August 1993. Ong completed his six-year term in August 1999 and was succeeded by President S.R. Nathan. Instead of being a symbolic figure as his predecessor, the elected President has been given more powers. In other words, the Prime Minister is no longer the most powerful person in Singapore, as he has to share some of his powers with the elected President.

Future Challenges

Democracy Singapore-style will not change significantly as long as the PAP government remains in power. In February 1995, the *New York Times* described Singapore's government as "clean and mean" and Taiwan's government as "filthy and free".[79] Samuel P. Huntington extended the comparison between Singapore and Taiwan thus:

> The freedom and creativity that President Lee [Teng Hui] has introduced in Taiwan will survive him. The honesty and efficiency that Senior Minister Lee [Kuan Yew] has brought to Singapore are likely to follow him to his grave.[80]

Huntington's unlikely prediction about the post-Lee era in Singapore illustrates his ignorance of the PAP government's commitment to clean government and its effective comprehensive anti-corruption strategy and the various successful measures taken by the Singapore Civil Service to enhance efficiency. As this emphasis on efficient and honest government during the past four decades has been supported by Singaporeans, it will endure for a long time.

In contrast to Huntington's pessimistic forecast, Raj Vasil has praised Singapore's "limited democracy" and its success in "producing the national development it had been deliberately designed to produce". According to Vasil:

> It is remarkable that the PAP rulers of Singapore, enjoying almost total power given them by the political system, have administered it without succumbing to any abuse of power, arbitrary rule, corruption, mismanagement or disregard for the interests of Singaporeans. They have always ruled the island state with exceptional integrity, dedication and respect for the rule of law.[81]

He concluded that "it is equally certain that Singapore is not likely to see a similar substantial transformation of its limited democracy for a considerable period of time" because "the system has worked extremely well and has produced remarkable national development".[82]

In his January 1995 address to PAP cadre members, Prime Minister Goh Chok Tong asked: "Will Singapore be as prosperous 30 years hence?" His answer was that while Singapore has done well so far, there is no guarantee that it would continue to be prosperous in the future unless it has a good government to deal with its long term problems.[83] In view of Singapore's small size and lack of natural resources, it is not surprising why the PAP leaders are constantly concerned with the city-state's long term survival and prosperity.

The 1985–87 economic recession in Singapore demonstrated clearly that there was a serious brain drain to other countries if there was negative or slow economic growth in the city-state. If there is also political unrest caused by racial and/or religious conflict, the many multi-national corporations in Singapore will move their regional headquarters to more politically stable countries, and talented Singaporeans will emigrate to countries like Australia, Canada or the United States. Thus, the worst case scenario for Singapore's long term survival would be the brain drain of talented Singaporeans to other countries to escape from economic recession and civil unrest.

In order to secure Singapore's long term survival and affluence, the PAP leaders must be able to deal effectively with three key issues and their challenges. First, the issue of *institutionalizing good government* in Singapore is to maintain the tradition of an honest and competent government established by the PAP government during the last 40 years through its commitment to meritocracy and an effective anti-corruption strategy, which has made corruption a "high risk, low reward" activity by minimizing both the incentives and opportunities for such behaviour by punishing those found guilty, regardless of their position or status in society.

The problem which the elected President is designed to solve is this: How to check the powers of the Prime Minister in Singapore's one-party dominant Parliament? Without certain safeguards, it would not be difficult for a corrupt prime minister to squander the nation's hard-earned official foreign reserves. With the institution of the elected President in place, the challenges associated with the institutionalization of good government in Singapore are twofold. The first challenge facing the PAP leaders is to attract, motivate and retain the "best and brightest" Singaporeans in political office, the public bureaucracy and the SAF in the face of tough competition from the private sector and other countries. The PAP government has relied on meritocracy and competitive salaries to persuade talented Singaporeans to pursue careers in politics, the civil service and the SAF. While the PAP has succeeded in finding suitable candidates from the private sector, it has been less successful in persuading those from the private sector and women to pursue a political career.

The second challenge faced by the PAP government in institutionalizing good government in Singapore is the need to maintain and preserve the tradition of honest and effective government. As there is no guarantee that future political leaders will remain honest and incorrupt, the current anti-corruption strategy, which has been effective in minimizing corruption in Singapore should be continued, periodically reviewed and fine-tuned to ensure its continued effectiveness. In short, the key to institutionalizing good government in Singapore is to succeed in persuading talented Singaporeans to join politics, the civil service and the SAF and to motivate them to behave ethically and rationally for the national interest.

The PAP leaders have dealt with the second issue of *maintaining political stability* by introducing the GRC scheme in 1988 and the Maintenance of Religious Harmony Act in 1990 to minimize the potential for racial and/or religious conflict. The third issue concerns the *need to enhance political participation* as Singaporeans have become affluent, better educated and informed, widely travelled, and with higher expectations. However, the need for maintaining political stability has to be balanced with the growing demand for political participation generated by economic growth, especially among the younger Singaporeans.

Thus, the third and most difficult challenge facing the PAP leaders is whether they will be able to balance the increasing demand for political participation with the need for maintaining political stability. This is a difficult task for the PAP leaders because they are concerned with the risks involved with political liberalization and might not be willing to satisfy completely the younger Singaporeans' demands for more political participation for fear that the satisfaction of these demands would undermine political stability and erode Singapore's competitiveness in the international arena.

Notes

1 Quoted in Kees Tamboer, "Albert Winsemius: 'founding father' of Singapore", *IIAS Newsletter* no. 9 (Summer 1996), p. 29.
2 *World Development Report 1998/99: Knowledge for Development* (Washington, D.C.: Oxford University Press for The World Bank, 1999), pp. 190–91, Table 1.
3 *Singapore 1998* (Singapore: Ministry of Information and the Arts, 1998), pp. 30–32; and *Singapore Facts and Pictures 2000* (Singapore: Ministry of Information and the Arts, 2000), p. 9.
4 See Michael Leifer, "Israel's President in Singapore: Political Catalysis and Transnational Politics", *Pacific Review* 1, no. 4 (1988) 341–52.
5 See "Habibie on ethnic Chinese", *Straits Times*, 10 February 1999, p. 24.
6 Michael Leifer, *Singapore's Foreign Policy: Coping with Vulnerability* (London: Routledge, 2000), pp. 37 and 39.
7 Jon S.T. Quah, "Controlled Democracy, Political Stability and PAP Predominance: Government in Singapore", in *The Changing Shape of Government in the Asia-Pacific Region*, ed. John W. Langford and K. Lorne Brownsey (South Halifax: Institute for Research on Public Policy, 1988), p. 127.
8 C.M. Turnbull, *A History of Singapore 1819–1988*, 2nd ed. (Singapore: Oxford University Press, 1989), p. 237.
9 *Singapore 1998*, p. 338, Appendix 6.
10 Jon S.T. Quah, "The Public Policy-making Process in Singapore", *Asian Journal of Public Administration* 6, no. 2 (December 1984): 113. For details of the composition of the present Cabinet, see *Singapore Facts and Pictures 2000* (Singapore: Ministry of Information and the Arts, 2000), p. 28.

11 Douglas V. Verney, "Analysis of Political Systems", in *Comparative Politics: A Reader*, ed. Harry Eckstein and David E. Apter (New York: The Free Press of Glencoe, 1963), p. 190.

12 Jon S.T. Quah, "Political Consequences of Rapid Economic Development in Singapore", in *Development in the Asia Pacific: A Public Policy Perspective*, ed. Jong S. Jun (Berlin: Walter de Gruyter, 1994), p. 408.

13 *Singapore 1992* (Singapore: Ministry of Information and the Arts, 1992), p. 36.

14 Turnbull, *A History of Singapore 1819–1988*, p. 251.

15 John Drysdale, *Singapore: Struggle for Success* (Singapore: Times Book International, 1984), p. 194.

16 The penalty for not voting is an administrative fee of S$5 to restore the non-voter's name on the electoral register.

17 *Straits Times*, 25 July 1984, p. 10.

18 Ibid., p. 1.

19 Jon S.T. Quah, "Singapore in 1984: Leadership Transition in an Election Year", *Asian Survey* 25, no. 2 (February 1985): 223.

20 Ahmad Osman, "Vote MPs by Team System proposed", *Sunday Times*, 25 January 1987, p. 1.

21 Ahmad Osman, "Proposed changes won't affect one-man-one-vote, says MP", *Sunday Times,* 25 January 1987, p. 13.

22 Jon S.T. Quah, "Singapore in 1987: Political Reforms, Control, and Economic Recovery", in *Southeast Asian Affairs 1988* (Singapore: Institute of Southeast Asian Studies, 1988), p. 234.

23 Quoted in "What the man in the street has to say", *Straits Times*, 12 February 1987, p. 10.

24 "Team MPs system is politically neutral, says Goh", *Straits Times*, 28 February 1987, p. 11.

25 Goh Chok Tong, "Building a Multiracial Nation", *Speeches: A Bi-Monthly Selection of Ministerial Speeches* 11, no. 2 (March–April 1987): 8–10.

26 Quah, "Singapore in 1987", p. 236.

27 "Team MPs proposal can ensure a continued multi-racial Parliament", *Straits Times,* 17 August 1987, p. 14.

28 *Straits Times*, 30 November 1989, p. 18.

29 *Straits Times,* 24 January and 30 March 1990.

30 Quah, "Political Consequences of Rapid Economic Development in Singapore", p. 415.

31 Pang Cheng Lian, *Singapore's People's Action Party: Its History, Organization and Leadership* (Singapore: Oxford University Press, 1971), pp. 2–3 and 5–6.

32 *Singapore 1998*, p. 338, Appendix 5.

33 Lee Kuan Yew, *The Singapore Story: Memoirs of Lee Kuan Yew* (Singapore: Times Editions, 1998), p. 663.

34 Jon S.T. Quah, "Meeting the Twin Threats of Communism and Communalism: The Singapore Response", in *Governments and Rebellions in Southeast Asia*, ed. Chandran Jeshurun (Singapore: Institute of Southeast Asian Studies, 1985), pp. 198–208.

35 Chua Sian Chin, "Communism — A Real Threat", in *Socialism That Works: The Singapore Way*, ed. C.V. Devan Nair (Singapore: Federal Publications, 1976), p. 18.

36 Quah, "Singapore in 1987", pp. 244–46.

37 *Singapore 2000* (Singapore: Ministry of Information and the Arts, 2000), p. 185.

38 Leong Ching, "S'poreans better off than in 1990", *Straits Times*, 29 December 1998, p. 3.

39 Hussin Mutalib, "Illiberal democracy and the future of opposition in Singapore", *Third World Quarterly* 21, no. 2 (2000): 314.

40 Jon S.T. Quah, "The 1980s: A Review of Significant Political Developments", in *A History of Singapore*, ed. Ernest C.T. Chew and Edwin Lee (Singapore: Oxford University Press, 1991), pp. 389–90.

41 Chan Heng Chee, "Singapore", in *Military-Civilian Relations in South-East Asia*, ed. Zakaria Haji Ahmad and Harold Crouch (Singapore: Oxford University Press, 1985), p. 136.

42 Lee Kuan Yew revealed that the Indian Prime Minister, Lal Bahadur Shastri, and President Nasser of Egypt ignored his request for assistance to build up Singapore's armed forces. See Lee Kuan Yew, *From Third World To First: The Singapore Story: 1965–2000* (Singapore: Times Media Private Limited, 2000), pp. 30–31.

43 Ibid., pp. 140–41, and 145–46.

44 Ibid., pp. 149–50.

45 Yong Mun Cheong, "The Military and Development in Singapore", in *Soldiers and Stability in Southeast Asia*, ed. J. Soedjati Djiwandono (Singapore: Institute of Southeast Asian Studies, 1988), p. 289.

46 Ducro Clement Chandran, "Bureaucrats and Politicians in a One-Party Dominant System: A Case Study of Singapore", B.Soc.Sc. Honours Thesis, Department of Political Science, National University of Singapore, 1999, pp. 71–72.

47 *Singapore 1998*, pp. 75, and 77–78.

48 Lee, *The Singapore Story*, p. 144.

49 R.S. Milne and Diane K. Mauzy, *Singapore: The Legacy of Lee Kuan Yew* (Boulder: Westview Press, 1990), p. 80.

50 Ibid., p. 80.

51 Eugene Kheng-Boon Tan, "Law and Values in Governance: The Singapore Way," *Hong Kong Law Journal* 30, Part 1 (2000): 106–107.

52 Quoted in ibid., p. 107.

53 Goh Chok Tong, "Our National Ethic", *Speeches* 12, no. 5 (September-October 1988), pp. 13–15.

54   *Straits Times*, 10 January 1989, p. 12.
55   See Jon S.T. Quah, ed., *In Search of Singapore's National Values* (Singapore: Times Academic Press for the Institute of Policy Studies, 1990).
56   *Shared Values*, Cmd 1 of 1991 (White Paper presented to Parliament by command of the President of the Republic of Singapore, 2 January 1991), p. 10, paragraph 52.
57   *Straits Times*, 16 January 1991, p. 1.
58   C. Wright Mills, *The Power Elite* (New York: Oxford University Press, 1956), pp. 3–4.
59   Peter S.J. Chen, "The Power Elite in Singapore", in *Studies in ASEAN Sociology: Urban Society and Social Change*, ed. Peter S.J. Chen and Hans-Dieter Evers (Singapore: Chopmen Enterprises, 1978), pp. 78–79. This paper was presented at a conference in Bangkok in May 1975.
60   Cherian George and Jason Leow, "Who runs Singapore?" *Sunday Times*, 26 April 1998, p. 36.
61   Jon S.T. Quah, "Public Administration in Singapore: Managing Success in a Multi-Racial City-State", in *Public Administration in the NICs: Challenges and Accomplishments*, ed. Ahmed S. Huque, Jermain T.M. Lam and Jane C.Y. Lee (Basingstoke: Macmillan Press Ltd., 1996), pp. 72–73.
62   Jon S.T. Quah, "Globalization and Singapore's Search for Nationhood", in *Nationalism and Globalization: East and West*, ed. Leo Suryadinata (Singapore: Institute of Southeast Studies, 2000), pp. 92–93.
63   *Report of the Cost Review Committee* (Singapore: SNP Publishers, 1993), pp. 34–35.
64   Linda Low and Ngiam Tee Liang, "An Underclass among the Overclass", in *Singapore: Towards a Developed Status*, ed. Linda Low (Singapore: Oxford University Press, 1999), pp. 235–36.
65   Quah, "Public Administration in Singapore", pp. 81–82.
66   Chan Heng Chee, *The Dynamics of One-Party Dominance: The PAP at the Grass-roots* (Singapore: Singapore University Press, 1976), p. 36.
67   Housing and Development Board, *Annual Report 1997/98* (Singapore: HDB, 1998), p. 74.
68   Christine A. Genzberger et al., *Singapore Business* (San Rafael: World Trade Press, 1994), pp. 17–18.
69   Simon S.C. Tay, "Human Rights, Culture, and the Singapore Example", *McGill Law Journal* 41, no. 4 (August 1996): 775–76.
70   Stella R. Quah, "Social Discipline in Singapore: An Alternative for the Resolution of Social Problems", *Journal of Southeast Asian Studies* 14 (1983): 287.
71   Albert O. Hirschman, *Exit, Voice and Loyalty* (Cambridge: Harvard University Press, 1970).
72   Peter Truell and Larry Gurwin, *False Profits: The Inside Story of BCCI, the World's Most Corrupt Financial Empire* (Boston: Houghton Mifflin Company, 1992), p. 96.

73   Lee Kuan Yew, "Can Singapore's Experience Be Relevant to Africa?" in *Can Singapore's Experience Be Relevant to Africa?* ed. Singapore International Foundation (Singapore: SIF, 1994), p. 5.

74   Ezra F. Vogel, "A Little Dragon Tamed", in *Management of Success: The Moulding of Modern Singapore*, ed. Kernial S. Sandhu and Paul Wheatley (Singapore: Institute of Southeast Asian Studies, 1989), pp. 1052–53.

75   Jon S.T. Quah, "Controlling Corruption in City-States: A Comparative Study of Hong Kong and Singapore", *Crime, Law and Social Change* 22 (1995): 394–96.

76   "PM: Pay well or we pay for it", *Straits Times*, 23 March 1985, pp. 1, 14–16.

77   Howard M. Leichter, *A Comparative Approach to Policy Analysis: Health Care in Four Nations* (Cambridge: Cambridge University Press, 1979), p. 42.

78   *Singapore 1998*, p. 338, Appendix 6.

79   *New York Times*, 5 February 1995, pp. E1 and E4, quoted in Samuel P. Huntington, "Democracy for the Long Haul," in *Consolidating the Third Wave Democracies: Themes and Perspectives*, ed. Larry Diamond et al. (Baltimore: Johns Hopkins University Press, 1997), p. 12.

80   Huntington, "Democracy for the Long Haul", p. 13.

81   Raj Vasil, *Governing Singapore: Democracy and National Development* (St Leonards: Allen and Unwin, 2000), p. 233.

82   Ibid., pp. 248–49.

83   Goh Chok Tong, "Will Singapore be as prosperous 30 years hence?" *Petir* (January–February 1995), pp. 7–13.

Further Reading

Arun, Mahizhnan and Lee Tsao Yuan, eds. *Singapore: Re-engineering Success.* Singapore: Institute of Policy Studies and Oxford University Press, 1998.

Ho Khai Leong. *The Politics of Policy-Making in Singapore.* Singapore: Oxford University Press, 2000.

Lee Kuan Yew. *The Singapore Story: Memoirs of Lee Kuan Yew.* Singapore: Times Editions, 1998.

———. *From Third World to First: The Singapore Story: 1965–2000.* Singapore: Times Edition, 2000.

Leifer, Michael. *Singapore's Foreign Policy: Coping with Vulnerability.* London: Routledge, 2000.

Low, Linda. *The Political Economy of a City-State: Government-made Singapore.* Singapore: Oxford University Press, 1998.

Milne, R.S. and Diane K. Mauzy. *Singapore: The Legacy of Lee Kuan Yew.* Boulder: Westview Press, 1990.

Quah, Jon S.T., Chan Heng Chee and Seah Chee Meow, eds. *Government and Politics of Singapore.* Rev. ed. Singapore: Oxford University Press, 1987.

Quah, Jon S.T., ed. *In Search of Singapore's National Values*. Singapore: Times Academic Press for the Institute of Policy Studies, 1990.

Sandhu, Kernial S. and Paul Wheatley, eds. *Management of Success: The Moulding of Modern Singapore*. Singapore: Institute of Southeast Asian Studies, 1989.

Tan, Kevin Y.L. and Lam Peng Er, ed. *Managing Political Change in Singapore. The Elected Presidency*. London: Routledge, 1997.

Vasil, Raj. *Asianising Singapore: The PAP's Management of Ethnicity*. Singapore: Heinemann Asia, 1995.

_____ . *Governing Singapore: Democracy and National Development*. St. Leonards: Allen and Unwin, 2000.

9

THAILAND
Reform Politics

John Funston

INTRODUCTION

Thailand is the only state in Southeast Asia to escape colonialism. Many elements of traditional society therefore remain, but civil society has made its presence felt since the dramatic student-led overthrow of a military government in 1973. Subsequent reform has advanced in fits and starts. The 1997 "people's constitution", passed after the onset of a dramatic economic crisis, is the most ambitious attempt yet to entrench democratic rule.

Popular versions of Thai history trace state origins to the Buddhist kingdom of Sukhothai, established in the mid thirteenth century. Driven out of China in a series of migrations, this is "the story of a conquering race claiming an empty territory as its home".[1] Under the legendary Ramkhamheng (1279–98), the kingdom expanded to include much of present-day Thailand. Historians no longer accept this account — archaeological findings confirm sophisticated civilisations centuries earlier, Sukhothai's control of areas beyond its immediate neighbourhood in northern Thailand is much in doubt, and present day "Thais" are seen not as a unique race but a mixture of Tai, Mon, Khmer, Chinese, Indian and others. Nonetheless the popular account continues to be taught in schools, and remains influential.

Ayudhya, founded 1351 just to the north of the current capital, Bangkok, soon eclipsed neighbouring states, and became a major player on the Southeast Asian mainland. With an economic base founded on both rice and international trade, Ayudhya exercized at least a loose suzerainty over an area extending beyond present-day borders. It established relations with a range of countries, from China to Europe, sending a diplomatic mission to Europe as early as 1608. Ayudhya's Kings stood at the apex of an elaborate hierarchy sanctified by both Hindu and Buddhist doctrines. The *sakdina* system accorded everyone a number of points, the highest attracting to those close to the King. This was linked, at least initially, to control over property, though the system was essentially about control over people and territorial aspects were never clear-cut as with European feudalism. In terms of current political culture, while Sukhothai has been linked to paternalism and authoritarianism, Ayudhya has been associated with more absolutist, hierachical and bureaucratic practices.[2]

Ayudhya suffered two major defeats at the hands of the Burmese, the first in the mid sixteenth century and the second some two centuries later. Following the latter, military leader Taksin defeated the Burmese in 1767, and set up in Thonburi, across the river from Bangkok. After allegedly going mad, he was executed and replaced by his leading general. The first of the still reigning Chakri dynasty moved the capital to its current location.

The new dynasty felt the pressures of an expanding Western colonialism. It benefited from being a natural buffer between British influences in Burma and Malaya, and the French in Indochina, but found it necessary to make concessions. In 1855 King Mongkut signed an agreement with British envoy Sir John Bowring, opening the country to Western trade and extending extraterritoriality to Europeans. The treaty was humiliating, but Thailand profited from involvement in the international economy through the export of rice. Following this, Thai kings embarked on reform of the bureaucracy and the legal system, sending students abroad to acquire a Western education, and employing Europeans to head new departments. Even these actions could not prevent France and Britain seizing more Thai-claimed territory in Laos, Cambodia, Burma and Malaya, during the late nineteenth and early twentieth centuries.

By 1932 absolute monarchy had been undermined by its own success in creating a Western educated élite anxious for change, and the impact of global depression. A small group comprising military and civilians, led by Phibun Songkram and Pridi Phanomyong respectively, seized power in a military coup. In subsequent years the military group predominated, frustrating Pridi's attempts to introduce democratic government. In 1938 Phibun became Prime Minister, and the following year changed the country's name from Siam to the more 'modern' Thailand, which it has remained except for a brief reversion to Siam during civilian rule in the 1940s. Military-led ultra-nationalism became entrenched under Phibun, and Thailand entered World War II on the side of Japan. When Japan's defeat loomed, parliament rejected government legislation in July 1944,

FIGURE 9.1

Thailand: Key Dates

1250	Legendary Sukhothai empire.
1351	Ayudhya empire.
1767	Thonburi/Bangkok empire.
1855	Bowring Treaty.
1932	Overthrow of absolute monarchy — key roles played by Phibun Songkram on military side, and Dr Pridi Phanomyong on the civilian side.
1938	First Phibun government.
1944	Phibun defeated in parliament. Followed by succession of pro-Pridi civilian governments.
1947	Pro Phibun coup in November. Phibun regains power following April.
1957	Sarit Thanarat coup. Prime Minister from 1958 till death in December 1963.
1963	Thanom Kittikatchorn becomes Prime Minister; Praphat Charusathien as deputy.
1973	50,000 strong student-led uprising on 14 October, forcing Thanom, Praphat (and Thanom's son Narong) into exile. Then three years of turbulent democracy, under caretaker administration led by Privy Councilor Sanya Thammasak, then elected governments led by Pramot brothers (Kukrit followed by Seni).
1976	Bloody coup on 6 October led by Kriangsak Chomanan. Installs right wing civilian government led by Thanin Kraivichien.
1977	Kriangsak becomes Prime Minister after second coup.
1980	Kriangsak resigns, and parliament elects Prem Tinsulanonda as Prime Minister.
1988	Prem stands down after election, and replaced by Chatichai Choonhavan.
1991	Chatichai ousted in coup. Respected civilian, Anand Panyarachun, installed as Prime Minister.
1992	Attempts by military leader Suchinda Kraprayoon to become Prime Minister opposed by mass protests. Military crackdown led to Black May. Anand again becomes caretaker Prime Minister until elections return coalition led by Chuan Leekpai's Democrats.
1995	Fall of Democrats and replacement by coalition led by Chat Phattana under Banharn Silpa-archa.
1996	Banharn government implodes, and new elections won by coalition led by Chavalit Yongchaiyut of the New Aspiration Party.
1997	Chavalit loses support after economic crisis sparked by devaluation of baht on 2 July. New pro-democracy constitution passed September. In November, parliament approves Chuan II government.
2000	First senate elections. House of Representatives completes longest term ever, before dissolved for 6 January 2001 elections.
2001	Thai Rak Thai big winner in general election. Impeached, controversial TRT leader, Thaksin Shinawatra, becomes Prime Minister.

ushering in a turbulent three years of democracy. Ten governments, under five prime ministers, held office during this period, most under the influence of Pridi, who spent the war years as head of the King's Privy Council and leader of the Free Thai anti-Japanese movement.

This interregnum was ended by a coup in November 1947, masterminded by Colonel Sarit Thanarat. Back as Prime Minister by April 1948 Phibun's second period in office was again marked by authoritarian rule, strong nationalistic indoctrination and intense conflict between factions within the military. As conflict within the ruling élite intensified, and public protest heightened, Sarit moved against Phibun in September 1957. Taking over as Prime Minister one year later, he instituted the most thoroughgoing absolutism ever witnessed, ruling by decree. No provision was made for elected parliamentarians, and the appointed parliament's only function was to draft a permanent constitution. A strong, charismatic leader, Sarit dispensed immediate economic benefits (lower electricity prices and bus fares) along with reorienting the economy along World Bank lines to build infrastructure and give more priority to private enterprise. He brought the young King back to centre-stage, benefiting indirectly from his popularity. And he plundered the state for personal profit — US$158 million in illegal assets (a staggering sum at the time) was discovered after his death in 1963.

No government before or after Sarit has matched his unchallenged authority. This heritage kept politically less adroit successors in office for a further decade. Generals Thanom Kittikatchorn and Praphat Charusathien eventually permitted a new constitution, and elections in November 1969, but then became impatient with parliamentary needling and dismissed it in November 1971. The self-serving nature of the government, and the absence of democratic opportunity, galvanized resistance from a growing educated and middle class. Some 500,000 students took to the streets in October 1973. Army leaders were divided over how to respond, but killed over 100 protestors in an attempt to regain control by force. Government leaders then heeded the King's advice that they flee the country. Supporting the students was a business class, largely Sino Thai, now sufficiently wealthy to loosen connections with former military patrons and seek power on its own.

A succession of short-lived caretaker and elected governments held power during the tumultuous democratic interlude from 1973 to 1976. In an overflow of pent-up frustrations students, rural groups and trade unions took their grievances to the streets. At the same time right wing vigilante groups spread terror, assassinating students, and the leaders of both rural associations and trade unions — and gained public support after the 1975 victory of communism in Indochina spread fear that Thailand might follow the same course. Dozens were killed in 1976 elections, the most violent on record. Finally, right wing groups and elements in the police and military launched a bloody attack on Thammasat University on 6 October, giving the military under the influence of General Kriangsak Chomanan a pretext to declare a coup.

The military installed as Prime Minister Thanin Kraivichien, a right wing civilian, but his attempts to emulate Sarit's dictatorial style alienated even the military, which ousted him one year later. Having rejected right wing extremism, communism loomed briefly as an alternative, strengthened by a rush of student activists to the jungle after the 1976 coup. However the Communist Party of Thailand disintegrated in the early 1980s, following China's withdrawal of support, internal dissension (linked to the influx of ideologically independent students, and decline of international communism), and an enlightened government 'open arms' policy.

Kriangsak became Prime Minister after the 1978 coup, and moved to implement a constitutional semi-democracy, until economic pressures forced his resignation in 1980. Parliament then elected army commander General Prem Tinsulanonda as Prime Minister. Backed strongly by the monarchy, Prem was returned twice more by parliament without standing for popular election, and remained in power until August 1988. Using his prerogative to select cabinet members from parliament or outside, he included trusted and competent non-political technocrats in key economic portfolios (finance and commerce), alongside parliamentarians from the major political parties. Cabinets changed frequently, and the government narrowly survived coup attempts in 1981 and 1985, but the period of Premocracy is now viewed nostalgically as a time of rare political stability and effective government.

In the subsequent decade Thailand had eight governments, one of the highest turnover rates in the world. Governments were empowered by a predominantly rural electorate, often electing candidates who paid the most money for this purpose, and were then brought down by clamour from the middle class in Bangkok. The Chatichai government, elected to office in 1988, represented both a high point in democracy and a high point in business influence. Chatichai Choonhavan was the first directly elected prime minister in twelve years, and most of his cabinet were parliamentarians. But the self-seeking nature of politicians, most from a provincial business background, was so pronounced that the ministry became known as the "buffet cabinet". This, and squabbling between coalition partners, soon brought his government into disrepute.

When the military staged a coup in 1991 public support for the government was non-existent. Coup-makers annointed Anand Panyarachun — a respected former top diplomat turned businessman — as prime minister. Following elections in 1992 the military sought to entrench its rule by persuading parliament to appoint army head General Suchinda Kraprayoon as prime minister. In mid-May half a million protesters took to the streets. An ensuing clash with the military left some fifty fatalities, and ended only after the King intervened. Suchinda stepped down, and Anand returned as caretaker a second time.

After the drama of 1992 politics remained unsettled. A Democrat-led government headed by Chuan Leekpai emerged from subsequent elections, but lost office two and a half years later following a land scandal. Elections followed in 1995 and 1996, with scandal-prone and ineffective coalitions led by Banharn Silpa-archa and former military head Chavalit Yongchaiyudh. Separately, NGO movements began mobilizing support for fundamental changes that would "clean up" politics, make it more democratic, and entrench civilian rule. A 99-member, partly elected, Constitution Drafting Assembly was convened for this purpose, and began its task in January 1997. The economic crisis that struck in July 1997 helped ensure quick parliamentary approval of the new constitution in September, and undermined the government. In November Chavalit resigned, and by a small margin parliament voted in a second government led by Chuan. Defying frequent predictions of its imminent demise, Chuan's reformist government created history by serving out all but a week of the remaining parliamentary term. Nevertheless, the bitter medicine prescribed for economic reform, and unfavourable international factors (particularly high oil prices) exacted a heavy toll, and the new *Thai Rak Thai* swept to power in January 2001 general elections.

Geographical Determinants

Thailand occupies a strategic location in mainland Southeast Asia. It is close to China and Vietnam, and has long land borders with Myanmar, Laos and Cambodia. In the South it is linked to island Southeast Asia by a narrow isthmus, and a border with Malaysia. This makes it a natural aviation hub, with Bangkok hosting the busiest airport in the region.

Thailand has four regions, which correspond with broad linguistic, ethnic and occupational differences. The fertile rice-growing Central region,

FIGURE 9.2

Thailand: Key Statistics

Land area:	514,000 sq. kilometres
Population:[a]	61,740,848 (2000)

GNP:[b] Current exchange rate — US$165.8 bn (1997); US$131.9 (1998)

Purchasing Power Parity — US$393 bn (1997); US$338 bn (1998)

GNP Per Capita:[b] Current exchange rate — US$2,740 (1997); US$2,160 (1998)

Purchasing Power Parity — US$6,490 (1997); US$5,524 (1998)

Income Distribution (1998):[b]

Gini Index	41.4
% share of income or consumption:	
Lowest 10%	2.8
Lowest 20%	6.4
2nd 20%	9.8
3rd 20%	14.2
4th 20%	21.2
Highest 20%	48.4
Highest 10%	32.4

Human Development Index (HDI) Ranking:[c]

World ranking	67 (1997); 76 (1998)
Value	0.753 (1997); 0.744 (1998)

Armed Forces:

Total no.[d]	306,000
Expenditure[d]	US$2 bn
% of GNP[b]	2.5% (1995)

Sources: [a] Official national sources.
   [b] World Bank, *World Development Indicators* (Washington, D.C., 1999 & 2000).
   [c] United Nations Development Programme (UNDP), *Human Development Report* (New York: Oxford University Press, 1999 & 2000).
   [d] International Institute for Strategic Studies (IISS), *The Military Balance, 1999–2000* (London: Oxford University Press, 1999).

with its capital of Bangkok, is often regarded as the cultural heartland of the country. The North is cooler, mountainous, agriculturally diversified, and home to earlier notable kingdoms based at Chiengmai, Thailand's second largest city. The Northeast is Thailand's driest, poorest and most populous region; its inhabitants share an ethnic identification with lowland Lao, and have a tradition of opposing control from Bangkok. The South has a number of coastal ports, with broader international links than other regions, and a significant ethnic Malay minority bordering Malaysia.

These circumstances have made Thailand a major exporter of agricultural products, which remained the major component of exports until a shift to exporting light industrial products in the 1980s. In recent decades industry and services have come to dominate Thailand's economy, and urbanisation has proceeded apace. By 1996 agriculture accounted for only 11 per cent of gross domestic product, though it still employed half the workforce.

Social — Hierarchy versus Civil Society

Thailand's different ethnic and regional groups have merged into a relatively homogeneous population. More than 70 per cent of the population are normally defined as Thai. Chinese make up around 15 per cent, but most have been assimilated into Thai society. Many leading public figures, including prime ministers, have had Chinese origins. Muslims make up 4 per cent of the population. Most are Malays in the four Southern provinces bordering Malaysia, but others are found in small pockets in Bangkok and throughout the central plains. Though irredentist sentiment in the South has often been strong, several have recently risen to top public positions, including that of parliamentary President (Wan Muhamad Noor Matha) and Foreign Minister (Surin Pitsuwan). Hill tribes number some 800,000, most of whom do not have Thai citizenship and are frequently mistreated by officialdom — they remain a blemish on an otherwise ethnically tolerant society. Apart from permanent residents there are around one million foreign labourers in the country, most illegals, from Myanmar and lesser numbers from Laos and Cambodia. Thailand has also hosted millions of refugees in recent decades, and still has around 100,000 from Myanmar.

More than 90 per cent of Thais are Buddhist, of the orthodox Theravada school. A close connection between the clergy (*sangkha*) and state has existed from pre-Ayudhya days, with each reinforcing the other. The temple is the social as well as religious centre of village activities. Most men will become monks and enter a temple, at least for a few days in their life. By some accounts Buddhism has had a part in reinforcing a hierarchical society, as high social status can easily be attributed to good deeds accumulated in previous incarnations (*karma*). But Thai Buddhism has always left open the possibility of individual improvement, and the monkhood has served as a direct means of upward mobility for the academically gifted from poor families. In recent years Buddhism has sometimes appeared to be in crisis. Unorthodox sects have flourished, many linking the religion more directly with material prosperity, and several charismatic monks have been implicated in money or sexual scandals. It remains, nonetheless, a central part of Thai identity. Leading monks are among the most revered public figures, and both clerical and lay theologians have looked to the religion to assist in reforming politics and supporting more sustainable economic development.

Thai society emphasizes hierarchy. Sociologist Niels Mulder has noted that "the concept of equality is unknown in Thai cultural tradition; ... all social relations are characterized by a superior-inferior aspect; [and] ... it is impossible to speak Thai without reference to relative status".[3] A high degree of economic inequality reinforces this divide. (See Figure 9.2) Society is therefore seen as vertically integrated, with patron-client relations providing the main form of social interaction. At the same time Thai society is widely regarded as "loosely structured", meaning a society in which "considerable variation of individual behaviour is sanctioned"[4] — implying a high degree of individualism, and even social mobility.

Sociologists have not satisfactorily resolved the conflicting nature of these different attributes, but generally place more stress on hierarchy. The continuing importance of traditional social leaders from royalty and the aristocracy is readily apparent, even from a cursory view of the social pages of Bangkok newspapers. Wealthy Thais can gain access to this circle by donations to royal charities, and receiving royal awards. Top bureaucrats, including the military, continue to be accorded great deference. And in rural areas, the *jao phor* (godfather) — who as the name suggests has often made their fortunes from questionable means — extend control over communities by a combination of intimidation and the respect that goes to such powerful individuals.

Both hierarchy and loose social structure have been seen as inhibiting the emergence of civil society, since they prevent horizontal cooperation. The 1973 uprising, and events since, have shown such views to be mistaken. Social values and organisation — and the real power that many leaders possess — may inhibit the formation of civil society, but have not been able to prevent it.

Civil society emerged in the 1970s with expansion of the middle class, and growing exploitation of both peasants and a nascent industrial labour force. The middle class grew following rapid economic growth in the 1960s, and was reflected initially in a burgeoning class of tertiary students — the group that led the overthrow of military rule in 1973. As economic growth continued white collar workers grew from around half a million in the 1960s to four and a half million by the late 1980s, and almost eight and a half million by the close of the century (26 per cent of the work-force). They provided leaders for a range of urban civil society organizations that promoted democracy and mobilized rural society against abuses by the state and the disruptive impact of commercial agriculture.

Women have traditionally held a relatively high place in Thai society. They have, for example, generally controlled household budgets, and had high representation in such areas as commerce, academia, and to a lesser extent the bureaucracy. Thailand has heroines who rescued the country from foreign subjugation (by Burma) in the past. Nonetheless their status is also reflected in the well-known epithet, that women are the "hind legs of the elephant". In politics women were not allowed to hold leadership positions in local government until a decade ago, and even now are only some 3 per cent of village heads. They made up 6 per cent of the 1996 House of Representatives, and around 10 per cent of the 2000 Senate.

Women have also suffered most from the numerous social ills that has accompanied turbo-charged growth. Prostitution expanded greatly in the 1960s because of United States military bases in the country for the Indochina War, and visiting troops on recreation. This was later reinforced by mass tourism, and increased supply caused by pressures to leave the countryside. Thailand has the worst AIDS problem in the region with around 740,000 HIV positive, notwithstanding international praise for control efforts. And it has a major drug problem. Heroin and amphetamine factories in neighbouring Myanmar have found a ready outlet for their product among Thailand's youth.

Economy — from Tiger Cub to Crisis

The Bowring treaty inducted Thailand into the international economy, bringing it riches as a rice exporter to neighbouring Western colonies. But in other respects Thailand remained something of a backwater until Sarit came to power in 1958 and committed the state to promoting rapid economic development. Polices introduced at this time, with World Bank assistance, reduced direct government intervention but upgraded communications and education, and introduced policies favouring import-substitution industrialization (behind high tariffs), and the export of agricultural products. High growth rates became the norm, assisted greatly by massive United States support during the Second Indochina War of the 1960s and early 1970s.

These policies remained in place until the mid 1980s. Then, as growth declined in the face of rising international oil prices, and a global downturn, technocrats changed track to emphasize the export of light industrial products. The baht was devalued some 15 per cent, foreign companies offered various investment incentives to set up export-oriented industries, and protectionist barriers gradually brought down. In the early 1990s financial services gained increased focus, with the opening of the capital account. Foreign direct investment surged, particularly Japanese following appreciation of the yen after the Plaza Accord of 1985. In the 1990s foreign capital increased in other forms, including portfolio investment and loans. Foreign companies spearheaded the export drive, but Thai companies were never far behind: Thailand relied less on foreign investment than most other countries in Southeast Asia. The World Bank proclaimed it an exemplar of the Asian miracle. *The Economist*, in 1995, touted it as the world's eighth largest economy by 2020.

What went wrong, and precipitated the crash of July 1997? Economists continue to debate causes, but broadly agree that a massive inflow of short-term international funds, particularly after Thailand liberalized its capital account in 1993, was of fundamental importance. Private debt leapt from US$30.5 billion in 1992 to US$92 billion in 1996. Financial institutions were ill equipped to handle this, creating a bubble economy with excess investment particularly in the property sector. Bank of Thailand (BOT) attempts to contain overheating by tightening monetary policy led to rising non-performing loans, causing concern over the viability of the financial sector, and eventually assaults on the currency by hedge funds together with the outflow of short-term capital. The BOT then sought to prop up the currency by buying U.S. dollars in a series of forward swap arrangements, a gamble that lost around US$10 billion in foreign reserves; it lost even more by injecting capital into financial institutions that slid ever deeper into debt. Corrupt and indecisive governments exacerbated these difficulties.

After Thailand floated the baht in July 1997 the currency plummeted, and the stock market went into free fall. The International Monetary Fund (IMF) had to be called in, and agreed on a US$17.2 billion loan — the second highest ever awarded to that time. The IMF introduced its standard package of tight monetary and fiscal policies, but also demanded major structural reforms, starting with the finance sector, and focused on increasing BOT supervisory capabilities, corporate governance, and liberalization.

Initially IMF intervention made things worse. Its insistence on hasty closure of financial institutions and strict fiscal and monetary policies pushed the country into recession. By January 1998 the baht had fallen to 54 against the U.S. dollar, 55 per cent of its pre-crisis value, and the stock market was down 60 per cent on its early 1997 level. Around this time the IMF accepted the need for change — in part because of Thai representations — and agreed to loosen fiscal and monetary policy. Slowly the economy stabilized, and after negative growth of 10.4 per cent in 1998 began to grow around April 1999. GDP expanded by 4.2 per cent in 1999, and is likely to be slightly more in 2000. Thailand did not require the last $3.7 billion from the IMF loan, and formally graduated from the programme in June 2000. Numerous large problems remain, with corporate and financial restructuring expected to take five to ten years. Still, while the difficulties of economic management in today's volatile global environment are not to be underestimated, wide-ranging reforms introduced since the crisis provide some hope that a basis for sustainable growth is now in place.

THE POLITICAL SYSTEM

Thailand, according to the first three sections of its Constitution, is a unitary kingdom, a democracy with the King as head of state, and vests sovereign power in the people.[5] In other words, it is a democracy with a constitutional monarchy and a unitary administration.

The current Constitution, approved by Parliament in September 1997 and promulgated by the King the following month, is Thailand's sixteenth in 65 years. Several provisions did not become operative immediately, but are being phased in after the passage of "organic laws" and the January 2001 election. It is the most detailed ever, containing twelve chapters and 336 sections, addressing particularly the role of the King, the rights and duties of the Thai people, the separation of powers between the legislature, executive and judiciary, and local government. It has similarities with liberal Constitutions in the past (1974 and 1991 after amendments in 1996), but also several unique features. Drawn up by an independent 99-member Constitution Drafting Assembly, whose representatives toured the country to seek public views, it is certainly the most democratic of all Thailand's constitutions. Many previous charters were drafted merely to legitimize military rule.

The Constitution commits the state to promote decentralization of power, and has a chapter on local government which provides for autonomy of local organizations in areas such as government, administration, personnel and finance. Thailand's local government comprises some 8,000 units, including the Bangkok Metropolitan Administration, Pattaya City, 74 Provincial Administration Organisations, municipalities and sub-districts (*tambon*). Four acts passed in 1999 set out arrangements for a 10-year programme to devolve power.[6] Schools, hospitals, agricultural promotion and a wide range of additional services will eventually be run by elected local organizations. The share of national budget allocated to this level will increase from 9 per cent to 20 per cent in 2001, and reach 35 per cent by 2010. The mechanism and details of this process still remain less than clear, causing anxiety among affected groups such as teachers and health professionals.

Traditionally, Thailand has been integrated bureaucratically through the Ministry of Interior. It has governors heading each of Thailand's 76 provinces, and other officials reaching down to the district and village level, facilitating strict central control over local units. Its reach has now been constrained, but it remains influential. Ultimately, a district officer unhappy with a *tambon* council may seek approval from the governor for its dissolution and new elections. At higher levels dissolution will require approval of the Minister of Interior, on advice from a governor.

The Constitution is not, of course, meant to be comprehensive. As noted a number of "organic laws" are linked to the constitution — including election laws, and the setting up of several independent agencies with oversight over areas such as corruption and human rights. Many other laws and traditional practices also shape the political system. And although the constitution is designated the "supreme law of the land", changing it would not seem to be a major obstacle. Proposals for amendment require the backing of Cabinet, or 20 per cent of the lower house, or 20 per cent of parliament as a whole. Amendment then requires only a simple parliamentary majority.

Head of State

The Thai King is a hereditary monarch. He is accorded a constitutional position of "revered worship", and cannot be exposed to "any sort of accusation or action". A separate law on *lèse majesté* ensures that this provision has strong state backing, if necessary. The King must be a Buddhist, but is also upholder of all religions. He heads Parliament, Cabinet, the judiciary and the armed forces. He opens and closes Parliament, approves all legislation, and issues Emergency Decrees; appoints all ministers together with military and civilian officials at the head of department level; and appoints senior judges, and exercises the power of clemency. In short, very little can be done without the King's signature. While the Constitution implies that the King acts on advice in such areas, it does recognize that he might refuse assent to a parliamentary bill. In such a case the bill would still be enacted if its is reaffirmed by two-thirds of Parliament (Section 94). To date the King has never refused assent to any bill.

The King does, however, have powers to "create titles and confer decorations", select his own Privy Council (up to 19 members) and determine his successor. The Privy Council has an advisory role to the King, and other responsibilities if succession issues are not clear-cut. The 1924 Palace Law on Succession is the main legislation governing succession, and may be amended by the King at his discretion. This mandates succession through male heirs, but since 1974 the Constitution has allowed that in the event of the King not naming a successor the Privy Council should decide, and "the name of a princess may be submitted" (Section 23). In an innovative blend of monarchism and democracy the successor will be approved by the National Assembly (parliament) and proclaimed by the Assembly's President.

The monarchy has independent wealth. The Bureau of the Crown Property is a major landowner in Bangkok and throughout the country. It also manages investments in numerous companies, most notably Thailand's largest indigenous corporate group, Siam Cement. Royal charities attract large donations from Thailand's wealthier citizens.

However, such a formal description of the monarch's legal position does little to convey the importance this institution has in Thai politics. For many years following the end of absolute monarchy in 1932 royal influence was on the wane. After Rama VII abdicated in 1935, Thailand had no resident adult monarch until 1950. And in the early 1950s the policies of Prime Minister Phibun — a participant in the 1932 coup — continued to sideline the King. That changed after General Sarit's coup in 1957. In a bid to improve his own legitimacy Sarit revived royal ceremonies, encouraged widespread exposure of the royal family's activities, forged closer links between the military and monarchy, and encouraged expansion of the monarchy's welfare and charity work.[7] The King's prestige has gone from strength to strength ever since.

From the 1950s King Bhumibol Adulyadej (Rama IX) has maintained a gruelling schedule of visits all over the country, identifying with problems faced by Thais from all walks of life, particularly in rural areas. He has not travelled abroad since the 1960s. In response to the economic crisis the King issued an appeal for greater focus on self-sufficiency in his annual birthday address on 4 December 1997. The speech, and the King's "New Theory" for developing rural self-sufficiency, based on his own rural development projects, were widely reproduced and distributed throughout the country. So also was the King's book *Mahajanaka* published (in English and Thai) in 1996, which bore a similar message. The ideas were immediately endorsed by economists, bureaucrats, military leaders, politicians, the media and others.

Like his predecessors, King Bhumibol is seen as having sacred powers. Houses, shops, vehicles and other places feature royal portraits, which are revered and worshipped and believed to bring good fortune. In addition, the current King has provided stability during years of turbulent political change. Though widely accepted as being above politics, at critical times he has intervened to resolve major conflicts — most notably during armed conflict between students and the military in 1973, and the military and a coalition of anti-government civilian groups in 1992.[8]

The Executive

The locus of power is with the Council of Ministers, or Cabinet, an organization that is collectively responsible to the National Assembly. It meets weekly, on Tuesdays, and major decisions are posted on the Internet. Recent cabinets have numbered 49 members, but since the January 2001 general election the upper limit is 36, including the Prime Minister. Unlike most countries, deputy ministers are as much a part of Cabinet as full ministers.

Partly because of its large size, but also for other reasons associated with the personalized nature of authority in Thailand, power does not rest with the Cabinet as a collective, but with powerful government ministers. As Thailand's foremost journalist has noted:

> No major decisions affecting the country have been made in this weekly ritual. Cabinet meetings serve only as a venue where Cabinet members pretend to deliberate on issues which don't need deliberation. Ministers are interested only in pushing their own recommendations, hoping that the other members would mind their own business while he minds his.[9]

The Prime Minister (PM) is the most important minister, but in democratic periods must make concessions to coalition partners.

Future Thai cabinets will be strictly separated from the legislature — an arrangement aimed at preventing ministers using their positions for electoral advantage. Previous Thai cabinets have had some members from outside parliament; under the current constitution, all must be. Prospective Prime Ministers must, however, be elected to the House of Representatives first. The House will then meet to select a nominee, and the result will be conveyed to the King by the House President, for his appointment. Established practice is to give the head of the party with the largest parliamentary representation first opportunity to form a government, and only look elsewhere if the party is unable to draw together a majority coalition. However, a Constitution Court ruling allowing parliamentarians to vote according to conscience rather than on party lines has introduced a new element of uncertainty.

Once a Prime Minister has been chosen he selects his Cabinet. This is a complicated process in which a balance has to be struck between coalition partners, and major power holders in society. Traditionally the main group outside political parties that must be taken into account is the military. This is not as essential now as in the past, when top military figures required — at the least — that the Defence Minister be an acceptable active or retired General, but it still must be handled carefully. The PM is free to select ministers from inside or outside parliament, but unlike previous constitutions elected representatives must immediately resign their parliamentary post.

Notwithstanding this clear separation between the executive and the legislature, the former does have a legislative role. The Cabinet may sponsor any bills it wishes, or call for a general debate. And finance bills require the PM's explicit backing. Cabinet can also issue Emergency Decrees with the force of law, though these must be endorsed by Parliament at the earliest possible moment. Or it may call for a referendum, thereby gaining support for its legislative agenda.

Ministers must have Thai nationality by birth, be at least 35 years old, and have university education to Bachelor's level. They may not be government officials — a provision directed particularly at excluding the military from any direct political role — and must divest shareholdings exceeding 5 per cent in any business firms. All personal and immediate family assets must be publicly declared on taking office, again on departure, and finally one year later. Ministers hold office for the term of the House of Representatives unless dismissed by the PM, or by a

---

FIGURE 9.3

Thailand: Government Ministries and Agencies

Office of the Prime Minister
including
  National Economic and Social Development Board
  Council of State
  Civil Service Commission
  Public Relations Department
  National Security Council
  National Intelligence Agency

Ministry of Defence

Ministry of Finance

Ministry of Foreign Affairs

Ministry of Agriculture and Co-operatives

Ministry of Transport and Communications

Ministry of Commerce

Ministry of Interior

Ministry of Justice

Ministry of Education

Ministry of Public Health

Ministry of Industry

Ministry of Science, Technology and Environment

Ministry of University Affairs

Ministry of Labour and Social Welfare

Independent Public Agencies
including
  Bureau of the Royal Household
  National Counter Corruption Commission
  Office of the Attorney-General
  Election Commission
  The Constitution Court
  National Human Rights Commission

parliamentary vote of no confidence, or by a vote of three fifths of the Senate after investigation by the National Counter Corruption Commission (NCCC).

Cabinet must comply with legislative requests for information. In addition it must deliver a statement of policies to the National Assembly within 15 days of taking office, and provide annual assessments of its performance thereafter.

Under the Cabinet are the Office of the Prime Minister (OPM) and 14 ministries (see Figure 9.3). Ministries are further divided into Departments, Divisions and Sub-Divisions. Since Prime Minister Sarit reorganized the OPM in the late 1950s its preeminence has been undisputed. Economic departments under it include the Budget Bureau and the National Economic and Social Development Board (the main economic planning agency). The National Security Council, chaired by the PM, is the main security organization, and its secretariat comes under the OPM. The National Intelligence Agency, the top body for political intelligence, comes under the Office. The Police were transferred there from the Interior Ministry in 1998, though with what has been reported as "independent status".

On economic matters, Finance is the most important ministry, having major responsibility for fiscal policy. It also works closely with the Bank of Thailand (BOT), which has the key role in determining monetary policy. The Governor of the BOT is responsible to the Finance Minister, who has exercised his authority by removing several Governors in recent years, but the BOT nonetheless has considerable autonomy. That was much in evidence in the recent economic crisis when the BOT failed to ensure proper supervision over banks and other financial institutions, and lost vast foreign reserves in a futile attempt to maintain the value of the baht — a major report faulted political leaders for not becoming more involved. A draft law approved by Cabinet in March 2000 seeks to strengthen independence by proscribing only that the bank "take into consideration" government policy needs, and ensuring that the Governor could only be sacked for serious crimes or negligence.[10] Commerce (covering domestic and international trade), Industry, and relevant sections of the OPM, also have weight on economic issues. The four ministries constitute the core of the Economic Cabinet that meets weekly on Mondays, the day before the Cabinet proper.

Two other ministries are particularly influential within Cabinet. Interior controls provincial and local administration, giving it a major say in any events outside Bangkok. These powers were greatly augmented until recently by its control over the police and elections. Police, as noted, has now gone to the OPM, while the new Constitution puts elections in the charge of an independent Election Commission. Defence was also a key portfolio in the past, because of the enormous political influence of the military, but its influence has been much eroded in recent years.

Public servants manning these ministries receive scant mention in the Constitution, beyond statements prohibiting their representation in legislative, executive and related bodies, and requiring that they be politically neutral. They numbered some 1,146,019 in 1994 (including local authorities, teachers and police, but not the military); and 1,775,854 in 1998 (including the military).[11] The bureaucracy is governed by the Civil Service Act 1992, and major policies affecting it are determined by the Civil Service Commission, chaired by the PM. It is intended to be an apolitical service, with only heads of departments being appointed by ministers.

Bureaucratic influence is more considerable than this might indicate. For many years Thailand was described as a "bureaucratic polity", with bureaucrats (including retirees) dominating cabinet, and appointed parliaments. In a seminal work published in 1966 Fred Riggs discovered that of 237 ministers in cabinets between 1932 and 1958, 184 were officials, 100 civilians and 84 military.[12] (A later study found that for the period 1959–1974 all but four of 145 ministers were bureaucrats, including 103 civilians.)[13] Riggs further documents how these officials sustained their political positions by strategic alliances with a pariah Sino-Thai business class, and the use of harsh repressive measures. Parliamentary powers were strictly curtailed and sometimes abolished. The draconian 1952 Act for the Prevention of Communist Activities (amended 1969 and 1979) allowed censorship of the media, and 210 days detention without court order for alleged communists, and another 270 days under court order pending trial.[14] Political parties were often banned or faced severe restrictions. Other means of extending influence included through around sixty state enterprises — including the tobacco monopoly, and services such as posts and telecommunications, and electricity — and delegated legislation. The Customs Tariff Act of 1960 contained only 13 articles, but "enabled the Ministry of Finance to issue over 300 ministerial notifications".[15]

The scope of bureaucratic influence has been reduced considerably since the time that Riggs wrote, particularly as internal and external threats from communism subsided in the 1980s. Several repressive laws remain on the books, but the more liberal constitution takes precedence over all else — the first time this has been written into the constitution. Bureaucrats are not as important as they once were in either the executive or the legislature. Their direct intervention in the latter ended when the last appointed Senate was dissolved in March 2000. But although the current Constitution rules out a direct political role both civilian and military bureaucracies (see below) retain an important influence, and will do so for a long time. Bureaucrats, particularly through the conservative Council of State under the OPM, still play a key role in drafting laws for parliamentary passage. Others have positions on supervisory bodies associated with areas such as commerce and communications. Technocrats in the bureaucracy retain a critical role in economic decision-making, as BOT mistakes contributing to the regional economic crisis illustrate. Moreover, bureaucrats still have much of the prestige they once had as the King's servants (*kharachakaan*), and a widely perceived right to exercise authority over the public. Government privatization programmes may eventually affect the influence of the public sector, but are only just beginning to make inroads. Ambitious plans for bureaucratic reform will reduce numbers, but if the reforms are successful more competent bureaucrats will remain valuable for their political masters.

Political Role of the Military and Police

The military has been at the forefront of Thai politics since the 1932 coup against absolute monarchy. Most of the time it has seized power, or reinforced its power, by the use or threat of force. There have been 22 successful or attempted coups to date. Nonetheless, military influence has slowly waned since student-led demonstrations toppled the military government in 1973. After three turbulent years the military returned to leadership, but soon sought a more cooperative relationship with civilian politicians. Prime Minister for most of the 1980s, General Prem had his base in the army and never stood for public office, but he was elected to power by Parliament and allowed a slow expansion of parliamentary influence. His successor had a military rank, but General Chatichai had been out of the army for two decades, and was an elected parliamentarian. He was toppled by a military coup in 1991, orchestrated by army strongman General Suchinda. However, when Suchinda sought to entrench his power by becoming Prime Minister he was opposed by popular demonstrations, and forced to withdraw. Chavalit Yongchaiyut, another former army head, was elected to power in 1996 general elections, after retiring from service several years earlier.

The 300,000-strong military is conscript based, though only a small fraction of the eligible age group are accepted at the annual intake. It is overwhelmingly an army-dominated institution. The Army Commander in Chief has direct control over troops, and is thus more important than the Supreme Commander (through current reform plans seek to change this). The road to the prime ministership followed a predictable pattern in past years, with field command then control over the Bangkok-based First Army (the coup army) featuring as key requirements — broken only in the mid 1980s when Chavalit, with a background in military intelligence, became army commander. The army had occasional success in clashes with a communist insurgency, but has not had a distinguished fighting record. By most accounts it came second best against the lowly rated Lao military during armed border clashes in the late 1980s.

Past constitutions were often crafted to allow the military an open political role. Some permitted government officials — military and civilian — to be appointed to cabinet, even to the highest level of PM. Others allowed appointment to the Senate, and gave this chamber powers to check the elected lower house. All such dispensations have been removed from the 1997 constitution. No active servicemen remained in parliament after the appointed Senate was dissolved in March 2000.

Nonetheless the military has several other means to ensure its political role will not be entirely eclipsed. As Prime Minister, Chavalit frequently sought to enhance his position by appearing in public with military leaders. The military retains extensive business interests, and connections with mass movements developed during the 1980s, that give it considerable power behind the scenes. Retired generals are often welcomed into political parties for just that reason. At the time of writing military officers were maneouvring to be included in a selection panel that will oversee the distribution of frequencies for radio and television, in a bid to retain some control over an area they once monopolised. And some may still harbour interventionist ambitions. Army leader General Surayud Chulanont twice warned of such a group in November 2000, after 60 senior officers paid a courtesy call on then opposition leader Thaksin Shinawatra the preceding month. (They professed nothing beyond friendship — some were colleagues of Thaksin, who started his career in the police force, in the Armed Forces Academies Preparatory School.)

Still, for the moment at least, the military seems prepared to maintain a low-key political presence. In 1997 military leaders urged Prime Minister Chavalit to support the new constitution before he was willing to do so. They accepted Prime Minister Chuan's decision to hold the Defence portfolio — only the second civilian to do so — with only minor murmurings of discontent. General Surayud has strongly reaffirmed support for the army remaining outside the political arena, and became the first general to resign from the Senate in support of this principle. Annual military promotions in September, once the high point of the annual political calendar, are now scarcely reported by the media. Military budgets have gone down along with other sectors in the wake of the economic crisis, and military reforms will, inter alia, see a reduction in military strength of around 72,000 by 2007.

The police force developed a para-military role and emerged as a rival to the army's political dominance in the 1950s, but after General Sarit's 1957 coup army men headed the police through to the mid 1970s. Since then police have had a much lower public profile. They often worked in close alliance with others in the Ministry of Interior, but never looked like an independent political force. Often they receive negative publicity for involvement in corruption, generally of a petty nature. Their 1998 transfer to the OPM made little initial difference, as they came under Deputy Prime Ministers who concurrently held the Interior portfolio, but in the long run the shift makes the chance of them playing an independent role even less likely.

The Legislature

The 1997 Constitution has given the legislature a strong basis for implementing its powers of legislation, control of finance, and calling the executive to account. The bicameral National Assembly comprises a 500-member House of Representatives, or lower house, and 200-member Senate, or upper house. Together they have a large degree of autonomy over their own affairs, and allow parliamentarians the usual legal immunity — though unlike some parliamentary systems, only comments directed at the Cabinet or Assembly members are privileged. The main session lasts 120 days, with provision for another shorter regular session and an extraordinary session if required.

The main powers rest with the House. It provides and approves the Prime Minister. Its President is President for the parliament as a whole. Apart from limited areas where a public initiative is possible (requiring the support of 50,000 voters), it has exclusive power to initiate all legislation, and predominant power to push it through. And it has considerable powers to call the executive to account.

Legislation forwarded from the House to the Senate must be deliberated on within 60 days, or 30 for a finance bill. If the Senate fails to act the bill passes. If the bill is either rejected or returned to the House in an amended form, a joint committee is established to resolve any differences. If that fails the bill may be "held back" for 180 days, after which the House will be able to impose its will if it remains committed.

The House preeminence is diluted somewhat by the requirement of a joint sitting for issues such as legislation on "crucial" government bills rejected by the House, and constitutional change, and approval of treaties. However, in such instances the House's numerical dominance gives it the main say.

The House has the major role in enforcing Cabinet accountability. As noted, Cabinet must provide it with an initial statement of policy, and an annual report of its achievements. One fifth of its members can file a motion of no confidence against a minister, and two fifths against the Prime Minister. Carriage of the motion, which requires a simple majority, leads to the ouster of the minister or, where the PM is involved, the government. Once a motion against the PM has been filed the government may not call an election until the debate has concluded. Such a motion is permitted only once a year — a requirement that inadvertently turned such debates into an annual event in recent times.

Members of both houses can question ministers, who may decline to answer only on grounds of security or national interest. Three fifths of the Senate may require the Cabinet to justify its performance in a general debate, at least once a year. And as noted, the Senate may hold ministers (and indeed other officials and parliamentarians) to account if the NCCC finds some basis for this, and if three fifths of the Senate vote in favour.

The Senate also plays a major role in relation to several new independent agencies and courts set up by the Constitution, including the NCCC, the Election Commission, the National Commission on Human Rights, and the Constitution Court. It takes the initiative to find members for such organisations, and must then approve them.

In sum, while the Senate is supposedly "non-political" (members must not belong to a political party, and are not even allowed to campaign for election) and less important than the House, it is by no means a rubber stamp. On its own, and in joint sittings with the House, it has considerable influence over legislation and cabinet accountability. And it has a crucial role establishing and overseeing important new independent agencies. The first elected Senate convened in August 2000.

Committees play an important role in Assembly proceedings. They are both ad hoc, to conduct in depth examination of legislation as it is before Parliament, and permanent, to address a wide range of topics under Parliament's purview. There are currently 23 standing committees in the House, and 16 in the Senate. These meet weekly during parliamentary sessions, and prepare occasional reports after bringing in outside experts to assist in deliberation and drafting. Small secretariats attached to each house also provide limited assistance.

A novel institution attached to parliament is the King Prajadhipok Institute, established in December 1994 as a division under the House secretariat, but later made an independent body under the supervision of the parliamentary president. The Institute provides seminars and courses on democracy for parliamentarians, administrators, local government members, business representatives and other public groups.

Since it was established in 1932 parliament has had a turbulent history, frequently being disposed of after military coups, and/or coming under the domination of government-appointed members. During times when reasonably free elections were permitted parliament has played a significant role in Thai politics, particularly in terms of proposing legislation and calling the government to account.[16] Its importance has gradually been consolidated. In the 1980s Constitutional amendments led to a more representative and independent legislature, governments changed hands according to parliamentary process, and the cut and thrust of parliamentary debate became an established feature of Thai life. These developments were set back by the 1991 military coup, but parliament again became important after popular demonstrations ousted the military-led government in 1992. The 1996–2000 House broke several records, including the longest-serving legislature ever — dissolved just seven days short of its four year term — and the greatest number of bills passed (287).

While parliamentary importance has been rising, there has also been a downside. Parliament has often been discredited by the corruption of democratically elected governments (though military governments have been no less guilty), the process of musical chairs whereby governments rapidly fall apart and are reformed, and the wild accusations, muck-raking and grandstanding of some of the leading personalities. The 1997 Constitution seeks to address these issues through a range of reforms, particularly by strengthening political parties and combating large-scale corruption.

Elections

National elections are organised and implemented by an independent five-member Election Commission. This is constituted by a complex selection process, involving a Senate-appointed ten-member selection panel (two judges, four university rectors and four political party representatives) and later approval by the Senate. Membership criteria include having Thai nationality by birth, a Bachelor's degree or equivalent, no political party affiliation, and being at least forty years old. Members are appointed by the King for a seven-year term. No reappointment is possible.

The Commission has wide-ranging powers to organise and ensure the smooth running of elections. Three organic bills to assist in this process passed parliament in early 1998, and were strengthened by amendments in 2000. The commission Chairman, chosen by members themselves, also serves as the Registrar for political parties.

Voting is compulsory, an innovation intended to make money politics more difficult. Convicted defaulters lose political rights for a few years. In the past electoral turnout has generally been less than 50 per cent, but reached 62 per cent in 1995 and 1996. Senate elections under the new system in 2000 saw a 72 per cent turnout in the first round, though this declined to 30 per cent in the final (fifth) round. The first round of general elections in January 2001 saw a 70 per cent turnout. Voters must have Thai nationality by birth, or citizenship for at least five years, and be at least 18 years old.

The vote for the House of Representatives is divided between 400 elected on a single constituency basis, and 100 on a nation-wide party list. Unlike a similar system in Japan candidates must choose between a constituency or the list; they may not contest both in the same election. For constituencies the electorate is divided into 400 equal parts, with some adjustments to ensure these do not cross provincial boundaries, and that every one of 76 provinces has at least one representative. Election here is determined on a first-past-the-post basis. Constitutional framers hope that single-member constituencies — as distinct from multiple members in the past — will help bond parties and public, thereby strengthening parties and reducing the influence of vote buying. To strengthen constituency links recent legislation even requires the candidate or party to pay for by-election costs if an elected representative resigns to accept ministerial office.

Election for the party list is determined by the overall national vote for each party, with parties being required to gain at least 5 per cent of the vote before winning any seats. (A party winning, say, 40 per cent of the vote would, therefore, end up with slightly more than 40 seats.) The purpose of the 5 per cent minimum is to encourage larger, nationally based parties, and thereby strengthen prospects for stability. In the event of a seat from the party list falling vacant — when parliamentarians resign to take a post in Cabinet, for example — the position will be filled by the next candidate on the party list without the need for another vote.

Candidates must be nationals by birth, at least 35 years old and have a Bachelor's degree or equivalent. They are elected for a four-year term, though the Prime Minister may call elections before this. Once parliament has been dissolved elections must be called within 60 days. Amongst possible reasons for parliamentarians loosing their seat mid term are resigning from, or being expelled from, their party — an attempt to provide more stability by ending the common practice of party hopping.

The Senate has 200 seats, based on provinces. Seat allocation reflects the proportion of a provincial electorate to voters in the country as a whole, though with each province having at least one senator. Bangkok has the largest allocation with 18, while 22 provinces have one. Voters may cast their ballot for one candidate only, regardless of the number of senators assigned to a province.

Candidates must be nationals by birth, have a Bachelor's degree or equivalent, be at least 40 years old, and not be a member of a political party. They are elected to a six-year term, and may be re-elected only once.

Senate elections, which began on 4 March 2000, provided the first test for those new electoral arrangements. The initial ballot was immediately hailed a success, by virtue of the 72 per cent turnout, peaceful, well-organised and transparent process, and better than expected elected representatives (less than half from 'traditional' backgrounds). The disqualification of 78 senators for fraud later that month did little to dim enthusiasm. Thereafter the process became messy as the second ballot for 78 positions resulted in 12 disqualifications. Eventually five balloting rounds were required, taking five months, before the Senate could convene. Nonetheless the willingness of the EC to demonstrate independence in acting against members of a previously untouchable rich and powerful elite was a most positive outcome. Subsequent legislative changes strengthened the hand of the EC, particularly in order to ensure elections for the House would be completed within the one month mandated by the constitution.[17]

The House elections followed a similar pattern. Many candidates sought to get around prohibitions on electoral fraud, but the EC outed four before the first round of voting on 6 January 2001, and 62 subsequently. Eight of the latter were given 'red cards' prohibiting them (or a party substitute) standing again; the rest, where evidence of fraud was not so strong, received 'yellow cards' and were permitted to recontest. (*Thai Rak Thai* was hardest hit, receiving five red and 27 yellow cards.) Parliament was convened on schedule, but the EC has said it will continue investigation of alleged fraud and may disqualify more. As with Senate elections the process was messy, accompanied by loud allegations of vote buying and other fraudulent behaviour, and angry protests by supporters of defeated candidates. Several shortcomings in electoral procedure were revealed, including a confusing ballot paper that resulted in ten per cent of constituency votes being declared invalid (compared to three per cent for the party list).

Nonetheless, many of the intended objectives of electoral reform were achieved. The 70 per cent turnout was the highest in a general election. EC arrangements were more effective than those of the Interior ministry previously. And the polls were the freest and fairest ever. Central counting in each constituency (rather than at polling stations) ensured that voting was kept secret, and other arrangements prevented ballot stuffing. As a result, many of Thailand's notorious rural political clans were defeated, and a higher proportion of younger candidates (many in their thirties) were elected. Parties gave much greater emphasis to policies than in previous elections. Above all the election succeeded in strengthening larger parties, reducing the potential for instability associated with unstable, multi-party coalitions. *Thai Rak Thai* emerged just short of a majority (248) and augmented this by absorbing 14 *Seritham* representatives after the election; the Democrats gained 128. Previous mid-sized parties became small parties (*Chat Thai* 41, New Aspiration Party 36, *Chat Pattana* 29), and former small parties lost comprehensively.

Elections at provincial, municipal and *tambon* levels are to be held every four years. The requirements for candidates and electors are not as demanding as the national level, notably candidates do not have to have university degrees and voting is not compulsory. Elections remain under the Interior ministry, but a new law is under consideration that may eventually put the EC in charge.

Elections have been a troublesome aspect of the Thai political system in the past. They allowed a wide discussion of political issues, with limited acts of violence, but were also associated with low voter turnout, vote buying (since the 1970s), and manipulation by the Interior ministry and local 'Mafia'. The system favoured a large number of minor parties, working against the interests of stability and predictability.[18] The 1997 Constitution seeks to address such problem areas. Some aspects are controversial, including the requirements of compulsory voting and a Bachelor's degree for all candidates. But outcomes from the first Senate and House elections under the new rules do suggest at least modest progress.

Judiciary

The Constitution establishes the judiciary as an autonomous arm of government. Until August 2000 it had come under the Justice portfolio, but now manages its own affairs, including budgeting for which purpose it is treated as a ministry. The main court structure has three levels, Courts of First Instance, Court of Appeal, and the Supreme Court of Justice. Appointments are by the King, on the advice of a Judicial Commission, comprising the President of the Supreme Court and twelve judges.

The Constitution also strengthens the basis for a parallel three-tier Administrative Court, first mentioned in 1996 Constitutional amendments but only recently given a legislative basis. Appointments are made on the same basis as regular courts. Its function is to adjudicate disputes between government departments and individuals, and between different government departments. It was established because bringing a case against the bureaucracy has hitherto been fraught with difficulties.

A new Constitution Court comprises five Supreme Court judges, two Administrative judges, five members of the public with legal qualifications, and three with political science qualifications. Selection of court members is managed by the Senate. Its responsibilities in relation to the constitution are broad, including for instance adjudication on official assets declarations where these have been found inaccurate by the NCCC. Additionally, the Constitution provides for a new "political crime division" attached to the Supreme Court, that would adjudicate criminal charges of corruption, malfeasance or misconduct involving public officers.

The modern Thai judiciary dates back to the introduction of Western law in the late nineteenth century. At the highest level it generally has a good reputation for integrity and competence. But there have been exceptions, and the judiciary as a whole is not highly regarded. Its dispensing of criminal justice in particular has often been questionable — trials sometimes drag on interminably, while on other occasions prosecution is mysteriously dropped. In some instances the absence of an up-to-date legal framework is a problem; sometimes courts appear too deferential to the rich and powerful.[19] It took more than twelve months after the economic crisis in July 1997 had revealed massive wrongdoing in the financial sector before any charges were laid, and more than three years on little progress has been made.

Political Parties

No particular type of party system is imposed on the Thai political system in any legislated form. The 1997 constitution does, however, introduce a number of reforms aimed at strengthening political parties, and thereby creating a more stable political environment.

Political parties have not always been prominent in recent political history, but when permitted Thailand has had a very fluid multi party system. Parties have been numerous (over 30 competed in the 2001 general election) weak, and organised around strong and wealthy individuals or sometimes political "dynasties". Thai political scientists often yearn for "real" political parties — well managed, mass based, and ideologically driven — but have failed to find them.[20]

The Democrats, Thailand's most successful party, is something of an exception. Established in 1946, its fortunes have fluctuated over the years, but at times of political openness it has been the party Thais have consistently turned to. Ideologically it is middle of the road, bringing together businessmen and professionals, idealists and pragmatists. Its main base is in the South, where it takes nearly all the seats, but it is sometimes successful in Bangkok, and has pockets of support throughout the country.

The Thais Love Thais or Thai Patriotic Party (*Thai Rak Thai*, or TRT) established in July 1998 by a reformist group led by telecommunications billionaire Thaksin Shinawatra, is currently the other major party. Initially it presented itself as more business savvy, and better able to defend Thai interests in a new global economy. After failing to make much headway, TRT changed tack in early 2000 and 'sucked' over one hundred parliamentarians from established, traditional parties. In the run-up to the general election TRT appealed to populism, with promises of B1 million payouts to rural villages, a three-year halt to repayments of rural loans, B30 medical consultations and a quick fix to the urban economy by buying over all bank non-paying loans. These offerings proved irresistible to an electorate still suffering from the 1997 economic crisis, and TRT swept all before it in January elections. Now it faces challenges delivering these promises without bankrupting the country, and maintaining unity in a party evenly divided between traditional politicians and new representatives. Above all it must allay public concerns about Thaksin's complicated financial arrangements, his purchase of a controlling share in the country's only independent television station, and NCCC findings that Thaksin falsely declared assets following a brief time in government in 1997. If the Constitution Court upholds NCCC findings, Thaksin will be forced to relinquish public office for five years.

Until 2000 the New Aspiration Party (NAP), headed by former Prime Minister Chavalit, was the main opposition party, winning two more seats than the Democrats in the 1996 election. It represents a coalition of generally right wing interests — particularly from provincial business, and the military — cobbled together by Chavalit and several provincial strongmen. Its base is the populous Northeast, and it has little support outside this region. Two other major parties, Chat Thai and Chat Pattana are very similar to NAP, though both are descended from a military faction associated with Prime Minister Phibun in the 1950s.

Thailand's growing middle class has supported a range of more reform-minded political parties over the years. These have sometimes enjoyed success in Bangkok, but have not been able to gain enough support to make major inroads. Some have adopted the tactics and eventually ideology of more traditional parties — such as the Social Action Party — while others — like Buddhist-oriented *Palang Dharma* — have virtually faded from the scene.

Thai political parties have traditionally disintegrated and re-formed very rapidly around election time. Parties sought to buy over potential election winners, and politicians scrambled to jump on whichever bandwagon appeared to have the greatest chance of success. Both NAP and TRT burst to the forefront in such a manner. After elections politicians moved to where the power was.

The 1997 constitution seeks to address the problems of political parties at different levels. Public funding is made available, based largely on representation at the previous election. The introduction of party lists and single electorates, and prohibition on party hopping, seek to consolidate the influence of larger parties, and improve party images by making them more accountable to the electorate. Extensive powers are vested in the EC, and other institutions such as the NCCC, in an attempt to counter corruption and thereby improve the public perception and legitimacy of parties.

Ideology

Thailand subscribes to no official ideology. The slogan "Nation, Religion and Monarchy" (*Chat, Sasana, Phramahakasat*) is repeated so frequently that it almost serves the same purpose. And Thailand has long had a tradition of nationalist education extolling the virtues of past Kings, warning of foreign dangers (particularly the colonial powers France and Britain, together with Myanmar), and stressing the virtues of national cohesion, Buddhism and an ordered (hierarchical) society.[21]

Civil Society and Human Rights

The growth of civil society has been one of the most profound changes in Thai politics over the past three decades, disproving several learned works claiming public apathy and unwillingness to resist authority. Civil society arrived unexpectedly with the mass student demonstrations and overthrow of the military government in 1973, and has been a force to be reckoned with since. Non Governmental Organisations (NGOs) moved out to the countryside, particularly in the 1980s. Business organisations found new ways of influencing the government through Joint Public and Private Sector Consultative Committees. Mass unrest flared anew in 1992 when 500,000 demonstrators forced another military-led government out of office. New pro-democracy, pro-environment and pro-human rights organisations flourished. And throughout this period the press played a critical role. Though not without shortcomings of its own — some journalists and papers were controlled by political factions — the print media joined the opposition to military dominance, and increasingly exposed corruption in official ranks. (Radio and television did not play the same role, since until recently all were government owned.)

Thailand's legal regulatory framework has gradually moved to accommodate these changes, and the 1997 constitution gives unprecedented support to civil society. The public may initiate legislation and impeach public officials, with the support of 50,000 electors at the national level and smaller numbers at lower levels. Amongst constitutional articles are establishment of:

- A National Commission on Human Rights
- An independent agency with representatives from consumers to draft laws, regulations and directives and to provide opinions on law enforcement to protect consumers
- A National Advisory Council on Economic and Social Affairs, to advise Cabinet
- An independent public organisation to allocate radio and television and other telecommunications frequency bands (i.e. diluting state — particularly military — domination in this area).

The constitution also strengthens civil society's active campaign against corruption by the establishment of organisations such as the EC, the NCCC, Constitution Court, Parliamentary Ombudsmen, and an independent audit authority (the Public Finance Commission). The EC, as noted, demonstrated its willingness to oppose the use of money politics when it disqualified rich and powerful politicians for electoral fraud. The NCCC did much the same though a landmark decision in March 2000, when it forced the resignation of Sanan Kachornprasart, the second most powerful politician in the country — Deputy Prime Minister and Minister of Interior — after finding he had concealed assets of around US$1 million. The Constitution Court later upheld the ruling, forcing Sanan out of politics for the next five years. The constitution also assists NGOs in rural areas by providing for fully elected local administration units. And it provides psychological support to civil society groups by endorsing "the right to peacefully oppose any attempt to seek administrative power through means which are not stipulated by the Constitution" (Section 65) — a thinly veiled reference to opposing any military coup.

Fundamental human rights are strongly affirmed in the constitution, under chapter 3 (Rights and Liberties of the Thai People) and chapter 5 (Directive Principles of Fundamental State Policies). In a number of instances these are qualified by exceptions if allowed by law in the interests of national security or public welfare. However the entrenched nature of such fundamental freedoms as freedom of speech, publication and assembly — and the negative reactions that any government would court by acting restrictively — give considerable reassurance that such prohibitions would not be undertaken lightly.

MAJOR POLITICAL ISSUES

Who Has Power?

Following the overthrow of the absolute monarchy in 1932, Thai politics was for many years dominated by the military and the civilian bureaucracy. In what was often described as a "bureaucratic polity", government sometimes assumed the forms of parliamentary democracy, but generally changed hands as the result of a military coup. Civilian bureaucrats were junior partners, indispensable for running ministerial portfolios that required technical expertise. The monarchy remained on the outer for many years. General Sarit revived it after his coup in 1957, and it has been an important actor in Thai politics ever since. Underpinning the system was a culture that most observers saw as quiescent, in which individuals sought political ends by means of patron-client relationships.

Economic growth and educational expansion initiated by Sarit brought new groups into the political arena. That was dramatically demonstrated when students held public demonstrations that felled a military government. Since 1973 power in Thailand has been dispersed between different groups

— political parties and parliament, the monarchy, military, civil bureaucracy and civil society.

Political parties and parliament are predominantly under the influence of business and professional leaders. There are, however, different type of representation in different parties. Bangkok business has aligned particularly with the Democrats. Though realistic about working in an environment where money matters, and in some instances not entirely immune to the allures of corruption, this group has generally identified its self-interest with pursue of a reformist agenda. It has also worked closely with professionals, such as Democrat leader Chuan who is a lawyer without business involvement.

Rural business elites, however, often dubbed *jao phor* (godfather) because of associations and political practice, are identified with the worst aspects of Thai politics — corruption, money politics, self-interested political dealing, and even political violence. They are particularly identified with parties such as *Chat Thai*, which led the infamous "buffet cabinet" under Chatichai, and Banharn and Chavalit administrations in the 1990s. TRT started out as a Bangkok-based reformist party, but made little headway until it expanded in 2000 by 'sucking' parliamentarians linked with rural business. It now represents the first alliance between Bangkok and rural business.

The 1990s involved a seesaw tussle between Bangkok and rural groups, with the Democrats leading much of the time under two Chuan administrations. In the longer term 1997 constitutional changes emphasising the importance of democracy, transparency and opposing corruption should strengthen the influence of city capital and its professional and other allies. The first elected senate has already tipped the balance a little in this direction. While members did include a number from rural business and other traditional backgrounds, reformers were in the majority.[22]

The monarchy remains an extremely powerful institution. The enthusiasm with which the public picked up the King's 1997 call for greater self-sufficiency is the most recent reminder of his influence. Nonetheless the King has, over the years, projected an image of being above politics, limiting involvement to occasional forays. Adoration for this long-reigning monarch is, also, to a considerable extent, addressed to the person rather than the institution per se. How Thailand will manage after the present King remains a matter of intense speculation.

For reasons noted earlier, the military is not the power it once was, but it remains important. Short of attempting another coup its main interests lie in preserving what powers it can in such areas as statutory boards, and in ensuring its budget. Similar circumstances affect the civilian bureaucracy, though its influence has not declined to the same extent because it retains a critical role in some supervisory bodies, and in drafting parliamentary laws. Still, when the Council of State sought bureaucratic control over organizations such as the NCCC and National Human Rights Commission public pressure forced it to draw back.

The people as a whole through civil society organizations and sometimes political parties are now exerting a major influence on politics. Civil society played a leading role in framing the new constitution, and is among its main beneficiaries. In particular, new independent institutions established under the Constitution have demonstrated a willingness to protect public interest. EC actions against fraud in the senate elections, and the NCCC actions against former Deputy Prime Minister Sanan, are particularly noteworthy examples.

Some analysts draw a sharp distinction between traditional and people's politics, arguing that the two are incompatible. By this argument, all members of élite families, military and civilian bureaucrats and businessmen, have interests fundamentally in conflict with those at the bottom of society. Unless the latter take power traditional top down politics will remain entrenched. In practice, however, many from such traditional backgrounds have been at the forefront of change in recent years, as members of civil society organizations and manning new independent bodies such as the EC. Perhaps the best-known example is former Prime Minister Anand, who led the drafting of the 1997 Constitution and has been an outspoken supporter of democratic reform. In such ways members of the traditional elite and grassroots leaders of NGOs have for the most part worked co-operatively together.

Who Benefits

In the decade before the 1997 economic crisis Thai growth rates were by some estimates the highest in the world. Sino-Thai entrepreneurs, most associated with commercial banks, built hugely successful conglomerates. And provincial business élites cornered markets in their regions and proceeded to use new riches to establish a political base. The middle class burgeoned, many making easy money with the expansion of the financial market and a bubble property economy. One telling statistic is that by the mid-1990s Thailand, without any wine-drinking culture, suddenly became the twelfth largest market for top quality Bordeaux wines, exceeding even some traditional wine-drinking European countries. Wine had become "a status symbol, alongside Rolex watches and Hermes handbags".[23]

Some benefits did filter down, as the poverty rate dropped from 34 per cent to 11 per cent between 1986 and 1996. Indeed if the international standard of US$1 per person per day is used, poverty dropped below 1 per cent.[24] A wide range of social indicators improved, with impressive achievements in such areas as basic literacy, population control (growth rates falling from more than 3 per cent in the 1960s to around 1 per cent) and low-cost basic medical treatment.

But the benefits were far from evenly spread, with a neglected rural sector paying a high price for such growth. Some peasants had been displaced from land from the beginning of commercial rice production in the mid nineteenth century, but problems escalated from the 1970s as room for agricultural expansion came to an end and the forces of commercialisation and globalisation impinged every more intrusively. Indebtedness and conflicts over land titles soared. Rural workers lost control over traditional resources as the city intruded into the countryside. Developers and the state seized land occupied by traditional right to plant eucalyptus forests, build housing and industrial estates, golf courses, resorts, irrigation and hydro-electric dams. Residue from industrial waste and pesticides poisoned waterways. Compensation was generally inadequate, and sometimes non-existent. Rural education and health were rudimentary compared to those in the cities. And the mass of people forced off the land to the cities, particularly Bangkok, found employment in low paying manufacturing jobs or the service industry. Worst affected were hill tribes, a majority of whom lacked even the protection of citizenship, and a million foreign labourers. While poverty reduction to the mid 1980s occurred without an increase in inequality, thereafter the gap widened. A World Bank study for 1988–1992 showed a sharp jump in the Gini coefficient from 0.485 to 0.536, and later studies show at best marginal gains.[25]

Turbo-charged growth also had severe environmental consequences, particularly but not confined to the rural areas. Forest cover declined from over 50 per cent in the 1960s to 25 per cent in 1995. The Chatichai government declared an end to commercial logging in 1989, but that was easily circumvented or rapacious loggers transferred their attention to Burma.[26] Traditional fishing grounds were lost because of massive over-fishing. Bangkok achieved notoriety as one of the world's most polluted and congested cities.

One account of Thailand's economic boom summarises the overall benefits as follows: "For society's top ten per cent, incomes tripled, amenities increased, horizons expanded to embrace the globe... Further down the social scale, the income gains were modest. At the bottom, they were meagre... Livelihoods were threatened by land-grabbers, polluting industries, government development projects, damaged ecology".[27]

How was this affected by the economic crisis? The socio-economic impact of the crisis was severe, though not to the extent, or in ways, expected. Official unemployment figures vary widely, but an upper-range figure of almost 2 million at peak (almost 6 per cent) is about the same total figure recorded during the downturn in the mid 1980s, when the workforce was 20 per cent smaller than today. By 2000 it had decline to around 4.2 per cent. One study of those living in extreme poverty showed an increase from 11.4 million in 1996 to 12.9 in 1998, but a decline to 7.9 million two years later.[28] Half the workforce that remains in agriculture benefited from high international prices for rice and other rural commodities (particularly 1997–98). Government attempts to cushion the impact by job creation initiatives — with Japanese and World Bank funds — were haphazardly directed, but did provide relief.

A unique feature of this economic downturn was its severe impact on sections of the middle class. Tens of thousands lost jobs in the financial sector. New graduates found it difficult to obtain work. Stock market and property investments vanished. Small businesses went bankrupt. And private education became more expensive, particularly for those with children abroad. Middle class Thailand had never experienced such a decline in previous economic downturns. The impact on this group strengthened the momentum for political and economic reform.

Extent of Legitimacy

Recent political history has demonstrated very considerable support for the institutions of a constitutional monarchy. The King enjoys enormous popular support, and his presence has been an important stabilising factor. Support for the monarchy has also gone hand in hand with support for democracy. The masses who put their lives on the line in 1973 and 1992 did so in defence of open, democratic rule. And such values are continually reinforced by Thailand's strong civil society.

Paradoxically, public support for individual governments has been low. New governments seldom have a honeymoon as long as three months before facing major public criticism. Deep cynicism about governments is reflected in the low turnout at elections, particularly among the more educated in Bangkok. Governments established with votes from the majority of rural electorates have come under sustained pressure from civil society groups in Bangkok, through attacks in the media and demonstrations in the streets. This has either forced the government's resignation or built an atmosphere of crisis that facilitated military intervention. The post-crisis Democrat-led coalition is the first government not be forced from office in such a manner. Chuan returned as Prime Minister in an atmosphere of high expectation, and enjoyed a much longer honeymoon than usual. Public opinion polls tracked a gradual disillusionment from late in his first year, but the media never mobilised full-scale opposition to the government, nor did Bangkokians take to the streets.

There has, arguably, been a structural obstacle to achieving legitimacy in Thailand, in that elections have not, in a direct way, determined the composition of government. No single party has won an electoral majority, so governments have had to be formed through a process of horse-trading. The willingness of parties to change policies after elections to participate in government, and individual elected representatives to jump parties for the same purpose, has reinforced perceptions that the link between elections and government is a tenuous one. Weak, venal and self-interested coalitions have then brought governments into further disrepute.

Government legitimacy has also been brought into question by concern about aspects of governance during the boom years — the growth of corruption, money politics, environmental degradation, policies promoting greater inequalities, and the lack of democracy. Civil society groups articulated these issues increasingly from the 1980s. By the mid 1990s many saw the answer in constitutional reform, leading to the establishment of a partly elected 99-member Constitution Drafting Assembly in January 1997. The economic collapse starting in July that year — although not entirely due to domestic developments — strengthened the argument for reform. At the beginning of the year parliament seemed disinclined to support initiatives proposed by civil society. In September the draft sped though Parliament with a 578–16 vote, after parliamentarians realized it had massive popular support.

The Constitution, and related reforms, seek to address both the structural problems of weak coalition governments and related governance problems. Many want quick results. A rather loud chorus from within the country and outside has begun to question reform commitment, and argue that nothing much has changed. That, however, underestimates the extent of change implemented already (see Governance section below), and broad popular support for continuing in the current direction. The current Constitution enjoys much higher legitimacy than those before it did.

Governance

During the high growth decade preceding the economic crisis, Thailand was held up as a model developing country by the World Bank and others. Its record for devising and implementing economic plans was rated highly, even if much was attributed to allowing the private sector to take the lead. Economic benefits had trickled down, reducing the numbers in poverty, improving incomes, and improving a wide range of additional social indicators. Some remaining problem areas were acknowledged, including one of the poorest records in the region for secondary education (only 25 per cent graduating), and ineffective, sometimes venal, governments. The latter was, however, seen as at least partly ameliorated by competent technocrats given charge of key economic portfolios, and top bureaucrats in institutions such as the BOT.

Nonetheless, as noted above, by the mid 1990s many Thais were worried by negative costs associated with rapid development. The crash of 1997 made the need to reexamine development policies an urgent one. Some, together with the King, gave greater priority to agriculture, self-sufficiency and sustainable development. Others viewed it as a problem of governance, defined as commitment to the rule of law, transparency, participation, accountability and cost effectiveness. Regular seminars and workshops were held throughout the country on improving governance in both the government and corporate sectors. Among the staunchest supporters were former Prime Minister, Anand Panyarachun, and two prominent members of civil society, physician Dr Prawase Wasi and Thirayuth Boonmee, a leader of the 1973 uprising against a military government. (Thirayuth even popularised the term *dhammarath* — taken from *dhamma* [Buddhist teachings] and *rath* [nation] — to reflect governance in the Thai language.) The Thailand Development Research Institute (TDRI), an influential, independent economic think tank, was tasked by the government with developing the concept. Based on TDRI recommendations Cabinet adopted governance as a national agenda in May 1999, requiring all government agencies to establish a plan to improve their work according to the five principles, and file an annual report to Cabinet for passing to Parliament.

The concern for improved governance was also apparent in other initiatives to promote economic, social and political change. Initial efforts after the crash focused on an extensive reorganisation of the BOT and financial sector. These went hand in hand with a raft of bills dealing with issues such as greater corporate transparency, strengthening the Stock Exchange of Thailand, and Securities and Exchange Commission, enforcement of bankruptcy, competition policy, money laundering, consumer protection, alien business (expanding businesses open to foreigners), the land code (allowing foreigners some access to land), labour reform, privatisation, bureaucratic, legal and education reforms. Many were part of an 11-bill package agreed on between Thailand and the IMF.

As the concept of governance implies, economic and political reform were seen as intertwined. Breaking the stranglehold of a small number of banks, and bringing more transparency to the corporate sector, for instance, was necessary for limiting opaque political-business linkages and corruption, and hence advance political reform. And areas normally seen as political reform — including a new constitution and a Freedom of Information Act — were also implemented to give government credibility and thus facilitate its economic planning and implementation roles.

Thailand has made many advances towards improved governance since the economic crisis. There have been logjams from so much legislation introduced at once, and some reforms were deflected by opposition from vested interests, but much has been achieved. That was true even in such contested areas as corruption, which organisations such as Transparency International reported was perceived as worse than before the crisis. Seminars on corruption held in August and September 2000 placed corruption in the public eye, but importantly these were organised by the government, or by civil society groups with full government cooperation. For an August seminar, the Civil Service Commission commissioned four separate surveys by independent consultants. "Nothing similar has ever happened before", commented columnist Chang Noi.[29] However the clearest evidence for progress against corruption were the actions taken by the EC against fraudulent senate candidates, and the NCCC and Constitutional Court against former Deputy Prime Minister Sanan. A short time ago such action against rich and powerful figures was inconceivable. They demonstrated that the new constitution, and independent agencies established as a result, do indeed have teeth.

GRADUAL, CONTESTED REFORM

Thailand entered the twentieth century as an absolute monarchy, independent but greatly influenced by the Western colonialism that surrounded it. The modernising reforms of Kings in the Chakri dynasty, and global depression, ended this system. But the 'revolution' of 1932 was essentially a change from one oligarchy to another, with the military dominant in alliance with civilian bureaucratic allies. This new disposition remained through to 1973, apart from brief periods when civilians led (1944–1947) or had influence (1947–1951, 1955 and 1969–1971). Royal influence remained subdued, until Sarit promoted the young King Bhumiphol after 1957. Political scientists defined Thailand as military dominated or a 'bureaucratic polity', which meant much the same thing.

The student-led overthrow of a military government in 1973 introduced a new era, in which civil society and civilian politicians (largely representing business interests) came to play a more important role. The King's stature continued to grow, and he frequently intervened during critical moments, never failing to influence events in the direction he desired. For the most part, however, he remained in the background providing a stabilising presence above the fray of intense political conflict. The military gradually became less influential, but against expectations ousted the elected Chatichai government in 1991. Anek Laothamatas described the system in the 1970s and 1980s as "liberal corporatism". While the military remained dominant in its own realm, economic decisions were taken by government agencies (ministers and officials) acting autonomously but in close cooperation with business interests. The government did not have the autonomy of the 'East Asia' model (Japan, South Korea, Taiwan and Singapore), but it was more than a 'soft' state.[30] Under this system growth rates took off in the late 1980s.

Liberal corporatism arguably worked best during the rule of Prime Minister Prem Tinsulanonda, and the short interlude of Anand Panyarachun. They kept corruption in check by appointing reputable non-political technocrats to key economic portfolios. At other times the model ran into problems as successive governments were tainted by corruption scandals, particularly administrations under the influence of provincial business elites.

In 1992 the military made a desperate attempt to reassert dominance, engineering the parliamentary election of General Suchinda as Prime Minister, but was thwarted by a mass public uprising. Thereafter the military continued to play a role, but only behind the scenes. Politics now focused on what Anek acknowledged to be the two main weaknesses of the liberal corporatist model, the exclusion of the public from policy making, and failure to consider socially relevant issues including environmental degradation and income inequality — and, it should be added, corruption. A growing civil society marshaled pressure in these areas at a time when revolving door governments seemed increasingly incapable of addressing them. Momentum for change built to the extent that by January 1997 a Constitution Drafting Assembly had been convened to undertake a major constitutional redraft. This process was given increased urgency by the economic collapse in July.

The subsequent 1997 Constitution, and related legislation, has made Thailand a much more open and democratic society. Economic and political reforms have weakened the hold of money politics, and the maintenance of self-serving links between business and politics. New laws, and independent institutions such as the EC, NCCC and Constitution Court have demonstrated they can defend democracy against powerful traditional interests. Civil society has been strengthened. The military has receded from the political limelight.

Further proof of change can be found in shifting public attitudes towards individuals and events that conservative groups frowned on in the past. The August 1999 funeral of former top bureaucrat and democratic activist Dr Puey Ungphakorn — twice forced to flee the country because of his opposition to military dictatorship — evoked a mass outpouring of emotion. On 14 October that year officials and members of the public attended a groundbreaking ceremony for the construction of a long-delayed memorial to those killed in the 1973 democratic uprising. The circumstances of military killings during Black May in 1992 are increasingly discussed; in June 2000 the military released a highly classified 600-page report on Black May, yielding to public pressure after issuing a heavily censored version a month earlier. And the 11 May 2000 birth centennial of early democrat Pridi Phanomyong — never before officially recognized — was marked by weeklong activities.

A reversion to old practices cannot be entirely ruled out. Traditional groups remain strong, and global economic forces highly volatile. But the many new laws and institutions adopted in recent years could not be easily dismantled, and an ever-strengthening civil society will resist backtracking.

Notes

1   *The Nation*, 14 August 1999.
2   Prudhisan Jumbala, *Nation Building and Democratization in Thailand: A Political History* (Bangkok: Chulalongkorn University, Social Research Institute, 1992), pp. 7–8.
3   J.A.N. Mulder, "Origin, Development, and Use of the Concept of 'Loose Structure' in the Literature about Thailand: An Evaluation", in *Loosely Structured Social Systems: Thailand in Comparative Perspective*, ed. H.D.

Evers (New Haven: Yale University Cultural Report Series No. 17, 1969), p. 19.

4 J.F. Embree, "Thailand — A Loosely Structured Social System", *American Anthropologist*, 52 (April 1950).

5 Available on web site <http://www.krisdika.go.th/law/text/lawpub/e11102540/text.htm>

6 For details, see Suvicha Pouaree, "Power to the people", *Bangkok Post*, 3 September 2000.

7 Thak Chaloemtiarana, *Thailand: The Politics of Despotic Paternalism* (Bangkok: Social Science Association of Thailand, 1979), pp. 309–34.

8 See Kobkua Suwannathat-Pian, "The Post-1972 Constitutions: Preliminary Analysis of Constitutional Monarchy a la Thailand". Paper presented to the Seventh International Conference on Thai studies, Amsterdam, 4–8 July 1999.

9 Sutichai Yoon, "Thai Talk: Cabinet ministers are yawn to rule", *The Nation*, 21 May 1999.

10 *The Nation*, 29 March, 2000.

11 John Halligan and Mark Turner, *Profiles of Government Administration in Asia* (Canberra: Commonwealth of Australia, 1995), pp. 166–67, and *The Nation*, 25 January 1999. The latter also gives a figure of 3,598,107, including "volunteers" and part-time local headmen.

12 F. W. Riggs, *Thailand: The Modernisation of a Bureaucratic Polity* (Honolulu: East-West Center Press, 1966).

13 Likhit Dhiravegin, *The Bureaucratic Elite of Thailand* (Bangkok: Thai Khadi Research Institute, Thammasat University, 1978), pp. 199 and 203.

14 Vitit Muntarbhorn, *Mass Media Laws and Regulations in Thailand* (Singapore: Asian Media Information & Communication Centre, 1998), pp. 10 and 45.

15 John Halligan and Mark Turner, *Profiles of Government Administration in Asia*, p. 172.

16 On earlier periods see David Morell, "Power and Parliament in Thailand: The Futile Challenge", Ph.D. thesis, Princeton University, 1974 and David Morell and Chai-anan Samadavanija, *Political Conflict in Thailand* (Cambridge, Massachusetts: Oelgeschlager, Gunn & Hain, 1981), pp. 121–23.

17 John Funston, "Political Reform in Thailand: Real or Imagined?" *Asian Journal of Political Science* 8, no. 2 (December 2000): 89–108.

18 See, for instance, chapters by Benedict R. Anderson, Suchit Bunbongkarn and Anek Laothamatas in *The Politics of Elections in Southeast Asia,* edited by R. H. Taylor (New York: Woodrow Wilson Center Press, 1996).

19 Pasuk Phongpaichit and Chris Baker, *Thailand's Boom and Bust* (Chiang Mai: Silkworm Books, 1998), pp. 300–305.

20 See Duncan McCargo, "Thailand's Political Parties: Real, authentic and actual", in *Political Change in Thailand. Democracy and Participation,* edited by Kevin Hewison (London: Routledge, 1997).

21 See Scot Barme, *Luang Wichit Wathakan and the Creation of a Thai Identity* (Singapore: ISEAS 1993).

22 John Funston, "Political Reform in Thailand: Real or Imagined?" See also, "Commentary" by Kanjana Spindler, *Bangkok Post*, 8 November 2000.

23 Stan Sesser, "How Thailand Kicked the Habit", *Asian Wall Street Journal*, 20–21 August 1999, p. P6.

24 World Bank, *Everyone's Miracle*. (Washington, D.C.: World Bank, 1997).

25 World Bank, *Poverty Reduction and the World Bank; Progress in Fiscal 1996 and 1997* (Washington, D.C.: World Bank, 1998), Annex A, p. 113. The figures cited for the Gini coefficient here are higher than most others, including World Bank statistics cited elsewhere in this chapter, but the trend is acknowledged by all writing on this topic. National Economic and Social Development Board statistics show the index declining from 49.9 in 1992 to 47.7 in 1996, then rising again to 48.1 in 1998.

26 Charnvit Kasetsiri, "Siam/Thailand — Burma/Myanmar: An Odd couple on Deforestation". Draft for discussion, ISEAS, Singapore, May 1998.

27 Pasuk Phongpaichit and Chris Baker, *Thailand's Boom and Bust*, p. 309.

28 Findings of economist Methi Krongkaew, reported in *The Nation*, 20 May 2000.

29 Chang Noi, "Corruption: codes of dishonour", *The Nation*, 4 September 2000.

30 Anek Laothamatas, *Business Associations and the New Political Economy of Thailand: From Bureaucratic Polity to Liberal Corporatism* (Boulder: Westview Press, 1992), especially pp. 153–71. See also Pasuk Phongpaichit and Chris Baker, *Thailand's Boom and Bust*.

Further Reading

Chaloemtiarana, Thak. *Thailand. The Politics of Despotic Paternalism*. Bangkok: Social Science Association of Thailand, 1979.

Girling, John L. S. *Thailand. Society and Politics*. Ithaca & London: Cornell University Press, 1981.

Hewison, Kevin, ed. *Political Change in Thailand. Democracy and Participation*. London: Routledge, 1997.

Jumbala, Prudhisan. *Nation-building and Democratization in Thailand: A Political History*. Bangkok: Chulalongkorn University, Social Research Institute, 1992.

Laothamatas, Anek. *Business Associations and the New Political Economy of Thailand. From Bureaucratic Polity to Liberal Corporatism*. Boulder: Westview Press, 1992.

McCargo, Duncan. *Chamlong Srimuang and the New Thai Politics*. London: Hurst, 1997.

Morell, David and Chai-anan Samadavanija, *Political Conflict in Thailand*. Cambridge, Massachusetts: Oelgeschlager, Gunn & Hain, 1981.

Muntarbhorn, Vitit. *Mass Media Laws and Regulations in Thailand.* Singapore: Asian Media Information & Communication Centre, 1998.

Phongpaichit, Pasuk and Chris Baker. *Thailand's Boom and Bust.* Chiang Mai: Silkworm Books, 1998.

————. *Thailand's Crisis.* Chiang Mai: Silkworm Books, 2000.

Riggs, F.W. *Thailand: The Modernisation of a Bureaucratic Polity.* Honolulu: East-West Center Press, 1966.

Wilson, David A. *Politics in Thailand.* Ithaca: Cornell University Press, 1962.

Xuto, Somsakdi, ed. *Government and Politics of Thailand.* Singapore: Oxford University Press, 1987.

10

VIETNAM
Doi Moi Difficulties

Thaveeporn Vasavakul

INTRODUCTION

As the region's first communist state, Vietnam has followed a different political trajectory from Southeast Asian neighbours. That path has been complicated by almost five decades of warfare, on its own territory until 1975 (and again briefly in 1979) then in Cambodia from the end of 1978. A glorious victory over the might of United States-led forces, then an ambiguous stalemate in Cambodia, has been followed by several setbacks in efforts to "win the peace" since the late 1980s.

Ho Chi Minh declared Vietnam's independence in September 1945, but failed to receive recognition from the international community. War between Ho's Democratic Republic of Vietnam (DRV) and France followed, and lasted until the French defeat at the battle of Dien Bien Phu in 1954. The subsequent Geneva Conference temporarily divided Vietnam into two military regroupment zones at the seventeenth parallel and endorsed a reunification of the two Vietnams through a general election in 1956. However, the United States, motivated by Cold War fears of communism, moved to support a separate southern state under the leadership of Ngo Dinh Diem. That maintained Vietnam's partition until the fall of Saigon in 1975. The DRV followed a socialist model of development, and after reunification this model was imposed on the newly-liberated South. The economic crisis that followed forced the leadership to implement reform measures which culminated in the official endorsement of the policy of *doi moi* (renewal) at the Sixth National Party Congress of the Vietnamese Communist Party (VCP) in 1986.

FIGURE 10.1

Vietnam: Key Political Dates

700BC	Early beginnings of Viet dynasties (northern Vietnam).
111BC	Chinese control, until 931/939 AD.
1010	Ly Dynasty.
1225	Tran Dynasty.
1407	Chinese occupation.
1427	Le Dynasty, until 1788 (Mac usurpers 1527–92).
1778	Tay Son Dynasty.
1802	Nguyen Dynasty. Unified South with North, and survived until 1945.
1859	Beginning of French advance, completed 1884.
1930	Yen Bai uprisings, followed by French destruction of the Vietnam Nationalist Party. Indochinese Communist Party founded by Nguyen Ai Quoc, later known as Ho Chi Minh.
1945	August revolution, following World War II. Declaration of independence in September. "Dissolution" of Communist Party.
1946	First national elections. Ho Chi Minh becomes President. Promulgation of first Constitution. Beginning of war with France.
1951	Revival of the communist party at Second Party Congress, under the name Vietnam Lao Dong Party.
1954	Dien Bien Phu victory and the Geneva Conference. Vietnam partitioned at 17th parallel, supposedly to prepare for elections and reunification. Beginning of American direct involvement in Vietnam.
1959	New socialist Constitution.
1960	Third Party Congress endorses the First Five-Year Plan (1961–65) and imposition of central planning.
1969	Death of Ho Chi Minh. Ton Duc Thang becomes President.
1973	Paris Peace Treaty, and U.S. withdrawal from Vietnam.
1975	Communist Democratic Republic of Vietnam defeats U.S.-allied Republic of Vietnam.
1976	Reunification of country as Socialist Republic of Vietnam. Party renamed Vietnamese Communist Party.
1979	Vietnam's occupation of Cambodia, war with China, and conflict with ASEAN.
1980	New socialist Constitution for entire country.
1986	Promulgation of *doi moi* at the Sixth Party Congress.
1989	Vietnamese troops withdrawn from Cambodia. Collapse of the Soviet bloc sparks debate over policy options.
1991	Policy of Vietnam befriending all, adopted at Seventh Party Congress. Normalization of relations with China. Cambodian settlement at Paris Conference.
1992	Promulgation of more liberal Constitution.
1994	Normalization of relations with the United States.
1995	Membership of ASEAN.
1997	Major rural unrest in Thai Binh and other provinces.
2001	Ninth Party Congress. The Central Committee of the CPV elects moderate Nong Duc Manh, Speaker of the National Assembly for the preceding nine years, as party General Secretary. Unrest in the Central Highlands.

Historic-Geographic Setting

Vietnam's land area of over 331,000 square kilometres makes it the fourth largest country in Southeast Asia, and it ties with the Philippines as the second largest in terms of population. The S-shape of Vietnam's continental territory is largely a product of the Viet's march to the south over the centuries. Originally, the Viet were concentrated in the northern part of the country. The eighteenth parallel, the area known as Transversal Pass *(Deo Ngang)*, was the traditional demarcation line between the Kingdom of Dai Viet and the Champa empire. After the Viet gained independence from China in the tenth century, they began to move southward, in the process taking over areas under the control of the kingdoms of the Champa and Cambodia. This left Vietnam sharing long boundaries with China (1,150 kms), Laos (1650 kms) and Cambodia (930 kms).

Vietnam consists of three distinct topographical characteristics: mountains, plains and sea. Hills and mountains form three quarters of Vietnam's land area. Vietnam has three plains systems, lying along the meridian and in a north-west-southeasterly direction. Each plain borders mountains or hills to the west and the sea to the east. The plains of Nam Bo, the largest, cover an area of 61,000 square kilometres and are part of the Mekong-Dong Nai river system. The second largest plains area is in northern Vietnam around the Red River delta and covers 16,000 square kilometres. The third is the coastal central plains, totaling around 14,000 square kilometres and consisting of the flat areas from Thanh Hoa to Thuan Hai provinces (a distance of 1000 kilometres), but these are cut by mountain formations running from the Truong Son range to the sea.

This setting has crucial implications for the structure of Vietnam's political system and its operation. The process of the march to the south that took place over centuries incorporated areas of economic, geographical, historical, and cultural diversity into Vietnam. The long borders raised questions related to cross-border economic exchange as well as national defence. The existence of an extensive mountainous region is a factor in defining ethnic, administrative, and development policies. Geographical as well as historical differences in the plains areas have fostered the sense of regionalism that the one-party state has to take into account in its administrative and economic planning.

Ethnic Make-up and Government-Minority Relations

Vietnam is currently listed as comprising 54 ethnic groups. In the 1990s, the Viet, also known as the Kinh, made up 87 per cent of the population.

The ten largest ethnic groups, according to a 1994 survey, are the Tay (1,190,000), Thai (1,040,000), Muong (914,000), Chinese (Hoa) (900,000), Khmer (895,000), Nung (705,000), Hmong (558,000), Dzao (474,000), Gia-rai (242,000), and E-de (195,000).[1] The minorities live mainly in the mountainous areas, occupying around two-thirds of the territory, while the Viet have settled in the plain areas along the coast.

Minorities played an important political role during the revolutionary period. Those in the northern provinces assisted the League for Vietnam's Independence (Viet Minh), a united front organization set up by Ho Chi Minh during the Japanese Occupation (1940–45), and the war of resistance with France (1946–54). Prior to 1945, the Viet Minh built its first resistance base in the North Eastern mountainous areas inhabited by the Nung. After war with France broke out in 1946 the Ho Chi Minh government moved its political headquarters to minority-inhabited areas north of Hanoi. In 1954, it waged a decisive battle at Dien Bien Phu, a Thai-inhabited area of the North West. The importance of these ethnic groups can be seen through the DRV's policies. At the end of the war in 1954, the DRV established autonomous zones for Thai and Hmong ethnic groups in the North West and another zone for the Tay and Nung in the North East of the Northern region. In these autonomous zones, minority leaders were allowed to handle their own affairs, including appointing local civil servants and raising a militia force.

Minorities in the Central Highlands and the Truong Son Mountain Range also played an important role during the American War period. After Vietnam was partitioned in two, the Central Highlands and the Truong Son Range became a contentious area owing to their strategic importance. During the regroupment period, thousands of Southern mountainous groups went to the North for training before returning in the late 1950s. By the early 1960s, the North succeeded in setting up regiments in the Central Highlands that were joined by minorities from the Hre, Gia-rai, Rhade, and Ba-na ethnic groups. A communist document captured by American advisers in 1963 indicated the communists' respect for local customs.[2]

The relationship between the Viet and the minorities turned sour for a brief period after 1975. Following liberation of Saigon, the autonomous zones in Northern Vietnam were abolished. Between 1975 and 1979, the Socialist Republic of Vietnam moved to impose the socialist model of development over the entire country. This involved the nationalization of free enterprises in the South including those owned by the Chinese, precipitating the exodus of Chinese entrepreneurs, technicians, and skilled workers, all of whom had played an important role in the economy. Some problems also erupted between the central government and the Central Highlanders. Between 1976 and 1981, several sources mentioned tribal-based resistance to communist rule in the highlands from the United Front for the Struggle of the Oppressed Races (FULRO). This short, difficult period eased from 1979, when the Sino-Vietnamese war broke out, with minorities in the Northern mountainous areas mobilized to fight the foreign invasion. The FULRO resistance reportedly faded in the 1990s.

Economy

The socialist economic system developed in the DRV (1945–76) consisted of three main components: public ownership (state and collective), central planning, and the rationing system. Change in the ownership system began in the agricultural sector when the Party leadership launched campaigns for rent and interest reductions and land reform between 1953 and 1956.[3] In 1958, the leadership moved to collectivize agriculture, setting up production co-operatives in which land and capital belonged to the collective. At the beginning, the size of the co-operative was small, consisting of a few hamlets with several hundred people. Later, it was expanded to cover one or more villages with several thousand people. Villagers were only allowed to keep 5 per cent of the land as private. The government invested in agricultural infrastructure such as irrigation and agricultural machinery, and supplied fertilizer and agricultural instruments to producers at below market prices. In return, the co-operative would deliver agricultural taxes and sell a certain amount of produce to the state at below market prices. Co-operative members were paid according to the amount of time spent on each task. The party leadership hoped that these arrangements would help increase production capacity and allow the state to extract surpluses from the agricultural sector to help expedite industrial undertakings. Also, after 1954, private industries in urban centres were nationalized and organized as state-private joint venture enterprises.[4]

The introduction of central planning began in 1960 when the Third Party Congress of the Communist Party endorsed the First Five-Year plan. The State Planning Commission and the State Prices Commission determined what was to be produced, how to produce it, who would produce it, how much material would be used, how much it would cost, and where it would be sold. A system of rationing was also introduced as a means for distribution of goods.[5]

This socialist model of economic development generated several problems. The first was the development policy itself, that overemphasized heavy industry. In most socialist countries, socialism is identified with industrial development, especially heavy industries such as steel or machinery manufacture to produce the equipment used to produce other goods. By implication, this is an economic system that does not emphasize consumption and consumer goods. The second was the distortion that the pricing system introduced into buying and selling, which had a major impact on producers' incentives. The third was the distortion of the role of the state in becoming overly involved in economic management. The fourth was a phenomenon of chronic shortages resulting from the lack of production supplies that was often associated with central planning. In the agricultural sector where the majority of the population worked, for example, there were three main problems. One was that prices paid to the co-operatives for their produce were in general very low, because of the belief that the government needed to extract agricultural surpluses to finance industrialization. Another problem was the residual character of remuneration given to the co-operative members. Before the final distribution to the peasants, a portion of the output would be sold to the state at below market prices, another would be delivered to the state as agricultural taxes, and yet another would be retained for the co-operative's general fund. This meant that the remainder for distribution among co-operative members was very small; and their incomes did not rise and may even have fallen below subsistence levels. This dampened the incentives for co-operative producers to continue their economic exchange with the state. Since they would not get much from the government anyway, they looked for opportunities to produce for their own consumption.[6]

After reunification in 1975, the system developed in North Vietnam was imposed on the newly-liberated south. By the end of the 1980s, economic crisis developed, leading to famine and food riots and a subsequent disregard for central instructions (known colloquially as fence breaking — *pha rao*).

The process of economic reform took place in two stages, the first from 1979 to 1985 and the second from 1986. During the first phase, the leadership adopted policies within the central planning framework. The Sixth Plenum of the Communist Party's Central Committee in August 1979 endorsed a multi-sector economy consisting of five elements: the state, collective, joint state-private, private, and individual sectors. It also endorsed the use of material incentives. Four major reform policies followed. In 1980, the leadership began to reform the old foreign trade system, moving more towards capitalist countries including Japan, Hong Kong, Singapore, and Taiwan. In 1981, it introduced an end-product system (*khoan san pham*) allowing households to contract directly with the co-operative to work on some of the tasks previously performed

FIGURE 10.2

Vietnam: Key Statistics

Land area:	331,689 sq kilometres
Population:[a]	77,311,000 (2000)

GNP:[b]   Current exchange rate   — US$24 bn (1997);
                                         US$26.5 bn (1998)
            Purchasing Power Parity — US$122 bn (1997);
                                         US$129 bn (1998)

GNP Per Capita:[b]   Current exchange rate   — US$310 (1997);
                                                 US$350 (1998)
                    Purchasing Power Parity — US$1,590 (1997);
                                                 US$1,689 (198)

Income Distribution (1998):[b]
            Gini Index   36.1
            % share of income or consumption:
            Lowest 10%   3.6
            Lowest 20%   8.0
            2nd 20%   11.4
            3rd 20%   15.2
            4th 20%   20.9
            Highest 20%   44.5
            Highest 10%   29.9

Human Development Index (HDI) Ranking:[c]
            World ranking   110 (1997); 108 (1998)
            Value   0.664 (1997); 0.671 (1998)
            Gini Index   41.4

Armed Forces:

            Total no.[d]   484,000
            Expenditure[d]   US$891 m
            % of GNP[b]   2.6% (1995)
            Gini Index   41.4

Sources: [a] Official national sources.
         [b] World Bank, *World Development Indicators* (Washington, D.C., 1999 & 2000).
         [c] United Nations Development Programme (UNDP), *Human Development Report* (New York: Oxford University Press, 1999 & 2000).
         [d] International Institute for Strategic Studies (IISS), *The Military Balance, 1999–2000* (London: Oxford University Press, 1999).

collectively. Land was contracted to the household for three years. This was the first sign of the party moving away from the co-operative and towards the individual household. Also in 1981, the leadership allowed state-owned enterprises (SOEs) to act independently, finding their own materials and selling what they wanted after they had fulfilled their plans. The fourth reform, focusing on pricing, was promulgated in October 1981, but was blocked by SOEs and southern provinces because they believed it meant they would have to pay more for supplies and labour. Of the four measures, the end-product system was the most successful and led to an increase in agricultural production.[7]

The second phase of economic reform began in 1986 at the Communist Party's Sixth Congress, with the introduction of *doi moi*. While previous congresses had emphasized heavy industry, the Sixth emphasized the development of foodstuffs, consumer goods, and export goods. The Congress also agreed to abolish central planning, relying instead on "socialist business accounting", which was another name for a market economy. In 1987, a foreign investment law was promulgated. In the same year, SOEs were instructed to follow business accounting principles. In 1988, the leadership granted decision-making power to households. Land tenure was extended from 15 to 19 years. The government relied on bargaining to determine state prices for food procurement. These were signs of decollectivization. From this time on, the co-operative disintegrated. In 1989, a two-price system was abolished in favour of market alone. Administrative prices were only maintained for the post-office, railway services, and telephone calls. In the 1990s, policy focused on the development of market factors (including land, labour, and capital). In 1993, the Land Law was promulgated, allowing the transfer of land-use rights. In 1994, a labour law was promulgated. By the mid-1990s, reform of the banking system was being discussed.

Doi moi brought with it economic success. In 1989, Vietnam exported rice for the first time since 1945. Between 1992 and 1998 the average annual GDP growth rate in Vietnam was 8.4 per cent — agricultural 4.5 per cent and industry by 13 per cent.[8]

THE POLITICAL SYSTEM

Vietnam has adopted a unitary, communist, one-party system. It has, however, permitted greater pluralism since the beginning of *doi moi* in 1986.

Vietnam has had four constitutions since 1946.[9] Each emerged in a specific political context and thus emphasized different features of the political system. The 1946 Constitution (7 chapters and 70 clauses), passed following Ho Chi Minh's declaration of independence in September 1945 and the first national elections in January 1946, was heavily influenced by that of France. The 1959 Constitution was written after Vietnam was partitioned in two, when the DRV was fully in the socialist orbit and the leadership had decided to follow a socialist path of development. With 10 chapters and 112 clauses, it was the first to reflect principles drawn from socialism. The 1980 Constitution was passed after Vietnam was reunified in 1975 and when the leadership was determined to develop the socialist economic model in the entire country. This constitution (12 chapters and 147 clauses) focused mainly on the development of socialism and emphasized the role of the state in economic, political, and social affairs. The 1992 Constitution first appeared as an amendment of the 1980 version, but later was adopted as a new constitution. It was drafted after the Vietnamese leadership had endorsed the policy of *doi moi* (renewal) in 1986. Although it retained the same structure of the 1980 Constitution (12 chapters, 147 clauses), it marked a major shift in political philosophy.

The 1992 Constitution differed from its predecessors in four main aspects. First, the constitution states that the Vietnamese Communist Party (VCP) is *one* of the leading forces, not *the* leading force. This implies power sharing, at least in theory, among different political institutions in the era of *doi moi*. It grants more power to the President, the National Assembly Standing Committee, and the Prime Minister than allowed in the 1980 constitution. Secondly, it broadens the class character of the regime, stating that it is based on alliances among workers, peasants and intellectuals. The incorporation of intellectuals reflects a major shift in the political philosophy given that the social group had never received official recognition in the past; both the 1959 and 1980 constitutions had mainly mentioned workers and peasants. Thirdly, while it continues to define human rights and citizenship rights broadly, including social, political, and economic aspects, it strengthens several of these rights. It emphasizes equal rights between men and women, contains a clause asking for the future promulgation of laws on human rights and, for the first time, pays attention to the procedural aspects of arrest and detention and proclaims the principle of innocence unless legally judged guilty by the court. Fourthly, the constitution departs from the 1959 and 1980 constitutions in that it has revived and recognizes additional rights to private property and economic activities, while downplaying previously recognized state provision for health care and education.

Below the national government Vietnam is divided into three administrative levels, province, district, and commune. There are currently 4 municipalities under direct control of the central government — Hanoi,

Ho Chi Minh City, Hai Phong and Da Nang — and 57 provinces. At each level, there are People's Councils whose members are elected in local elections organized every five years. The 1992 constitution, following practices adopted earlier, indicates that Councils are representative agencies of the local people, entitled to form People's Committees to oversee day-to-day work, organize activities in the local areas, determine the budget, and rescind illegal decisions of lower-level people's councils and committees. However, people's councils resolutions are based on laws from above and have to fulfil the tasks assigned to the locality by the upper levels. A 1994 revised law on local government stipulates that People's Committees are representatives of the central government.

Only the National Assembly is granted the authority to amend the constitution, with at least two-thirds of the deputies required to present the amendment motion.

Head of State

Between 1945 and 1969, the Presidency played a prominent role on the Vietnamese political stage. The 1946 constitution endorsed a political system which gave enormous power to the President, Ho Chi Minh himself, in ways somewhat similar to the French presidential system. The President, elected by parliament (the People's Parliament), was both head of state and the government. He chose the Prime Minister from parliament, though parliament then had to endorse this. The new Prime Minister then nominated his Ministers, all of whom had to be from parliament, and required parliamentary endorsement. The President, however, could nominate non-parliamentary members to become Under-Secretaries (Deputy Ministers). In addition to appointing the Prime Minister and signing decrees appointing members of the Cabinet, the President commanded the armed forces, appointed or dismissed commanders of the land army, navy, and air force, presided over the Government's Council, and promulgated all laws passed by parliament.

The 1959 Constitution provided the Presidency with even more power. While the parliament (National Assembly) still elected the President, he was not required to be an Assembly deputy. In implementing decisions of the Assembly and its Standing Committee, the President promulgated laws and decrees and appointed or removed Prime Ministers, Vice-Prime Ministers and members of the Council of Ministers. He could proclaim a state of war, order general or partial mobilization, and declare martial law. The President of the DRV was the Supreme Commander of the armed forces and President of the National Defense Council, with power to

---

FIGURE 10.3

Vietnam: Cabinet and Ministerial-Level Agencies

Prime Minister
Deputy Prime Ministers (four)

Ministries and Ministerial-Level Agencies
Agriculture and Rural Development
Construction
Culture and Information
Defence
Education and Training
Finance
Foreign Affairs
Health
Industry
Public Security
Justice
Labour, War Invalids, and Social Welfare
Fisheries
Planning and Investment
Science, Technology and Environment
Trade
Transport and Telecommunication
Ethnic Minorities and Mountain Regions Commission
Government Commission for Organization and Personnel
State Inspectorate
Government Office
Sport and Youth Commission
State Bank
Planning Committee

---

appoint or remove the Vice-President and members of the National Defense Council. If necessary, he had the power to attend and preside over the meetings of the Council of Ministers, as well as Special Political Conferences. These conferences comprised the President and Vice-President of the DRV, the Chairman of the Standing Committee of the National Assembly, the Prime Minister, and other relevant persons. The Presidency was linked directly to the National Assembly, whose jurisdiction was larger than that of the Soviet and Chinese National Assemblies. It was, according to the 1959 constitution, responsible for legislation; election or removal of the Council of State, National Defense Council, Nationalities Commission, and Council of Ministers; and appointment of such officers as Procurator-General of the Supreme People's Control Commission and Chief Justice of the Supreme Court. The Presidency thus held the reins of power shared by the various branches of state and party institutions.

After Ho's death in 1969, the then Vice-President, Ton Duc Thang, a veteran party member from southern Vietnam, became President and remained in the position until his death in 1980. Because of his southern affiliations, he represented constituencies from south of the seventeenth parallel. However, his Presidential role was mainly symbolic. Since Thang was neither a full nor alternate member of the party's influential Politburo, power was broadly distributed among Politburo members.

The 1980 constitution abolished the old office of the Presidency found in the 1946 and 1959 constitutions, replacing the Presidency with a new body called the Council of State (*Hoi Dong Nha Nuoc*, or COS). This was a political body consisting of a President, Vice-President, Secretary, and members. The President of the COS was concurrently Commander of the Armed Forces, and chairman of the top security body, the National Defense Council. All COS members worked collectively as the Standing Committee of the National Assembly, and as representatives of Vietnam in both domestic and international affairs. Because of the latter function, the COS was called a collective presidency.

The COS served as the National Assembly Standing Committee, getting deputies to meet or making suggestions on the passage of particular laws. It then supervised the implementation of laws, making sure that laws passed by the National Assembly were implemented by the Council of Ministers (cabinet).

Ton Duc Thang was President of the COS until his death in March 1980, when the former chairman of the southern National Liberation Front, Nguyen Huu Tho who was one of the Vice-Presidents became President. In June 1981, veteran party leader Truong Chinh was elected to the post.

The 1992 constitution split the position of the Council of State into that of the President and the National Assembly Standing Committee. The President is the head of state and represents the SRV internally and externally. He is elected by the National Assembly from among its members, for a term of office that follows the Assembly. The constitution does not mention any limit on the number of re-elections, and the implication seems to be that if a former President is re-elected another term as a National Assembly deputy he has a chance to be re-elected as President a second time. This, however, has not yet happened. As listed in the constitution, the President's responsibilities are numerous: to promulgate laws and decree-laws; to command the armed forces and chair the National Defense Council; to propose to the National Assembly to elect, release from duty or remove from office, the Vice-President, the Prime Minister, the President of the Supreme Peoples' Court, the Head of the Supreme People's Office of Supervision and Control and their deputies; and to grant amnesties.

In theory, then, the powers of the President are considerable, though much of the time he would be acting on advice from the party or, sometimes, other institutions such as the National Assembly. Seven people have held this office: Ho Chi Minh (1945–69), Ton Duc Thang (1969–80), Nguyen Huu Tho (1980–81), Truong Chinh (1981–87), Vo Chi Cong (1987–92), Le Duc Anh (1992–97), and Tran Duc Luong (1997–2002). However, the extent of power wielded by the office depends on the office holder. Ho Chi Minh was the most powerful President. Among those serving as Ho Chi Minh's successors, Truong Chinh and and Le Duc Anh were influential figures. Truong Chinh was the General Secretary of the Vietnam Worker's Party in the 1950s and the second person in the Politiburo from the 1960s to the 1980s. Le Duc Anh was a military officer and senior party official who commanded Vietnam's operations in Cambodia in the 1980s. Both were in a position to exercise power through the Presidential office. Ton Duc Thang, Nguyen Huu Tho, Vo Chi Cong, and Tran Duc Luong were less influential. They represented certain political, social, and regional constituencies. Thang was a veteran revolutionary active among workers in southern Vietnam during the French period. Nguyen Huu Tho was the chairman of the National Liberation Front for South Vietnam that was active prior to 1975. Vo Chi Cong was a key party veteran in charge of military affairs in Zone V in central Vietnam during the American War period. Tran Duc Luong, the current office holder, is a geologist from Central Vietnam and represents the intellectual circle. These Presidents had a more symbolic role, and gave greater emphasis to the position's ceremonial aspects.

The President is assisted by one or more Vice Presidents, also elected by the National Assembly. The office does not appear to be independently influential, but one of the holders would replace the President should the encumbent die in office.

The Executive

Prior to the period of *doi moi*, executive power rested firmly with Ho Chi Minh until his death in 1969 and with top Political Bureau members after that. Since *doi moi* efforts have been made to increase the role of ministers, and the government bureaucracy, largely as a result of the need to develop strong institutions to help promote economic development.

The 1992 constitution granted the Prime Minister a major role in cabinet, with the power to appoint ministers and restructure government agencies. The constitutions also allows the Prime Minister to dismiss the chairmen and deputy chairmen of the People's Committees of the provinces and the municipalities (generally controlled by the party machine), although he cannot appoint them. In the early 1990s, during the second term of Vo Van Kiet (1992–97), the Prime Minister's economic power base was strengthened in other ways. He was granted powers to deal with smuggling, a major activity involving middle-ranking government agencies as well as the non-government sector that was believed to deprive the central government of lawful tax revenue. The Prime Minister also came to control the state oil company (PetroVietnam) and the Tourism Department. He was able to force through the north-south power line in the face of provincial opposition, and the State Treasury was able to win over the provinces on tax matters. Finally, the shake-up of foreign investment approvals procedures in January 1995 also indicated the rise of ministerial power. However, the Prime Minister was not always successful. His move to impose a stricter ban on timber exports was dropped in face of resistance from military and provincial interests.

Prior to *doi moi*, the government bureaucracy was dominated by the party since party members either controlled or assumed governmental positions. Under *doi moi* major reforms of government administration were carried out during the term of Prime Minister Vo Van Kiet. Government ministries now have increased power and are accountable to the Prime Minister rather to party leaders. In January 1995, the Eighth Plenum of the Central Committee officially endorsed public administration reform, focusing on restructuring organization of the government bureaucracy, simplifying administrative procedures, and rebuilding the civil service. Rule by law has become a major mechanism governing the operation of the state and state-society relations.

Bureaucratic reform involved first and foremost separation of economic and administrative functions of state institutions. Under central planning, government agencies at all levels had been entitled to own production enterprises of various sizes. Generally translated as "line ministries", these government agencies provided economic and administrative direction to SOEs and served as their advocates where SOEs came into conflict with specialized agencies such as the Ministries of Finance and Labor. To separate state-owned enterprises from their line ministries, the Prime Minister set up experimental economic conglomerates in March 1994 which became models for sixteen newly-merged large economic conglomerates in 1995. The General Director of each conglomerate's management board was appointed by the Prime Minister, and their funding was distributed by the General Department for the Management of State Investment Capital, attached to the Ministry of Finance.

Another concrete measure in building an administrative apparatus was the reduction of administrative links by the merging of ministries and government agencies at different levels. The current number of ministries and ministerial-level organizations totals 24. (See Figure 10.3). The leadership also moved to reform administrative procedures. In 1995, reforms touched on budget allocation and distribution of basic state investment fund, direct foreign investment, immigration, construction permits and certificates, import and export, the setting up of companies and commercial registration, and the handling of citizens' petitions. The major strategy was to reduce the number of administrative and economic "intermediaries" to simplify the regulation of government-business relations, ease government-society tension, and reduce corruption. Emphasis was also given to the handling of citizens' petitions, particularly those that involved administrative abuses.

The final aspect of administrative reform dealt with a new civil service system. Under socialism, mass organization cadres, state cadres, and some sections of party cadres had all been considered state workers or "civil servants". Reform involved the design of a professional civil servant system and a civil service code, a new salary system, a new recruitment process based on examination instead of allocating tasks, and the retraining of old cadres.[10] While the VCP's Organization Committee formerly monopolized personnel matters for both the party and government machinery, it now shares power with the Government Committee on Organization and Personnel.

In summary, the state executive in Vietnam since *doi moi* is very different to that which preceded it. The VCP no longer monopolizes power. It continues to provide guidelines, and decides major policy directions, but does not deal with the day-to-day administration. It still issues decrees, but whereas these were once immediately law now they must be approved by the National Assembly. All the top executive positions are assumed by party members, but at lower levels non-party personnel play an important role. Complex economic areas are increasingly turned over to experts, and their activities defined by law rather than party fiat.

Political Role of the Military and Police

The Vietnam People's Army (VPA) was founded in December 1944 as the People's Liberation Armed Forces. Its size grew from a mere 34 members in 1944 to a peak in 1987 of 1.26 million, with reserves numbering 2.5 million, a border defense force of 60,000, and various paramilitary groups totaling an additional 1.5 million.[11] As in other socialist countries, the VPA structure is fully integrated into two systems of control: the state and the party. At the head of the state are the Ministry of Defense, the National Defense Council, the office of the commander in chief, and five military directorates (Political; Technical; Economic and Defense Industry; Rear Services; and Intelligence). At the head of the Vietnamese Communist Party are the Political Bureau, the Party Central Committee, and the Central Military Party Committee.[12]

The late 1980s represented a turning point for the VPA. Changed international circumstances and the endorsement of *doi moi*, led to the end of almost five decades of continuing war and military conflict. In 1987, the Politburo issued Resolution no. 2 calling for the withdrawal of forces from Cambodia and Laos and a reduction of the VPA's size by half through demobilization.[13] In 1989, Vietnam announced its complete withdrawal of troops from Cambodia, ending more than ten years of military conflict. Between 1988 and 1993, the size of the armed forces was cut in half, from around 1 million to 500,000. The end of the Cold War contributed to these changes — the rise of Mikhail Gorbachev and his new foreign policy led to a drastic cut in Soviet military assistance to Vietnam.

Despite its changing role in national defense, the VPA has remained an important political actor, in close association with the VCP. Between 1989 and 1991, during crisis in the communist bloc, the VPA supported the Party, rejecting political pluralism and condemning the intervention of imperialist forces in the internal affairs of socialist countries. The 1992 constitution affirmed the VPA as a backbone of the national defense system. Generals Le Duc Anh and Doan Khue were elected to the Politburo, and Le Duc Anh, who had been in charge of Vietnam's military operations in Cambodia, assumed the position of President in 1992.

The VPA has also developed vested economic interests in the one-party system. In the 1980s and 1990s, it was able to both expand and legalize its involvement in economic activities. Military-owned businesses were divided into defense industries, defense-related economic enterprises, and exclusively commercial enterprises. Defense industries were firms producing weapons and other military equipment; these firms were part of the VPA structure. Defense-related economic enterprises coordinated economic development with defense needs by producing goods and providing material and welfare for civilians in areas of strategic importance. Exclusively commercial enterprises were firms within the military that produced goods for civilian use similar to other SOEs. Military-owned enterprises reportedly have done well compared with other SOEs.

Overall, the VPA's role has shifted from focusing mainly on national reunification and defence, to maintaining domestic political stability under party rule and promotion of economic development. Growing VPA participation in domestic security affairs and its increasing role in the economy have reinforced interlocking ties between the military, party and state. Greater openness under *doi moi* has not led to further differentiation between military and civil affairs.[14]

In Vietnam, police, crime-detention, and law enforcement activities have been treated collectively as related to "public security". These are handled by several organisations: the People's Security Force (PSF) or People's Police; the People's Public Security Force (PPSF) or the People's Security Service (PSS) at the village level; and the People's Armed Security Force (PASF). The PSF, set up in 1962, carries out normal police functions in urban areas. The PPSF or PSS at the village level deal with sensitive security issues, and are under the control of the party. The PASF, established in 1959, operates chiefly in the villages and rural areas. It has a broader function than the PSF, since it is also concerned with insurgency threats and organized counter revolutionary activities. It consists of party security cadres and VPA personnel and is more heavily armed and more mobile than ordinary police.

Police and internal security have come under the jurisdiction of the Ministry of Interior or the Ministry of Public Security. When the DRV was established in 1945, police and internal security functions were under the jurisdiction of the Ministry of Interior. In 1954 the Ministry of Public Security was set up to take charge of police and security functions. After Vietnam was reunified in 1975 the Ministry of Interior again took over, but after *doi moi* was launched in May 1998 the National Assembly replaced the name "Ministry of Interior" with "Ministry of Public Security". The new ministry has responsibilities for police and internal security affairs while allocating other non-security affairs to other ministries. Nonetheless, internal security monitoring has continued to be largely in the hands of the VPA and the VCP.

The Legislature

A unicameral National Assembly has been part of national affairs since shortly after the founding of the Democratic Republic of Vietnam. The first National Assembly was elected in January 1946, and because of wartime conditions operated until 1959. Since then elections have been held at five-yearly intervals. Three institutions have been central to its activities, the Standing Committee, Nationalities Council, and Specialized Committees.

The National Assembly Standing Committee was first set up in 1956 to supervise the government ministries, and was only endorsed as the representative of the National Assembly by the 1959 constitution. In 1980 it was replaced by the Council of State (COS). However, since COS functioned both as the National Assembly Standing Committee and as the head of state, power was overly concentrated in one institution. The 1992 constitution replaced it with the Presidency and a reconstituted Standing Committee. The National Standing Committee now serves as the permanent secretariat of the National Assembly. It consists of the National Assembly chairman, vice chairman and members. Among other duties, it decided on issues such as appointments, demotions or expulsions of ministers when the National Assembly is not in session. Its Chairman is responsible for organizing National Assembly meetings, and joint meetings with the chairman of the Nationalities Council and the chairmen of the National Assembly committees.

The National Assembly currently has seven permanent committees and one Council to assist in specific areas: a Legal Committee; Economic and Budgetary Committee; National Defense and Security Committee; Culture, Education, and Youth Committee; Social Issues Committee; Science, Technology and Environment Committee; and Foreign Affairs Committee. They mainly perform advisory role and some are more active than the others. The Nationalities Council, first endorsed by the 1980 constitution, also has an important role. In 1961, the National Assembly had set up a committee for nationalities to help it with minority affairs. The 1992 constitution expanded the role and authority of the Council. It attends meetings organized by various agencies on minority questions and has to be consulted before the government promulgates laws on minorities.

The National Assembly meets twice a year. Before 1975, its main function was to symbolize national unity; a number of seats were reserved for representatives from the south. Its legislative role was minimal since it merely endorsed laws prepared by the party, often afer these were issued as decrees. Similarly, extensive powers ostensibly vested in it to make important appointments, such as the President and Prime Minister, were in reality exercised by the party. In the period of reform in the 1990s the Assembly became more actively involved in making decisions in controversial areas that were formerly under the jurisdiction of the Politburo. Its law-making functions have been enhanced, elaborating party decrees and turning them into legislation. Assembly deputies are now often outspoken in questioning the performance of the government and individual ministers. Since 1998, National Assembly meetings have been televised.

Elections

Vietnam has held 10 election since 1945, in 1946, 1960, and subsequently at five-yearly intervals. Elections at national level for the National Assembly and at local level for the various People's Councils have generally taken place on the same day, for an elected term of five years. The most recent law governing National Assembly elections was the revised version of the 1992 elections law, passed in April, 1997. This allows citizens aged 18 or over the right to vote, and those aged 21 or over the right to stand in an election.

The National Assembly Standing Committee determines the election date and is required to announce this date at least 60 to 90 days in advance. The next step is the setting up of an Election Council for the National Assembly election, and local councils for the election of People's Councils. Members of these bodies consist of representatives of social organizations, party organizations, and the state. These councils are responsible for announcing a list of candidates, examining and resolving petitions or denunciations related to candidates, if any, collecting results, and announcing final results. They organize elections for 450 Assembly deputies, up to 100 for municipal and provincial councils, 50 at the district level and 30 for communes.

The new law spells out the qualifications of candidates, stressing loyalty to the fatherland and the Constitution as well as a commitment to the tasks of industrializing and modernizing the country as outlined by the VCP. In addition, candidates are expected to be "thrift-minded, incorruptible, just and impartial, and exemplary in upholding the law, to firmly struggle against all signs of bureaucratic arrogance, authoritarianism, corruption, and acts of violation of the law". Approved "independent" candidates are allowed, but VCP members normally comprise a majority of candidates. The Fatherland Front must give final authorization to set up a candidate list. It must coordinate a range of different organizations: party, labour unions, peasant associations, women's associations, and Ho Chi Minh youth groups. The current law also allows self nomination, although self-nominated candidates must still be introduced to their work places by the Fatherland Front. In order to arrive at a final list of candidates, the Fatherland Front has to organize three consultative meetings. These are occasions to finalize the number of candidates each organization can nominate and to introduce the candidates to the work places to test their popularity. Selected candidates contact with the work place and in their residential areas during political consultative meetings. The revised law also allows the candidates to launch final "election campaigns" through meeting-with-voter conferences and the mass media. Elected candidates are expected to maintain close and regular contact with their constituencies and to take an active part in National Assembly activities.

Judiciary

The Supreme People's Court is the highest judicial organ of the SRV. It operates independently from the Ministry of Justice, and supervises and directs the work of local People's Courts and Military Tribunals. Local People's Courts are found at each administrative level except at the commune level, where members of the communes' administrative committees also do judiciary work.

The Supreme People's Court tries cases involving high treason or other crimes of a serious nature and reviews cases originating with the lower courts. Economic, labour, and administrative courts are set up within the supreme, provincial, and municipal courts. Under the 1992 constitution, judges are appointed by the President for a five-year term, on advice from the National Assembly. This practice replaced the previous one which allowed the People's Council to elect judges on the same level.

An independent Supreme People's Office of Supervision and Control, and its district and precinct agencies, has been created to ensure that ministries, armed forces, state employees, and citizens are not violating laws. Its second role is to exercise the power of public prosecution to ensure that all crimes are discovered in good time. Its underlying philosophy is that internal security problems develop as a result of a breakdown in social discipline and that the restoration of discipline is best achieved with a system of self-control or self-discipline. There is ongoing discussion regarding responsibilities of the agencies and how to strengthen their prosecution role.[15]

Since *doi moi* the Ministry of Justice has moved to strengthen investigative bodies and reorganized them into five systems, two belonging to the people's police, two under the Ministry of Defence, and one belonging to the People's Organ of Control. The judicial support agencies have also been strengthened. In most provinces and cities, there are bar associations and public notary offices. Legal consultancy and service offices have been created.

Vietnam's judicial system has been strengthened by *doi moi*, and its emphasis on the rule of law. Courts now play a greater role in areas formerly considered outside their jurisdiction, such as cases involving corruption. The system, however, is vastly overloaded, causing long delays in trial. It also lacks an adequate legislative framework to address the many complicated economic changes that have come with liberalization. The Vietnam courts have not yet become independent enough to work on cases that are political in nature.

One-Party System

Vietnam is one of the few socialist or communist countries to retain a one-party system since the collapse of the Soviet bloc in the late 1980s. The Vietnamese Communist Party (VCP), first known as the Indochinese Communist Party, was founded in 1930. It was, in theory, dissolved between November 1945 and February 1951, but continued as the Association of Marxist Studies Group. In 1951 it was reconstituted as the Viet Nam Lao Dong Party (Vietnam Workers Party) and renamed the Vietnamese Communist Party in 1976. Membership has increased from 211 in 1930, to 5,000 in 1945, 760,000 in 1951, and 2,218,742 in 1996.

The structure of the party, based on principles of "democratic centralism", has remained the same since foundation. Basic units are local party cells (*chi bo*) containing between three and ten members. The next level is the district committee, followed by provincial and municipal organizations. Above them is the Central Committee (*Truong Uong Dang*, or CC), which meets at least twice a year at plenums that often concentrate on a particular theme. Committee membership increased gradually from 19 elected at the Second National Party Congress in 1951 to 170 at the Eighth Congress in 1996.

The CC elects a Political Bureau (or Politburo) to represent it when it is not in session, and this is where real power lies. Policy and other decisions taken at this level are transmitted down the ranks of party and state. Within this small group, as with communist parties elsewhere, the General Secretary is the most powerful office holder. The Bureau's size has expanded in parallel to that of the CC, increasing from seven in 1951 to 15 in 1996 and 2001. Until 1996 the party Secretariat was responsible for day-to-day work for the Bureau. A Politbureau Standing Board then replaced it, but the Secretariat was revived by the Ninth Congress in 2001.

Congresses, now five-yearly events, are attended by party members elected from lower party levels. Normally, each congress approves long-term policy direction, and often endorse policies that mark turning points. The first Congress met in 1935 to confirm the Comintern line of emphasizing class struggle in the colonial countries. The second met in 1951 to re-establish the Indochinese Communist Party that had been dissolved in 1945 as the Vietnam Lao Dong Party. This Congress also provided for the setting up of separate parties in Laos and Cambodia and renewed class-based politics as seen in subsequent land reform policies. The Third Congress met in 1960 after it had become clear that there would be no election to reunify the North and South. It endorsed the building of socialist industrialization in the North and armed struggle in the South. The Fourth Congress in 1976 endorsed the reunification of Vietnam and changed the party name to VCP. It continued to endorse socialist industrialization and central planning. The Fifth Congress in March 1982 responded to economic crisis in 1979 and slowed down socialist transformation. The Sixth Congress in 1986 endorsed *doi moi* and changed Vietnam's development strategies. The Seventh Congress in 1991 met after the fall of the Soviet Bloc. It endorsed socialism, while promising openness. The Eighth Congress in 1996 showed signs of the rise of conservatism in several policy areas.The Ninth Congress in 2001 reflected an attempt to strike a balance between extreme conservatism and reformism.

In the past, all congresses elected a new General Secretary. The Eighth Congress that met in 1996 was the first at which no new General Secretary was elected; this was done at the Fourth Plenum of the Central Committee that met at the end of 1997. The first member of an ethnic minority was elected General Secretary by the Ninth Congree, which also passed a resolution restricting this office to two terms.

Historically, the "party-state" concept, which signified party penetration of the government apparatus, began in the early 1950s and was institutionalized after 1954. Under state socialism, party members played an important role at all levels of the government apparatus. The higher echelons of government were almost entirely dominated by party members particularly, at ministerial level. The main decision-making bodies thus were not the agencies of government itself, but those of the party. The party also oversaw the government agencies through its specialized party committees. For example, the Politburo oversaw the working of the State Planning Commission in formulating economic policies. The Central Party Organization committee, an agency under the Central Committee, played an important role in government personnel matters. The External Relations committee of the party oversaw the work of the Foreign Ministry, while its Central Economic committee worked with the relevant ministries on economic issues. In addition, there were party committees responsible for propaganda, science and education, culture and ideology, and the interior. Finally, to oversee the government apparatus, the party set up party organizations in the government bureaucracy. The 1935 Party Statute of the first Congress, stipulating rules and regulations governing party membership, structure, and responsibilities, endorsed *dang doan* (party groups) as a means to "expand party influence and implement party policies in workers' associations, peasant associations, and popular organizations". The 1951 Statute assigned party committees at different levels to set up and lead *dang doan* in government agencies and mass organizations. The 1960 Statute reserved a separate chapter for *dang doan*, signifying its institutionalization. After reunification, the 1976 Party Statute introduced a second type of party organization, the committee of party workers (*ban can su*), to serve as a link between the party and executive and juridical administrative units, while retaining *dang doan* for elected representative bodies (the National Assembly and the People's Councils) and mass organizations. The 1982 Statute abolished *ban can su* in government and legal administrative units, leaving direct leadership of these units to party cadres or through party committees. This entity, however, was revived in 1992.

Once *doi moi* was endorsed in 1986, the party moved to share power with other political agencies. As noted, the new division of labour was officially endorsed by the 1992 Constitution, which confirmed the VCP as only one of many leading forces in politics and society. All former party committees in charge of economic areas have been merged into a single economic committee. The party no longer runs economic branches, and its main job is to conduct research on theoretical problems and economic principles. It now has only nine specialized central committees under the Central Committee: the Central Party Organizational Committee, the Central

Economic Committee, the Central Committee for Internal Affairs, the Central Science and Educational Committee, the Committee on Culture and Ideology, the Central Committee for External Affairs, the Central Control Commission, the Central Financial Management Committee, and the Central Committee for Popular Mobilization. The most authoritative party committee is that on Culture and Ideology. It deals with problems concerning the mass media, intellectuals, and literature, all areas where the Government has no real power.[16]

However, party directives remain a policy compass, and party organizations within the state agencies have been retained, if not expanded. For example, the June 1992 Congress revived the importance of both *dang doan* and *ban can su*. In the National Assembly, *dang doan* oversee the activities of Assembly deputies who were party members, and mobilize non-party members to follow the party line. The party remains committed to the building of the state apparatus, and working with state agencies through *ban can su* which would report to the Politburo and Secretariat on government decisions and implementation. At the local government level, party committee heads or deputies generally became chairpersons of the People's Councils. Party cadres would also assume the headship of specialized branches in local government.

Post *doi moi*, however, the VCP can no longer be considered monolithic. Party leaders disagreed over strategies for state and party building, manifested in the debates prior to Congresses of the 1990s. A series of developments during the past decade also reflected the process of sector competition, negotiations, and mobilization for policy support. They took the form of policy advances, policy rectifications, continuous ideological campaigns and counter campaigns, personnel reshuffling, and character assassination.[17] These developments have also served to mitigate the absolution of Vietnam's "one-party rule".

State Ideology

Vietnam's constitution proclaims communism and Ho Chi Minh's thought the official state ideology. It is, in fact, a blend of marxism and nationalism, with Ho Chi Minh's thoughts officially incorporated after *doi moi*.

The prominent role of Marxism-Leninism, even after the collapse of socialism, is largely a product of the fact that this ideology came to Vietnam as an anti-colonial solution. Marxism-Leninism made it possible for Vietnamese intellectuals and anti-colonial activists to imagine Vietnam as an independent country in an anti-imperialist context. It universalized the Vietnamese experience of French colonialism, offering a workable definition of the nature of French colonialism and the means to overthrow it. It emphasized the need for an organization that would allow the anti-colonial movement to mobilize supporters. The Vietnamese communist movement's international connections also helped the movement survive French suppression, using sanctuaries outside the reach of the French colonial regime, in places such as Moscow and southern China.

Marxism-Leninism permeated every aspect of Vietnam's nationalist discourse. It mixed with a Vietnamese nationalist grammar, in which peasant-based ideologies, and certain elements of peasant culture, were highlighted and treated as popular culture or the culture of the working people (*nhan dan lao dong*). In discussing peasant culture, official writings cautioned that peasant culture contained both bad and good elements, and the positive aspects needed to be emphasized. The peasant family was seen as a stable social unit engaged in agricultural activities. Internal family relations should be marked by equality, reciprocity, and mutual sacrifice between husband and wife on the one hand and between older and younger brothers on the other. The major intra-family work ethic to be stressed was the equal distribution of responsibilities. These horizontal and fraternal aspects of internal family relations were extended to cover the relationship among friends, societal members, and people from different ethnic groups.

The spirit of patriotism was another aspect of peasant culture highlighted as an element of popular tradition. Popular sayings eulogized heroes who led the resistance to foreign invasion and extolled peasants' contribution to that resistance. The peasant resentment of injustice, seen in popular sayings deriding greedy mandarins, Taoist priests, and Buddhist monks, was also promoted.

National history was represented as the history of both patriotism and class struggle. The former could be seen from the Viet's and the minorities' resistance to attempts to invade and conquer made by successive Chinese dynasties and French colonialism. The latter was exemplified by peasant rebellions against exploitative land policies imposed by the courts between the eleventh and the nineteenth centuries. The new socialist working ethics were not presented as new, but as an outgrowth of popular working traditions.

In the process of cultural reformulation and political transformation, the communist movement appeared as both an historical and cultural force. The rise of the Communist Party, the August Revolution, the war against the return of French colonialism, domestic transformation after the

Revolution, and the building of the Democratic Republic of Vietnam were all treated as events manifesting both the continuing class struggle and the thrust for national unity. The Communist Party represented the fusion of nationalist and anti-exploitation forces and as a result was capable of mobilizing collective action by the Viet and the minorities in every part of the country.[18]

This interpretation has not gone unchallenged. During a period of openness from 1987–89 Vietnam's intellectuals questioned the doctrinaire nature of these beliefs and supported greater freedom of individual rights. (See below.) Difficulties making the transition from war to peace have also led to some cynicism. However for most Vietnamese VCP achievements — particularly in wars against France, then the United States and its allies — lend substance to ideological claims. In the 1990s, to respond to criticism, the VCP leadership added to this ideology by elevating Ho Chi Minh's teachings from "advice" to "thought". This reflected an attempt to emphasize Ho's pragmatism and internationalism when Vietnam was moving from central planning to a market economy and into a globalized world.

Civil Society and Human Rights

Prior to *doi moi*, no independent space existed for social organizations independent of the state. The VCP leadership organized society into mass organizations controlled by the party. The Fatherland Front (*Mat Tran To Quoc*) was and remains the umbrella organization of mass organizations which originally included the Vietnamese Confederation of Trade Unions, the Women's Union, the Ho Chi Minh Youth Union, and the Peasants' Union. These mass organizations had a dual function, both to implement party and government policies, and to act as a transmission belt sending information to the party. During the period of *doi moi*, two additional organizations, the Union for the Elderly and the Association of Vietnamese Veterans, were added. The leadership continued to view all mass organizations as a means of organizing civil society and linking the party-state with society.

Now these state-sponsored organizations no longer monopolize the socio-cultural scene. A new popular civil space emerged following economic liberalization. This new space is occupied by associations built upon family connections. After decollectivization allowed the household to become an independent economic unit, household and clan relations (*dong ho*) grew into important social institutions. In the lowland Vietnamese areas, ancestor worship, family records, clan-based funds and clan rules mushroomed. The new space is also occupied by the elderly, village heads and village customs. In urban centers, there are new economic and social associations, focusing on: production, planting, husbandry and technical transfer; philanthropic associations working to eradicate poverty; associations promoting education, agriculture, industry, forestry, and services.[19]

While the party-state leadership has been tolerant of popular associations focusing on economic and social affairs, it has been less tolerant of political, intellectual and religious groups that expressed disagreement with the leadership's policies. In the wake of the collapse of the socialist bloc between 1989 and 1991, prior to and after the Seventh National Party Congress in 1991 and the Eighth National Party Congress in 1996, middle-ranking party members and technocrats voiced their opinions on the future and appropriateness of one-party rule. The leadership's response to party members with opposite views was harsh. Middle-ranking party members who advocated political pluarlism were expelled from the Party on the grounds of violating democratic centralism.[20]

The leadership has sometimes allowed broader freedom of expression among the circles outside the party. During the open period from 1987 to 1989, General Secretary Nguyen Van Linh called for Vietnamese intellectuals to support *doi moi* by "looking straight at the truth". Following his call, Vietnamese writers cum intellectuals became critical of the regime's policies. Many writings directly challenged the ideology of socialist nationalism which had developed during the DRV period. Tran Manh Hao's *Ly than* (Alienation) depicted the communist party's intrusion into the private life of its cadres. Nguyen Huy Thiep's writings questioned the Party's monopoly of truth. He discarded the traditional methods of providing a happy ending or a moral theme to his stories, replacing them with inconclusive endings for readers to interpret according to their taste. Vietnamese writers did not restrict their criticism to the Party, some even attempting to put Ho Chi Minh on trial. Tran Huy Quang's *Linh nghiem* (Prophecy) published in Van Nghe in July 1992, was the first piece alluding directly to Ho Chi Minh, interpreting his "journey of discovery" as a failure. Writers not only attacked the Party's monopoly of truth and power, they also questioned the benefits of the class struggle. Duong Thu Huong's *Nhung thien duong mu* (Foggy Paradises) portrayed the impact of the class war waged during land reform and the impact of its mistakes on the lives of three women. Contrary to the conventional view of nationalism which identified war as a "glorious" and "heroic" act, Bao Ninh's *Noi buon chien tranh* (Sorrow of War) described war as a source of misery, sorrow, separation, inhumanity and atrocities. War, once portrayed as a collective heroic undertaking, was recast in terms of individual losses and sufferings. Writers also wrote about individualism, individual freedom, family relationships, humanism, love, and female sexual freedom, all of which were once thought to reflect the "petty bourgeois" mentality. Nguyen Van Linh, however, withdrew his support for such openness in 1989 when the political situation in Eastern Europe became unstable and one-Party rule was challenged. Some of these critical writers were then censored or put under surveillance.

The Vietnamese Government has also been less than tolerant of religious establishments, even though it has recognized six official religions: Buddhism, Confucianism, Islam, Catholicism, Protestantism, Cao Dai, and Hoa Hao. Following victories in 1954 over the French and in 1975 over the US-backed South Vietnam, communist authorities took control of thousands of properties which belonged to Buddhist, Catholic and other religious groups. Some religious property has been returned in recent years, but the issue remains contentious. Groups such as the indigenous Cao Dai faith face continued land grabs by authorities. A circular issued in the first part of 2000 by the Central Land Department and the Party Central Committee on Religious Affairs specified that land-use rights of all property currently occupied by religious organizations or places of worship would be given to the religious bodies. The regulations applied only to the 21,000 legally recognized religious properties or places of worship in the nation, including pagodas, churches, monasteries, graveyards, temples and mosques. They forbade any readjustment of the land site from the current boundaries or transfer of title of the land certificates, and implied that religious property and lands once handed over to the government would belong to the state.[21]

The relationship between the party-state and some of the official religious establishments has often been difficult. Catholics number some 10% of the population. Many Catholics were driven underground in the hard line period of communist rule until the 1990s, but now openly display their faith. Still authorities continue to place restrictions on Church activities, training and social activities and publications. The *Hiep Thong* (Communion), published by the Conference of Bishops in Hanoi the only bulletin published by the Church — was closed in October 2000. Property belonging to the Catholic Church has been seized: the government recently confiscated the lands of the Thien An Monastery near Hue for the construction of an amusement park. Protestants of the ethnic Hmong community in the Central Highlands have been intimidated and forced to abandon their faith.

Other faiths fared no better. In a letter sent secretly to U.S. President Bill Clinton dated 5 November 2000, prominent Buddhist leader Thich Quang Do called on the President to speak out in favour of human rights and religious freedom during his forthcoming visit to Vietnam. According to his account, in September 2000 six members of the Hoa Hao Buddhist sect were condemned to prison sentences of up to three years for sending a Petition to the Government protesting against the harassment of Hoa Hao followers. Cao Dai dignitaries and followers have been detained: one received a two-year sentence simply because she tried to meet the UN Special Rapporteur on Religious Intolerance during his visit to Vietnam. The Unified Buddhist Church is outlawed, its educational and social institutions seized, and all activities prohibited.[22] A range of additional unauthorized religious groups (sects) routinely encounter government crackdowns.

In the 1990s, the party leadership allowed some freedom of expression in the mass media circles. Only a certain number of topics remained out of bounds, including stories related to Ho Chi Minh's personal life, individual party leaders, and internal conflict or disagreement within the leadership. However, leaders have been wary of other avenues of expression, and in particular sought to restrict and control the use of the Internet in the last years of the 20th century.

MAJOR POLITICAL ISSUES

Who Has Power?

It is possible to argue that in Vietnam from the 1990s, no one political institution has monopolized power. The party, the state executive (including the civilian bureaucracy) the army, and increasingly the National Assembly, are all important actors. Since *doi moi*, constellations of power are based on a mixture of sectoral interests, personality, and bureaucratic authority.

The importance of the VCP in the 1990s stemmed from its weight of "tradition" and its claim to post-central planning indispensability. Under the state socialist system, one of its major tasks was to mobilize production units to fulfil plans and provide assistance for state officials to implement party directives. During the reform period, however, this mobilization role became increasingly irrelevant since the economic activities of production units were driven by cost-benefit calculation rather than ideological campaigns. Under the market system it moved to share political power with other institutions, but retained its claim to provide general guidelines on policy issues. At the Seventh Congress in 1991, Nguyen Van Linh, the out-going General Secretary who had been credited with pushing *doi moi* forward, asserted that the VCP was an historically rooted movement that had brought both national independence and revolutionary gains. The state executive (cabinet) and its bureaucracy, traditionally merged with the party as seen in the label "party-state", developed into a separate entity. Under the state socialist system, politics and economics meshed and the party-state assumed both administrative and economic responsibilities. During *doi moi*, economic reform necessitated the building of a law-governed state to provide a framework for market-based economic activities. Ministers and the bureaucracy were thus granted more autonomy.[23] The VPA also became more influential in the 1990s. Although a significant institution prior to reunification, its representation in the VCP Central Committee declined after the Fourth Congress in 1976. In the late 1980s and early 1990s, however, during the crisis in the communist bloc, it supported the VCP single-party system, and its role in the party subsequently increased. In addition, to cope with a reduced budget since the late 1980s, it converted its army divisions into economic units. At present, it reportedly runs around 200 state-registered businesses, including four major corporations involved in electronics, computing and telecommunications.

Despite the importance of these institutions, none is monolithic. The label "one-party rule" notwithstanding, by the mid-1990s, the VCP had become ideologically divided. The period between the Sixth and the Eighth Congresses (1986–96) saw the rise of two-dimensional sectoral interests within the VCP. The first centered around provincial party members and the second around cadres in the party work section. The rising prominence of provincial cadres had its roots in the economic liberalization that unfolded after 1979 and their increasing command of economic resources. The party work section represented the traditional legacy of the socialist system. After the collapse of the Soviet bloc, the work section developed a close relationship with the Chinese Communist Party. It resorted to the vocabulary of socialist ideology and national culture as its weapons. Tension among different sectors in the VCP can be seen through the leadership's disagreement over strategies for state and party building in the post-central planning era manifested in the debates prior to the Eighth National Congress in June 1996 and in the documents endorsed by the Congress itself.

The government bureaucracy was also fragmented. Vietnamese reformists writing about central-local government relations identified economic and administrative tension stemming from a power vacuum during the period of transition from plan to market. For example, local governments imported and exported freely and refused to share revenue with the central government. They also exploited natural resources for personal interests as well as with foreigners. Administratively, local government often issued regulations contradictory to those of the central government, or did not elaborate decisions issued by the central government. Currently, central-local government relations are a crucial dimension that needs attention in analyzing the executive and its bureaucracy.

Finally, the VPA itself is not monolithic either. Differences among army officials centre around strategies to modernize the armed forces, either completely relying on modern technology or continuing to rely on the doctrine of people's war, and the extent to which the VPA should get involved in economic management.

Who Benefits?

As with communist systems everywhere, leading party members benefit most in terms of controlling power, and a wide range of perquisite that come with that. In some cases the benefits have multiplied since the beginning of *doi moi*. Several studies show that those in power used their political power to accumulate economic wealth, with abuse of power taking such forms as appropriation of state property, illegal dealings, and corruption. Other accounts show that the means to acquire wealth has been institutionalized, and those who have acquired wealth under the one-party system have been able to ensure it is inherited by their children and networks of relatives.[24] In mid-1997 several thousand villagers in Thai Binh province staged violent protests against excessive taxation demands and corrupt officials.

Relative rapid economic growth since *doi moi* has benefitted every sector of society. However, the gap between their rich and poor has also widened. The government, with assistance from internal financial agencies and donors, has intensified campagins for hunger eradication and poverty reduction. Its success remains to be seen not the least because there have been cases in which fund is embezzled and misused.

Minority groups have again begun to feel deprived. In early 2001, rural unrest broke out in the minority-inhabited provinces of Dac Lac and Pleiku. According to the Ministry of Foreign Affairs, demonstrators marched through downtown Pleiku in response to the arrest of two men who were charged with "undermining national unity". State-controlled news agencies reported that protestors damaged a number of official buildings and that 20 people were arrested following demonstrations. Despite the attempt of the state-controlled media to downplay the conflict, residents reported that the demonstrators were drawn from a whole range of different ethnic groups, including the region's largest — the Jarai, Ede and Bahnar — who between them numbered more than 600,000 people. The demonstration was precipitated by anger among all minority groups at the government's confiscation of their ancestral lands to make way for Vietnamese settlers to plant coffee. This policy further exacerbated the ethnic imbalance already fostered by the communist government's now abandoned policy of settling hundreds of thousands of ethnic Vietnamese in so-called New Economic Zones in the 1980s. Residents also said the anger of the minority groups had been further inflamed by government repression of Protestant groups which had built up a large following among the ethnic minorities in recent years.

Legitimacy

By the 1990s, the party based its claim to legitimacy on a combination of collective leadership, rule by law, and continued economic growth while maintaining social equality. The concept of collective leadership developed in the 1970s meant that no one leader became prominent. Unlike their predecessors, however, the current leaders came from different backgrounds. They advanced their political careers through their expertise, connections, and networks of patronage cultivated during the period of political and economic changes in the 1980s and 1990s, rather than by their contributions to wars and revolution. The sectoral representation of the leadership in major political bodies meant that bargains could be struck and material benefits distributed. This has helped guarantee leadership stability, at least for the present.

However in the long run the legitimacy of this system depends on maintaining economic growth and establishing a firmer legal basis for its role. So far attempts at economic and political reforms have vacillated between slow progress and paralysis. (See section on Governance below.) Economic growth slowed as a result of the regional economic crisis in 1997. Inequalities between the rich and poor and conflict between government and society have widened. Public alienation has even taken the form of violent protests.

In the absence of free elections and public opinion polls, measuring the extent of the current government's legitimacy is almost impossible.

As the successor to a regime that achieved a remarkable military victory over the United States and its allies it still has some traditional legitimacy to call on. But a mixed or even poor record in areas such as the economy, human rights, and participation means that its legitimacy might be under challenge.

Governance

In the 1990s, the one-party state emphasized the promotion of economic growth, social equity, and grass roots participation. Vietnam witnessed a steady economic growth rate, averaging almost 9% during the first half of the 1990s, but the GDP growth rate reportedly only averaged 6.9% during the second half of the decade. The level of economic growth in Vietnam depended on the international context of development. The financial crisis that began in Thailand in 1997 and spread to other countries began to affect Vietnam in 1998. The country avoided the worst aspects of the crisis because it had not been integrated into international financial markets. It had also maintained strict controls on foreign exchange transactions and restricted private capital flow. But the negative spill-over effects eventually reached Vietnam in the second half of 1998. Vietnam relies on direct foreign investment for capital. Foreign investment that had been slow because of the unfavorable investment climate dropped even further. Vietnam was put under pressure by the large devaluations in the crisis-stricken countries. Local goods could not compete with legal and smuggled imports from the countries affected by the crisis in the region. The Fourth Plenum in December 1997 mentioned the financial crisis, although it did not explore its impact on Vietnam. To respond to the crisis, the Plenum endorsed the mobilization of internal resources (*noi luc*) for economic development. One concern arose from the fact that foreign direct investment made up almost 49 per cent of all the capital in Vietnam, when in other countries the level of foreign capital did not exceed 20 per cent. The level of foreign debt to the percentage of GDP was also too high, indicating the lack of independence in the economy. However, the Plenum argued that the emphasis on internal resources did not mean the abandonment of foreign cooperation. Further emphasis was put on agriculture, rural development, poverty alleviation, and unemployment. In the context of the domestic and international situation of 1997 and 1998, these represented some of the very few options that might maintain domestic economic and political stability and lead to further growth in a time of declining foreign direct investment.

Economic development thus far has led to an increase in inequality, particularly between rural and urban areas. There is, now, an attempt to address these issues with international assistance and through poverty alleviation programs. Vietnam's economic reforms have also brought about new types of economic conflict between the one-party state and different social sectors. The collapse of the socialist bureaucracy during the transition from plan to market left a void that was not immediately filled by the setting up of a new legal and administrative system. This gave government officials opportunities to pursue financial gains. There have even been cases in which law enforcement agencies acted as violators of the people's economic rights.

Corruption has emerged as a major problem, with a lack of concrete measures to deter it. The mid-term party conference in 1994 listed corruption as the main internal threat to national security. The conflict between government agencies and different sectors of society was mirrored in petitions and letters of criticism lodged by citizens in the 1990s. The 1959, 1980, and 1992 Constitutions of Vietnam had granted citizens the right to file complaints. Petitions lodged between 1992 and 1994 were concerned with economic and social problems related to land, housing, and taxation. Complaints also dealt with false charges, illegal arrests and unfair treatment and trial. Statistics collected in the early 1990s show that cadres at the commune, quarter, precinct and district levels, as well as directors of state enterprises, were main targets.

The party-state, in the first part of the 1990s, tried to address these grievances by expediting the process of handling petitions and letters of criticism. Further political reform was carried out in response to the Thai Binh unrest in 1997. The Third Plenum of the Central Committee called for the promotion of direct grass-roots democracy. For example, every organ, enterprise, ward and village was to be open about its plans for action, financial collection and spending, and profit sharing. If necessary, "referenda" could be held at the basic level. The Plenum called for the improvement of the quality of representative democracy by improving the electoral system. It also called for the continuation of administrative reform and the reform of cadre work to upgrade the cadres' moral commitment. These emphases were not new, merely reinforcing earlier VCP Congress resolutions. Further steps include a Politburo Directive in February 1998 on the building and implementation of grassroots democracy. Emphasis was given first to the commune administrative level in rural areas and the ward level in urban areas, and in state-owned enterprises. In March, the Standing Committee of the National Assembly circulated for public comments a draft law on the rights of Vietnamese citizens to petition and denounce wrong doings by state officials.[25] How far such attempt to reform meets public expectations remains to be seen.

CHANGING WITH CAUTION

The twentieth century saw Vietnam move from one political system to another. Each change came into being to cope with socio-economic difficulties the old system had been unable to deal with. The one-party state in the 1990s was more open and inclusive, and substantially different from that developed prior to *doi moi*. Yet, at the turn of the century doubts remain about whether reform thus far is sufficient in providing a basic framework for economic development and in guaranteeing human rights. There are also signs that the system itself has generated conflict between the government and society in general, and within different social groups in various forms. Further reform is needed to ensure that the system itself can continue to serve as a positive engine for economic growth, social equality, and the expansion of grassroots participation.

Which direction the one-party state will likely take in the early 21st century can in part be deduced from the Ninth National Congress of the Vietnamese Communist Party's political report entitled: "Bring into full play the strength of the whole nation, continue the renovation work, accelerate industrialisation and modernisation, build and defend the socialist homeland of Vietnam." An earlier version was circulated and discussed by over two million Party members and the Party Committees' Congresses at all levels, delegates of the National Assembly, the Fatherland Front at various levels, the revolutionary veterans and intellectuals. The 11th plenum of the Eighth Party Central Committee corrected the earlier version after receiving feedback, approved the new version, and publicized it on the occasion of the 71st founding anniversary of the VCP to solicit opinions from the people.

The political report recaptures both conservative and reformist rhetoric that had persisted throughout the 1990s. It cites the founding of the Indochinese Communist Party, the August Revolution of 1945, and the two resistance wars against France and the United States as major political events that had transformed Vietnam's political life as a nation-state. It recognizes that Vietnam would be substantially transformed in the 21st century as the country comes into contact with modern technology and globalization. Vietnam had to continue to cooperate with the international community to promote its own domestic economic growth and help solve cross-national problems. Yet, it warns that the capitalist economic system would continue to breed conflict over the means of production and class struggle, and reiterated the four dangers outlined by the mid-term party conference in 1994: economic regression; socialist deviation; corruption; and peaceful evolution.

In assessing the general situation during the past 15 years, the report endorsed policies of renovation adopted by the Sixth to Eighth National Party Congresses. However, it pointed to the slow implementation of the somewhat conservative Eighth Congress resolutions as the main cause for a slower rate of growth, chronic cultural and social problems, corruption among party and government officials, slow administrative reform, and a lack of consensus over important policy issues. One full section discusses Vietnam' s road to socialism, confirming that the Vietnamese people and the Party are determined to follow the socialist path based on the ideological foundation of Marxism-Leninism and Ho Chi Minh's Thought. However, it downplayed the notion of domestic class struggle, highlighting instead unity of forces in the process of modernization and industralization. It mapped out the general goals of the strategy for the socio-economic development in the ten coming years, aiming to establish a modern industralized country by 2020. While supporting a market economy, it emphasized the role of the state in leading the economy to maintain a balance between plan and market. The report emphasizes national defence and security, but balances this by emphasising the importance of consolidating Vietnam's position in international relations and expanding its foreign relations.

The report not only reflected the incorporation of agendas from various political sectors within and outside the VCP, as normally practised, but also the VCP's attempt to find its own development model in the post-socialist era. However, it is likely that further *doi moi* reform in Vietnam will continue to be slow because bargaining and compromise among different interests have become more complicated. Paralysis has ensued when no meaningful agreement can be reached. In the past, a stalemate was often broken only when the party leadership was confronted with domestic or international pressure that forced decision. Decollectivization was not carried out until 1988 when rural production dropped, and the administrative prices system was not abandoned until 1989 when it became clear that Soviet aid would be cut. Reform of the public administration was endorsed in 1995, to some extent because of pressure from the World Bank and the IMF, but there has been little progress since. The Asian financial crisis that took place in 1997 had spillover effects on Vietnam, but did not have enough impact to precipitate a fundamental structural change of the Vietnamese political system.

Notes

1   Dang Nghiem Van, Chu Thai Son, and Luu Hung, *Ethnic Minorities in Vietnam* (Hanoi: The Gioi, 2000), pp. 266–75.

2   Bernard Fall, *The Two Vietnams* (London: Pall Mall Press, 1967).

3   At the end of 1955, during the last wave of land reform, which covered villages in the newly-liberated areas in the Red River Delta, local cadres misclassified peasants, treating middle-income peasants as rich, and rich peasants as landlords. This was the only time that major violence occurred under the DRV regime. The Party tried to rectify the errors by rehabilitating those who had been misclassified and a number of Politburo and Central Committee members responsible for land reform were demoted. See Edwin Moise, *Land Reform in China and North Vietnam: Consolidating the Revolution at the Village Level* (Chapel Hill: University of North Carolina Press, 1983).

4   For more information, see Melanie Beresford, *Vietnam: Politics, Economics, and Society* (London and New York: Pinter Publishers, 1988).

5   See Adam Fforde and Stefan De Vylder, *From Plan to Market: The Economic Transition in Vietnam* (Boulder: Westview Press, 1996).

6   See Christian White, "Agricultural Planning, Price Policy, and Cooperatives in Vietnam", *World Development* 13, no. 1: 97–114.

7   Fforde and De Vylder, *From Plan to Market*.

8   *Vietnam Attacking Poverty* (Hanoi: Joint Report of the Government-Donor NGO Working Group, 1999), p. 44.

9   For further information on Vietnam's four constitutions, please see Van Phong Quoc Hoi, *Hien Phap nam 1946 va su ke thua, phat trien trong cac hien phap Viet Nam* (The 1946 constitution and its impact on the development of subsequent Vietnamese constitutions) (Hanoi: Chinh Tri Quoc Gia, 1998); and *Hien Phap Viet Nam* (1959, 1980 va 1992) (Vietnam's Constitutions: 1959, 1980, 1992) (Hanoi: Chinh Tri quoc Gia, 1995).

10 See Thaveeporn Vasavakul, "Politics of the Reform of State Institutions in the Post-Socialist Era", in *Vietnam Assessment: Creating a Sound Investment Climate*, ed. Suiwah Leung (Singapore: ISEAS, 1996), pp. 42–67.

11 Carlyle Thayer, *The Vietnam People's Army under Doi Moi* (Singapore: ISEAS, 1994), p. 2.

12 For further discussion on the Vietnam People's Army, see Thaveeporn Vasavakul, "Vietnam: From Revolutionary Heroes to Red Entrepreneurs", in *Coercion, and Governance: The Declining Political Role of the Military in Asia*, ed. Muthiah Alagappa (Stanford: Stanford University Press, forthcoming).

13   Thayer, *The Vietnam People's Army under Doi Moi*, pp. 14–17.

14   Vasavakul, "Vietnam: From Revolutionary Heroes to Red Entrepreneurs", in *Coercion and Governance*, ed. Alagappa.

15   *Hien Phap Viet Nam* and Uong Chu Luu, "Legal Development and Socio-Economic Reform in Vietnam", paper presented to the Regional Symposium on Law, Justice and Open Society in ASEAN, 6–9 October 1997, Thailand.

16   Dang Phong and Melanie Beresford, *Authority Relations and Economic Decision Making in Vietnam* (Copenhagen: NIAS, 1998).

17   See detailed discussion in Thaveeporn Vasavakul, "Sectoral Politics and Strategies for State and Party Building from the VII to the VIII Congress of the Vietnamese Communist Party (1991–96)", in *Doi Moi Ten Years After the 1986 Party Congress,* ed. Adam Fforde (Canberra: Department of Political and Social Change, RSPAS, 1997), pp. 81–135.

18   This section is drawn from Thaveeporn Vasavakul, "Vietnam: The Changing Model of Legitimation", in *Political Legitimacy in Southeast Asia: The Quest for Moral Authority,* ed. Muthiah Alagappa (Stanford, CA.: Stanford University Press, 1995), pp. 257–89.

19   See detailed discussion in Thaveeporn Vasavakul, "Vietnam: Sectors, Classes, and the Transformation of a Leninist State", in *Driven by Growth: Political Change in the Asia-Pacific Region,* ed. James W. Morley, (revised edition) (New York: M.E. Sharpe, 1999), pp. 59–82.

20   Vasavakul, "Vietnam: The Changing Model of Legitimation".

21   "Vietnam to seal fate on religious property", *Deutsche Presse-Agentur,* 2 November 2000.

22   "Vietnam — Thich Quang Do's Letter to President Clinton", International Buddhist Bureau, 48 rue Parmentier — 94450 Limeil Brevannes (France).

23   For detailed discussion, see Vasavakul, "Politics of the Reform of State Institutions in the Post-Socialist Era".

24   See for example, Gerald Greenfield, "The Development of Capitalism in Vietnam", in *Between Globalism and Nationalism,* ed. Ralph Miliband and Leo Panitch (London: Merlin Press, 1994), pp. 203–34; Gabriel Kolko, *Anatomy of a Peace* (London and New York: Routledge, 1997).

25   See Vasavakul, "Vietnam: Sectors, Classes, and the Transformation of a Leninist State".

Further Reading

Dang Phong and Melanie Beresford. *Authority Relations and Economic Decision-Making in Vietnam.* Copenhagen: NIAS, 1998.

De Vylder, Stefan and Adam Fforde. *From Plan to Market: The Economic Transition in Vietnam.* Boulder, Co: Westview Press, 1996.

Duiker, William. *Ho Chi Minh.* St. Leonards: Allen & Unwin, 2000.

Fforde, Adam, ed. *Doi Moi: Ten Years After the Sixth Party Congress.* Canberra: Department of Political and Social Change, Australian National University, 1997.

Huynh Kim Khanh. *Vietnamese Communism, 1925–1945.* Ithaca: Cornell University Press, 1982.

Hy Van Luong. *Revolution in the Village: Tradition and Transformation in North Vietnam, 1925-1988.* Hawaii: University of Hawaii Press, 1992.

Kerkvliet, Benedict and Doug Porter, eds. *Vietnam's Rural Transformation.* Boulder: Westview Press, 1995.

Liljestrom, Rita et al. *Profit and Poverty in Rural Vietnam: Winners and Losers of a Dismantled Revolution.* Surrey: Curzon, 1998.

Litvack, Jennie I. and Dennis A. Rondinelli. *Market Reform in Vietnam: Building Institutions for Development.* Westport, Connecticut and London: Quorum Books, 1999.

Marr, David and Christine P.White, eds. *Postwar Vietnam: Dilemmas in Socialist Development.* Ithaca: Southeast Asia Program, Cornell University, 1988.

Marr, David, ed. *The Mass Media in Vietnam.* Canberra: Department of Political and Social Change, RSPAS, ANU, 1998.

Porter, Gareth. *Vietnam: The Politics of Bureaucratic Socialism.* Ithaca: Cornell University Press, 1993.

Rambo, Terry, Robert Reed, Le Trong Cuc, and Michael Digregorio. *The Challenges of Highland Development in Vietnam.* Hawaii: East-West Center, 1995.

Turley, William and Mark Selden, eds. *Reinventing Vietnamese Socialism: Doi Moi in Comparative Perspective.* Boulder: Westview, 1993.

CONCLUSION

Southeast Asia is a heterogeneous entity. Historians and anthropologists have discerned underlying similarities, ranging from Indian-influenced notions of society and kingship (except for the Sinicized northern Vietnam, and untouched areas of the Philippines), a common animistic underlay to Buddhist, Islamic and Christian religions, traditional occupations based largely on rice farming and fishing, rice-based diets, housing (using stilts), and social relations that, *inter alia*, give a relatively high status to women. But these similarities pale by contrast with the region's diversities.

When the first tentative moves towards regionalism emerged with the formation of ASEAN in 1967, the five founding members were deeply divided by history, race, language and religion. All except Thailand had been under colonial rule just one or two decades earlier, with separate masters except for British rule of Malaysia and Singapore. Malays in Indonesia and Malaysia were overwhelmingly Muslim, while those in the Philippines were predominantly Christian; Thais were Buddhist; and Chinese Singaporeans Buddhist, Taoist and Christian. Economies were fragile, particularly Indonesia's, where annual per capita income of only US$50 was less than a third that of other ASEAN partners. And Indonesia's population of more than 100 million, was over three times the size of the next largest state, and fifty times as large as Singapore. Political systems included different forms of military rule in Indonesia and Thailand, a U.S.–style presidential system in the Philippines, and Westminster-derived parliamentary systems in Malaysia and Singapore. All, however, were politically unstable, under siege from communist and ethnic opponents. Divisions within and between Southeast Asia countries — which loomed even larger when neighbours in Indochina and Burma (Myanmar) were taken into account — led commentators at the time to describe the region as the Balkans of Asia.

Three decades on, members of the now 10-country ASEAN (possibly soon 11 if East Timor joins) are no less diverse. The Key Statistics for each country tell part of the story. Populations now range from Indonesia's 220 million to 325 thousand in Brunei, GNP per capita from US$30,000 in Singapore to $260 in Cambodia, and rankings on the Human Development Index are from 24 for first world Singapore to 140 for Laos. In economic terms the divide is particularly between older ASEAN members and Cambodia, Laos, Myanmar, Vietnam (CLMV), with many analysts referring to a two-tier organization.

TABLE C.1

Southeast Asian Political Systems

Monarchy	Military Rule	Communism	Semi-Democracy	Democracy
Brunei	Myanmar	Vietnam	Malaysia	Thailand
		Laos	Singapore	Philippines
			Cambodia	Indonesia

Southeast Asia's current political systems, in most respects, share this diversity (see Table C.1). A neo-traditional monarchical form of government persists in Brunei. Military rule has been imposed in Myanmar. Years after communist regimes have collapsed in other parts of the world, they continue in Vietnam and Laos. The remaining governments represent various forms of semi democracy or democracy. Malaysia, Singapore and perhaps now Cambodia, employ many democratic practices, particularly regular elections, but do not permit others such as freedom of speech, assembly and association to the extent normally considered essential for a democracy. Thailand, the Philippines and Indonesia have a much wider degree of political liberty, though privileged élites in these countries sometimes subvert democracy, and in Indonesia's case continued violence and killings may negate its democratic claims.

Labelling Southeast Asia's governments according to such a commonly used classification gives some indication of the region's diversity, but does not take explanation very far. Moreover different institutional arrangements have not precluded as least some convergence in the area of political practice. The remainder of these concluding remarks will draw together judgements made on political institutions and practices in the preceding chapters.

Distribution of Power — Centre versus Periphery

Throughout Southeast Asia political power is heavily concentrated in the hands of national governments. Only one country, Malaysia, is a federation, but even here most powers are centralized. The political dominance of the ruling *Barisan Nasional* (BN) coalition has helped entrench federal rule. The party has controlled most state assemblies since independence, and ensured all BN state leaders are selected by the Prime Minister. At lower levels municipal officials are appointed by state governments (since 1964), and have few independent powers.

The Philippines, Thailand and Indonesia all have legislation providing for a considerable devolution of power to provinces and/or smaller local government units. This has already been put into practice in the Philippines, giving more members of Filipino society a larger role in local government and policy making. Devolution is just beginning in Thailand and Indonesia, with many uncertainties about how it will work in practice. Cambodia is in the process of drafting devolution laws.

In Myanmar power is centralized in the hands of senior junta members. Powerful regional commanders may, however, sometimes be in a position to defy central administrative authorities, particularly when they out-rank ministers or officials. Communist centralization prevails in Vietnam and Laos. In Brunei the monarchy is all-powerful, though a degree of popular participation is allowed with occasional election of village heads.

Heads of State

The current ceremonial heads of Southeast Asian countries are presidents (Indonesia, Philippines, Singapore, Vietnam, Laos), monarchies (Thailand, Malaysia, Cambodia, Brunei) or the military (Myanmar). The presidents of Indonesia and the Philippines are also heads of government, along with Myanmar's military junta head and Brunei's monarch. Presidents of Vietnam, Laos and Singapore are not — prime ministers hold this post — but those in Vietnam and Laos may exercise considerable influence if they hold important posts in the communist party. Singapore's president has a largely symbolic role, but also has some executive responsibilities, particularly in relation to safeguarding national financial reserves. The remaining monarchs play mainly ceremonial or symbolic roles, but exert varying degrees of influence over government affairs. The Thai King has intervened on several occasions, and come to be regarded as an important safeguard of stability in that country.

Executives

Institutional arrangements, traditional value systems (emphasizing patronage and neo-feudalism) and political evolution, have combined to ensure that most Southeast Asian countries have strong executives. In Malaysia, Singapore and the communist states Vietnam and Laos, the government, ruling party, and administration (civil and military) are intertwined with few countervailing forces. Myanmar and Brunei are similar in this respect, however neither allow a significant role for political parties. Business is a subordinate part of this nexus in Malaysia and Singapore, signified in the former by proud use of the term Malaysia Inc. Civil society has recently begun to offer resistance to executive dominance in Malaysia, but for the moment the executive remains strong.

Executive dominance is not as apparent in Thailand, Philippines and Cambodia. Particularly in the former two, parliament has some influence, civil society is stronger, major parties do not have such a dominant role, and new independent organizations provide some protection for individual rights against the executive. Politicians and businessmen may work in close collaboration, but alliances are dispersed rather than all centring on the government. In some cases less efficient bureaucracies also pose a practical limitation on the extent of executive dominance.

Indonesia, arguably, is the one country where the executive is weak. Although it still has much strength in relation to other political forces, new executive bodies have yet to gain widespread acceptance since Soeharto's ouster. The military has been greatly weakened, though efforts to impose civilian control over the military have triggered new military-civilian rivalries.

Executive control usually centres around the head of government and his/her cabinet. In Malaysia and Singapore these officials must be members of parliament. In Cambodia they need not be, but must come from a political party that has parliamentary representation. Other countries are not prescriptive. In most countries there is at least some parliamentary involvement in selecting ministers, though frequently once a head of government is chosen he/she has a free hand in selecting the cabinet. The Philippines, Myanmar and Brunei are exceptions, the first because its president is directly elected by the people, and the others because they do not have a legislature. Where parliament "selects" the head of government ministers are generally collectively responsible to parliament. Elsewhere they are responsible to the head of government.

A notable feature of Southeast Asian executives in recent years is the extent to which the influence of the military and other security forces has declined, at least in the original ASEAN 5. For many decades the military had a dominant influence in Indonesia and Thailand, and a major role in the Philippines under Marcos' martial law. The military in these countries is still an important player, as a cursory look at military titles among members of cabinet and legislatures will reveal. But it now has a subordinate role, with generals forced to adopt new strategies such as contesting elections after retirement. The recent economic crisis has reinforced this change, since many of the domestic problems seen as contributing to this were linked to the profligate ways of military officials. It is too early to predict that the military will never again seek to grab power in these countries, but its influence does appear to be on a seminal wane. The same cannot be said of Myanmar, Vietnam and Laos, where the military is either dominant or remains very influential.

Legislatures

As executives in the region are strong, so are legislatures, or parliaments, weak. They are in abeyance in Myanmar and Brunei, and elsewhere seldom fulfil traditional roles assigned to them, namely to pass laws, control the purse strings, and act as a check against the executive. Parliaments in Malaysia and Singapore, and communist countries, have been used primarily to endorse government or ruling party proposals. In the Malaysia and Singapore they have also occasionally been used as a safe outlet for the grievances of backbenchers or opposition members. Parliaments in Thailand, Indonesia, the Philippines and Cambodia have sometimes stood up to the executive, and may increasingly do so as new arrangements and practices consolidate.

Parliaments are bicameral, except for unicameral assemblies in Vietnam, Laos and Singapore. They are elected or appointed in different ways (see section on Elections below), and a different division of labour between the two houses is found in bicameral legislatures. The upper house has a minor role in Malaysia and Cambodia. It is less influential than the lower house in Thailand and the Philippines, but in both countries has a very important watchdog role vis a vis the executive. In Indonesia the "upper house" (MPR) is the supreme body in the country, though since the "lower house" (DPR) is the main body within the MPR this is not a bicameral parliament in the conventional sense.

Elections

Elections play some role in governmental arrangements for all Southeast Asian countries, though currently suspended in both Myanmar and Brunei. Public elections are mainly confined to legislatures, with the exception of the Philippines and Singapore where presidents are directly elected. For the most part elections are on a first-past-the-post or plurality basis — meaning the candidate with the most votes wins, whether or not he/she has more than 50 per cent of votes — for single-member constituencies. A form of proportional representation exists based on provinces in Indonesia, at the national level for Cambodia, and at the national level for party list components of the lower house in Thailand and the Philippines. Multiple constituencies exist at the national level for the Philippines senate, and at the provincial level for the Thai senate.

There are wide differences in terms of the extent to which elections can be considered free and fair. The Commission on Elections in the Philippines (COMELEC), and similar independent public bodies in Thailand and Indonesia, have made progress in ensuring the credibility of the electoral process in these countries. They have been assisted by strong NGOs, such as the National Movement for Free Elections (NAMFREL) in the Philippines and PollWatch in Thailand. Nonetheless, abuse of process by such means as money politics and intimidation have sometimes negated the influence of these independent bodies.

Elections in Malaysia and Singapore have generally been regarded as free. Any one may contest, and the voter's choice is assumed to be accurately reflected in the vote count — though the extent to which this remains true is now being questioned in Malaysia. But elections are not fair, since the ruling party is able to use its control over government machinery and the media to influence voters' decisions. The process is taken even further in Vietnam and Laos, where the party permits only approved candidates to contest.

Judiciary

The judiciary in most Southeast Asian countries tends to be sensitive to the executive. There have been few cases of it standing as a "third arm" of government, defending the constitution and upholding the law against a powerful executive. The Philippines judiciary arguably did, when it acted to facilitate the transfer of presidential power from Joseph Estrada to Gloria Macapagal Arroyo in January 2001. Intervening at a critical moment, when other institutions were paralysed and hundreds of thousands were massed in the streets, the Supreme Court approved Arroyo's swearing in, providing a legal basis for presidential change.

Leading judicial members are appointed by different arrangements, most allowing considerable say by the executive. Thailand is an exception, with appointments made by the judiciary itself. However the executive often acts on advice of, or selects from nominees proposed by, others: the Judicial Bar Council in the Philippines, the Council of Rulers in Malaysia, parliament (DPR) in Indonesia, and the Supreme Council of Magistracy in Cambodia. Most judiciaries come under line departments for administrative purposes, though both Thailand and Indonesia have some independence. Fiscal autonomy is also generally limited.

The judiciary, and the broader legal framework within which it operates, have been among the most problematic aspects of government in the region. A perceived lack of judicial independence, and in some cases outright venal behaviour, has deterred foreign investment and sometimes attracted international condemnation.

Political Parties

Every country has at least one political party, though in Myanmar and Brunei they play no part in the administration. Elsewhere there are different forms of one party systems, one party dominant and multi party. Vietnam and Laos allow only the communist party. Malaysia and Singapore have one party dominant systems, though in Malaysia's case UMNO is part of the multi-party BN coalition. Cambodia appears headed in a similar direction. Thailand, the Philippines and Indonesia have multi party systems.

The one party and one party dominant systems have what some regard as "real" parties — well managed, mass based, and ideologically driven. Elsewhere parties are generally looser arrangements, formed around strong and wealthy patrons. Often their main function is to seek a part in government, then reap the rewards of office.

Ideology

Six of the countries have official ideologies, taught in schools and public information settings, and reiterated with varying frequency in an attempt to help legitimize governments and government policies. In Vietnam and Laos, communism no longer provides the rationale for state economic monopoly, as it once did, but continues as a justification for tight control of a one party state. Singapore's "shared values", and the doctrines of *Pancasila* and *Rukunegara* in Indonesia and Malaysia respectively, encourage respect for a pluralistic, multireligious and multicultural society — as does the Indonesian motto of "unity in diversity". Under Soeharto the *Pancasila* requirement of belief in one God was also used to justify strong opposition to communism, equated with atheism.

Both Malaysia and Thailand have what might be considered "unofficial" ideologies in the slogans *Bangsa, Agama, Negara* (race, religion, nation) and *Chat, Sasana, Phramahakasat* (nation, religion, monarchy). Cambodia uses almost the same terminology as Thailand, *Cheat, Sasna, Mohaksath*. All have similarities with the Brunei official ideology of *Melayu, Islam, Beraja* (Malay, Islamic, Monarchy). These ideologies or slogans have generally been used to reinforce a conservative political ideology, one that is Malay-centred in the Malaysian and Brunei cases.

Neither the Philippines or Myanmar has such ideologies. In its place the Philippines has a looser commitment to liberal-democratic values, as expressed in the country's constitution. Myanmar's military junta justifies its existence by the alleged imperative of national salvation.

Civil Society and Human Rights

Economic boom conditions in non-communist Southeast Asia during the 1980s and 1990s created massive social change, which in most cases led to more pluralistic societies, including stronger media and NGOs. The newly strengthened civil societies sometimes sought to advance public interest by acting against the state, and at other times worked cooperatively with it. Civil society influence grew most dramatically in the Philippines, Thailand and Indonesia. It also burgeoned in Malaysia, though in recent times this has been mainly in opposition to the state, hardly ever in a cooperative relationship.

Civil society influence has been somewhat weaker in Cambodia, which missed the economic boom, and Singapore, where the state has generally directed it towards the government's agenda. It is even weaker in the Brunei and remaining CLMV countries, where governments have strongly resisted the emergence of any potential alternative centres of power.

Human rights issues have become controversial in recent years, when plans to admit Myanmar to ASEAN (realized in 1997) coincided with greater global interest in human rights and democracy in the aftermath of the Cold War. Prior to that the killing fields of Cambodia attracted some attention, and the case of East Timor, but generally the issue was not prominent. While the Cold War continued the West was generally unwilling to take too strong a stand where non-communist partners were concerned.

All countries in the region have human rights problems, ranging from the prevention of basic freedoms of assembly, expression and association, to laws allowing detention without trial, and sometimes extending to brutality on the part of security forces — particularly in CLMV countries. These attract strong criticism in publications such as annual country Human Rights Reports by the United States State Department. Government-sponsored Human Rights Commissions established in Indonesia, Philippines, and Malaysia have operated with varying degrees of independence and effectiveness. Thailand will soon have a similar body. Though not discussed in the forgoing chapters there have also been moves to establish human rights dialogues with Western countries, both bilaterally and through ASEAN; and ASEAN is slowly giving greater attention to this issue, including establishment of a Human Rights Mechanism.

Who Rules?

As noted in discussion of the executives, governments in Southeast Asia generally are in the hands of a few. In Vietnam and Laos government is controlled by party leaders, the *nomenklatura*. Control is also clear cut in both Myanmar and Brunei, resting with the military and monarchy respectively. Malaysia and Singapore, and to a lesser extent Cambodia, have strong party-based leadership, interlinked with the bureaucracy (civil and military) and business.

Thailand, Philippines and Indonesia differ slightly. Elites remain influential in all — traditional/aristocratic, and leaders in the military and business. But they are counterbalanced by elite pluralism, robust civil societies, and institutions that limit the role of the military and provide independent support for the public — such as election commissions, ombudsmen and counter corruption agencies. Parliaments are also becoming stronger and providing a check on the executive.

At the onset of the Asian economic crisis some analysts, and U.S. officials, predicted that existing autocratic regimes would fall and democratic rule emerge triumphant. With the exception of Indonesia — whose future remains uncertain — nothing along these lines happened. In Thailand the crisis did reinforce moves towards greater democracy, but this was already in progress beforehand. Estrada's ouster in the Philippines was for illegal not autocratic behaviour. Elsewhere effects have been more subtle, but at least in the short run have tended to reinforce existing authoritarian rule.

Who Benefits?

In countries governed by a few it is hardly surprising that benefits have gone disproportionately to a few. Members of the inner circle in the non-communist countries, now often labeled cronies, made vast profits and joined the international jet set. Inequality — always high except in the shared poverty of countries such as Laos and Vietnam — has been exacerbated in recent decades, with the Gini index on an upward trend. The recent economic crisis aggravated poverty and inequality, though the effects were not as dire as predicted at its outset.

Nonetheless benefits did flow down in the Asian "miracle" countries, with improvements across a wide range of social indicators. Though many problems remain, especially for those left behind in agriculture, the poor have benefited from a massive reduction in poverty, improved literacy, low-cost health services, family planning and the like. These gains were not, as some critics claim, a mirage. Some even jumped to the middle class, which burgeoned dramatically as economies moved away from agriculture to industry and services.

Socialist countries, and for many years politically troubled Philippines, by contrast, could not develop sufficiently high growth rates to lift living standards. In CLMV countries failed attempts to promote centrally planned economies, aggravated by wartime devastation in Cambodia and security problems elsewhere, led by the 1990s to attempts to emulate non-socialist economic prescriptions.

Legitimacy

Southeast Asian governments have used different approaches to enhance legitimacy, with outcomes that have diverged widely. For the most part the respective national political systems appear broadly legitimate, with the probable exception of Myanmar. In Indonesia, and to a lesser extent in other countries such as Philippines and Thailand, the existing framework has also been challenged by secessionist minorities. Elsewhere there have been few pressures for wholesale change, but in many countries questions about the legitimacy of particular governments.

Regional governments are perhaps best known for seeking legitimacy based on effectiveness. Indeed much has been written about an unspoken social contract between governments and the people to deliver material progress, in return for the public accepting constraints on individual liberty. The economic crisis pulled this prop away from Soeharto's Indonesia and made it more difficult for governments in Thailand, Philippines and Malaysia, and successors to Soeharto in Indonesia. CLMV governments were not so acutely affected, but lost expected benefits from opening up their economies because foreign investment — much of it sourced from crisis-hit neighbours — dried up. Even Brunei was shaken a little, when the economic crisis contributed to multi-billion dollar losses at the hands of former finance minister Prince Jefri.

Other bases of legitimacy outlined by Max Weber were also invoked. Most governments sought to use traditional symbols and associations to justify their rule — none more than Brunei which claims a system of government linked to centuries of monarchical rule. There are no towering charismatic figures in the region today, such as Indonesia's Sukarno or Vietnam's Ho Chi Minh in the past. Malaysia's Dr Mahathir was once viewed in a similar light, but is now widely blamed for the recent dramatic erosion of Malay support. Former Philippines film star President Estrada came to power on a wave of popular adulation, but was forced out of office by People Power II less than three years later. Nonetheless in the highly personalized world of Southeast Asia politics charisma remains an important factor, at least in terms of leadership in political parties. Legal-based legitimacy is widely acknowledged throughout the region, though efforts to reduce this to a process of regular elections have been resisted by civil society.

At the time of writing questions were being asked about the legitimacy of governments in Indonesia, Philippines, Malaysia, Thailand and Myanmar. Except, possibly, for Indonesia, this did not appear to presage major realignments, as existing institutions appeared strong enough to cope with change.

Governance

Governance, meaning the extent to which governments are effective, honest, equitable, transparent and accountable, has been central to much debate about the Southeast Asian region in the past decade. The ability of the Asian miracle economies to plan and implement policies that raised living standards for all once drew unanimous praise. But having been held up as a model of governance by the boosters of this concept, particularly the World Bank, the economic crisis was then attributed to a failure of governance, particularly because of corruption. Singapore's relative resilience, on the other hand, was widely attributed to successful governance.

Such a mono-causal explanation for the economic crisis is clearly inadequate — an under-regulated international financial system, private sector failures, and premature opening of capital accounts before establishing adequate regulatory mechanisms, were no less responsible. Nonetheless, a failure of governance was as a contributing factor, and acknowledged as such in most Southeast Asian countries. In Thailand, for instance, this resulted in widespread debate over how public welfare might be improved by more transparency, reducing corruption, increasing accountability and establishing an adequate legal framework. In Indonesia the term *reformasi* served as a synonym for good governance. The extent to which concrete steps were taken varied from country to country, but in virtually all cases the issue became part of political discussion, and governments gave at least rhetorical support to improving governance.

A discernible shift in the notion of governance since about the time of the crisis has been to associate it with building civil society, democracy and even human rights. That has been welcomed in more democratic countries — Thailand, Philippines and Indonesia — and Singapore's response included opening a "speakers corner". Elsewhere this trend has not been welcomed, at least in official circles.

Wither Southeast Asia?

At the beginning of this new millennium most Southeast Asian countries had emerged from colonialism for half a century or less. Different historical and geopolitical circumstances created a wide range of political systems at inception, and institutional diversity has remained ever since.

Yet despite such diversity, by the late 1980s four non-communist states — Indonesia, Thailand, Malaysia and Singapore — had begun to converge in some areas of political practice. Each had strong executives, and though they retained outward forms of democracy its practice was constrained. They pursued high-growth economic policies, following an industry-based export growth path pioneered earlier by Japan and other newly industrializing Asian economies. Economic benefits trickled down, even as inequality worsened, social problems multiplied and the environment suffered. These countries tapped into foreign direct investment and foreign markets, and ensured close cooperation between government, business and labour (as in Malaysia Inc). High economic growth conferred legitimacy, and was frequently invoked as a rationale for limiting democracy.

Outside this group, political instability sidelined the Philippines for many years, but it moved decisively towards this model after President Ramos came to power in 1992. CLMV countries began tentative moves in this direction from the mid 1980s, but intensified efforts in the 1990s, joining ASEAN in an attempt to fast track the process. Even Brunei had some similarities, but based its politics on a neo-traditional Sultanate, and used petroleum riches to ensure a trickle down.

The economic crisis that began in 1997 raised profound uncertainties about this model. It weakened claims of legitimacy based on delivery of economic benefits, even if subsequent recovery has been somewhat better than anticipated. Indeed, autocratic leadership, cronyism and a lack of transparency were among the factors widely blamed for triggering the crisis. Citizens have, therefore, been demanding more say in running governments, more sustainable economic and environmental policies, more attention to inequality and social safety nets, and better governance — meaning not just the capacity to ensure high economic growth, but also a proper environment for the rule of law, greater transparency in government operations (particularly dealings with the private sector), support for civil society, better protection of human rights, and opposition to corruption. External influences reinforced these concerns. Agencies such as the IMF and World Bank required governance reforms in the countries they assisted to overcome the crisis. Western countries gave a higher foreign policy priority to economics, democracy, human rights and the environment. International civil rights groups supported their counterparts in Southeast Asia. And the international media highlighted flaws in the old system. Communication changes such as the fax, mobile phone and Internet also helped Southeast Asian citizens to organize, and enabled anti government groups to get their message widely disseminated.

Nowhere were the effects of these changes more keenly felt than in Indonesia, where the long-running Soeharto regime fell, and a more democratic governmental system replaced it. In the Philippines greater concerns over corruption led to the first ever impeachment of a president, and eventually his overthrow by People Power II. Malaysia encountered unprecedented unrest, and the defection of a majority of Malays to the opposition. In a country where the basis of the ruling party's legitimacy has always been Malay support, that has left large uncertainties about the future. In Thailand the changes reinforced pressures for more democracy and better governance.

CMLV countries were not as directly affected by the crisis, however, it served as a warning that they might not be able to replicate the miracle others had achieved. It also deprived them of much foreign investment, most of which came from ASEAN neighbours. Apparent attempts by the junta in Myanmar to move towards an Indonesia-style system were de-legitimized by the fall of Soeharto. Though not immune from internal and international pressures to change, the immediate reaction in these countries has generally been to batten down.

Where these developments will ultimately lead remains uncertain. Better governance, including more democracy, have been widely touted as the way forward, but it is not the panacea many believe. Changing legal frameworks and reforming bureaucracies requires enormous effort, and will be opposed at every step by entrenched interests. Greater democracy can provide opportunities for extremists of all types, and even facilitate money politics. Democracy is often slow and messy, making citizens disillusioned and attracted to an imagined simpler past. Finance houses and investors do not like democratic delays and uncertainty. And when governments are threatened, their usual instinct is to move further away from democracy.

Nonetheless, gradual change in the direction of improved governance and greater democracy is likely, particularly in the ASEAN 5 countries. International pressures in this direction are likely to increase. Even more importantly, an increasingly influential civil society in these countries is pressing for such change. Lacking such civil societies, and disturbed by the social upheaval that accompanied the economic crisis, the remaining Southeast Asian countries are likely to follow at a more measured pace.

INDEX